MW00638249

Verse by Verse Commentary on the Gospel of

MATTHEW

Enduring Word Commentary Series
By David Guzik

The grass withers, the flower fades,
but the word of our God stands forever.
Isaiah 40:8

Commentary on Matthew

Copyright ©2019 by David Guzik

Printed in the United States of America
or in the United Kingdom

Print Edition ISBN: 1-56599-027-7

Enduring Word

5662 Calle Real #184

Goleta, CA 93117

Electronic Mail: ewm@enduringword.com

Internet Home Page: www.enduringword.com

All rights reserved. No portion of this book may be reproduced in any form (except for quotations in reviews) without the written permission of the publisher.

Scripture references, unless noted, are from the New King James Version of the Bible, copyright ©1979, 1980, 1982, Thomas Nelson, Inc., Publisher.

Contents

Matthew 1 - The Genealogy and Birth of Jesus Christ 5

Matthew 2 – Wise Men from the East, Escape to Egypt and Back Again 18

Matthew 3 - The Ministry of John the Baptist 32

Matthew 4 - The Temptation of Jesus and His First Galilean Ministry 44

Matthew 5 - The Sermon on the Mount 58

Matthew 6 - The Sermon on the Mount (Continued) 91

Matthew 7 - The Sermon on the Mount (Continued) 108

Matthew 8 - Healing, Teaching, and Miracles 122

Matthew 9 - Jesus Ministers and Heals 140

Matthew 10 - The Sending of the Twelve 156

Matthew 11 – Not the Messiah they Expected Him to Be 170

Matthew 12 - The Religious Leaders Continue to Reject Jesus 180

Matthew 13 - The Kingdom Parables 197

Matthew 14 - Jesus Displays Authority over Nature 214

Matthew 15 - Jesus Corrects the Pharisees and Ministers to Gentiles 226

Matthew 16 - Revealing Who Jesus Is and What He Came to Do 238

Matthew 17 - Jesus Transfigured, Triumphant, and Taxed 252

Matthew 18 – Qualities and Attitudes of Kingdom Citizens 264

Matthew 19 - On Marriage, Divorce, Riches, and Discipleship 279

Matthew 20 - Jesus Teaches of Grace, Greatness, and Service 293

Matthew 21 - The Beginning of Jesus' Last Week 305

Matthew 22 - Jesus Answers and Asks Difficult Questions 320

Matthew 23 - Woes to the Scribes and the Pharisees 332

Matthew 24 - Jesus' Olivet Discourse 345

Matthew 25 - Jesus' Olivet Discourse (Part 2) 363

Matthew 26 - Jesus' Betrayal and Arrest 378

Matthew 27 - Jesus' Trial, Death, and Burial 405

Matthew 28 - A Risen Lord Jesus and His Commission 435

Bibliography 445

To Sirena

Matthew 1 - The Genealogy and Birth of Jesus Christ

A. The Genealogy of Jesus Christ.

1. (1) Matthew presents his theme in the first verse: Jesus as the fulfillment of prophecy and of Israel's expectation.

The book of the genealogy of Jesus Christ, the Son of David, the Son of Abraham:

a. **The book of the genealogy of Jesus Christ**: So, Matthew begins his account of the life of Jesus Christ. From the statement in the ancient Greek text, it is difficult to tell what **the book of the genealogy** refers to.

i. "The first two words of Matthew, *biblos genseos*, may be translated 'record of the genealogy,' 'record of the origins,' or 'record of the history'" (Carson). There is a sense in which each meaning is valid.

- In Matthew 1:1-17 we have the "record of the genealogy."
- In Matthew 1:18-2:23 we have the "record of the origins."
- In the entire Gospel of Matthew we have the "record of the history."

ii. As a former tax collector (also called "Levi"), Matthew was qualified to write an account of Jesus' life and teachings. A tax collector of that day must know Greek and be a literate, well-organized man. Some think that Matthew was the "recorder" among the disciples and took notes of Jesus' teaching. We might say that when Matthew followed Jesus, he left everything behind – except his pen and paper. "Matthew nobly used his literary skill to become the first man ever to compile an account of the teaching of Jesus." (Barclay)

iii. "We know that he was a taxgatherer and that he must therefore have been a bitterly hated man, for the Jews hated the members of

their own race who had entered the civil service of their conquerors."
(Barclay)

b. **The Son of David, the Son of Abraham**: In this overview of explaining
the lineage of Jesus, Matthew clearly and strongly connects him to some of
the greatest men in the history of the Old Testament. Matthew begins his
account of the life of **Jesus Christ** with the record of the lineage of Jesus
from the patriarch **Abraham**.

i. Though most New Testament scholars believe that the Gospel of
Matthew was not the first of the four written, it is well placed as the
first book of the New Testament. There are many reasons why Matthew
belongs first among the gospel accounts.

- "It is a remarkable fact that, among the variations in the order
  in which the Gospels appear in early lists and texts, the one
  constant factor is that Matthew always comes first." (France)

- In the early days of Christianity, many people thought that the
  Gospel of Matthew was the first written.

- The early Christians rightly saw the Gospel of Matthew as
  important because it has some significant portions of Jesus'
  teaching that are not included in other gospels, such as a fuller
  version of the Sermon on the Mount.

- It was the only one of the synoptic gospels (Matthew, Mark,
  and Luke) to have an apostolic author - Matthew (who was
  also known as Levi), who was a former tax collector before he
  followed Jesus as a disciple.

- "Matthew's Gospel was in fact far more quoted in Christian
  writings of the second Christian century than any other."
  (France)

- The Jewish flavor of the Gospel of Matthew makes for a logical
  transition between the Old and New Testaments. For these
  reasons, the early church placed it first in order among the four
  gospel accounts.

ii. The Jewish character of this Gospel is evident in many ways. There
are many indications that Matthew expected that his readers would be
familiar with Jewish culture.

- Matthew doesn't translate Aramaic terms such as *raca* (Matthew
  5:22) and *corban* (Mark 7:11).

- Matthew refers to Jewish customs without explanation (Matthew
  15:2 to Mark 7:3-4; see also Matthew 23:5).

- Matthew starts his genealogy with Abraham (Matthew 1:1).

- Matthew presents the name of Jesus and its meaning in a way that assumes the reader knows its Hebrew roots (Matthew 1:21).

- Matthew frequently refers to Jesus as the "Son of David."

- Matthew uses the more Jewish phrase "Kingdom of Heaven" instead of "Kingdom of God."

iii. Yet significantly, the Gospel of Matthew also triumphantly ends with Jesus commanding His followers to make disciples of all the nations (Matthew 28:19-20). So the Gospel of Matthew is deeply rooted in Judaism, but at the same time is able to look beyond; it sees the gospel itself as more than a message for the Jewish people; rather it is a message for the whole world.

iv. We also see that Matthew is deeply critical of the Jewish leadership and their rejection of Jesus. To say that Matthew is "pro-Jewish" is incorrect; it is better to say that he is "pro-Jesus," and presents Jesus as the authentic Jewish Messiah, whom sadly many of the Jewish people (especially the religious establishment) rejected.

v. Some early church commentators and modern scholars say that Matthew originally wrote his gospel in Hebrew, and it was then translated into Greek. Yet there is no concrete evidence for this theory, such as the discovery of an early Hebrew manuscript of Matthew.

vi. More modern theories about the Gospel of Matthew say that he wrote in the style of Jewish *midrash* literature, which creates imaginary stories as a running commentary on the Old Testament. Certain writers use the *midrash* example to say that Matthew wrote about many events that never happened, but he wasn't lying because he never intended to tell the truth, and his audience never believed that he was. These are unconvincing theories, and analysis shows more differences than similarities between Matthew and *midrashim*. "Jewish Midrashim... present stories as illustrative material by way of commenting on a running Old Testament text. By contrast Matthew 1-2 offers no running Old Testament text." (Carson)

c. **Son of David**: Throughout his work, Matthew presents Jesus as the kingly Messiah promised from David's royal line (2 Samuel 7:12-16).

i. The Old Testament prophesied that the Messiah would be the **Son of David**; in the very first sentence, Matthew points to Jesus as the fulfillment of Old Testament prophecy.

d. **Son of Abraham**: Matthew not only connected Jesus to David, but back yet further to **Abraham**. Jesus is the Seed of Abraham in whom all nations would be blessed (Genesis 12:3).

2. (2-16) Jesus' Genealogy through Joseph.

Abraham begot Isaac, Isaac begot Jacob, and Jacob begot Judah and his brothers. Judah begot Perez and Zerah by Tamar, Perez begot Hezron, and Hezron begot Ram. Ram begot Amminadab, Amminadab begot Nahshon, and Nahshon begot Salmon. Salmon begot Boaz by Rahab, Boaz begot Obed by Ruth, Obed begot Jesse, and Jesse begot David the king. David the king begot Solomon by her *who had been the wife* of Uriah. Solomon begot Rehoboam, Rehoboam begot Abijah, and Abijah begot Asa. Asa begot Jehoshaphat, Jehoshaphat begot Joram, and Joram begot Uzziah. Uzziah begot Jotham, Jotham begot Ahaz, and Ahaz begot Hezekiah. Hezekiah begot Manasseh, Manasseh begot Amon, and Amon begot Josiah. Josiah begot Jeconiah and his brothers about the time they were carried away to Babylon. And after they were brought to Babylon, Jeconiah begot Shealtiel, and Shealtiel begot Zerubbabel. Zerubbabel begot Abiud, Abiud begot Eliakim, and Eliakim begot Azor. Azor begot Zadok, Zadok begot Achim, and Achim begot Eliud. Eliud begot Eleazar, Eleazar begot Matthan, and Matthan begot Jacob. And Jacob begot Joseph the husband of Mary, of whom was born Jesus who is called Christ.

a. **Abraham... Joseph**: This genealogy establishes Jesus' claim to the throne of David through his adoptive father Joseph. This is not blood lineage of Jesus through Mary, but the legal lineage of Jesus through Joseph. The Gospel of Luke provides Jesus' blood lineage through Mary.

i. "The Jews set much store by genealogies, and to Jewish Christians the Messiahship of Jesus depended on its being proved that he was a descendant of David." (Bruce)

ii. There are some genuine problems in sorting out the details of this genealogy and reconciling some points to both Luke's record and those found in the Old Testament.

iii. The author is persuaded that Matthew records the genealogical record of Joseph, and Luke the record of Mary; but this is not accepted without dispute by some. "Few would guess simply by reading Luke that he is giving Mary's genealogy. The theory stems, not from the text of Luke, but from the need to harmonize the two genealogies. On the face of it, both Matthew and Luke aim to give Joseph's genealogy." (Carson)

iv. Nevertheless, genealogical difficulties should not prevent us from seeing the whole. Matthew Poole acknowledged that there were some problems with the genealogies, and in reconciling the records of Matthew and Luke, yet he rightly observed:

- The Jews kept extensive genealogical records, and so it is not unwise to trust such records.

- We should remember Paul's warnings about striving over genealogies and not get into arguments about them (1 Timothy 1:4 and 6:4; Titus 3:9).

- If the Jewish opponents of Jesus could have demonstrated that He was not descended from David, they would have disqualified His claim to be Messiah; yet they did not and could not.

v. "And therefore it is the most unreasonable thing imaginable for us to make such little dissatisfactions grounds for us to question or disbelieve the gospel, because we cannot untie every knot we meet with in a pedigree." (Poole)

vi. The Jewish interest in genealogies could sometimes be a dangerous distraction. Therefore Paul warned Timothy to guard against those who were fascinated by *endless genealogies* (1 Timothy 1:4), and he gave a similar warning to Titus (Titus 3:9).

vii. "With one or two exceptions these are the names of persons of little or no note. The later ones were persons altogether obscure and insignificant. Our Lord was 'a root out of dry ground'; a shoot from a withered stem of Jesse. He set small store by earthly greatness." (Spurgeon)

b. **Tamar… Rahab… Ruth… her who had been the wife of Uriah**: This genealogy is noted for the unusual presence of four women. Women were rarely mentioned in ancient genealogies, and the four mentioned here are worthy of special note as examples of God's grace. They show how God can take unlikely people and use them in great ways.

- **Tamar**: She sold herself as a prostitute to her father-in-law Judah to bring forth **Perez and Zerah** (Genesis 38).

- **Rahab**: She was a Gentile prostitute, for whom God took extraordinary measures to save from both judgment and her lifestyle of prostitution (Joshua 2; 6:22-23).

- **Ruth**: She was from Moab, a Gentile, and until her conversion out of the covenant of Israel (Ruth 1).

- **Her who had been the wife of Uriah**: Bathsheba (who is mentioned by implication in Matthew 1:6) was an adulteress, infamous for her sin with David (2 Samuel 11). "Matthew's peculiar way of referring to her, 'Uriah's wife,' may be an attempt to focus on the fact that Uriah was not an Israelite but a Hittite." (Carson)

i. These four women have an important place in the genealogy of Jesus to demonstrate that Jesus Christ was not royalty according to human perception in the sense that He did not come from a pure aristocratic background.

ii. These four women have an important place in the genealogy of Jesus to demonstrate that Jesus identifies with sinners in His genealogy, even as He will in His birth, baptism, life, and His death on the cross. "Jesus is heir of a line in which flows the blood of the harlot *Rahab*, and of the rustic *Ruth*; he is akin to the fallen and to the lowly, and he will show his love even to the poorest and most obscure." (Spurgeon)

iii. These four women have an important place in the genealogy of Jesus to show that there is a new place for women under the New Covenant. In both the pagan and the Jewish culture of that day, men often had little regard for women. In that era, some Jewish men prayed every morning thanking God that they were not Gentiles, slaves or women. Despite that, women were regarded more highly among the Jews than they were among the pagans.

iv. "By far the most amazing thing about this pedigree is the names of the women who appear in it." (Barclay)

v. "Men and women, notorious for their evil character, lie in the direct line of his descent. This was permitted, that He might fully represent our fallen race." (Meyer)

c. **Jacob begot Joseph the husband of Mary, of whom was born Jesus who is called Christ**: Matthew wanted to make it clear that Joseph was not the father of Jesus; rather he was the **husband of Mary**.

i. "The new phraseology makes it clear that Matthew does not regard Jesus as Joseph's son physically…The genealogy is clearly intended to be that of Jesus' 'legal' ancestry, not of his physical descent." (France)

3. (17) Matthew's Organization of the Genealogy.

So all the generations from Abraham to David *are* fourteen generations, from David until the captivity in Babylon *are* fourteen generations, and from the captivity in Babylon until the Christ *are* fourteen generations.

a. **Fourteen generations...fourteen generations...fourteen genera-**
tions: Here Matthew made it clear that this genealogy is not complete.
There were not actually fourteen generations between the points indicated,
but Matthew edited the list to make it easy to remember and memorize.

i. For example, Matthew 1:8 says *Joram begot Uzziah*. This was Uzziah,
King of Judah, who was struck with leprosy for daring to enter the
temple as a priest to offer incense (2 Chronicles 26:16-21). Uzziah
was not the immediate son of Joram; there were three kings between
them (Ahaziah, Joash, and Amaziah). Yet as Clarke rightly says, "It is
observed that omissions of this kind are not uncommon in the Jewish
genealogies."

b. **So all the generations**: The practice of skipping generations at times
was common in the listing of ancient genealogies. Matthew did nothing
unusual by leaving some generations out.

i. Another of the royal line that Matthew passed over was in between
Josiah and Jechoniah (Matthew 1:11), and his name was *Jehoakim* (2
Chronicles 36:5-8). Jehoakim was so wicked that through the Prophet
Jeremiah, God promised that no blood descendant of his would sit on
the throne of Israel (Jeremiah 36:30-31). This presented a significant
problem: If someone was a blood descendant of David through
Jehoakim, he could not sit on the throne of Israel and be the king and
the Messiah because of this curse recorded in Jeremiah 36:30-31. But
if the conqueror was not descended through David, he could not be
the legal heir of the throne because of the promise made to David and
the nature of the royal line.

ii. This is where we come to the differences in the genealogies of Matthew
and Luke. Matthew recorded the genealogy of *Joseph, the husband of*
Mary, of whom was born Jesus who is called Christ (Matthew 1:16). He
began at Abraham and followed the line down to Jesus, *through Joseph.*
Luke recorded the genealogy of Mary: *being, (as was supposed) the son*
of Joseph (Luke 3:23). He began with Jesus and followed the line back
up, all the way to Adam, *starting from the unmentioned Mary.*

iii. Each genealogy is the same as it records the line from Adam (or
Abraham) all the way down to David. But at David, the two genealogies
separated. If we remember the list of David's sons in 2 Samuel 5, we
see that Satan focused his attention on the descendants of the royal
line through Solomon – and this was a reasonable strategy. According
to Matthew 1:6, *Joseph's* line went through Solomon (and therefore
Jehoakim, the cursed one). Jesus was the *legal* son of Joseph, but not
the *blood* son of Joseph – so the curse on Jehoakim did not affect

him. Joseph did not contribute any of the "blood" of Jesus, but he did contribute his legal standing as a descendant of the royal line to Jesus. *Mary's* line – the blood line of Jesus – did not go through Solomon, but through a different son of David, named Nathan (Luke 3:31). Mary was therefore not part of that blood curse on the line of Jehoiakim.

B. The Birth of Jesus Christ.

1. (18) Mary, while engaged to Joseph, is found to be with child as a result of a miraculous conception by the Holy Spirit.

Now the birth of Jesus Christ was as follows: After His mother Mary was betrothed to Joseph, before they came together, she was found with child of the Holy Spirit.

a. **Now the birth of Jesus Christ was as follows**: Matthew doesn't really tell us about the *birth* of Jesus; Luke does that. Matthew instead tells us *where Jesus came from*, and it tells the story through the eyes of Joseph.

b. **After His mother Mary was betrothed to Joseph**: There were essentially three steps to marriage in the Jewish world of Jesus' time.

- *Engagement*: This could happen when the bride and groom to be were quite young, and was often arranged by the parents.

- *Betrothal*: This made the previous engagement official and binding. During the time of betrothal the couple were known as husband and wife, and a betrothal could only be broken by divorce. Betrothal typically lasted a year.

- *Marriage*: This took place after the wedding, after the year of betrothal.

c. **She was found with child of the Holy Spirit**: Matthew plainly (without the greater detail found in the Gospel of Luke) presents the virginal conception and subsequent birth of Jesus. However, the virgin birth was difficult for people to believe back then, even as it is also doubted now by some.

i. We should consider what a great trial this was for a godly young woman like Mary, and for Joseph her betrothed. "Her situation was the most distressing and humiliating that can be conceived. Nothing but the fullest consciousness of her own integrity, and the strongest confidence in God, could have supported her in such trying circumstances, where her reputation, her honour, and her *life* were at stake." (Clarke)

ii. The truth of the supernatural conception of Jesus was disbelieved by many then and was later twisted into lies about the parentage of Jesus. References are made to these suspicions in passages like John 8:19

and 8:41. Lies spread that Mary had become pregnant from a Roman soldier. Here, Matthew set the story straight - both then and now.

iii. "There was no other way of his being born; for had he been of a sinful father, how should he have possessed a sinless nature? He is born of a woman, that he might be human; but not by man, that he might not be sinful." (Spurgeon)

2. (19) Joseph seeks a quiet divorce.

Then Joseph her husband, being a just *man*, and not wanting to make her a public example, was minded to put her away secretly.

a. **Joseph her husband**: The previous verse told us that *Mary was betrothed to Joseph*. This comment shows that even though they were not formally married, Joseph was still considered Mary's **husband** by betrothal.

b. **Being a just man, and not wanting to make her a public example**: Being **just man**, Joseph knew that if Mary had been unfaithful to him it would be impossible to go through with the marriage. Yet his nature as a **just man** also did not want to make this an unnecessary hardship or stigma upon Mary. Joseph made the understandable decision to seek a quiet divorce.

c. **To put her away secretly**: This refers to breaking an engagement by divorce. In Jewish culture of that time, a betrothal was binding and one needed a divorce to break the arrangement.

i. "Their being betrothed was a thing publicly taken notice of, and he could not put her away so privately but there must be witnesses of it; the meaning therefore must be, as privately as the nature of thing would bear." (Poole)

ii. "When we have to do a severe thing, let us choose the tenderest manner. Maybe we shall not have to do it at all." (Spurgeon)

3. (20-21) An angel speaks to Joseph in a dream, convincing him not to divorce Mary.

But while he thought about these things, behold, an angel of the Lord appeared to him in a dream, saying, "Joseph, son of David, do not be afraid to take to you Mary your wife, for that which is conceived in her is of the Holy Spirit. And she will bring forth a Son, and you shall call His name JESUS, for He will save His people from their sins."

a. **Behold, an angel of the Lord appeared to him in a dream**: This was not *the* Angel of the LORD, but simply *an* angel of the Lord. Perhaps it was Gabriel, who is prominent in the announcements made to Mary and

Zacharias (Luke 1:19 and 1:26). Yet those were actual angelic visitations; this was presented to Joseph **in a dream**.

> i. The dream came **while he thought about these things**. Joseph was understandably troubled by Mary's mysterious pregnancy, her future, and what he should do towards her. Though he had decided to *put her away secretly*, he was not comfortable with that decision.

b. **Joseph, son of David**: The address **son of David** should have alerted Joseph that something was particularly significant about this message. **Son of David** is a reference to Joseph's legal lineage to the throne of David.

c. **That which is conceived in her is of the Holy Spirit**: It seems that Mary had not told Joseph that she was pregnant by the Holy Spirit. This shouldn't surprise us; how could she (or how could anyone except God) explain such a thing? This angelic word to Joseph was persuasive.

> i. There is no explanation as to *how* this happened, other than what we have in Luke 1:35. "This wonderful conception of our Saviour is a mystery not much to be pried into, and is therefore called an overshadowing, Luke 1:35." (Trapp)

> ii. "There is no hint of pagan deity-human coupling in crassly physical terms. Instead, the power of the Lord, manifest in the Holy Spirit who was expected to be active in the Messianic Age, miraculously brought about the conception." (Carson)

d. **You shall call his name JESUS**: The name **JESUS** ("The Salvation of Yahweh") was fairly common in that day (Josephus mentions 12 different men named "Jesus" in his writings), but it is supremely blessed in our day. As was later said by the Apostle Peter, there is *no other name under heaven by which men must be saved* (Acts 4:12).

> i. "The name which the angel commanded Joseph to give to Mary's Child was one that was common at the time…its full significance was 'The Salvation of Jehovah.'" (Morgan)

e. **For He will save His people from their sins**: The angelic messenger briefly and eloquently stated the work of the coming Messiah, Jesus. He will come as a *savior*, and come to **save His people from their sins**.

> i. This description of the work of Jesus reminds us that Jesus meets us *in* our sin, but His purpose is to save us **from** our sins. He saves us first from the *penalty* of sin, then from the *power* of sin, and finally from the *presence* of sin.

> ii. "Salvation *from sins* is an element in the Old Testament hope (*e.g.* Isaiah 53; Jeremiah 31:31-34; Ezekiel 36:24-31) and in later Messianic

expectation…but not the dominant one. Its isolation here warns the reader not to expect this Messiah to conform to the more popular hope of a national liberator." (France)

iii. Wonderfully, it says "**His people**." If it had said, "God's people," we might have thought it was reserved for the Jewish people alone. But it isn't belonging to Abraham that brings salvation from sin; it is belonging to Jesus, being one of **His people**.

4. (22-23) The virgin birth as the fulfillment of prophecy.

So all this was done that it might be fulfilled which was spoken by the Lord through the prophet, saying: "Behold, the virgin shall be with child, and bear a Son, and they shall call His name Immanuel," which is translated, "God with us."

a. **That it might be fulfilled**: This is the first use of this important phrase which will become a familiar theme throughout Matthew.

b. **"Behold, the virgin shall be with child, and bear a Son, and they shall call His name Immanuel"**: Matthew rightly understood that the supernatural conception of Jesus was prophesied in Isaiah 7:14.

i. There has been some measure of controversy regarding this quote from Isaiah 7:14, primarily because the Hebrew word *almah can* be translated as either **virgin** *or* "young woman."

ii. We know the Isaiah passage speaks of Jesus because it says **the virgin shall be with child**, and that conception would be *a sign* to David's entire house. Those who deny the virgin birth of Jesus like to point out that the Hebrew word in Isaiah 7:14 translated **virgin** (*almah*) can also be translated as "young woman." The idea is that Isaiah was simply saying that a "young woman" would give birth, not a virgin. While the *near fulfillment* of the Isaiah prophecy may have reference to a young woman giving birth, the *far* or *ultimate fulfillment* clearly points to a woman miraculously conceiving and giving birth. This is especially clear because the Old Testament never uses the word in a context other than **virgin** and because the Septuagint translates *almah* in Isaiah 7:14 categorically **virgin** (*parthenos*).

c. **Immanuel**: This title of Jesus refers to both His deity (***God*** with us) and His identification and nearness to man (**God *with us***).

i. Jesus is truly **Immanuel**, *God with us*. "Christ, indeed, was not called by this name Immanuel that we anywhere read of…but the import of this name is most truly affirmed and acknowledged to be fully made good in him." (Trapp, on Isaiah 7:14)

ii. "In what sense then, is Christ GOD WITH US? Jesus is called Immanuel, or *God with us*, in his *incarnation*; *God with us*, by the influences of his *Holy Spirit*, in the *holy sacrament*, in the *preaching* of his *word*, in *private prayer*. And *God with us*, through every *action* of our life, that we begin, continue, and end in his name. He is *God with us*, to *comfort*, *enlighten*, *protect*, and *defend* us, in every time of *temptation* and *trial*, in the hour of *death*, in the day of *judgment*; and *God with us* and *in us*, and we *with* and *in* him, to all eternity." (Clarke)

iii. We can deeply meditate on the meaning of this name – **Immanuel**.

- It shows how low God bent down to save man; He added the nature of one of His own creatures to His own divine nature, accepting the weaknesses, frailties and dependency that the creature experiences.

- It shows what a great miracle it was that God could add a human nature to His own and still remain God.

- It shows the compatibility between the unfallen human nature and the divine nature; that the two could be joined shows that we are truly made in the image of God.

- It shows that we can come to Him; if He has come to us, then we can come to Him. "Then, if Jesus Christ be 'God with us,' let us come to God without any question or hesitancy. Whoever you may be you need no priest or intercessor to introduce you to God, for God has introduced himself to you." (Spurgeon)

iv. "John Wesley died with that upon his tongue, and let us live with it upon our hearts. – 'The best of all is God with us.'" (Spurgeon)

5. (24-25) Joseph marries Mary after the angelic announcement.

Then Joseph, being aroused from sleep, did as the angel of the Lord commanded him and took to him his wife, and did not know her till she had brought forth her firstborn Son. And he called His name JESUS.

a. **Did as the angel of the Lord commanded**: Joseph's obedience is notable. He did not doubt nor waver; he instantly understood the truth and the importance of the angelic messenger that came to him in the dream.

b. **Did not know her till she had brought forth her firstborn Son**: The words **did not know her till** imply that Joseph and Mary had normal marital relations after Jesus' birth.

i. This emphasizes that Jesus was conceived miraculously. "Matthew wants to make Jesus' virginal conception quite unambiguous, for he adds that Joseph had no sexual union with Mary until she gave birth to Jesus." (Carson)

ii. This also denies the Roman Catholic dogma of the perpetual virginity of Mary. "The marriage was thus formally completed, but not consummated before the birth of Jesus. The Greek expression for *not until* would normally suggest that intercourse did take place after the end of this period…There is no biblical warrant for the tradition of the 'perpetual virginity' of Mary." (France)

iii. This is an unbiblical doctrine which did not appear earlier than the fifth century after Jesus. It should be placed with the dogmas of Mary's Immaculate Conception, assumption into heaven, and present role as a mediator for believers. Each one of these is man's invention, meant to exalt Mary in an unbiblical manner.

c. **And he called His name Jesus:** They did what God told them to do. Though it was a fairly common name, it had a genuinely great meaning and would come to be the greatest name, the name above all names.

Matthew 2 – Wise Men from the East, Escape to Egypt and Back Again

A. Wise men from the East come to honor Jesus.

1. (1-2) The wise men arrive in Jerusalem.

Now after Jesus was born in Bethlehem of Judea in the days of Herod the king, behold, wise men from the East came to Jerusalem, saying, "Where is He who has been born King of the Jews? For we have seen His star in the East and have come to worship Him."

a. **After Jesus was born in Bethlehem**: Matthew actually tells us little about the birth of Jesus; Luke 2 records these familiar details. What Matthew tells us regards something that happened **after Jesus was born in Bethlehem**.

i. **Bethlehem** was the ancestral home of David, the great king of Israel and founder of their royal dynasty; however, it was not a large or significant town. "Bethlehem was quite a little town six miles to the south of Jerusalem. In the olden days it had been called Ephrath or Ephratah." (Barclay)

ii. "A stir begins as soon as Christ is born. He has not spoken a word; he has not wrought a miracle; he has not proclaimed a single doctrine; but 'when Jesus was born,' at the very first, while as yet you hear nothing but infant cries, and can see nothing but infant weakness, still his influence upon the world is manifest. 'When Jesus was born, there came wise men from the east,' and so on. There is infinite power even in an infant Savior." (Spurgeon)

b. **In the days of Herod the king**: This was the one known as *Herod the Great*. Herod was indeed great; in some ways great as a ruler, builder and administrator; in other ways great in politics and cruelty.

i. "He was wealthy, politically gifted, intensely loyal, an excellent administrator, and clever enough to remain in the good graces of

18

successive Roman emperors. His famine relief was superb and his building projects (including the temple, begun 20 B.C.) were admired even by his foes. But he loved power, inflicted incredibly heavy taxes on the people, and resented the fact that many Jews considered him a usurper. In his last years, suffering an illness that compounded his paranoia, he turned to cruelty and in fits of rage and jealousy killed close associates." (Carson)

ii. "Augustus, the Roman Emperor, had said, bitterly, that it was safer to be Herod's pig than Herod's son. (The saying is even more epigrammatic in Greek, for in Greek *hus* is the word for a *pig*, and *huios* is the word for a *son*)." (Barclay)

iii. The reign of Herod also gives us a chronological marking point. "*Jesus was born* before the death of *Herod* the Great, which is probably to be dated in 4 BC; the exact date of Jesus' birth is unknown." (France)

c. **Wise men from the East came**: These travelers are called **wise men**, which in the ancient Greek is *magoi*. Misconceptions and legends abound about these wise men. They were not kings but **wise men**, which means they were astronomers. There were not only three, but probably a great company. They seem to have come not on the birth night, but probably several months later.

i. "In later centuries down to New Testament times, the term [*magoi*] loosely covered a wide variety of men interested in dreams, astrology, magic, books thought to contain mysterious references to the future, and the like." (Carson)

ii. Being **from the East**, they would have been among Jews who were exiled from Judah and Israel centuries before. "That many Jews were mixed with this people there is little doubt; and that these eastern *magi*, or philosophers, astrologers, or whatever else they were, might have been *originally* of that class, there is room to believe. These, knowing the promise of the Messiah, were now, probably, like other believing Jews, waiting for the consolation of Israel." (Clarke)

iii. There was a general expectation of a messiah or great man from Judea. Not very long after Jesus was born, the Roman historian Seutonius wrote: "There had spread over all the Orient an old and established belief, that it was fated at that time for men coming from Judea to rule the world." Tacitus, another Roman historian of the general period, wrote: "There was a firm persuasion...that at this very time the East was to grow powerful, and rulers coming from Judea were to acquire universal empire." (Cited in Barclay)

iv. "The tradition that the Magi were kings can be traced as far back as Tertullian (died c. 225). It probably developed under the influence of Old Testament passages that say kings will come and worship the Messiah (cf. Psalms 68:29, 31; 72:10-11; Isaiah 49:7; 60:1-6)." (Carson)

v. Church traditions even tell us their names - supposedly Melchior, Caspar, and Balthasar. You can see their supposed skulls in the great cathedral at Cologne, Germany.

d. **Came to Jerusalem**: Guided by the astronomical phenomenon mentioned following, they came to the area and expected to find answers in **Jerusalem**. They expected that the leaders and people of this capital city of the Jews would be even more interested than they were. Matthew does not tell us specifically that the star guided them to Jerusalem.

i. "A comparable visit by eastern Magi to Nero in AD 66 vouches for the probability of this story." (France) "There is not the slightest need to think that the story of the coming of the Magi to the cradle of Christ is only a lovely legend. It is exactly the kind of thing that could easily have happened in the ancient world." (Barclay)

ii. "It has been truly remarked that the shepherds did not miss their way; they came to Christ at once, while the wise men, even with a star to guide them, yet missed their way, and went to Jerusalem instead of to Bethlehem, and enquired at the palace of Herod, instead of at the stable where the Christ was born." (Spurgeon)

e. **Where is He who has been born King of the Jews?** They traveled this great distance to honor a **King**; yet there is a little irony in their great effort to honor the **King of the Jews**. At that time the Jewish people were often despised and dishonored because of their unique customs and beliefs, and also often because of their success and prosperity. They were often thought of as a low, troublesome, and conquered race. It was remarkable that they would trouble themselves so much to honor an infant **King**, but even more so a **King of the Jews**.

i. "They said, 'Where is he that is born King of the Jews?' 'Jews?' Who cared for Jews? Even in those days, Jews were the subject of contempt, for they had aforetime been carried captive into the east. Although they are the very aristocracy of God, his chosen people, yet the nations looked down upon the Jews." (Spurgeon)

ii. Significantly, they say this one **has been born King of the Jews**. It is a strange thing for a baby to be born a king. Usually they are princes for a long time before they are kings. "His kingly status was not conferred on him later on; it was from birth." (Carson)

f. **For we have seen His star in the East**: There are many different suggestions for the natural origin of this remarkable star. Some say it was a conjunction of Jupiter and Saturn; some, other planetary conjunctions; others suggest a supernova; and some think of comets or a specifically created unique star or sign.

> i. Whatever it was, it is significant that God met them in their own medium: He guided the astronomers by a star. This was also in fulfillment of Numbers 24:17: *A Star shall come out of Jacob; a Scepter shall rise out of Israel.* This was widely regarded by ancient Jewish scholars as a Messianic prediction.

> ii. Notice, it was **His star**: "The star was Christ's star itself, but it also led others to Christ. It did this very much because it moved in that direction. It is a sad thing when a preacher is like a sign-post pointing the way but never following it, on his own account. Such were those chief priests at Jerusalem: they could tell where Christ was born, but they never went to worship him; they were indifferent altogether to him and to his birth." (Spurgeon)

g. **And have come to worship Him**: The wise men came first to Jerusalem, assuming that the leaders of the Jews would be aware and excited about the birth of their Messiah. The wise men are about to find that this wasn't the case at all.

2. (3) Herod is troubled at the news brought by the wise men.

When Herod the king heard *this*, he was troubled, and all Jerusalem with him.

> a. **When Herod the king heard this, he was troubled**: Herod was constantly on guard against threats to his rule, especially from his own family. He assassinated many family members whom he suspected of disloyalty. His being **troubled** is completely in character.

> i. Herod, who wanted to be accepted by the Jews whom he ruled, was not a Jew at all but an Edomite, and Rome recognized him as a vassal king over Judea. The Jews tempered their great hatred of him with admiration for his building projects, such as the magnificent improvements made to the second temple.

> ii. Barclay reminds us of what a bloody, violent ruler Herod was: "He had no sooner come to the throne than he began by annihilating the Sanhedrin...he slaughtered three hundred court officers...he murdered

his wife Mariamne, and her mother Alexandra, his eldest son Antipater, and two other sons, Alexander and Arisobulus."

b. **He was troubled, and all Jerusalem with him**: The fact that **all Jerusalem** was **troubled** with Herod is significant. This was due either to the fact that the people of Jerusalem rightly feared what sort of paranoid outburst might come from Herod upon hearing of a rival king being born, or because of the size and dignity of this caravan from the East.

i. This trouble is again testimony to the greatness of Jesus, even as a young child. "Jesus of Nazareth is so potent a factor in the world of mind that, no sooner is he there in his utmost weakness, a now-born King, than he begins to reign. Before he mounts the throne, friends bring him presents, and his enemies compass his death." (Spurgeon)

3. (4-6) Herod is instructed regarding the Messiah's coming by the chief priests and scribes.

And when he had gathered all the chief priests and scribes of the people together, he inquired of them where the Christ was to be born. So they said to him, "In Bethlehem of Judea, for thus it is written by the prophet:

'But you, Bethlehem, *in* the land of Judah,
Are not the least among the rulers of Judah;
For out of you shall come a Ruler
Who will shepherd My people Israel.'"

a. **All the chief priests and the scribes**: This was the first contact the religious leaders had with Jesus. They understood the Biblical information correctly, but failed in application to their lives.

i. **Chief priests** would especially include those who once held the office of High Priest; Herod changed the High Priest often because it was largely a political appointment.

ii. **Scribes**: "The 'teachers of the law,' or 'scribes' as other English versions call them, were experts in the Old Testament and in its copious oral tradition. Their work was not so much copying out Old Testament manuscripts (as the word 'scribes' suggests) as teaching the Old Testament." (Carson)

b. **So they said to him, "In Bethlehem of Judea"**: Quoting Micah 5:2, the chief priests and scribes understood that the Messiah would be born in **Bethlehem of Judea**, distinguishing it from another town of the same name further north.

i. From this passage in Micah, they understood not only that the Messiah would be born in **Bethlehem**, but also that He would be **a Ruler who will shepherd My people Israel**.

ii. Sadly, these experts had the right information but seem personally uninterested in meeting the Messiah for themselves.

iii. "Had they met with the shepherds of Bethlehem, they had received better intelligence than they could from the learned scribes of Jerusalem." (Trapp)

4. (7-8) True to character, Herod attempts to use wise men to find the child that he may kill Him.

Then Herod, when he had secretly called the wise men, determined from them what time the star appeared. And he sent them to Bethlehem and said, "Go and search carefully for the young Child, and when you have found *Him*, bring back word to me, that I may come and worship Him also."

a. **Determined from them what time the star appeared**: Because Herod later commanded that all boys two and younger be killed in the area, we can assume that the wise men first saw the star a year or so previously (on the night Jesus was born). Their journey from the East to Judea was not quick, and they may have left as soon as logistics allowed.

i. Herod heard a good Bible study about the birthplace of the Messiah, but it did him no good. "When the earth-king dabbles in theology, it bodes no good to truth. Herod among the priests and scribes is Herod still. Some men may be well instructed in their Bibles and yet be all the worse for what they have discovered." (Spurgeon)

b. **Bring back word to me, that I may come and worship Him also**: The irony is strong. Herod claimed a desire to **worship** Jesus, when he really wanted to kill Him.

i. "Mark that the wise men never promised to return to Herod; they probably guessed that all this eager zeal was not quite so pure as it seemed to be, and their silence did not mean consent." (Spurgeon)

5. (9-12) The wise men present gifts to Jesus and leave without informing Herod.

When they heard the king, they departed; and behold, the star which they had seen in the East went before them, till it came and stood over where the young Child was. When they saw the star, they rejoiced with exceedingly great joy. And when they had come into the house, they saw the young Child with Mary His mother, and fell down and worshiped

Him. And when they had opened their treasures, they presented gifts to Him: gold, frankincense, and myrrh. Then, being divinely warned in a dream that they should not return to Herod, they departed for their own country another way.

a. **Behold, the star which they had seen in the East went before them**: The star continued to guide them, apparently re-appearing. We can surmise that the star appeared some months before, guiding them to the general area, and then they visited Jerusalem to gain more information. Then the **star** appeared again to specifically guide them. This was an obviously supernatural phenomenon.

> i. "We believe it to have been a luminous appearance in mid-air; probably akin to that which led the children of Israel through the wilderness, which was a cloud by day and a pillar of fire by night. Whether it was seen in the daylight or not we cannot tell." (Spurgeon)

> ii. **And stood over where the young Child was**: Adam Clarke says that this is more literally, *stood over the head of the child*. In his thinking, it was some kind of meteor that guided them to the very house where Jesus was. He goes on to say that this idea of a star-like shine associated with the head of Jesus gave rise to the idea of the *halo* in ancient and medieval art.

> iii. "The words *came to rest* mean literally 'came and stood', and can mean only that the star itself moved to guide the Magi." (France)

b. **They saw the young Child with Mary His mother**: We notice that Jesus here is called a **young Child**, likely being between 6 and 18 months old. We also notice that (against custom) the **Child** is mentioned before the **mother**.

> i. "Joseph haply was at work, or otherwise absent, lest the wise men should mistake him for the true father of the child." (Trapp)

c. **When they had opened their treasures, they presented gifts to Him: gold, frankincense, and myrrh**: It was common – especially in the East – that one would never appear before royalty or a person of importance without bringing **gifts**. Considering who these wise men believed the **young Child** to be, it is not surprising that they gave such lavish gifts.

> i. The idea that there were three wise men comes from the fact that there were three gifts. We may say that gold speaks of royalty, incense speaks of divinity, and myrrh speaks of death. Yet it is almost certain that the Magi did this unawares; they simply wanted to honor the King of the Jews.

d. **They presented gifts to Him**: The precious gifts were not presented to Mary or Joseph, but to Jesus Himself. Yet undeniably, the infant Jesus did not use or spend any of these precious gifts, but His parents used them, hopefully wisely, on His behalf and benefit.

i. In the same way, when we give to Jesus today, we do not give to Him directly, but to His people, who use those gifts on His behalf and benefit – and hopefully wisely.

ii. "How useful this gold was to Joseph in the following months! It helped him to defray the cost of the journey into Egypt and back, and to maintain his precious charges there. The Heavenly Father knew what those needs would be, and met them by anticipation." (Meyer)

e. **Fell down and worshipped Him**: More important than their gifts is the fact that they worshipped Jesus. It must have been a curious sight to see these impressive dignitaries bowing before a young child.

i. We see here three different responses to Jesus; one may say that all people respond in one of these three ways.

- Herod displayed an open hatred and hostility toward Jesus.
- The chief priests and the scribes were indifferent toward Jesus, all the while retaining their religious respectability.
- The wise men sought out Jesus and worshipped Him - even at great cost.

ii. In comparing the visit of the wise men to the earlier visit of the shepherds (Luke 2:15-20), we see:

- Jesus came to the Jew first, then to the Gentile.
- Jesus came to the humble and ignorant first, then the honorable and learned.
- Jesus came to the poor first, then the rich.

iii. We should learn from the wisdom of these wise men.

- They were not satisfied with looking at the star and admiring it; they *did* something about the star, and set out and followed it.
- They persevered in their search and in following after the star.
- They were not discouraged in the search by clergy and doubtful religious leaders.
- They rejoiced at the star.
- When they arrived at the destination the star led them to, they entered in.

- When they entered in, they worshipped.

- They sensed an urgency to worship Him *now* and not wait until later.

- When they worshipped, it was to give something – not empty-handed adoration.

iv. We see a wonderful pattern: "Those who look for Jesus will see him: those who truly see him will worship him: those who worship him will consecrate their substance to him." (Spurgeon)

f. **Being divinely warned in a dream that they should not return to Herod, they departed for their own country another way**: Their worship is also manifested in obedience. They are obedient to the heavenly dream and leave without serving as Herod's informants.

B. The flight to Egypt and the return to Nazareth.

1. (13-15) Joseph, Mary, and Jesus find refuge in Egypt.

Now when they had departed, behold, an angel of the Lord appeared to Joseph in a dream, saying, "Arise, take the young Child and His mother, flee to Egypt, and stay there until I bring you word; for Herod will seek the young Child to destroy Him." When he arose, he took the young Child and His mother by night and departed for Egypt, and was there until the death of Herod, that it might be fulfilled which was spoken by the Lord through the prophet, saying, "Out of Egypt I called My Son."

a. **Arise, take the young Child and His mother, flee to Egypt**: The command was urgent, and came right when the wise men **had departed**. It would not have sounded *completely* strange to Joseph that they should find refuge in **Egypt**. There was a large Jewish community in Egypt. It wasn't strange that the Holy Spirit would guide Joseph to take the family there.

i. "Egypt was a natural place to which to flee. It was nearby, a well-ordered Roman province outside Herod's jurisdiction; and, according to Philo (writing circa A.D. 40), its population included about a million Jews." (Carson)

b. **Herod will seek the young Child to destroy Him**: This response is consistent with both the character of Herod and humanity in general. It doesn't speak well of humanity to notice that when God added humanity to His deity and came to earth – in the most non-threatening manner possible – the almost immediate reaction of one section of humanity was to try as hard as they could to murder Him.

c. **When he arose, he took the young Child and His mother by night**: Joseph's rapid (leaving the very **night** of the dream) and complete obedience is impressive. It is unlikely that Joseph ever imagined such events when he first was betrothed to Mary of Nazareth.

> i. "We are not told into what part of Egypt Joseph went, nor how long he stayed there: some say six or seven years; others but three or four months." (Poole)

d. **Out of Egypt I called My Son**: In the process, another prophecy was fulfilled. At first glance, we might wonder how this prophecy from Hosea 11:1 is fulfilled in Jesus. But Matthew makes it clear that even as Israel as a nation came out from Egypt, so would the Son of God.

2. (16-18) The Massacre of the Innocents.

Then Herod, when he saw that he was deceived by the wise men, was exceedingly angry; and he sent forth and put to death all the male children who were in Bethlehem and in all its districts, from two years old and under, according to the time which he had determined from the wise men. Then was fulfilled what was spoken by Jeremiah the prophet, saying:

"A voice was heard in Ramah,
Lamentation, weeping, and great mourning,
Rachel weeping *for* her children,
Refusing to be comforted,
Because they are no more."

a. **He sent forth and put to death all the male children who were in Bethlehem and in all its districts**: Though there are no exact descriptions of this event in secular history, it is entirely in character with Herod's well-known ruthlessness.

> i. "Incredible? Anything is credible of the man who murdered his own wife and sons. This deed shocks Christians; but it was a small affair in Herod's career, and in contemporary history." (Bruce)

> ii. Especially in his last years Herod was cruel and suspicious. When he knew that his death was approaching, Herod had many Jewish leaders of Jerusalem arrested on false charges. He ordered that as soon as he died, they should all be killed - he knew well no one would mourn his own death, so he was determined that *some* tears be shed when he died.

> iii. "Actually, the story is in perfect harmony with what we know of Herod's character in his last years…The death of a few children (perhaps a dozen or so; Bethlehem's total population was not large) would hardly have been recorded in such violent times." (Carson)

b. **A voice was heard in Ramah, lamentation, weeping, and great mourning**: This quotation from Jeremiah 31:15 originally referred to the mourning of Israel's mothers during the conquest and captivity of the nation. Here **Rachel** is a representation of Bethlehem's mothers.

> i. "This prophecy was literally fulfilled when Judah was carried into captivity; there was then a great mourning in the tribes of Benjamin and Judah, for their children that were slain and carried away into captivity. It was now fulfilled, that is, verified, a second time." (Poole)

> ii. "Rachel was to the Hebrew fancy a mother for Israel in all time, sympathetic in all her children's misfortunes." (Bruce)

3. (19-21) The return to Israel.

But when Herod was dead, behold, an angel of the Lord appeared in a dream to Joseph in Egypt, saying, "Arise, take the young Child and His mother, and go to the land of Israel, for those who sought the young Child's life are dead." Then he arose, took the young Child and His mother, and came into the land of Israel.

a. **Arise, take the young Child and His mother**: God spoke to Joseph again in a dream, through **an angel of the Lord**. We also notice Joseph's quick obedience.

b. **The young Child...the young Child...the young Child**: Repeatedly, **the young Child** is given first place in the account.

c. **And came into the land of Israel**: The Messiah might spend a few years in Egypt, a refugee from the murderous Herod, but He would certainly come back **into the land of Israel**.

> i. There have been some who falsely teach that Egyptian magicians or sorcerers influenced Jesus and His later miracles were really just Egyptian tricks. It is important to note that there is no *evidence* for such claims, and significant evidence *against* such claims. Particularly, the teaching and style of ministry of Jesus is completely influenced by Old Testament Judaism, not by Egyptian mysticism.

4. (22-23) Fearing the evil son of Herod (Archelaus), the family settles north in Nazareth.

But when he heard that Archelaus was reigning over Judea instead of his father Herod, he was afraid to go there. And being warned by God in a dream, he turned aside into the region of Galilee. And he came and dwelt in a city called Nazareth, that it might be fulfilled which was spoken by the prophets, "He shall be called a Nazarene."

a. **When he heard that Archelaus was reigning over Judea**: Joseph had good reason to be cautious regarding **Archelaus**. This son of Herod proved to be such an incompetent and violent ruler, that at the plea of the Jews of Judea, the Romans deposed him for misrule and replaced him with a governor appointed by Rome in AD 6.

> i. This **Archelaus** was as cruel as his father Herod the Great, but without any of his greatness. "A man of kindred nature, suspicious, truculent (Jospehus, Antiquities, 17,11,2), to be feared and avoided by such as had cause to fear his father." (Bruce)

> ii. "His brother Herod Antipas is reported of a much milder disposition, and more inactive temper. So Joseph, not without the direction of God, goeth into his own province, which was Galilee." (Poole)

b. **Being warned by God in a dream, he turned aside into the region of Galilee**: Again receiving guidance by a divine dream, Joseph settled outside of the much more religious region of Jerusalem and Judea, and into the populous region of **Galilee**, which had a much more significant Gentile population than Judea or Jerusalem.

> i. "Schanz, taking a hint from Augustine, suggests that Joseph wished to settle in Jerusalem, deeming that city the most suitable home for the Messiah, but that God judged the despised Galilee a better training school for the future Saviour of publicans, sinners and Pagans." (Bruce)

c. **And he came and dwelt in a city called Nazareth**: It was remarkable that Joseph came back to Nazareth, the hometown of Mary and presumably Joseph (Luke 1:26-27). It was remarkable because Nazareth was an *unremarkable* town, and because it was where everyone knew Mary and Joseph and the strange circumstances surrounding the birth of their son.

> i. Nazareth was an unwalled, unprotected town with a somewhat bad reputation; Nathaniel wondered if anything good could come from Nazareth (John 1:46). In God's plan, Jesus came from a small, insignificant place that, if it had any reputation, it was a bad one. This is where Jesus grew up and matured into adulthood.

d. **That it might be fulfilled which was spoken by the prophets, "He shall be called a Nazarene"**: Of all of Matthew's references to the Old Testament and the prophets, this is one of the most interesting. There is no specific passage found in the Old Testament that says in the given words, **"He shall be called a Nazarene."**

> i. Some think that Matthew meant, *the Messiah would be a Nazirite*. To be a Nazirite was to commit one's self to a special vow of consecration, as described in Numbers 6:1-21. When under the vow, people regarded

themselves as especially devoted to God, leaving their hair uncut, drinking no wine and eating no grape products, and avoiding any kind of contact with anything dead. Certainly Jesus was a remarkably consecrated man, but it seems that Matthew only hints at the idea of a *Nazirite* from a distance and instead focuses on the connection to the town of **Nazareth**.

ii. Yet what specific prophecy from the Old Testament tells us that the Messiah would come from **Nazareth**? France notes that there is something peculiar in the way Matthew worded this reference. "It should be noted, however, that the formula introducing the quotation differs from the regular pattern in two ways: it refers not to a single prophet but to *the prophets*, and it concludes not with 'saying' but with 'that'. This suggests that it is not meant to be a quotation of a specific passage, but a summary of a theme of prophetic expectation...Thus it has been suggested that Matthew saw in the obscurity of Nazareth the fulfillment of Old Testament indications of a humble and rejected Messiah." (France)

iii. If there *was* any specific passage in Matthew's mind, it was likely Isaiah 11:1: *There shall come forth a Rod from the stem of Jesse, and a Branch shall grow out of his roots.* The Hebrew word translated *Branch* sounds like "Nazir" (*neser*). "Jerome, following the Jewish scholars of his time, believed the reference to be mainly to Isaiah 11, where mention is made of a branch that shall spring out of Jesse's root...The epithet **Nazarene** will thus mean: 'the man of Nazareth, the town of the little shoot'." (Bruce)

iv. "He meant that the prophets have described the Messiah as one that would be despised and rejected of men. They spoke of him as a great prince and conqueror when they described his second coming, but they set forth his first coming when they spoke of him as a root out of a dry ground without form or comeliness, who when he should be seen would have no beauty that men should desire him. The prophets said that he would be called by a despicable title, and it was so, for his countrymen called him a Nazarene." (Spurgeon)

v. "God by his singular providence so ordered it, that he who was the antitype to all the Nazirites, and the true *Nazir*, or person separated, should be educated at Nazareth, a poor contemptible town." (Poole)

e. **He shall be called a Nazarene**: In the plan of God the Father, inspired by God the Spirit, and embraced by God the Son, the Messiah grew up in the somewhat despised town. Indeed, Jesus would become known as "Jesus of Nazareth" and His followers "Nazarenes."

i. When Jesus revealed Himself to Paul on the road to Damascus – obviously after His resurrection and ascension and seating at the right hand of God the Father in glory – He introduced Himself to Paul saying, *I am Jesus of Nazareth* (Acts 22:8).

ii. In Acts 24:5, the prosecutors of Paul said this to his judge: *We have found this man a pestilent fellow, and a mover of sedition among all the Jews throughout the world, and a ringleader of the sect of the Nazarenes.*

iii. "Certainly he has long been called a '*Nazarene*,' both by Jews and violent unbelievers. Spitting on the ground in disgust, many a time has his fierce adversary hissed out the name '*Nazarene*,' as if it were the climax of contempt." (Spurgeon)

iv. "There is always some city or village or another whose inhabitants seem to be the butt of every joke and the object of scorn. The people of such places are thought to be low, uncultured, not-very-smart. That is the kind of place Nazareth was." (Spurgeon)

v. Growing up in Nazareth, Jesus would mature in boyhood and then in His young adulthood. He would fulfill the responsibilities expected of an eldest son; and then at some time Joseph disappeared from the scene and Jesus became the "man of the family." He worked His trade, supported His family, loved His God, and proved Himself utterly faithful in a thousand small things before He formally entered His appointed ministry. Yet no one would be intimidated to meet a man from Nazareth; the tendency would be to immediately think one's self *better* than a person from Nazareth.

Matthew 3 - The Ministry of John the Baptist

A. The public ministry of John the Baptist.

1. (1-2) The message of John the Baptist.

In those days John the Baptist came preaching in the wilderness of Judea, and saying, "Repent, for the kingdom of heaven is at hand!"

a. **In those days John the Baptist came**: Matthew introduces us to one of the fascinating characters of the New Testament. This was the John born to Zacharias and Elisabeth, whose miraculous birth to this too-old couple was announced, along with his call to be the forerunner of the Messiah, in Luke 1.

i. **In those days**: "It is a general term that reveals little chronologically but insists that the account is historical." (Carson)

b. **Preaching in the wilderness of Judea, and saying, "Repent"**: John's message was a call to repentance. Some people think that repentance is mostly about *feelings*, especially feeling sorry for your sin. It is wonderful to feel sorry about your sin, but **repent** isn't a "feelings" word. It is an *action* word. John told his listeners to make a change of the mind, not merely to feel sorry for what they had done. Repentance speaks of a change of direction, not a sorrow in the heart.

i. Is repentance something we must *do* before we can come to God? Yes and no. Repentance does not describe something we must do before we come to God; it describes what coming to God is like. If you are in New York, and I tell you to come to Los Angeles, I don't really need to say "Leave New York and come to Los Angeles." To come to Los Angeles *is* to leave New York, and if I haven't left New York, I certainly haven't come to Los Angeles. We can't come to the **kingdom of heaven** unless we leave our sin and the self-life.

ii. The call to repentance is important and must not be neglected. It is entirely accurate to say that it is the *first word of the gospel.*

- **Repent** was the *first word* of John the Baptist's gospel (Matthew 3:1-2).

- **Repent** was the *first word* of Jesus' gospel (Matthew 4:14 and Mark 1:14-15).

- **Repent** was the *first word* in the preaching ministry of the twelve disciples (Mark 6:12).

- **Repent** was the *first word* in the preaching instructions Jesus gave to His disciples after His resurrection (Luke 24:46-47).

- **Repent** was the *first word* of exhortation in the first Christian sermon (Acts 2:38).

- **Repent** was the *first word* in the mouth of the Apostle Paul through his ministry (Acts 26:19-20).

iii. The **wilderness** John preached in wasn't exactly desert. "It is hot and, apart from the Jordan itself, largely arid, though not unpopulated." (Carson)

c. **For the kingdom of heaven is at hand**: John wanted people to know that **the kingdom of heaven** was *near* - as close as your **hand**. It wasn't as distant or as dreamy as they had imagined. This is why John was so urgent in his call to repentance. If the **kingdom of heaven is at hand**, then we must get ready *now*.

i. John's main message wasn't "You're a sinner, you need to repent." John's main message was *"Messiah the King is coming."* The call to repentance was the *response* to the news that the King and His kingdom were coming – indeed, already here in one sense.

ii. Some dispensationalists see a difference between the **kingdom of heaven** and the *kingdom of God*, the dominant terms used in Mark and Luke. The idea is that the *kingdom of God* is a now-present spiritual kingdom, but the **kingdom of heaven** refers to the coming millennial earth in its splendor. A much better explanation is that Matthew simply used the term **kingdom of heaven** instead of *kingdom of God* so as to avoid offence to Jewish readers, who often rejected direct references to God and would refer to His dwelling place instead of Him directly.

iii. Adam Clarke gives a further idea: "But why is it called the *kingdom of* HEAVEN? Because God designed that his kingdom of grace here should resemble the kingdom of glory above. And hence our Lord teaches us to pray, Thy will be done on earth, as it is in heaven."

2. (3-4) The identity of John the Baptist.

For this is he who was spoken of by the prophet Isaiah, saying:

"The voice of one crying in the wilderness:
'Prepare the way of the LORD;
Make His paths straight.'"

And John himself was clothed in camel's hair, with a leather belt around his waist; and his food was locusts and wild honey.

a. **Prepare the way of the LORD**: Matthew used this passage from Isaiah 40:3 to identify John the Baptist as the prophesied forerunner of the Messiah. In this role, John's purpose was to **prepare** hearts for the Messiah, and to bring an awareness of sin among Israel so they could receive the salvation from sin offered by the Messiah (Matthew 1:12).

   i. "According to John 1:23, the Baptist once applied this passage to himself. Here Matthew does it for him." (Carson)

b. **Make His paths straight**: The passage Matthew quotes from (Isaiah 40:3) has in mind building up a great road for the arrival of a majestic king. The idea is to fill in the holes and knock down the hills that are in the way.

   i. "The idea is taken from the practice of eastern monarchs, who, whenever they entered upon an expedition, or took a journey through a desert country, sent *harbingers* before them, to prepare all things for their passage; and *pioneers* to *open* the *passes*, to *level* the *ways*, and to *remove* all *impediments*." (Clarke)

   ii. The idea of preparing the way of the LORD is a word picture, because the real preparation must take place in our hearts. Building a road is very much like the preparation God must do in our hearts. They are both expensive, they both must deal with many different problems and environments, and they both take an expert engineer.

   iii. Jesus was the coming Messiah and King, and John the Baptist was the one **crying in the wilderness**, and through his message of repentance, he worked to **prepare the way of the LORD**. We often fail to appreciate how important the *preparing* work of the LORD is. Any great work of God begins with great *preparation*.

   iv. "Men's hearts were like a wilderness, wherein there is no way; but as loyal subjects throw up roads for the approach of beloved princes, so were men to welcome the Lord, with their hearts made right and ready to receive him." (Spurgeon)

   v. In Isaiah 40:3 the way of Yahweh is prepared and made straight; in Matthew 3:3 it is the way of Jesus. This identification of Jesus with

Yahweh is common in the New Testament (as in Exodus 13:21 and 1 Corinthians 10:4; Isaiah 6:1 and John 12:41).

c. **Clothed with camel's hair, with a leather belt**: In his personality and ministry, John the Baptist was patterned after the bold Elijah (2 Kings 1:8), who fearlessly called Israel to repentance.

i. "Both Elijah and John had stern ministries in which austere garb and diet confirmed their message and condemned the idolatry of physical and spiritual softness." (Carson)

ii. In the spirit of today's age, John's ministry would have been very different. He wouldn't start in the wilderness. He wouldn't dress funny. He wouldn't preach such a straightforward message. He would use marketing surveys and focus groups to hone his message and presentation. John wasn't motivated by the spirit of today's age, but by the Spirit of God.

iii. It wasn't that John the Baptist was *trying to be* this Elijah-like forerunner predicted in Malachi 4:5, as if he decided on his own to make this his destiny and public image. John knew the words spoken to his father Zacharias before he was born: *He will also go before Him in the spirit and power of Elijah, "to turn the hearts of the fathers to the children," and the disobedient to the wisdom of the just, to make ready a people prepared for the Lord.* (Luke 1:17) This is simply who John the Baptist *was*, and one might say he was this before he was even created in the womb.

iv. "His diet, though limited, was nutritious and readily available in the wilderness." (France)

iv. "Lord, let not my meat, my drink, or garments, hinder me in thy work!" (Spurgeon)

3. (5-6) The success of John's ministry.

Then Jerusalem, all Judea, and all the region around the Jordan went out to him and were baptized by him in the Jordan, confessing their sins.

a. **Then Jerusalem, all Judea, and all the region around the Jordan went out to him**: John's ministry met with wonderful response. There were many people who recognized their sinfulness, their need to get ready for the Messiah, and were willing to *do* something about it.

i. Under the blessing of God, John's message of repentance and call to prepare for the Messiah bore great fruit. "Baptism was for sinners, and no Jew ever conceived of himself as a sinner shut out from God.

Now for the first time in their national history the Jews realized their own sin and their own clamant need of God. Never before had there been such a unique national movement of penitence and of search for God." (Barclay)

ii. "His preaching created a widespread revival movement, and his followers constituted a significant group within Judaism which maintained its separate existence beyond the New Testament period." (France)

iii. Josephus actually wrote more about John the Baptist than he did about Jesus. The influence of John the Baptist is evident decades after his ministry began, as seen in Acts 18:25 and 19:3.

iv. **All Judea, and all the region**: "The term *all* here twice repeated, is enough to let us know, that it is often in Scripture significative no further than *many*, for it cannot be imagined that every individual person in Jerusalem and the region about Jordan went to hear John the Baptist, but a great many did." (Poole)

b. **And were baptized by him**: With baptism, John offered a ceremonial washing that confessed sin and *did something* to demonstrate repentance. Before we can gain the kingdom of heaven, we must recognize our poverty of spirit (Matthew 5:3). This type of awareness of sin is the foundation for most revivals and awakenings.

i. Baptism simply means to "immerse or overwhelm." John didn't sprinkle when he **baptized**. As was the custom in some other Jewish ceremonial washings, John completely immersed those he baptized. "Naturally, therefore, the baptism was not a mere sprinkling with water, but a bath in which his whole body was bathed." (Barclay)

ii. Baptism was practiced in the Jewish community already in the form of ceremonial immersions, but typically it was only among Gentiles who wished to become Jews. For a Jew in John's day to submit to baptism was essentially to say, "I confess that I am as far away from God as a Gentile and I need to get right with Him." This was a real work of the Holy Spirit.

iii. John's baptism might have been related to the Jewish practice of baptizing Gentile converts, or to some of the ceremonial washings practiced by the Jews of that day. Though it may have some links, at the same time it was *unique* - so unique that John simply became known as "the Baptizer." If there were a lot of people doing that, it wouldn't be a unique title.

iv. "John's baptism was an innovation. The nearest contemporary parallels are the self-baptism of a Gentile on becoming a proselyte, and the repeated ritual washings (also self-administered) at Qumran." (France)

v. Christian baptism is like John's in the sense that it demonstrates repentance, but it is also more. It is being *baptized into Christ*, that is, into His death and resurrection (Romans 6:3).

c. **Confessing their sins**: This was another important aspect, and is a partner to the call to repentance. These Jewish people were very serious about getting right with God.

i. "The participle means, *while confessing*; not, provided they confessed. This confession of sins by individuals was a new thing in Israel. There was a collective confession on the great day of atonement, and individual confession in certain specified cases (Numbers 5:7), but no great spontaneous self-unburdenment of penitent souls – every man apart. It must have been a stirring sight." (Bruce)

ii. "The '*Confessing their sins*' which went with baptism in the Jordan gave it its meaning. Apart from the acknowledgement of guilt, it would have been a mere bathing of the person without spiritual significance." (Spurgeon)

4. (7-12) John's confrontation with the Pharisees and Sadducees.

But when he saw many of the Pharisees and Sadducees coming to his baptism, he said to them, "Brood of vipers! Who warned you to flee from the wrath to come? Therefore bear fruits worthy of repentance, and do not think to say to yourselves, 'We have Abraham as *our* father.' For I say to you that God is able to raise up children to Abraham from these stones. And even now the ax is laid to the root of the trees. Therefore every tree which does not bear good fruit is cut down and thrown into the fire. I indeed baptize you with water unto repentance, but He who is coming after me is mightier than I, whose sandals I am not worthy to carry. He will baptize you with the Holy Spirit and fire. His winnowing fan *is* in His hand, and He will thoroughly clean out His threshing floor, and gather His wheat into the barn; but He will burn up the chaff with unquenchable fire."

a. **When he saw many of the Pharisees and Sadducees coming**: This is our introduction to these two important groups in first-century Judaism. These two groups were very different and often in conflict. Together they represented the leadership of Judaism.

i. Matthew Poole pointed out four things about the Pharisees.

- They believed that one was made righteous by keeping the law, and they believed themselves to be righteous in this way.

- They often misinterpreted the law.

- They held many traditions to be of equal authority to Scripture.

- They were often hypocrites in their practice, neglecting the core and spirit of the law for aspects of outward observance.

ii. Bruce called the Pharisees "Legal precisians, *virtuosi* in religion." Of the Sadducees, he said they were "Men of affairs and of the world, largely of the sacerdotal class."

b. **Brood of vipers! Who warned you to flee from the wrath to come**: John accused these leaders of wanting to *appear* anxious for the Messiah, but not truly repenting and preparing their hearts. Therefore John demanded **fruits worthy of repentance**.

i. "Many Pharisees and Sadducees may have come for baptism with the ostentation that characterized their other religious activities... they were showing the world how ready they were for Messiah, though they had not truly repented." (Carson) John reminded them that real repentance will show itself in life. It has to be a matter of *living* repentance, not just *talking* repentance.

ii. "You come here and thrust yourselves into a crowd of penitents, but this is not enough, true repentance is not a barren thing...you must bring forth the fruits of holiness, fruits that may answer the nature of true repentance." (Poole)

iii. Of course most of the Jewish people believed in **the wrath to come**; the difference was the targets of that judgment. "They conceived of the judgment as concerning the heathen peoples; he thought of it as concerning the godless in Israel." (Bruce)

iv. We can learn much from John the Baptist's preaching, "**Flee from the wrath to come**."

- This wrath is the **wrath** of *God*.

- This wrath is fair and well deserved.

- This wrath is often ignored or disregarded because it is not immediate; it is **to come**.

- This wrath is not any less certain just because it is delayed and is **to come**.

- This wrath is terrible when it comes because it is God's wrath.

- This wrath cannot be stood against; the only way to survive is to successfully **flee** from it.

v. What John told them to do is also instructive: **flee**.

- To **flee** implies *immediate action*.
- To **flee** implies *swift action*.
- To **flee** implies *straight movement with no diversions*.

c. **Do not think to say to yourselves, "We have Abraham as our father"**: John warns them to stop trusting in their Jewish heritage because they must truly repent, not simply trust in Abraham's merits.

i. It was widely taught in that day that Abraham's merits were plenty for any Jew's salvation and that a Jewish person *couldn't* go to hell. John points out that these Pharisees and Sadducees are of a different family; they are a **brood of vipers** - meaning a family associated with serpents!

ii. **Even now the ax is laid to the root of the trees**: "It has been well observed, that there is an allusion here to a woodman, who, having marked a tree for excision, lays his axe at its root, and strips off his outer garment, that he may wield his blows more powerfully, and that his work may be quickly performed." (Clarke)

iii. "No mere pruning and trimming work did John come to do; he was the handler of a sharp axe that was to fell every worthless tree." (Spurgeon)

d. **I indeed baptize you with water unto repentance**: John's baptism was one of **repentance**. In this regard, it was not identical to Christian baptism or *baptism into Christ* (Romans 6:3), which includes a demonstration of repentance and cleansing, but also recognizes the believer's identification with Jesus' death, burial, and resurrection (Romans 6:3-4).

e. **Whose sandals I am not worthy to carry**: John recognizes his own place before Jesus. He is one **not worthy to carry** the **sandals** of Jesus, and he did not consider himself far above those whom he has called to repentance, and he knew where he stood in relation to Jesus (instead of becoming proud of the crowds he drew and the response he saw).

i. In saying this, John put himself lower in relation to Jesus than a normal disciple of a normal rabbi. "A Rabbi's disciple was expected to act virtually as his master's slave, but to remove his shoes was too low a task for even a disciple (*Ketuboth* 96a)."

f. **He will baptize you with the Holy Spirit and fire. His winnowing fan is in His hand, and He will thoroughly clean out His threshing**

floor: John warns them to prepare for the Messiah's coming, because He is coming with judgment.

i. **Baptize you with the Holy Spirit**: This is the promised out-pouring of the Spirit promised with the New Covenant (Ezekiel 37:14).

ii. **And fire**: To baptize with **fire** means to bring the fires of judgment, which will purify the pure, but destroy the wicked like **chaff**. **Chaff** is the worthless residue of a wheat stalk after the kernel of grain has been removed. These proud and unrepentant leaders were just as useless to God. "Purification by *fire* was also a prophetic hope (Isaiah 4:4; Zechariah 13:9; Malachi 3:2; *cf.* Isaiah 1:25). John therefore predicts a real cleansing, in contrast with his own merely outward token." (France)

iii. "A winnowing fork tossed both unto the air. The wind blew the chaff away, and the heavier grain fell to be gathered up from the ground. The scattered chaff was swept up and burned and the threshing floor cleared." (Carson)

iv. The Jewish leaders thought that the Messiah would come with judgment, but only against Israel's enemies. They were blind in their self-righteous confidence that only others needed to get right with God. Many today have the same idea. "John the Baptist is sadly needed to-day. Much of what we call Christianity is but christianized heathenism…we need that John the Baptist should come with his stern words about the axe, the winnowing-fan, and the fire. Nothing less will avail to prepare the way for a new coming of Christ." (Meyer)

B. John's ministry in baptizing Jesus.

1. (13-14) Jesus comes to John for baptism.

Then Jesus came from Galilee to John at the Jordan to be baptized by him. And John *tried to* prevent Him, saying, "I need to be baptized by You, and are You coming to me?"

a. **Then Jesus came from Galilee to John at the Jordan to be baptized**: This is a significant emergence of Jesus from His many years of obscurity. These first works in His public ministry carry great meaning in understanding the rest of His ministry.

b. **Jesus came**: No one compelled Jesus to be baptized. He came to John of His own choice. There are some old and false traditions (mentioned in Barclay) that Jesus was baptized because of pressure from His mother and brothers. Since everyone else was doing it, they thought He should also.

c. **I need to be baptized by You, and are You coming to me**: John recognized the inherent irony in this situation. Jesus had nothing to repent of, and it would be more appropriate for Jesus to baptize John.

> i. It was as if John said to Jesus, "I need your Spirit-and-fire baptism, not you my water-baptism." (France)

2. (15) Jesus allows Himself to be baptized by John.

But Jesus answered and said to him, "Permit *it to be so* now, for thus it is fitting for us to fulfill all righteousness." Then he allowed Him.

a. **It is fitting for us to fulfill all righteousness**: Jesus understood why this seemed strange to John, but it was nevertheless necessary **to fulfill all righteousness**. It wasn't that this one act in itself fulfilled all righteousness, but it was another important step in the overall mission of Jesus to identify with fallen and sinful man, a mission that would only finally be fulfilled at the cross.

> i. Yet it would be easy for any onlooker to think that Jesus was just another sinner being baptized; so He identified with sinful man. "Christ's baptism might create misunderstanding, just as His associating with publicans and sinners did. He was content to be misunderstood." (Bruce)

b. **Then he allowed Him**: The purpose was for Jesus to completely identify Himself with sinful man. This is exactly what He did in His birth, His upbringing, and His death. So here, as John **allowed Him** to be, Jesus stood in the place of sinful man.

> i. "In baptism He confessed, as His own, sins which He had not committed, and repented of them before God. He was numbered with the transgressors and bore the sins of many." (Morgan)

> ii. There is also a sense in which this was an important new beginning for Jesus; not in the sense of turning from sin, but in making a break with His previous life. "In accordance with the symbolic significance of the rite as denoting death to an old life and rising to a new, Jesus came to be baptized in the sense of dying to the old natural relations to parents, neighbors, and earthly calling, and devoting Himself henceforth to His public Messianic vocation." (Bruce)

3. (16-17) The Divine witness to Jesus' status as the Son of God.

When He had been baptized, Jesus came up immediately from the water; and behold, the heavens were opened to Him, and He saw the Spirit of God descending like a dove and alighting upon Him. And

suddenly a voice *came* from heaven, saying, "This is My beloved Son, in whom I am well pleased."

a. **The heavens were opened**: It was important for God the Father to publicly demonstrate that Jesus' baptism was not just like anyone else's, in the sense of being a display of repentance. It was *not* a display of repentance, but instead it was a righteous identification with sinners, motivated by love, was *well pleasing* to the Father.

b. **The Spirit of God descending like a dove**: This was a dramatic experience with the Holy Spirit, with the **Spirit of God** coming upon Jesus in a way that could actually be seen (somewhat similar to the coming of the Spirit of God upon the gathered disciples in Acts 2:1-4).

i. Luke 3:22 says it like this: *And the Holy Spirit descended in bodily form like a dove upon Him.* In some way the Spirit was present, and "flew down" upon Jesus **like a dove**. Whatever exactly it was, it was real. John 1:32-34 indicates that John the Baptist *saw* this phenomenon and understood what it meant.

ii. This was not a temporary gift of the **Spirit of God**. John the Baptist's testimony in John 1:32-33, when he said that he saw *the Spirit descend from heaven like a dove, and He remained upon Him.* Jesus was about to begin His public ministry, and He would do it in the power of the **Spirit of God**. "It was the Spirit of God who gave success to Jesus Christ's ministry." (Spurgeon)

iii. How a **dove** represents the work of the Holy Spirit:

- Like a dove, the work of the Holy Spirit can be swift.
- Like a dove, the work of the Holy Spirit can be soft and gentle.
- Like a dove, the work of the Holy Spirit brings peace.
- Like a dove, the work of the Holy Spirit is harmless.
- Like a dove, the work of the Holy Spirit speaks of love.

c. **This is My beloved Son, in whom I am well pleased**: When this voice of God the Father spoke from heaven, everyone knew that Jesus was not just another man being baptized. They knew Jesus was the perfect (**in whom I am well pleased**) Son of God, identifying with sinful man. By this, everyone knew that Jesus was different. Jesus was baptized so to be identified *with* sinful man, but He was also baptized to be identified *to* sinful man.

i. Luke 3:21 tells us that the heavens were opened while Jesus prayed. "As he was praying; for prayer is the key of heaven, wherewith we may

take out of God's treasury plentiful mercy for ourselves and others."
(Trapp)

ii. In this God the Father also expressed His approval of Jesus' life
up to this point. "By the divine proclamation at the baptism God
announced the presence of the King, and set the seal of His approval
on the years already lived." (Morgan)

d. **The Spirit of God descending...My beloved Son**: We should not miss
the obvious point: *God the Father loves God the Son, and communicated
that love by God the Holy Spirit.* Here we see the love relationship and
cooperation between the Persons of the Trinity, in one occasion when the
Father, the Son and the Holy Spirit were all manifested at the same time.

i. "God so loved his Son, that he gave him all the world for his
possession, Psalm 2; but he so loved the world, that he gave Son and
all for its redemption." (Trapp)

ii. There is no suggestion that Jesus *became* the Son of God with this
experience. "We need not assume that Jesus had no previous experience
of the Spirit; the vision symbolizes his commissioning for his Messianic
work, not a new spiritual status." (France)

Matthew 4 - The Temptation of Jesus and His First Galilean Ministry

A. Jesus is tempted in the wilderness.

1. (1-2) Jesus is led to the place of temptation.

Then Jesus was led up by the Spirit into the wilderness to be tempted by the devil. And when He had fasted forty days and forty nights, afterward He was hungry.

a. **Then Jesus was led up by the Spirit into the wilderness to be tempted**: After identifying with sinners in His baptism, Jesus then identified with them again in severe temptation. This was a necessary part of His ministry, so He truly was **led up by the Spirit into the wilderness**.

i. It was a remarkable contrast between the glory following Jesus' baptism and the challenge **to be tempted by the devil**.

- Then the cool waters of the Jordan; now the barren wilderness.
- Then the huge crowds; now solitude and silence.
- Then the Spirit rests like a dove; now the Spirit drives Him into the wilderness.
- Then the voice of the Father calling Him "Beloved Son"; now the hiss of Satan the tempter.
- Then anointed; now attacked.
- Then the water of baptism; now the fire of temptation.
- First the heavens opened; now hell.

ii. Jesus did not need to be tempted to help Him grow. Instead, He endured temptation both so that He could identify with us (Hebrews 2:18 and 4:15), and to demonstrate His own holy, sinless character.

iii. The Holy Spirit cannot tempt us (James 1:13), but the Holy Spirit may lead us to a place where we will be tempted. This is not to prove something to God (who knows all things), but to prove something to us and to the spiritual beings watching us.

b. **Tempted by the devil**: Temptation is a certainty for everyone. Yet Jesus' temptation was more severe. It was more severe because He was tempted directly by **the devil** himself, while we contend mainly with lesser demons. It was also more severe because there is a sense in which temptation is "relieved" by giving in, and Jesus never did yield. Therefore He bore levels of temptation we will never know by experience.

i. Many commentators believe it is improper to refer to this section as the *temptation* of Jesus, because the word *peirazo* is more often and more accurately translated *testing* instead of temptation. "*Peirazein* has a quite different element in its meaning. It means *to test* far more than it means *to tempt* in our sense of the word." (Barclay)

ii. "Luther's remark stands true, that prayer, meditation, and temptation, are the three best instructors of the gospel minister." (Spurgeon)

c. **He had fasted forty days and forty nights, afterward He was hungry**: Matthew points out both the barren desert (the Judean **wilderness** was and is exactly that), and Jesus' severe physical condition after such a long fast. It is said that when hunger pains return after such a fast (**He was hungry**), it indicates the subject is beginning to starve to death.

i. "Here was the Divine power miraculously seen, in upholding the human nature of Christ without any thing to eat: this was a miracle." (Poole) Yet it was a miracle also evident in the lives of Moses (Exodus 34:28) and Elijah (1 Kings 19:8). It was supernatural, but not beyond human capacity when enabled by the Spirit of God.

d. **Forty days and forty nights**: This is a familiar period of testing in the Bible, both in the days of Noah and for Israel in the wilderness. Jesus will succeed where Israel as a nation failed.

i. "Our Saviour was tempted all that forty days' space, saith St. Luke; but these three worst assaults were reserved to the last."

ii. This wasn't self-denial just for the sake of self-denial, or worse yet for the sake of building spiritual pride. This was a period of forced dependence upon God the Father. We remember: *He learned obedience through the things which He suffered* (Hebrews 5:8).

2. (3-4) The first temptation: an appeal to the lust of the flesh.

Now when the tempter came to Him, he said, "If You are the Son of God, command that these stones become bread." But He answered and said, "It is written, 'Man shall not live by bread alone, but by every word that proceeds from the mouth of God.'"

a. **When the tempter came**: Notice that Matthew writes *when* **the tempter came**. In our lives, it is not a question of *if* the tempter will come, but **when** he will come. We will face temptation until we go to glory.

    i. "But let us do what we will, we shall be tempted. God had one Son without sin, but he never had a son without temptation." (Spurgeon)

    ii. We should consider what preceded the temptation of Jesus:

- He was in an especially devout frame of mind before His temptation.

- He was engaged in an act of public obedience to His Father's will before His temptation.

- He was in an exceedingly humble frame of mind before His temptation.

- He was blessed by a heavenly assurance of His Sonship before His temptation.

- He was filled with the Holy Spirit before His temptation.

- He was completely separated from the world before His temptation.

b. **If You are the Son of God**: The question asked by Satan is more literally "*since* **You are the Son of God**," instead of "*if* **You are the Son of God**." Satan did not question Jesus' deity; he challenged Him to prove it or demonstrate it through miraculous works.

c. **Command that these stones become bread**: This was a temptation to use God's gifts for selfish purposes. Satan suggested that Jesus use His miraculous powers to provide food for Himself.

    i. "Sonship of the living God, he suggested, surely means Jesus has the power and right to satisfy his own needs." (Carson)

    ii. This wasn't a temptation to miraculously create great riches or luxuries, only **bread**. The Bible has many accounts of miraculous provision, some at the hands of Jesus. Yet Jesus would not **command that these stones become bread**, especially at the instigation of Satan.

    iii. We might say that Jesus was being tested through His strengths, through His gifts. Would He allow His strengths to become traps? "He bids the Lord prove his Sonship by catering for himself; and yet that would have been the surest way to prove that he was not the Son of God." (Spurgeon) We could say that the same temptation came to Jesus on the cross (Matthew 27:40).

d. **But He answered**: Jesus didn't silently disagree with Satan, **He answered** him - and He answered him from the Word of God. When Jesus quoted Deuteronomy 8:3, Jesus shows that **every word that proceeds from the mouth of God** should be more precious to us than food itself.

   i. What Satan suggested made sense - "Why starve yourself to death?" But what **is written** makes even more sense.

   ii. "Hunger represents human wants, and the question was: whether Sonship was to mean exemption from these, or loyal acceptance of them as part of the Messiah's experience." (Bruce)

   iii. It isn't that Jesus refused supernatural help in feeding Himself; He was more than happy to eat what the angels brought Him when the time of testing was over (Matthew 4:11). It wasn't a matter of refusing supernatural help; it was a matter of submitting to His Father's timing and will in all things.

e. **It is written**: By relying on the power and truth of God's Word, Jesus was willing to fight this battle as a man; He could have easily rebuked Satan into another galaxy, but resisted him in a way that we can imitate and identify with.

   i. Jesus used *Scripture* to battle Satan's temptation, not some elaborate spiritual power inaccessible to us. Jesus fought this battle as fully man, and He drew on no "special resources" unavailable to us. "Out flashed the sword of the Spirit: our Lord will fight with no other weapon. He could have spoken new revelations, but chose to say, '*It is written*.'" (Spurgeon)

   ii. He could have stood against Satan with a display of His own glory; He could have stood against Satan with logic and reason. Instead, Jesus used the word of God as a weapon against Satan and temptation.

   • He used a weapon that one can use when they are all alone.

   • He used a weapon to defend His Sonship.

   • He used a weapon to defeat temptation.

   • He used a weapon that was effective because He *understood it*.

   ii. We effectively resist temptation in the same way Jesus did: by countering Satan's seductive lies by shining the light of God's truth upon them. If we are ignorant of God's truth, we are poorly armed in the fight against temptation.

3. (5-7) The second temptation: an appeal to the pride of life.

Then the devil took Him up into the holy city, set Him on the pinnacle of the temple, and said to Him, "If You are the Son of God, throw Yourself down. For it is written:

'He shall give His angels charge over you,'

and,

'In *their* hands they shall bear you up,
Lest you dash your foot against a stone.'"

Jesus said to him, "It is written again, 'You shall not tempt the LORD your God.'"

a. **If You are the Son of God, throw Yourself down**: Satan tempted Jesus to "force" the Father into a supernatural event. Satan appealed to the desire within every man to sense approval from God and to have that approval publicly demonstrated.

i. **Set Him on the pinnacle of the temple**: The **pinnacle of the temple** arose some 200 feet from the floor of the Kidron Valley. A leap from there, and the appearance of the promised angelic protection, would be a remarkable spectacle.

ii. "The devil's suggestions was of an artificially created crisis, not of trusting God in the situations which result from obedient service." (France)

iii. "This was the very method that the false Messiahs who were continually arising promised…These pretenders had offered sensations which they could not perform. Jesus could perform anything he promised. Why should he not do it?" (Barclay)

iv. Jesus just had this kind of spectacular demonstration at His baptism (Matthew 3:17), but that must have seemed far away after forty days and nights of fasting in the wilderness.

b. **For it is written**: The devil can use this phrase also. We can trust that the devil has memorized the Bible himself, and is an expert at quoting it out of its context to confuse and defeat those he tempts. Here the devil quoted Psalm 91:11-12, and took it out of its context to say, "Go ahead, Jesus; if You do this the Bible promises angels will rescue You, and it will be spectacular self-promotion."

i. "Satan borrowed our Lord's weapon, and said, "*It is written*'; but he did not use the sword lawfully. It was not in the nature of the false fiend to quote correctly. He left out the necessary words, 'in all thy ways': thus he made the promise say what in truth it never suggested." (Spurgeon)

- This text is *falsely quoted*, because the devil left out the words, "*To keep you in all your ways.*" To test God in this way was *not* of Jesus' way; it was not of the way of the Savior or Messiah. "God had never promised, nor ever given, any protection of angels in sinful and forbidden ways." (Poole)

- This text is *wrongly applied*, because it was not used to teach or encourage, but instead to deceive. "Making this word a promise to be fulfilled upon Christ's neglect of his duy; extending the promise of special providence as to dangers into which men voluntarily throw themselves." (Poole)

ii. Jesus understood from His knowledge of the *whole counsel of God* (Acts 20:27) that Satan was twisting this passage from Psalm 91. Jesus knew how to rightly divide the word of truth (2 Timothy 2:15). Sadly, many are willing to believe anyone who quotes from the Bible today. A preacher can pretty much say whatever he wants if he quotes a few proof-texts, and people will assume that he really speaks from the Bible. It is important for each Christian to know the Bible for themselves, and not to be deceived by someone who quotes the Bible but not accurately or with correct application.

c. **It is written again, "You shall not tempt the LORD your God."** Jesus replied with Scripture, but applied correctly. He knew that attempting to force or manipulate God the Father into such a demonstration would **tempt** God, which the Scriptures strictly forbid.

i. This warns us against demanding something spectacular from God to prove His love or concern for us. He has already given the ultimate demonstration of His love for us at the cross (Romans 5:8), and He can do nothing more "spectacular" than that.

ii. "The focus is again on his relationship to God. As Son of God, he could surely claim with absolute confidence the physical protection which God promises in Psalm 91:11-12…The Son of God can live only in a relationship of trust which needs no test." (France)

4. (8-10) The third temptation: an appeal to the lust of the eyes.

Again, the devil took Him up on an exceedingly high mountain, and showed Him all the kingdoms of the world and their glory. And he said to Him, "All these things I will give You if You will fall down and worship me." Then Jesus said to him, "Away with you, Satan! For it is

written, 'You shall worship the LORD your God, and Him only you shall serve.'"

a. **All these things I will give You**: Essentially, this vision invited Jesus to take a shortcut around the cross. Jesus came to win **all the kingdoms of the world and their glory** back from Satan's domain, and Satan offers them to Jesus, if He will only **fall down and worship** him.

> i. It again may seem a small thing; Jesus could lay claim to **all the kingdoms of the world and their glory**, and do so without enduring the cross. "The danger is greatest when the end is *good*." (Bruce)

> ii. All He would have to do is give Satan what he has been longing for ever since he fell from glorious to profane: **worship** and recognition from God Himself. This is a revealing insight into Satan's heart; worship and recognition are far more precious to him than the possession of **the kingdoms of the world and their glory**. He is still the one who said *I will ascend into heaven, I will exalt my throne above the stars of God; I will also sit on the mount of the congregation on the farthest sides of the north; I will ascend above the heights of the clouds, I will be like the Most High.* (Isaiah 14:13-14)

> iii. "If the words, *all the kingdoms of the world*, be taken in a literal sense, then this must have been a visionary representation, as the highest mountain on the face of the globe could not suffice to make evident even one hemisphere of the earth, and the other must of necessity be in darkness." (Clarke)

> iv. If we can't exactly say how Satan showed Jesus this, we can say with some certainty what Satan *did not* show Jesus: "Satan offers the kingdoms of the world and their 'splendor' without showing their sin." (Carson)

b. **I will give You**: Evidently, Satan *has* authority over this world and its governments. The temptation could not have been real unless there is some real sense that Satan does "possess" **all the kingdoms of the world and their glory**.

> i. Adam and his descendants gave the devil this authority. God gave Adam the earth as a stewardship (Genesis 1:28-30), and Adam willingly turned it over to Satan. After that, all Adam's descendants cast their vote of approval by their personal sin.

> ii. Of course, ultimately, all things belong to God; but God allows Satan to function as *the god of this age* (2 Corinthians 4:4) for a purpose. This is why the fallen world is in the mess it is.

iii. "The tempter does not dare to mention Sonship in this case; for that would have laid the blasphemous suggestion too bare. No son of God can worship the devil." (Spurgeon)

c. **Away with you, Satan! For it is written**: Jesus replied with Scripture again, and commanded the devil to leave. In the same way we can *resist the devil and he will flee from you* (James 4:7). It worked for Jesus (**Then the devil left Him**) and it will work for us.

i. "The word of God hath a power in it to quail and to quash Satan's temptations, far better than that wooden dagger, that leaden sword of the Papists, their holy water, crossings, grains, dirty relics…It is not the sign of the cross, but the word of the cross, that overthrows Satan." (Trapp)

ii. The temptations of Jesus also remind us that *it is no sin to be tempted, as long as the temptation is resisted.* Even horrible temptations – Jesus was tempted to worship Satan – are not in themselves sin if they are resisted.

5. (11) The devil leaves and angels come to Jesus.

Then the devil left Him, and behold, angels came and ministered to Him.

a. **Then the devil left Him** means that Jesus won. He won because He recognized Satan's mode of attack: lies and deception. Primarily, Satan is a deceiver, and for those who live in light of the cross, deception is his only tool, because demonic powers were disarmed at the cross of their "real" weapons and power (Colossians 2:15). But deception is extremely effective at leading us into sin, and at causing us to live lives of fear and unbelief.

i. Jesus showed the only effective counter to deception: God's truth, not man's wisdom. First, we must see temptation for what it is - a lie. Then, we must combat temptation with the Word of God. Then, we must always build ourselves up in the truth, and have it in our heart.

ii. Each passage Jesus quoted back to Satan in this section comes from Deuteronomy chapters 6 and 8. It is not unreasonable to suppose that Jesus was meditating on those very passages, and He fought Satan with the fresh bread He fed on. We should make sure we always have some fresh bread to answer Satan with.

iii. "It is noteworthy that all the passages quoted by our Lord are from the Book of Deuteronomy, which book has been so grievously assailed by the destructive critics. Thus did our Lord put special honor upon that part of the Old Testament which he foresaw would be most attacked. The past few years have proved that the devil does not like

Deuteronomy: he would fain avenge himself for the wounds it caused him on this most memorable occasion." (Spurgeon)

iv. Jesus thought this was important for us to know; only He could have told the Gospel writers what happened when He was tempted in the Judean wilderness. We need to learn from this; to learn how *we* can overcome temptation, but even more importantly how *Jesus* overcame temptation on our behalf and succeeded as the sinless Son of God where Adam and Moses and all others had failed.

b. **Behold, angels came and ministered to Him**: God never forsakes those who endure through temptation. Even as **angels came and ministered to** Jesus, God will find a way to minister to us and meet our needs as we endure temptation.

i. "The angelic help of Psalm 91:11, which Jesus refused to call for illegitimately, is now appropriately given. *Ministered* implies particularly the provision of food, and again the experience of Elijah seems to be recalled (1 Kings 19:5-8)." (France)

ii. "These holy beings might not come upon the scene while the battle was being fought, lest they should seem to divide the honors of the day; but when the duel was ended, they hastened to bring food for the body, and comfort for the mind of the champion King." (Spurgeon)

B. The first Galilean ministry of Jesus.

1. (12-16) Fulfilling prophecy, Jesus brings light to the region of Galilee.

Now when Jesus heard that John had been put in prison, He departed to Galilee. And leaving Nazareth, He came and dwelt in Capernaum, which is by the sea, in the regions of Zebulun and Naphtali, that it might be fulfilled which was spoken by Isaiah the prophet, saying:

"The land of Zebulun and the land of Naphtali,
***By* the way of the sea, beyond the Jordan,**
Galilee of the Gentiles:
The people who sat in darkness have seen a great light,
And upon those who sat in the region and shadow of death
Light has dawned."

a. **When Jesus heard that John had been put in prison, He departed to Galilee**: John 3:22 and 4:1-2 indicate that the first ministry Jesus did with His disciples was a baptizing ministry at the Jordan. Sometime after that and after the arrest of John the Baptist, Jesus went to Galilee to begin His itinerant ministry in that region.

i. John's Gospel (John 1:19-2:12) records an early ministry in Galilee and in Judea before Jesus went to Galilee as mentioned here. This early Judean ministry included the earliest call of the disciples and the wedding at Cana (in Galilee), and the first cleansing of the temple followed by His interview with Nicodemus (in Judea). Then John tells us what happened when Jesus traveled north to Galilee through Samaria, and met a Samaritan woman at a well.

ii. It was the imprisonment of **John** that prompted this. "Galilee was the tetrarchy of Herod, who had imprisoned John. Into that region, our Lord went to continue the ministry of the man thus silenced… Thus it has ever been, and still is. Evil may silence a voice, but it cannot prevent the proclamation of the Word. If John is imprisoned, then Jesus takes up the message." (Morgan)

b. **He departed to Galilee**: The region of **Galilee** was a fertile, progressive, highly populated region. According to figures from the Jewish historian Josephus, there were some 3 million people populating Galilee, an area smaller than the state of Connecticut.

i. In an area of about 60 by 30 miles, Josephus says that there were some 204 villages with none having less than 15,000 people. That gives a population of more than 3 million for the region.

ii. Galilee was predominately Gentile in its population, but with a large number of Jewish cities and citizens. Also, Galilee was known as an incredibly fertile region. Many successful farms took advantage of the good soil.

c. **Leaving Nazareth, He came and dwelt in Capernaum**: This was because the people rejected Jesus in His own hometown (Luke 4:16-30). It was significant that Jesus made His home in Capernaum and not in Nazareth.

i. Matthew may have been particularly interested in **Capernaum** because it was where he himself lived (Matthew 9:1-9). Peter also had a house in Capernaum (Matthew 8:14, Mark 1:29 and 2:1).

ii. Yet **leaving Nazareth**, Jesus did not go to live and make His home in Jerusalem or Judea. Going to Jerusalem would seem to be smarter career planning for the Messiah, but Jesus **dwelt in Capernaum**. "This migration to Capernaum is not formally noted in the other Gospels, but Capernaum appears in all the synoptists as the main centre of Christ's Galilean ministry." (Bruce)

iii. "Here he dwelt in a house, either let or lent him; for of his own he had not where to rest his head, Matthew 8:20. Here he paid tribute as an inhabitant; and hither he resorted and retired himself, when he was tired." (Trapp)

d. **That it might be fulfilled which was spoken by Isaiah the prophet**: As is his custom, Matthew sees Jesus' ministry in Galilee as a fulfillment of prophecy. **Light** has come to this region, largely populated by Gentiles, and Isaiah 9:1-2 predicted this of the ministry of the Messiah.

> i. "In despised Galilee, the place where people live in darkness (i.e., without the religious and cultic advantages of Jerusalem and Judea)… here the light has dawned." (Carson)

> ii. "*Galilee of the Gentiles* was now an even more appropriate description than in Isaiah's day, as successive movements of population had given it a predominately Gentile population until a deliberate Judaizing policy was adopted by the Hasmonaean rulers, resulting in a thoroughly mixed population." (France)

2. (17) A general description of the message of Jesus.

From that time Jesus began to preach and to say, "Repent, for the kingdom of heaven is at hand."

a. **Jesus began to preach**: One might say that this was the main occupation of Jesus. He did heal and minister to many miraculously; but on the whole, it seems fair to say that Jesus was a preacher and teacher who healed, more than He was a healer who also preached and taught. This is the priority of Jesus' ministry as stated in Matthew 4:23.

> i. **Preach**: "The word in Greek is *kerussein*, which is the word for a herald's proclamation from a king. *Kerux* is the Greek word for herald, and the herald was the man who brought a message direct from the king." (Barclay)

b. **Repent**: The gospel Jesus preached began the same place that the gospel John preached began - with a call to *repentance* (Matthew 3:2). In fact, since Jesus waited until John *had been put in prison* (Matthew 4:12), He probably saw Himself as picking up where John left off. But Jesus would go further than John ever did, because John announced the coming of the Messiah, and Jesus is the Messiah.

c. **For the kingdom of heaven is at hand**: Some people make elaborate distinctions between **the kingdom of heaven** and *the kingdom of God*. There actually seems to be no difference at all, especially in light of the Jewish custom of often not even naming God directly, but referring to Him by the place where He lives **heaven** - a custom that Matthew, a Jew writing to Jews, often employs.

3. (18-22) Four men are called as disciples.

And Jesus, walking by the Sea of Galilee, saw two brothers, Simon called Peter, and Andrew his brother, casting a net into the sea; for they were fishermen. Then He said to them, "Follow Me, and I will make you fishers of men." They immediately left *their* nets and followed Him. Going on from there, He saw two other brothers, James *the son* of Zebedee, and John his brother, in the boat with Zebedee their father, mending their nets. He called them, and immediately they left the boat and their father, and followed Him.

a. **Saw two brothers... casting a net into the sea**: This was not the first time Jesus met these men, and other gospels describe previous encounters (John 1:35-42 and Luke 5:3), but this is when Jesus called them to leave their professions and follow Him with a full-time commitment.

i. "Its fishing industry was prosperous, and its *fishermen* not necessarily poor (Zebedee's family employed workers, Mark 1:20)." (France)

ii. God usually calls people as they are busy doing something. Jesus called the apostles as they were **casting a net into the sea** or **mending their nets**. "They were busy in a lawful occupation when he called them to be ministers: our Lord does not call idlers but *fishers*." (Spurgeon)

- Saul was looking for his father's donkeys.
- David was keeping his father's sheep.
- The shepherds were guarding their flocks.
- Amos was farming in Tekoa.
- Matthew was working at the tax collector's table.
- Moses was tending his father-in-law's flock.
- Gideon was threshing wheat.

b. **Follow Me, and I will make you fishers of men**: In that day, it was customary for a rabbi to have disciples; there was nothing cult-like about Jesus asking these men to be with Him constantly and to learn from Him. In some aspects, Jesus offered them a traditional education at the feet of a rabbi; in other aspects, this was very different from a normal rabbinical education.

i. **Follow Me** "would immediately suggest the disciples of a Rabbi... who literally followed him around to absorb his teaching, though this was by their own choice, not by his summons." (France)

ii. "He, however, went further than John, who could only announce and point to another. Jesus immediately followed the announcement with the word spoken to individuals, 'Follow Me,' thus claiming the position of King. (Morgan)

c. **They immediately left their nets… And immediately they left the boat and their father, and followed Him**: The *immediate* response of these disciples is a great example to us. Then the first disciples did what all disciples of Jesus should do: they **followed Him**.

i. Following Jesus means leaving some things behind. The Samaritan woman left her pitcher, Matthew left his tax table, and blind Bartimaeus left his cloak to follow Jesus.

4. (23-25) A description of Jesus' ministry in Galilee.

And Jesus went about all Galilee, teaching in their synagogues, preaching the gospel of the kingdom, and healing all kinds of sickness and all kinds of disease among the people. Then His fame went throughout all Syria; and they brought to Him all sick people who were afflicted with various diseases and torments, and those who were demon-possessed, epileptics, and paralytics; and He healed them. Great multitudes followed Him; from Galilee, and *from* Decapolis, Jerusalem, Judea, and beyond the Jordan.

a. **Teaching in their synagogues**: The customs of the synagogue in that day gave Jesus many opportunities to teach, because they would often give a visitor – especially a distinguished one – a chance to speak.

i. "After the address there came a time for talk, and questions, and discussion. The synagogue was the ideal place in which to get a new teaching across to the people." (Barclay)

b. **Teaching… preaching the gospel of the kingdom**: The difference between **teaching** and **preaching** is one of emphasis and manner, not of content.

i. "Preaching is the uncompromising proclamation of certainties; teaching is the explanation of the meaning and significance of them." (Barclay)

c. **All kinds of sickness and all kinds of disease**: Jesus' ability to heal those with all different kinds of diseases demonstrates that He has authentic power over the damage done by the fall of man. His authority over demons (**and those who were demon-possessed**) shows He has authentic power over all creation.

i. This is the first mention of the **demon-possessed** in the New Testament, and the concept is rarely recorded in the Old Testament (Saul was one example, who was troubled by a spirit, as in 1 Samuel

18:10, 19:9). There is obviously much more record of demon possession on the pages of the New Testament than either in the Old Testament or in the contemporary western world. Many suggestions have been offered for this fact.

- Some believe that God gave the devil greater allowance to afflict man in this way, to give greater evidence of Jesus' credentials as Messiah.

- Some believe that God allowed the devil a greater allowance to afflict man in this way to rebuke the Sadducees, who did not believe in supernatural beings such as angels and demons.

- Some believe that there was no greater allowance in those days at all, and that there is the same amount of demon possession today, although it is not recognized as such.

- Some believe that there is simply far less demon possession in cultures that have been under the influence of the gospel for hundreds of years, and far more in pagan and/or animistic cultures.

- Some believe that Satan himself is not interested in a strategy of widespread demon possession of humans in the contemporary western world, because he finds anonymity and spiritual skepticism more effective tools.

d. **Great multitudes followed Him**: Jesus had a purpose for allowing such dramatic miracles to attract **great multitudes**. He wanted to teach the multitudes, not simply to impress them with miracles.

i. "With every allowance for the exaggeration of a popular account, this speaks to an extraordinary impression." (Bruce)

ii. "Christ's *fame* spread very far doubtless, because of the good he did, and the miracles he wrought...*all* here again can signify no more than very many that were indisposed and ill affected as to their bodily health." (Clarke)

iii. "People from all these areas 'followed' Jesus. Despite contrary arguments 'follow' does not necessarily indicate solid discipleship. It may, as here, refer to those who at some particular time followed Jesus around in his itinerant ministry and thus were loosely considered disciples." (Carson)

Matthew 5 - The Sermon on the Mount

A. Introduction to the Sermon on the Mount.

1. (1) Jesus prepares to teach His disciples.

And seeing the multitudes, He went up on a mountain, and when He was seated His disciples came to Him.

a. **And seeing the multitudes**: The previous section mentioned that *great multitudes followed Him*, coming from many different regions (Matthew 4:25). In response to this, Jesus **went up on a mountain**.

i. It is wrong to think that Jesus **went up on a mountain** to remove Himself from the multitudes. It is true that Jesus gave this teaching to His disciples, but this use of the term is probably broad, including many among the *great multitudes* that *followed Him* mentioned in Matthew 4:25. By the end of the Sermon on the Mount, people in general heard His message and were amazed (Matthew 7:28).

ii. Luke says that this same basic material was, on a different occasion, spoken to *a crowd of His disciples and a great multitude of people from all Judea and Jerusalem, and from the seacoast of Tyre and Sidon, who came to hear Him and be healed of their diseases* (Luke 6:17). Yet, in the beginning of the teaching, Luke writes: *Then He lifted up His eyes toward His disciples, and said* (Luke 6:20). The sense of this is much the same as in Matthew; that this sermon was spoken to the disciples of Jesus, but *disciples* in a broad sense of those who had followed Him and heard Him; not in the narrow sense of only the Twelve.

iii. "Jesus was not monastic in spirit, and He had not two doctrines, one for the many, another for the few, like Buddha. His highest teaching… was meant for the million." (Bruce)

iv. "A crypt or cavern would have been out of all character for a message which is to be published upon the housetops, and preached to every creature under heaven." (Spurgeon)

b. **When He was seated**: This was the common posture for teaching in that culture. It was customary for the teacher to sit and the hearers to stand.

i. "Sitting was the accepted posture of synagogue or school teachers (Luke 4:20; cf. Matthew 13:2; 23:2; 24:3)." (Carson)

ii. Now in Matthew's record Jesus will speak and teach; it is God speaking but no longer through an inspired human personality like Jeremiah or Isaiah or Samuel; now the truth of God spoke through the exact personality of God.

c. **His disciples came to Him**: This again probably has in mind a group much larger than the Twelve, who to this point have not been introduced as a group in this Gospel.

i. "He ascends the hill to get away from the crowds below, and the disciples, now a considerable band, gather about Him. Others may not be excluded, but the disciples are the audience proper." (Bruce)

2. (2) Jesus begins to teach.

Then He opened His mouth and taught them, saying:

a. **Then He opened His mouth**: This means that Jesus used his voice in a strong way to teach this crowd. He spoke with energy, projecting His thoughts with earnestness.

i. "It is not superfluous to say that 'he opened his mouth, and taught them,' for he had taught them often when his mouth was closed." (Spurgeon)

ii. "He began to speak to them with freedom, so as the multitude might hear." (Poole) "Jesus Christ spoke like a man in earnest; he enunciated clearly, and spake loudly. He lifted up his voice like a trumpet, and published salvation far and wide, like a man who had something to say which he desired his audience to hear and feel." (Spurgeon)

iii. "In Greek, it is used of a solemn, grave and dignified utterance. It was used, for instance, of the saying of an oracle. It is the natural preface to a most weighty saying." (Barclay)

b. **And taught them, saying**: What they heard was a message that has long been recognized as the sum of Jesus' - or anyone's - ethical teaching. In the Sermon on the Mount, Jesus tells us how to live.

i. It has been said if you took all the good advice for how to live ever uttered by any philosopher or psychiatrist or counselor, took out the foolishness and boiled it all down to the real essentials, you would be left with a poor imitation of this great message by Jesus.

ii. The Sermon on the Mount is sometimes thought of as Jesus' "Declaration of the Kingdom." The American Revolutionaries had their *Declaration of Independence*. Karl Marx had his *Communist Manifesto*. With this message, Jesus declared what His Kingdom is all about.

iii. It presents a radically different agenda than what the nation of Israel expected from the Messiah. It does not present the political or material blessings of the Messiah's reign. Instead, it expresses the spiritual implications of the rule of Jesus in our lives. This great message tells us how we will live when Jesus is our Lord. "In the first century there was little agreement among Jews as to what the messianic kingdom would be like. One very popular assumption was that the Roman yoke would be shattered and there would be political peace and mounting prosperity." (Carson)

iv. It is important to understand that the Sermon on the Mount does not deal with salvation as such, but it lays out for the disciple and the potential disciple how regarding Jesus as King translates into ethics and daily living.

v. It can't be proved, but in my opinion, the Sermon on the Mount was Jesus' "standard" sermon. It was the core of His itinerant message: a simple proclamation of how God expects us to live, contrasting with common Jewish misunderstandings of that life. It may be that when Jesus preached to a new audience, He often preached this sermon or used the themes from it.

vi. Yet we can also regard this as Jesus training the disciples in the message He wanted them to carry to others. It was His message, meant to be passed onto and through them. "In the Sermon on the Mount, Matthew shows us Jesus instructing his disciples in the message which was his and which they were to take to men." (Barclay) In the Gospel of Luke, the material similar to the Sermon on the Mount comes immediately after Jesus chose the Twelve.

vii. Barclay also points out that the verb translated **taught** is in the imperfect tense, "Therefore it describes repeated and habitual action, and the translation should be: 'This is what he used to teach them.'"

viii. It is clear that the Sermon on the Mount had a significant impact on the early church. The early Christians make constant reference to it and their lives display the glory of radical disciples.

B. The Beatitudes: the character of kingdom citizens.

The first portion of the Sermon on the Mount is known as the Beatitudes, which means "The Blessings" but can also be understood as giving the believer his "be - attitudes" - the attitudes he should "be." In the Beatitudes, Jesus sets forth both the *nature* and the *aspirations* of citizens of His kingdom. They *have* and are *learning* these character traits.

All of these character traits are marks and goals of *all* Christians. It is not as if we can major in one to the exclusion of others, as is the case with spiritual gifts. There is no escape from our responsibility to desire every one of these spiritual attributes. If you meet someone who claims to be a Christian but displays and desires none of these traits, you may rightly wonder about their salvation, because they do not have the character of kingdom citizens. But if they claim to have mastered these attributes, you may question their honesty.

1. (3) The foundation: poverty of spirit.

"Blessed *are* the poor in spirit, for theirs is the kingdom of heaven.

a. **Blessed**: Jesus promised blessing to His disciples, promising that the **poor in spirit** are **blessed**. The idea behind the ancient Greek word for **blessed** is "*happy*," but in the truest, godly sense of the word, not in our modern sense of merely being comfortable or entertained at the moment.

i. This same word for *blessed* - which in some sense means "happy" - is applied to God in 1 Timothy 1:11: *according to the glorious gospel of the blessed God.* "Makarios then describes that joy which has its secret within itself, that joy which is serene and untouchable, and self-contained, that joy which is completely independent of all the chances and changes of life." (Barclay)

ii. In Matthew 25:34, Jesus said that on the Day of Judgment He would say to His people, *Come, you blessed of My Father, inherit the kingdom prepared for you from the foundation of the world.* On that day, He will judge between the blessed and the cursed – He both knows and explains what are the requirements for the blessed one. We can also say that no one was ever blessed more than Jesus; He knows what goes into a blessed life.

iii. "You have not failed to notice that the last word of the Old Testament is '*curse*,' and it is suggestive that the opening sermon of our Lord's ministry commences with the word 'Blessed.'" (Spurgeon)

iv. "Note, also, with delight, that *the blessing is in every case in the present tense*, a happiness to be now enjoyed and delighted in. It is not 'Blessed *shall* be,' but 'Blessed *are*.'" (Spurgeon)

b. **The poor in spirit**: This is not a man's confession that he is by nature insignificant, or personally without value, for that would be untrue. Instead, it is a confession that he *is* sinful and rebellious and utterly without moral virtues adequate to commend him to God.

i. The **poor in spirit** recognize that they have no spiritual "assets." They know they are spiritually bankrupt. We might say that the ancient Greek had a word for the "working poor" and a word for the "truly poor." Jesus used the word for the *truly poor* here. It indicates someone who must *beg* for whatever they have or get.

ii. Poverty of spirit cannot be artificially induced by self-hatred; the Holy Spirit and our response to His working in our hearts bring it about.

iii. This beatitude is *first*, because this is where we *start* with God. "A ladder, if it is to be of any use, must have its first step near the ground, or feeble climbers will never be able to mount. It would have been a grievous discouragement to struggling faith if the first blessing had been given to the pure in heart; to that excellence the young beginner makes no claim, while to poverty of spirit he can reach without going beyond his line." (Spurgeon)

iv. *Everyone* can start here; it isn't first blessed are the pure or the holy or the spiritual or the wonderful. Everyone can be **poor in spirit**. "Not what I have, but what I have not, is the first point of contact, between my soul and God." (Spurgeon)

c. **For theirs is the kingdom of heaven**: Those who are **poor in spirit**, so poor they must beg, are rewarded. They receive **the kingdom of heaven**, because poverty of spirit is an absolute prerequisite for receiving the kingdom of heaven, and as long as we harbor illusions about our own spiritual resources, we will never receive from God what we absolutely need to be saved.

i. "The kingdom of heaven is not given on the basis of race, earned merits, the military zeal and prowess of Zealots, or the wealth of a Zacchaeus. It is given to the poor, the despised publicans, the prostitutes, those who are so 'poor' they know they can offer nothing and do not try. They cry for mercy and they alone are heard." (Carson)

ii. "The poor in spirit are lifted from the dunghill, and set, not among hired servants in the field, but among princes in the kingdom...

'Poor in spirit;' the words sound as if they described the owners of nothing, and yet they describe the inheritors of all things. Happy poverty! Millionaires sink into insignificance, the treasure of the Indies evaporate in smoke, while to the poor in spirit remains a boundless, endless, faultless kingdom, which renders them blessed in the esteem of him who is God over all, blessed for ever." (Spurgeon)

iii. The call to be **poor in spirit** is placed first for a reason, because it puts the following commands into perspective. They cannot be fulfilled by one's own strength, but only by a beggar's reliance on God's power. No one mourns until they are **poor in spirit**; no one is meek towards others until he has a humble view of himself. If you don't sense your own need and poverty, you will never hunger and thirst after righteousness; and if you have too high a view of yourself, you will find it difficult to be merciful to others.

2. (4) The godly reaction to poverty of spirit: mourning.

Blessed *are* those who mourn, for they shall be comforted.

a. **Blessed are those who mourn**: The ancient Greek grammar indicates an intense degree of mourning. Jesus does not speak of casual sorrow for the consequences of our sin, but a deep grief before God over our fallen state.

i. "The Greek word for *to mourn*, used here, is the strongest word for mourning in the Greek language. It is the word which is used for mourning for the dead, for the passionate lament for one who was loved." (Barclay)

ii. The weeping is for the low and needy condition of both the individual and society; but with the awareness that they are low and needy because of sin. **Those who mourn** actually **mourn** over sin and its effects.

iii. This mourning is the *godly sorrow* that *produces repentance to salvation* that Paul described in 2 Corinthians 7:10.

b. **For they shall be comforted**: Those who **mourn** over their sin and their sinful condition are promised comfort. God allows this grief into our lives as a path, not as a destination.

i. Those who **mourn** can know something special of God; the fellowship of His sufferings (Philippians 3:10), a closeness to the Man of Sorrows who was acquainted with grief (Isaiah 53:3).

3. (5) The next step: meekness.

Blessed *are* the meek, for they shall inherit the earth.

a. **Blessed are the meek**: It is impossible to translate this ancient Greek word *praus* (**meek**) with just one English word. It has the idea of the proper balance between anger and indifference, of a powerful personality properly controlled, and of humility.

i. In the vocabulary of the ancient Greek language, the **meek** person was not passive or easily pushed around. The main idea behind the word "**meek**" was strength under control, like a strong stallion that was trained to do the job instead of running wild.

ii. "In general the Greeks considered meekness a vice because they failed to distinguish it from servility. To be meek towards others implies freedom from malice and a vengeful spirit." (Carson)

iii. "*The meek*, who can be angry, but restrain their wrath in obedience to the will of God, and will not be angry unless they can be angry and not sin, nor will be easily provoked by others." (Poole)

iv. "The men who suffer wrong without bitterness or desire for revenge." (Bruce)

v. The first two beatitudes are mostly *inward*; the third deals with how one relates to one's fellow man. The first two were mainly *negative*; the third is clearly positive.

vi. To be **meek** means to show willingness to submit and work under proper authority. It also shows a willingness to disregard one's own "rights" and privileges. It is one thing for me to admit my own spiritual bankruptcy, but what if someone else does it for me? Do I react meekly? This **blessed** one is meek:

- They are meek before God, in that they submit to His will and conform to His Word.

- They are meek before men, in that they are strong – yet also humble, gentle, patient, and longsuffering.

vii. "Our word *meek* comes from the old Anglo-Saxon *meca*, or *meccea*, a *companion* or *equal*, because he who is of a *meek* or *gentle* spirit, is ever ready to associate with the meanest of those who fear God, feeling himself *superior* to none; and well knowing that he has nothing of spiritual or temporal good but what he has received from the mere bounty of God, having never *deserved* any favour from his hand." (Clarke)

b. **For they shall inherit the earth**: We can only be **meek**, willing to control our desire for our rights and privileges because we are confident God watches out for us, that He will protect our cause. The promise "**they**

shall inherit the earth" proves that God will not allow His **meek** ones to end up on the short end of the deal.

i. "It looks as if they would be pushed out of the world but they shall not be, 'for they shall inherit the earth.' The wolves devour the sheep, yet there are more sheep in the world than there are wolves, and the sheep, continue to multiply, and to feed in green pastures." (Spurgeon)

ii. "The meek of England, driven by their native land by religious intolerance, have inherited the continent of America." (Bruce)

iii. "I had only to look upon it, all as the sun shone upon it, and then to look up to heaven, and say, 'My Father, this is all thine; and, therefore, it is all mine; for I am an heir of God, and a joint-heir with Jesus Christ.' So, in this sense, the meek-spirited man inherits the whole earth." (Spurgeon)

iv. Through the first three beatitudes we notice that the *natural* man finds no happiness or blessedness in spiritual poverty, mourning or meekness. These are only a blessing for the *spiritual* man, those who are new creatures in Jesus.

4. (6) The desire of the one who has poverty of spirit, mourning for sin, and meekness: righteousness.

Blessed *are* those who hunger and thirst for righteousness, for they shall be filled.

a. **Blessed are those who hunger**: This describes a profound hunger that cannot be satisfied by a snack. This is a longing that endures and is never completely satisfied on this side of eternity.

- This passion is *real,* just like hunger and thirst are real.
- This passion is *natural,* just like hunger and thirst are natural in a healthy person.
- This passion is *intense,* just like hunger and thirst can be.
- This passion can be *painful,* just like real hunger and thirst can cause pain.
- This passion is a *driving force,* just like hunger and thirst can drive a man.
- This passion is a *sign of health,* just like hunger and thirst show health.

b. **Hunger and thirst for righteousness**: We see Christians hungering for many things: power, authority, success, comfort, happiness - but how many **hunger and thirst for righteousness**?

i. It is good to remember that Jesus said this in a day and to a culture that really knew what it was to be hungry and thirsty. Modern man – at least in the western world – is often so distant from the basic needs of hunger and thirst that they also find it difficult to hunger and thirst after righteousness.

ii. "'Alas!' says he, 'it is not enough for me to know that my sin is forgiven. I have a fountain of sin within my heart, and bitter waters continually flow from it. Oh, that my nature could be changed, so that I, the lover of sin, could be made a lover of that which is good; that I, now full of evil, could become full of holiness!'" (Spurgeon)

iii. How does this hunger and thirst for righteousness express itself?

- A man longs to have a righteous nature.
- A man wants to be sanctified, to be made more holy.
- A man longs to continue in God's righteousness.
- A man longs to see righteousness promoted in the world.

iv. "He hungers and thirsts after righteousness. He does not hunger and thirst that his own political party may get into power, but he does hunger and thirst that righteousness may be done in the land. He does not hunger and thirst that his own opinions may come to the front, and that his own sect or denomination may increase in numbers and influence, but he does desire that righteousness may come to the fore." (Spurgeon)

c. **For they shall be filled**: Jesus promised to *fill* the hungry; to fill them with as much as they could eat. This is a strange filling that both satisfies us and keeps us longing for more.

5. (7) Blessing to the merciful.

Blessed *are* the merciful, for they shall obtain mercy.

a. **Blessed are the merciful**: When this beatitude addresses those who will show mercy, it speaks to those who have already received mercy. It is mercy to be emptied of your pride and brought to poverty of spirit. It is mercy to be brought to mourning over your spiritual condition. It is mercy to receive the grace of meekness and to become gentle. It is mercy to be made hungry and thirsty after righteousness. Therefore, this one who is expected to show mercy is one who has already received it.

- The merciful one will show it to those who are weaker and poorer.
- The merciful one will always look for those who weep and mourn.

- The merciful one will be forgiving to others, and always looking to restore broken relationships.

- The merciful one will be merciful to the character of other people, and choose to think the best of them whenever possible.

- The merciful one will not expect too much from others.

- The merciful one will be compassionate to those who are outwardly sinful.

- The merciful one will have a care for the souls of all men.

b. **For they shall obtain mercy**: If you want mercy from others - especially God - then you should take care to be **merciful** to others. Some people wonder why God showed such remarkable mercy to King David, especially in the terrible ways in which he sinned. One reason God gave him such mercy was because David was notably merciful to King Saul, and on several occasions was kind to a very unworthy Saul. In David, the **merciful** obtained **mercy**.

6. (8) Blessing to the pure in heart.

Blessed *are* the pure in heart, for they shall see God.

a. **Blessed are the pure in heart**: In the ancient Greek, the phrase **pure of heart** has the idea of straightness, honesty, and clarity. There can be two ideas connected to this. One is of inner moral purity as opposed to the image of purity or ceremonial purity. The other idea is of a single, undivided heart – those who are utterly sincere and not divided in their devotion and commitment to God.

  i. "Christ was dealing with men's spirits, with their inner and spiritual nature. He did this more or less in all the Beatitudes, and this one strikes the very center of the target as he says, not 'Blessed are the pure in language, or the pure in action,' much less 'Blessed are the pure in ceremonies, or in raiment, or in food;' but 'Blessed are the pure *in heart*.'" (Spurgeon)

b. **For they shall see God**: In this, the **pure of heart** receive the most wonderful reward. They shall enjoy greater intimacy with God than they could have imagined. The polluting sins of covetousness, oppression, lust, and chosen deception have a definite *blinding* effect upon a person; and the one **pure of heart** is freer from these pollutions.

  i. "For though no mortal eye can see and comprehend the essence of God, yet these men shall by an eye of faith *see* and enjoy *God* in this life, though in a glass more darkly, and in the life to come face to face." (Poole)

- The heart-pure person can see God in nature.
- The heart-pure person can see God in Scripture.
- The heart-pure person can see God in his church family.

ii. "One day, at an hotel dinner table, I was talking with a brother-minister about certain spiritual things when a gentleman, who sat opposite to us, and who had a serviette tucked under his chin, and a face that indicated his fondness for wine, made, this remark, 'I have been in this world for sixty years, and I have never yet been conscious of anything spiritual.' We did not say what we thought, but we thought it was very likely that what he said was perfectly true; and there are a great many more people in the world who might say the same as he did. But that, only proved that *he* was not conscious of anything spiritual; not that others were not conscious of it." (Spurgeon)

iii. Ultimately, this intimate relationship with God must become our greatest motivation for purity, greater than a fear of getting caught or a fear of consequences.

7. (9) Blessing to the peacemakers.

Blessed *are* the peacemakers, for they shall be called sons of God.

a. **Blessed are the peacemakers**: This does not describe those who *live* in peace, but those who actually bring about peace, overcoming evil with good. One way we accomplish this is through spreading the gospel, because God has entrusted to us the *ministry of reconciliation* (2 Corinthians 5:18). In evangelism we make peace between man and the God whom they have rejected and offended.

i. "The verse which precedes it speaks of the blessedness of 'the pure in heart, for they shall see God.' It is well that we should understand this. We are to be 'first pure, then peaceable.' Our peaceableness is never to be a compact with sin, or an alliance with that which is evil. We must set our faces like flints against everything which is contrary to God and his holiness. That being in our souls a settled matter, we can go on to peaceableness towards men." (Spurgeon)

ii. We commonly think of this peacemaking work as being the job of one person who stands between two fighting parties. This may be one way this is fulfilled; but one can also end a conflict and be a **peacemaker** when *they* are party to a conflict; when they are the injured or the offending party.

iii. "It is the devil who is a troublemaker; it is God who loves reconciliation and who now through his children, as formerly through his only begotten Son, is bent on making peace." (Stott)

b. **For they shall be called sons of God**: The reward of **peacemakers** is that they are recognized as true children of God. They share His passion for peace and reconciliation, the breaking down of walls between people.

i. He is blessed by God; though the peacemaker may be ill-treated by man, he is blessed by God. He is blessed to be among the children of God, adopted into His family, surrounded by brothers and sisters through the ages.

ii. "Now therefore, although it be, for the most part, a thankless office (with men) to interpose, and to seek to take up strife, to piece those again that are gone aside and asunder… yet do it for God's sake, and that ye may (as ye shall be after awhile) be called and counted, not meddler and busybodies, but sons of God." (Trapp)

iii. "And he sometimes putteth himself between the two, when they are very angry, and taketh the blows from both sides, for he knows that so Jesus did, who took the blows from his Father and from us also, that so by suffering in our stead, peace might be made between God and man." (Spurgeon)

8. (10-12) The world's reception of these kind of people: persecution.

Blessed are those who are persecuted for righteousness' sake, for theirs is the kingdom of heaven.

"Blessed are you when they revile and persecute you, and say all kinds of evil against you falsely for My sake. Rejoice and be exceedingly glad, for great *is* your reward in heaven, for so they persecuted the prophets who were before you.

a. **Blessed are those who are persecuted**: These blessed ones are persecuted for **righteousness' sake** and for Jesus' sake (**for My sake**), not for their own stupidity or fanaticism. Peter recognized that suffering might come to some Christians for reasons other than their faithfulness to Jesus (1 Peter 4:15-16), and this is not what Jesus addressed here.

i. The character traits described in the Beatitudes are not valued by our modern culture. We don't recognize or give awards to the "Most Pure in Heart" or "Most Poor in Spirit." Though our culture doesn't think much of these character traits, they do describe the character of the citizens of God's kingdom.

ii. "So the King adds an eighth beatitude, and that a double one, for those who because of their loyalty endure suffering." (Morgan)

b. **Blessed are you when they revile and persecute you, and say all kinds of evil against you falsely for My sake**: Jesus brings insults and spoken malice into the sphere of persecution. We cannot limit our idea of persecution to only physical opposition or torture.

i. In Matthew 5:10 they are persecuted for righteousness' sake; in Matthew 5:11 they are persecuted for the sake of Jesus. This shows that Jesus expected that their righteous lives would be lived after His example, and in honor to Him.

ii. It did not take long for these words of Jesus to ring true to His followers. Early Christians heard many enemies **say all kinds of evil against** them **falsely for** Jesus' **sake**. Christians were accused of:

- Cannibalism, because of gross and deliberate misrepresentation of the practice of the Lord's Supper.

- Immorality, because of gross deliberate misrepresentation of weekly "Love Feast" and their private meetings.

- Revolutionary fanaticism, because they believed that Jesus would return and bring an apocalyptic end to history.

- Splitting families, because when one marriage partner or parent became a Christian there was often change and division in the family.

- Treason, because they would not honor the Roman gods and participate in emperor worship.

c. **Rejoice and be exceedingly glad**: Literally, we could translate this phrase to say that the persecuted should "leap for joy." Why? Because the persecuted will have great **reward in heaven**, and because the persecuted are in good company: the **prophets** before them were also persecuted.

i. "A strong word of Hellenistic coinage, from to leap much, signifying irrepressible demonstrative gladness...It is the joy of the Alpine climber standing on the top of the snow-clad mountain." (Bruce)

ii. Trapp names some men who did in fact **rejoice** and were **exceedingly glad** when persecuted. George Roper came to the stake leaping for joy, and hugged the stake he was to be burned at like a friend. Doctor Taylor leapt and danced a little as he came to his execution, saying when asked how he was, "Well, God be praised, good Master Sheriff, never better; for now I am almost home...I am even at my Father's house." Lawrence Saunders, who with a smiling face embraced the stake of his execution and kissed it saying, "Welcome the cross of Christ, welcome everlasting life."

iii. Yet the world persecutes these good people because the values and character expressed in these Beatitudes are so opposite to the world's manner of thinking. Our persecution may not be much compared to others, but if *no one* speaks evil of you, are these Beatitudes traits of your life?

C. Where Jesus wants His disciples to display their discipleship.

1. (13) The followers of Jesus should be like salt.

"You are the salt of the earth; but if the salt loses its flavor, how shall it be seasoned? It is then good for nothing but to be thrown out and trampled underfoot by men."

a. **You are the salt of the earth**: Disciples are like **salt** because they are *precious*. In Jesus' day, salt was a valued commodity. Roman soldiers were sometimes paid with salt, giving rise to the phrase "worth his salt."

b. **You are the salt of the earth**: Disciples are like **salt** because they have a preserving influence. Salt was used to preserve meats and to slow decay. Christians should have a preserving influence on their culture.

c. **You are the salt of the earth**: Disciples are like **salt** because they add flavor. Christians should be a "flavorful" people.

i. "Disciples, if they are true to their calling, make *the earth* a purer and more palatable place." (France)

d. **If the salt loses its flavor...it is then good for nothing**: Salt must keep its "saltiness" to be of any value. When it is no good as salt, it is **trampled under foot**. In the same way, too many Christians lose their "flavor" and become good for nothing.

i. "Most salt in the ancient world derived from salt marshes or the like, rather than by evaporation of salt water, and therefore contained many impurities. The actual salt, being more soluble than the impurities, could be leached out, leaving a residue so dilute it was of little worth." (Carson)

2. (14-16) The followers of Jesus should be like light.

"You are the light of the world. A city that is set on a hill cannot be hidden. Nor do they light a lamp and put it under a basket, but on a lampstand, and it gives light to all *who are* in the house. Let your light so shine before men, that they may see your good works and glorify your Father in heaven."

a. **You are the light of the world**: Jesus gives the Christian both a great compliment and a great responsibility when He says that *we* are the light of the world, because He claimed that title for Himself as He walked this earth (John 8:12 and John 9:5).

 i. **Light of the world** means that we are not only light-receivers, but also light-givers. We must have a greater concern than only ourselves, and we cannot live only to ourselves; we must have someone to shine to, and do so lovingly.

 ii. "This title had been given by the Jews to certain of their eminent Rabbis. With great pomposity they spoke of Rabbi Judah, or Rabbi Jochanan, as the lamps of the universe, the lights of the world. It must have sounded strangely in the ears of the Scribes and Pharisees to hear that same title, in all soberness, applied to a few bronzed-faced and horny-handed peasants and fishermen, who had become disciples of Jesus." (Spurgeon)

 iii. Jesus never challenged us to *become* salt or light. He simply said that we *are* - and we are either fulfilling or failing that given responsibility.

 iv. A key thought in both the pictures of salt and light is *distinction*. Salt is needed because the world is rotting and decaying, and if our Christianity is also rotting and decaying, it won't be any good. Light is needed because the world is in darkness, and if our Christianity imitates the darkness, we have nothing to show the world. To be effective we must seek and display the Christian *distinctive*. We can never affect the world for Jesus by becoming like the world.

 v. "Poor world, poor world, it is dark, and gropes in midnight, and it cannot get light except it receives it through us!...To be the light of the world surrounds life with the most stupendous responsibilities, and so invests it with the most solemn dignity. Hear this, ye humble men and women, ye who have made no figure in society, ye are the light of the world. If ye burn dimly, dim is the world's light, and dense its darkness." (Spurgeon)

b. **Let your light so shine before men**: The purpose of light is to illuminate and expose what is there. Therefore light must be exposed before it is of any use - if it is hidden **under a basket**, it is no longer useful.

 i. "Christ knew that there would be strong temptation for the men that had it in them to be lights to hide their light. It would draw the world's attention to them, and so expose them to the ill will of such as hate the light." (Bruce)

ii. "Christ never contemplated the production of secret Christians, - Christians whose virtues would never be displayed, - pilgrims who would travel to heaven by night, and never be seen by their fellow-pilgrims or anyone else." (Spurgeon)

iii. The figures of salt and light also remind us that the life marked by the Beatitudes is not to be lived in isolation. We often assume that those inner qualities can only be developed or displayed in isolation from the world, but Jesus wants us to live them out before the world.

c. **A city that is set on a hill cannot be hidden**: Such a city is prominent and can't be hidden. If you see such a city from a distance, it is hard to take your eyes off of it. In the same way, Jesus wanted the people of His kingdom to live visible lives that attracted attention to the beauty of God's work in the life.

i. "It is as much as if our Saviour should have said, You had need be holy, for your conversation cannot be hid, any more than a city can that is built upon a hill, which is obvious to every eye. All men's eyes will be upon you." (Poole)

ii. "Not far from this little hill [where Jesus taught] is the city *Saphet*, supposed to be the ancient *Bethulia*. It stands upon a very *eminent* and *conspicuous* mountain, and is SEEN FAR and NEAR. May we not suppose that Christ alludes to this city, in these words of his, *A city set on a hill cannot be hid*?" (Maundrell, cited in Clarke)

d. **Nor do they light a lamp and put it under a basket, but on a lampstand**: The idea of a **lampstand** gives the sense that we are to be *intentional* about letting this light shine. Even as lamps are placed higher so their light can be more effective, we should look for ways to let our light shine in greater and broader ways.

i. "What a lamp-stand was found for Christianity in the martyrdoms of the Coliseum, in the public burnings by pagans and papists, and in all the other modes by which believers in Christ were forced into fame." (Spurgeon)

ii. "The text says that the candle gives light to all that are in the house. Some professors give light only to a part of the house. I have known women very good to all but their husbands, and these they nag from night to night, so that they give no light to them. I have known husbands so often out at meetings that they neglect home, and thus their wives miss the light." (Spurgeon)

iii. "The venerable Bede, when he was interpreting this text, said that Christ Jesus brought the light of Deity into the poor lantern of our humanity, and then set it upon the candlestick of his church that the whole house of the world might be lit up thereby. So indeed it is." (Spurgeon)

e. **That they may see your good works and glorify your Father in heaven**: The purpose in letting our **light so shine** by doing **good works** is so that others will glorify God, not ourselves.

> i. "The object of our shining is not that men may see how good we are, nor even see us at all, but that they may see grace in us and God in us, and cry, 'What a Father these people must have.' Is not this the first time in the New Testament that God is called our Father? Is it not singular that the first time it peeps out should be when men are seeing the good works of his children?" (Spurgeon)

> ii. Jesus pointed to a breadth in the impact of disciples that must have seemed almost ridiculous at the time. How could these humble Galileans salt the *earth*, or light the *world*? But they did.

> iii. The three pictures together are powerful, speaking of the effect of Jesus' disciples in the world:

> - Salt is the opposite of corruption, and it prevents corruption from getting worse.
> - Light gives the gift of guidance, so that those who have lost their way can find the path home.
> - A city is the product of social order and government; it is against chaos and disorder.

> iv. Bruce comments on this first reference to God as **Father**: "God, we learn, as Father delights in noble conduct; as human fathers find joy in sons who acquit themselves bravely."

D. The law and true righteousness.

1. (17-18) Jesus' relation to the law.

"Do not think that I came to destroy the Law or the Prophets. I did not come to destroy but to fulfill. For assuredly, I say to you, till heaven and earth pass away, one jot or one tittle will by no means pass from the law till all is fulfilled."

a. **Do not think that I came to destroy the Law or the Prophets**: Jesus here began a long discussion of the law, and wanted to make it clear that He did not oppose what God gave Israel in what we call the Old Testament. He did not come to **destroy** the word of God, but to free it from the way the Pharisees and Scribes had wrongly interpreted it.

i. "The Jews of Jesus' day could refer to the Scriptures as 'the Law and the Prophets' (Matthew 7:12, 11:13, 22:40; Luke 16:16; John 1:45; Acts 13:15, 28:23; Romans 3:21); 'the Law…the Prophets, and the Psalms (Luke 24:44); or just 'Law' (Matthew 5:18; John 10:34, 12:34, 15:25; 1 Corinthians 14:21)." (Carson)

ii. "To show that he never meant to abrogate the law, our Lord Jesus has embodied all its commands in his own life. In his own person there was a nature which was perfectly conformed to the law of God; and as was his nature such was his life." (Spurgeon)

iii. **For assuredly**: "*Truly* (Greek *Amen*), *I say to you* is Jesus' own signature: no other teacher is known to have used it…It serves, like the prophets' 'Thus says the LORD', to mark a saying as important and authoritative." (France)

b. **I did not come to destroy but to fulfill**: Jesus wanted to make it clear that He had authority apart from the Law of Moses, but not in contradiction to it. Jesus added nothing to the law except one thing that no man had ever added to the law: perfect obedience. This is certainly one way Jesus came **to fulfill** the law.

i. Even though He often challenged man's interpretations of the law (especially Sabbath regulations), Jesus never broke the law of God.

ii. "A greater than the Old Testament, than Moses and the prophets, is here. But the Greater is full of reverence for the institutions and sacred books of His people. He is not come to disannul either the law or the prophets." (Bruce)

iii. "Jesus fulfills the Law and the Prophets and they point to him, and he is their fulfillment." (Carson)

- Jesus **fulfilled** the doctrinal teachings of the **Law** and the **Prophets** in that He brought full revelation.
- Jesus **fulfilled** the predictive prophecy of the **Law** and the **Prophets** in that He is the Promised One, showing the reality behind the shadows.
- Jesus **fulfilled** the moral and legal demands of the **Law** and the **Prophets** in that He fully obeyed them and He reinterpreted them in their truth.
- Jesus **fulfilled** the penalty of the **Law** and the **Prophets** for us by His death on the cross, taking the penalty we deserved.

iv. The Apostle Paul wrote on this theme: *For Christ is the end of the law for righteousness to everyone who believes* (Romans 10:4).

v. "In a word, Christ completed the law: 1st. In *itself*, it was only the *shadow*, the *typical representation*, of good things to come; and he *added* to it that which was necessary to make it perfect, HIS OWN SACRIFICE, without which it could neither satisfy God, nor sanctify men. 2dly. He completed it *in himself* by submitting to its types with an exact obedience, and verifying them by his death upon the cross. 3dly. He completes this law, and the sayings of his prophets, *in his members*, by giving them grace to love the Lord with all their heart, soul, mind, and strength, and their neighbour as themselves; for this is all the *law* and the *prophets*." (Clarke)

c. **One jot or one tittle will by no means pass from the law till all is fulfilled**: The **jot** and the **tittle** were small marks in Hebrew writing. Jesus here told us that not only the *ideas* of the word of God are important, but also the *words themselves* – even the letters of the words – are important. This shows us how highly God regards His word.

i. The **jot** refers to *yod* (׳), the smallest letter in the Hebrew alphabet; it looks like half a letter.

ii. The **tittle** is a small mark in a Hebrew letter, somewhat like the crossing of a "t" or the tail on a "y."

- The difference between *bet* (ב) and *kaf* (כ) is a **tittle**.
- The difference between *dalet* (ד) and *resh* (ר) is a **tittle**.
- The difference between *vav* (ו) and *zayin* (ז) is a **tittle**.

iii. "Though all earth and hell should join together to hinder the accomplishment of the great designs of the Most High, yet it shall all be in vain-even the sense of a single letter shall not be lost. The *words* of God, which point out his designs, are as unchangeable as his *nature* itself." (Clarke)

iv. **Till all is fulfilled**: This is true in a few different senses.

- It is the assurance that Jesus Himself fulfilled the law by His perfect obedience.
- It is the assurance that Jesus Himself fulfills the law in us by His perfect obedience (Romans 8:4).
- It is the assurance that God's plan will never be set aside until all things are fulfilled at the end of the age.

2. (19-20) The disciple's relationship to the law.

"Whoever therefore breaks one of the least of these commandments, and teaches men so, shall be called least in the kingdom of heaven; but

whoever does and teaches *them,* he shall be called great in the kingdom of heaven. For I say to you, that unless your righteousness exceeds *the righteousness* of the scribes and Pharisees, you will by no means enter the kingdom of heaven."

a. **Whoever therefore breaks one of the least of these commandments**: The **commandments** are to be obeyed as explained and fulfilled by Jesus' life and teaching, not as in the legalistic thinking of the religious authorities of Jesus' day. For example, sacrifice is commanded by the law, but it was fulfilled in Jesus, so we do not run the danger of being **called least in the kingdom of heaven** by not observing animal sacrifice as detailed in the Law of Moses.

b. **Whoever does and teaches them, he shall be called great in the kingdom of heaven**: The Christian is done with the law as a means of gaining a righteous standing before God. One passage that explains this is Galatians 2:21: *For if righteousness comes through the law, then Christ died in vain.* However, the law stands as the perfect expression of God's ethical character and requirements.

i. The law sends us to Jesus to be justified, because it shows us our inability to please God in ourselves. But after we come to Jesus, He sends us back to the law to learn the heart of God for our conduct and sanctification.

c. **Unless your righteousness exceeds the righteousness of the scribes and Pharisees, you will by no means enter the kingdom of heaven**: Considering the incredible devotion to the law shown by the **scribes and Pharisees**, how can we ever hope to exceed their righteousness?

i. The Pharisees were so scrupulous in their keeping of the law that they would even tithe from the small spices obtained from their herb gardens (Matthew 23:23). The heart of this devotion to God is shown by modern-day Orthodox Jews. In early 1992, tenants let three apartments in an Orthodox neighborhood in Israel burn to the ground while they asked a rabbi whether a telephone call to the fire department on the Sabbath violated Jewish law. Observant Jews are forbidden to use the phone on the Sabbath, because doing so would break an electrical current, which is considered a form of work. In the half-hour it took the rabbi to decide "yes," the fire spread to two neighboring apartments.

ii. The life of Paul shows what the righteousness of the Pharisees was like: Acts 23:6, 26:5; Philippians 3:5.

iii. We can exceed their **righteousness** because our righteousness exceeds that of **the scribes and Pharisees** in *kind,* not *degree.* Paul describes the two kinds of righteousness in Philippians 3:6-9: *Concerning the righteousness which is in the law,* [I was] *blameless. But what things were gain to me, I have counted loss for Christ. But indeed, I count all things loss…that I may gain Christ, and be found in Him, not having my own righteousness, which is from the law, but that which is through faith in Christ, the righteousness which is from God by faith.*

iv. Though the righteousness of the scribes and Pharisees was impressive to human observation, it could not prevail before God (Isaiah 64:6).

v. So then, we are not made righteous by keeping the law. When we see what keeping the law *really* means, we are thankful that Jesus offers us a different kind of righteousness.

E. Jesus interprets the law in its truth.

In this section, Jesus shows the true meaning of the law. But this isn't Jesus against Moses; it is Jesus against false and superficial interpretations of Moses. In regard to the law, the two errors of the scribes and Pharisees were that they both restricted *God's commands (as in the law of murder) and* extended *the commands of God past His intention (as in the law of divorce).*

1. (21-22) Jesus interprets the law against murder.

"You have heard that it was said to those of old, 'You shall not murder, and whoever murders will be in danger of the judgment.' But I say to you that whoever is angry with his brother without a cause shall be in danger of the judgment. And whoever says to his brother, 'Raca!' shall be in danger of the council. But whoever says, 'You fool!' shall be in danger of hell fire."

a. **You have heard it said**: These people had not really studied the Law of Moses for themselves. All they had was the teaching on the law from the scribes and Pharisees. In this particular matter, the people had heard the scribes and Pharisees teach **"You shall not murder."**

i. When Jesus said, "**…it was said to those of old**," He reminds us that something isn't true just because it is old. And if it is not true, its antiquity is no credit to it. "Antiquity disjointed from verity is but filthy hoariness; and deserveth no more reverance than an old lecher, which is so much the more odious, because old." (Trapp)

b. **But I say to you**: Jesus shows His authority, and does not rely on the words of previous scribes or teachers. He will teach them the true understanding of the Law of Moses.

i. "What a King is ours, who stretches his scepter over the realm of our inward lusts! How sovereignly he puts it: '*But, I say unto you*'! Who but a divine being has authority to speak in this fashion? His word is law. So it ought to be, seeing he touches vice at the fountain- head, and forbids uncleanness in the heart." (Spurgeon)

c. **Whoever is angry with his brother without a cause shall be in danger of the judgment**: The teaching of the scribes and Pharisees (**"You shall not murder"**) was true enough. Yet they also taught that anything *short* or murder might be allowed. Jesus corrects this, and makes it clear that it is not only those who commit the *act* of murder who are in danger of judgment, those who have a murderous intent in the heart are also **in danger of the judgment**.

i. Jesus exposes the essence of the scribes' heresy. To them, the law was really only a matter of *external performance*, never the heart. Jesus brings the law back to the matters of the heart. "The supervision of the Kingdom does not begin by arresting a criminal with blood-red hands; it arrests the man in whom the murder spirit is just born." (Morgan)

ii. We should emphasize that Jesus is *not* saying that anger is as bad as murder. It is profoundly morally confused to think that someone who shouts at another person in anger has sinned as badly as someone who murders another person in anger. Jesus emphasized that the law condemns *both*, without saying that the law says they are the *same things*. The laws of the people could only deal with the outward act of murder, but Jesus declared that His followers understood that God's morality addressed not only the end but also the beginning of murder.

iii. Barclay, commenting on the specific ancient Greek word translated **angry**: "So Jesus forbids for ever the anger which broods, the anger which will not forget, the anger which refuses to be pacified, the anger which seeks revenge."

iv. "The words 'without cause' probably reflect an early and widespread softening of Jesus' strong teaching. Their absence does not itself prove there is no exception." (Carson)

c. **And whoever says to his brother, "Raca!" shall be in danger of the council**: To call someone **"Raca"** expressed contempt for their intelligence. Calling someone a **fool** showed contempt for their character. Either one broke the *heart* of the law against murder, even if it did not commit murder.

i. Commentators have translated the idea behind **Raca** as "nitwit, blockhead, numbskull, bonehead, brainless idiot." "*Raca* is an almost untranslatable word, because it describes a tone of voice more than anything else. Its whole accent is the accent of *contempt*...It is the word of one who despises another with an arrogant contempt." (Barclay)

ii. "These are not uncommon or particularly vulgar words...but they suggest an attitude of angry contempt." (France)

iii. "In these words of Jesus against anger and contempt there is an aspect of exaggeration. They are the strong utterance of one in whom all forms of inhumanity roused feelings of passionate abhorrence. They are of the utmost value as a revelation of character." (Bruce)

2. (23-26) More on problem personal relationships.

"Therefore if you bring your gift to the altar, and there remember that your brother has something against you, leave your gift there before the altar, and go your way. First be reconciled to your brother, and then come and offer your gift. Agree with your adversary quickly, while you are on the way with him, lest your adversary deliver you to the judge, the judge hand you over to the officer, and you be thrown into prison. Assuredly, I say to you, you will by no means get out of there till you have paid the last penny."

a. **Leave your gift there before the altar, and go your way**: Jesus considers it far more important to be reconciled to a brother than to perform a religious duty. Jesus says we must **first be reconciled to your brother**. We can't think that our service towards the Lord justifies bad relationships with others. We should do what Paul commanded in Romans 12:18: *If it is possible, as much as depends on you, live peaceably with all men.*

b. **Agree with your adversary quickly**: Jesus commands us to **quickly** settle anger and malice with another. When we ignore it or pass it off, it genuinely imprisons us (**and you be thrown into prison**).

i. Paul expresses the same idea in Ephesians 4:26-27 (*do not let the sun go down on your wrath*). When we hold on to our anger against another, we then sin – and we *give place to the devil*.

c. **Assuredly, I say to you, you will by no means get out of there till you have paid the last penny**: Jesus here spoke with figures of speech. The ultimate penalty one pays at the hands of the **judge**, the **officer**, and in the **prison** could never be satisfied with money (**the last penny**). Yet the reality suggested by these strong figures of speech reminds us that the suffering of eternity is indeed eternal.

i. "Let our merit-mongers first go to hell for their sins, and stay all eternity there; then afterward, if God will create another eternity, they may have liberty to relate their good works, and call for their wages...A child with a spoon may sooner empty the sea than the damned in hell accomplish their misery." (Trapp)

3. (27-28) Jesus interprets the law against adultery.

"You have heard that it was said to those of old, 'You shall not commit adultery.' But I say to you that whoever looks at a woman to lust for her has already committed adultery with her in his heart."

a. **You have heard that it was said to those of old**: Now, Jesus deals with what they had **heard** regarding the law of adultery. Of course, the teachers of the day taught that **adultery** itself was wrong. But they applied the law only to the actions, not to the heart.

b. **Whoever looks at a woman to lust for her has already committed adultery with her in his heart**: Jesus explains that it is possible to commit adultery or murder in our heart - or mind, and this also is sin and prohibited by the command against adultery.

i. With the words, "**whoever looks at a woman**," Jesus located the origin of lust back to the *eyes*. This is true according to Biblical statement (such as Job 31:1) and life-experience. "When one seemed to pity a one-eyed man, he told him he had lost one of his enemies, a very thief, that would have stolen away his heart." (Trapp)

ii. However, it is important to understand that Jesus *is not* saying that the act of adultery and adultery in the heart are the same thing. More than a few people have been deceived on this point and say, "I've already committed adultery in my heart, so I may as well do it in practice." The act of adultery is *far worse* than adultery in the heart. Jesus' point is not to say they are the same things, but to say they are both sin, and both prohibited by the command against adultery.

iii. Some people only keep from adultery because they are afraid to get caught, and in their heart they commit adultery every day. It is good that they keep from the act of adultery, but it is bad that their heart is filled with adultery.

iv. This principle applies to much more than men looking at women. It applies to just about anything we can covet with the eye or mind. "These are the most searching words concerning impurity that ever were uttered." (Morgan)

c. **Adultery... in his heart**: Since Jesus considers adultery in the heart a sin, we know what we *think about* and allow our heart to *rest on* is based on *choice*. Many believe they have no choice - and therefore no responsibility - for what they think about, but this contradicts the clear teaching of Jesus here. We may not be able to control *passing* thoughts or feelings, but we certainly do decide where our heart and mind will *rest*.

i. "Imagination is a God-given gift; but if it is fed dirt by the eye, it will be dirty. All sin, not the least sexual sin, begins with the imagination. Therefore what feeds the imagination is of maximum importance in the pursuit of kingdom righteousness." (Carson)

ii. It is also important to distinguish between temptation to sin and sin itself. "The look is supposed to be not casual but persistent, the desire not involuntary or momentary, but cherished with longing." (Bruce)

iii. Jesus, though tempted in all ways (Hebrews 4:15), endured such temptations but did not yield to such sin. He was able to see women as other than objects for His gratification. "He was tempted in all points as we are, but desire was expelled by the mighty power of a pure love to which every woman was a daughter, a sister, or a betrothed: a sacred object of tender respect." (Bruce)

4. (29-30) Our attitude in the war against sin.

"If your right eye causes you to sin, pluck it out and cast *it* from you; for it is more profitable for you that one of your members perish, than for your whole body to be cast into hell. And if your right hand causes you to sin, cut it off and cast *it* from you; for it is more profitable for you that one of your members perish, than for your whole body to be cast into hell."

a. **If your right eye causes you to sin, pluck it out**: Here Jesus uses a figure of speech, and did not speak literally. Sadly, some have taken it so and have mutilated themselves in mistaken efforts in the pursuit of holiness. For example, the famous early Christian named Origen castrated himself on the principle of this passage.

i. The trouble with a literal interpretation is that it does not go far enough! Even if you did cut off your hand or gouge out your eye, you could still sin with your other hand or eye. When all those are gone, you can especially sin with your mind.

ii. "Mutilation will not serve the purpose; it may prevent the outward act, but it will not extinguish desire." (Bruce)

b. **It is more profitable for you that one of your members perish, than for your whole body to be cast into hell**: Jesus simply stressed the point that one must be willing to sacrifice to be obedient. If part of our life is given over to sin, we must be convinced that it is more profitable for that part our life to "die" rather than to condemn our whole life.

i. This is the one thing many are unwilling to do, and that is why they remain trapped in sin, or never come to Jesus. They never get beyond a vague wish to be better.

ii. "The salvation of our souls is to be preferred before all things, be they never so dear and precious to us; and that if men's ordinary discretion teacheth them for the preservation of their bodies to cut off a particular member, which would necessarily endanger the whole body, it much more teacheth them to part with any thing which will prejudice the salvation of their souls." (Poole)

5. (31-32) Jesus interprets the law concerning divorce.

"Furthermore it has been said, 'Whoever divorces his wife, let him give her a certificate of divorce. But I say to you that whoever divorces his wife for any reason except sexual immorality causes her to commit adultery; and whoever marries a woman who is divorced commits adultery."

a. **It has been said, "Whoever divorces his wife, let him give her a certificate of divorce"**: In Jesus' day, many people interpreted the Mosaic permission for divorce (Deuteronomy 24:1) as granting virtually any reason as grounds for divorce. Some rabbis taught this even extended to allowing a man to divorce his wife if she burnt his breakfast.

i. "Moses insisted upon '*a writing of divorcement*,' that angry passions might have time to cool and that the separation, if it must come, might be performed with deliberation and legal formality. The requirement of a writing was to a certain degree a check upon an evil habit, which was so engrained in the people that to refuse it altogether would have been useless, and would only have created another crime." (Spurgeon)

ii. Yet in Jesus' day, this permission of Deuteronomy 24:1 had become an instrument of cruelty against wives. "The scribes busied themselves solely about getting the bill of separation into due legal form. They did nothing to restrain the unjust caprice of husbands; they rather opened a wider door to licence." (Bruce)

iii. In that time, the permissible grounds for divorce were debated:

- School of Shammai: "Restricted the 'some indecency' of Deuteronomy 24:1 to refer only to a sexual misdemeanour authenticated by witnesses." (France)

- School of Hillel: "Reputedly took it of any cause of complaint, even including burning the dinner." (France)

b. **Whoever divorces his wife for any reason except sexual immorality**: The issue of divorce revolved around a strict or loose interpretation of the word *uncleanness* in Deuteronomy 24:1. Those who wanted to make divorce easy had a loose interpretation. Jesus makes it plain that the idea of *uncleanness* is **sexual immorality**, not anything the wife might do to displease the husband.

> i. **Sexual immorality** "translates *porneia*, the root meaning of which is 'fornication', but it is used more widely, so that it could include premarital unchastity, subsequently discovered." (France)

> ii. The teaching of Jesus on marriage and divorce is further explained in Matthew 19, but here we see the intent of Jesus: getting back to the intent of the law, instead of allowing it to be used as easy permission for divorce.

> iii. "The Matthaean exceptive clause is not therefore introducing a new provision, but making explicit what any Jewish reader would have taken for granted when Jesus made the apparently unqualified pronouncements of Mark 10:9-12." (France)

> iv. This emphasis of Jesus on the permanency of marriage and the wrong of unjustified divorce went against the thinking of many in both the Jewish and the Gentile cultures. "In Greece we see a whole social system based on relationships outside marriage; we see that these relationships were accepted as natural and normal, and not in the least blameworthy." Roman culture came to adopt this attitude towards marriage. (Barclay)

c. **Causes her to commit adultery**: An illegitimate divorce gives place to **adultery** because God doesn't recognize the divorce, and sees a new relationship as bigamous. It is possible for a person to have a divorce that is recognized by the *state*, but not by *God*. If that person goes on to marry someone else, God considers that relationship **adultery** because He sees them as still married.

6. (33-37) Jesus interprets the law concerning oaths.

"Again you have heard that it was said to those of old, 'You shall not swear falsely, but shall perform your oaths to the Lord.' But I say to you, do not swear at all: neither by heaven, for it is God's throne; nor by the earth, for it is His footstool; nor by Jerusalem, for it is the city of the great King. Nor shall you swear by your head, because you cannot make one hair white or black. But let your 'Yes' be 'Yes,' and your 'No,' 'No.' For whatever is more than these is from the evil one."

a. **You have heard that it was said to those of old, "You shall not swear falsely"**: The scribes and Pharisees had twisted the law *You shall not take the name of the LORD your God in vain* (Exodus 20:7) to permit taking virtually every other name in a false oath.

b. **Do not swear at all**: Jesus reminds us that God is part of every oath anyway; if you swear by **heaven**, **earth**, **Jerusalem**, or even **your head**, you swear by God - and your oath must be honored.

> i. "Again an unqualified statement, to be taken not in the letter as a new law, but in the spirit as inculcating such a love of truth that so far as we are concerned there shall be no need of oaths." (Bruce)

c. **But let your "Yes" be "Yes"**: Having to swear or make oaths betrays the weakness of your word. It demonstrates that there is not enough weight in your own character to confirm your words. How much better it is to let your **"Yes" be "Yes"** and **"No" be "No."**

> i. Some have taken this word of Jesus as more than an emphasis on truth-telling and honesty as an absolute prohibition of all oaths. This is misguided, because oaths are permitted under certain circumstances, as long as they are not abused and used as a cover for deception.

> - God Himself swears oaths: Hebrews 6:13 and Luke 1:73.
> - Jesus spoke under oath in a court: Matthew 26:63-64.
> - Paul made oaths: Romans 1:9, 2 Corinthians 1:23, Galatians 1:20, 2 Thessalonians 2:5.

> ii. "The truly good man will never need to take an oath; the truth of his sayings and the reality of his promises need no such guarantee. But the fact that oaths are still sometimes necessary is the proof that men are not good men and that this is not a good world." (Barclay)

7. (38-42) Jesus interprets the law of retribution.

"You have heard that it was said, 'An eye for an eye and a tooth for a tooth.' But I tell you not to resist an evil person. But whoever slaps you on your right cheek, turn the other to him also. If anyone wants to sue you and take away your tunic, let him have *your* cloak also. And whoever compels you to go one mile, go with him two. Give to him who asks you, and from him who wants to borrow from you do not turn away."

a. **You have heard that it was said, "An eye for an eye and a tooth for a tooth"**: The Mosaic law did teach *an eye for an eye and a tooth for a tooth* (Exodus 21:24). But over time religious teachers moved this command out of its proper sphere (a principle *limiting* retribution for the civil government) and put it in the wrong sphere (as an *obligation* in personal relationships).

b. **But whoever slaps you on your right cheek, turn the other to him also**: Here, Jesus presents the fullness of the **eye for an eye** law, and how its idea of limiting revenge extends into the principle of accepting certain evils against one's self.

i. When a person insults us (**slaps you on the right cheek**), we want to give them back what they gave to us, plus more. Jesus said we should patiently bear such insults and offences, and not **resist an evil person** who insults us this way. Instead, we trust God to defend us. France points out that ancient Jewish writings say that striking someone with the back of the hand – a severe insult – was punishable by a very heavy fine, according to Mishnah *BK* 8:6.

ii. It is wrong to think Jesus means evil should never be resisted. Jesus demonstrated with His life that evil should and must be resisted, such as when He turned tables in the temple.

iii. "Jesus is here saying that the true Christian has learned to resent no insult and to seek retaliation for no slight." (Barclay) When we think how Jesus Himself as insulted and spoken against (as a glutton, a drunk, an illegitimate child, a blasphemer, a madman, and so forth) we see how He lived this principle Himself.

iii. It is wrong to think that Jesus means a physical attack cannot be resisted or defended against. When Jesus speaks of a slap **on your right cheek**, it was culturally understood as a deep insult, not a physical attack. Jesus does not mean that if someone hits across the right side of our head with a baseball bat, we should allow them to then hit the left side. "If a right-handed person strikes someone's right cheek, presumably it is a slap by the back of the hand, probably considered more insulting than a slap by the open palm." (Carson) 2 Corinthians 11:20 probably has in mind this kind of "insult slap."

iv. It is also wrong to think Jesus means that there is no place for punishment or retribution in society. Jesus here speaks to personal relationships, and not to the proper functions of government in restraining evil (Romans 13:1-4). I must turn my cheek when I am personally insulted, but the government has a responsibility to restrain the evil man from physical assault.

c. **If anyone wants to sue you and take away your tunic, let him have your cloak also**: Under the Law of Moses, the outer cloak could not be taken from someone (Exodus 22:26; Deuteronomy 24:13).

i. "Jesus' disciples, if sued for their tunics (an inner garment like our suit but worn next to the skin), far from seeking satisfaction, will gladly part with what they may legally keep." (Carson)

ii. "Yet even in a country where justice can be had, we are not to resort to law for every personal wrong. We should rather endure to be put upon than be forever crying out, 'I'll bring an action.'" (Spurgeon)

d. **Whoever compels you to go one mile, go with him two**: Positively, we are told to take command of evil impositions by making a deliberate choice to give more than we are required. At that time, Judea was under Roman military occupation. Under military law, any Roman soldier might command a Jew to carry his soldier's pack for one mile - but only one mile. Jesus here says, "Go beyond the one mile required by law and give another mile out of a free choice of love." This is how we transform an attempt to manipulate us into a free act of love.

i. "The Jews fiercely resented such impositions, and Jesus' choice of this example deliberately dissociates him from militant nationalists. Rather than resisting, or even resenting, the disciple should volunteer for a further *mile*." (France)

ii. "The old said, Insist on your own right, and loving your neighbor, hate your enemy, and so secure your safety. The new says, Suffer wrong, and lavish your love on all." (Morgan)

e. **Give to him who asks of you**: The only limit to this kind of sacrifice is the limit that love itself will impose. It isn't loving to give in to someone's manipulation without our transforming it into a free act of love. It isn't always loving to give or to not resist.

i. We might say that Paul repeated this idea of Jesus: *Do not be overcome by evil, but overcome evil with good.* (Romans 12:21)

8. (43-47) Jesus interprets the law of love towards your neighbor.

"You have heard that it was said, 'You shall love your neighbor and hate your enemy.' But I say to you, love your enemies, bless those who curse you, do good to those who hate you, and pray for those who spitefully use you and persecute you, that you may be sons of your Father in heaven; for He makes His sun rise on the evil and on the good, and sends rain on the just and on the unjust. For if you love those who love you, what reward have you? Do not even the tax collectors do the same? And if you greet your brethren only, what do you do more *than others?* Do not even the tax collectors do so?"

a. **You have heard that it was said, "You shall love your neighbor and hate your enemy"**: The Mosaic Law commanded *you shall love your neighbor*

(Leviticus 19:18). Yet some teachers in the days of Jesus added an opposite – and evil – misapplication: an equal obligation to **hate your enemy**.

> i. "They generally looked upon all the uncircumcised as not their neighbours, but their enemies, whom the precept did not oblige them to love." (Poole)

b. **But I say to you, love your enemies**: Instead, Jesus reminds that in the sense God means it, *all people* are our neighbors, even our enemies. To truly fulfill this law we must **love**, **bless**, **do good** and **pray** for our enemies - not only our friends.

> i. Jesus understood we *will* have enemies, yet we are to respond to them in love, trusting that God will protect our cause and destroy our enemies in the best way possible, by transforming them into our friends.

> ii. "The disciple's attitude to religious persecution must go beyond non-retaliation to a positive *love*." (France)

> iii. "A hard task, I must needs say, but, hard or not hard, it must be done, be it never so contrary to our foul nature and former practice." (Trapp)

c. **That you may be sons of your Father in heaven**: In doing this, we are imitating God, who shows love towards *His* enemies, by sending **rain on the just and on the unjust**.

> i. "You see our Lord Jesus Christ's philosophy of nature. He believed in the immediate presence and working of God. As the great Son of God he had a very sensitive perception of the presence of his Father in all the scenes around him, and hence he calls the sun God's sun- 'He maketh his sun to rise.'" (Spurgeon)

> ii. "As though he did not regard human character at all, God bids his sun shine on good and bad. As though he did not know that any men were vile, he bids the shower descend on just and unjust. Yet he does know, for he is no blind deity. He does know; and he knows when his sun shines on yonder miser's acres that it is bringing forth a harvest for a churl. He does it deliberately. When the rain is falling yonder upon the oppressor's crops, he knows that the oppressor will be the richer for it, and means that he should be; he is doing nothing by mistake and nothing without a purpose." (Spurgeon)

> iii. "What does God say to us when he acts thus? I believe that he says this: 'This is the day of free grace; this is the time of mercy.' The hour for judgment is not yet, when he will separate between the good and the bad; when he will mount the judgment seat and award different portions to the righteous and to the wicked." (Spurgeon)

iv. This is an *example* – that we also are to love our enemies and bless them if we can. In doing so, we show ourselves to **sons of** our **Father in heaven**. "We are made sons by regeneration, through faith in the Son; but we are called to make our calling and election sure – to approve and vindicate our right to that sacred name. We can only do this by showing in word and act that the divine life and principles animate us." (Meyer)

d. **For if you love those who love you, what reward have you**: What *do* you do more than the sinner? We should regard it as no matter of virtue if we merely return the love that is given to us.

i. Remember, Jesus here taught the character of the citizens of His kingdom. We should expect that character to be different from the character seen in the world. There are many good reasons *why* more should be expected from Christians than others:

- They claim to have something that others do not have; they claim to be renewed, repentant, and redeemed by Jesus Christ.
- They do in fact have something that others do not have; they are in fact renewed, repentant, and redeemed by Jesus Christ.
- They have a power that others do not have; they can do all things through Christ who strengthens them.
- They have the Spirit of God dwelling within them.
- They have a better future than others do.

9. (48) The conclusion to the true interpretation of the law: **be perfect**.

"Therefore you shall be perfect, just as your Father in heaven is perfect."

a. **Therefore you shall be perfect**: If a man could live the way Jesus has told us to in this chapter, he would truly be **perfect**.

- He would never hate, slander or speak evil of another person.
- He would never lust in his heart or mind, and not covet anything.
- He would never make a false oath, and always be completely truthful.
- He would let God defend his personal rights, and not take it upon himself to defend those rights.
- He would always love his neighbors, and even his enemies.

b. **Just as your Father in heaven is perfect**: If a man could keep just what Jesus said here, he would truly have a righteousness greater than the scribes and the Pharisees (Matthew 5:20), the very thing we must have to enter into God's Kingdom. But there is only one man who has lived like this:

Jesus Christ. What about the rest of us? Are we left out of the Kingdom of God?

i. "Jesus is saying that the true direction in which the law has always pointed is not towards mere judicial restraints, concessions rising out of the hardness of men's hearts…nor even to the 'law of love'…No, it pointed to all the perfection of God, exemplified by the authoritative interpretation of the law." (Carson)

ii. We see that in this section Jesus was not *primarily* seeking to show what God requires of the Christian in his daily life. True, Jesus has revealed God's ultimate standard, and we must take it to heart. But His *primary* intent was to say, "If you want to be righteous by the law, you must keep the whole law, internal and external - that is, you must be **perfect**."

iii. Jesus has demonstrated that we need a righteousness that is apart from the law (Romans 3:21-22). As Paul put it in Romans 3:21-22: *But now the righteousness of God apart from the law is revealed, being witnessed by the Law and the Prophets, even the righteousness of God, through faith in Jesus Christ, to all and on all who believe.*

iv. What is our current relation to the law, as truly interpreted? We are exposed as guilty sinners who can never make ourselves righteous by doing good works - which was exactly the view held by most people in Jesus' day, and in our own day.

v. Finally, when it comes to understanding the interpretation and the demands of the law, we do well to remember another aspect of Jesus' teaching on the law: in focusing on the command to love God and our neighbor, we will rightly understand the demands and details of the law (Matthew 22:37-40). The Apostle Paul wrote much the same thing: *Now the purpose of the commandment is love from a pure heart, from a good conscience, and from sincere faith.* (1 Timothy 1:5)

Matthew 6 - The Sermon on the Mount (Continued)

A. Doing good to please God.

1. (1) Jesus' warning against doing good to be seen by others.

"Take heed that you do not do your charitable deeds before men, to be seen by them. Otherwise you have no reward from your Father in heaven."

a. **Take heed that you do not do your charitable deeds before men**: **Charitable deeds** is actually the word *righteousness*. Jesus tells us to not do righteous things for the sake of display or image (**to be seen by them**).

i. Jesus has just clearly shown God's righteous standard; perhaps He anticipated the thought "Wouldn't everybody be impressed if I was like that?" So here Jesus addressed the danger of cultivating an *image* of righteousness. It is almost impossible to do spiritual things in front of others without thinking what their opinion is of us as we do those things, and how they are thinking better or worse of us as we do what we do.

ii. This does not contradict His previous command to *let your light so shine before men* (Matthew 5:16). Although Christians are to be seen doing good works, they must not do good works *simply* to be seen.

b. **Otherwise you have no reward from your Father in heaven**: The idea is when we do righteous deeds for the attention and applause of men, their attention and applause is our reward. It is much better to receive a **reward from your Father in heaven**.

i. There are some who say, "All that is important is the *doing* of the deed. *How* I do it is much less important than the doing of it." It is true that in some cases it would be better to do the right thing in the wrong way or out of the wrong motive than to do the wrong thing, but Jesus' point is clear: *God cares about how we do our good works, and with what motive we do them.*

ii. Jesus thus begins to deal with three spiritual disciplines: giving, prayer, and fasting. "These three were (and are) the most prominent practical requirements for personal piety in mainstream Judaism... These same three activities, together with the specifically Islamic requirements of the Hajj and recitation of the creed, constitute also the Five Pillars of Islam." (France)

2. (2-4) Examples of the wrong kind of giving and the right kind of giving.

"Therefore, when you do a charitable deed, do not sound a trumpet before you as the hypocrites do in the synagogues and in the streets, that they may have glory from men. Assuredly, I say to you, they have their reward. But when you do a charitable deed, do not let your left hand know what your right hand is doing, that your charitable deed may be in secret; and your Father who sees in secret will Himself reward you openly."

a. **When you do a charitable deed, do not sound a trumpet**: It was a custom for some in Jesus' day to draw attention to their giving so they would be known as generous. Today, people do not **sound a trumpet** to project the image of generosity, but they still know how to call attention to their giving.

i. There aren't good examples in ancient literature of people actually announcing their giving with the sound of a trumpet. It may be what Jesus had in mind was the gifts given during feast times, which were signaled by the blast of a trumpet. "These occasions afforded golden opportunities for ostentation." (Carson)

ii. Yet the idea of doing a **charitable deed** – giving alms and charity – was deeply established in the Jewish mind. "To give alms and to be righteous were one and the same thing. To give alms was to gain merit in the sight of God, and was even to win atonement and forgiveness for past sins." (Barclay)

b. **As the hypocrites do**: Such performers are rightly called **hypocrites**, because they are actors, acting the part of pious, holy people when they are not. It is not having a standard that makes someone a hypocrite; it is falsely claiming to live by that standard when you in fact do not, or when you have a double standard that makes one a hypocrite.

i. "In older Greek a *hypocrites* ('hypocrite') was an actor, but by the first century the term came to be used for those who play roles and see the world as their stage." (Carson)

ii. "There are religious actors still, and they draw good houses." (Bruce)

iii. "Oh, let us rather seek to be good than seem to be so." (Trapp)

c. **Assuredly, I say to you, they have their reward**: Jesus tells the one who gives so he can hear the applause of others that he should enjoy the applause, because that will be all the reward that he will receive. There will be no reward in heaven for the one who did it for the motive of an earthly reward.

i. It is *all* they will receive. "It would be better to translate it: 'They have received payment in full.' The word that is used in the Greek is the verb *apechein*, which was the technical business and commercial word for receiving payment in full." (Barclay)

d. **Do not let your left hand know what your right hand is doing**: Instead, our giving is to be - if it were possible - even hidden from ourselves. Though we cannot really be ignorant about our own giving, we can deny ourselves any indulgent self-congratulation.

i. "Keep the thing so secret that even you yourself are hardly aware that you are doing anything at all praiseworthy. Let God be present, and you will have enough of an audience." (Spurgeon)

e. **That your charitable deed may be in secret**: If someone finds out that we have given something, do we automatically lose our reward? The issue is really a matter of *motive*. If we give for our own glory, it doesn't matter if no one finds out and we will still have no reward from God. But if we give for God's glory, it doesn't matter who finds out, because your reward will remain because you gave for the right motive.

f. **Our Father who sees in secret will Himself reward you openly**: Jesus pointed out the great value of doing good deeds for the glory of God. It is much better to receive our return from God, who rewards much more generously and much more **openly** than men do.

i. God does see in **secret**. "We should ever remember that the eye of the Lord is upon us, and that he sees not only the *act*, but also every motive that led to it." (Clarke)

ii. We should not miss the strength of the promise – these things done the *right way* will *certainly* be rewarded. We can be sure of that, even when it doesn't feel like it.

3. (5-6) Examples of the wrong kind of prayer and the right kind of prayer.

"And when you pray, you shall not be like the hypocrites. For they love to pray standing in the synagogues and on the corners of the streets, that they may be seen by men. Assuredly, I say to you, they have their

reward. But you, when you pray, go into your room, and when you have shut your door, pray to your Father who *is* in the secret *place;* and your Father who sees in secret will reward you openly."

a. **And when you pray, you shall not be like the hypocrites**: Jesus assumed that His disciples would give, so He told them the right way to give (Matthew 6:1-4). He also assumed that His disciples would **pray**, and it was important that they not pray in the same manner as the **hypocrites**.

i. "There are no dumb children in God's house; the least he hath can ask him blessing. All are not alike gifted, but every godly man prayeth unto thee, saith David, Psalm 32:6." (Trapp)

b. **For they love to pray standing in the synagogues and on the corners of the streets**: There were two main places where a Jew in Jesus' day might pray in a hypocritical manner. They might pray at the synagogue at the time of public prayer, or on the street at the appointed times of prayer (9 a.m., noon, and 3 p.m.).

i. "In synagogue worship someone from the congregation might be asked to pray publicly, standing in front of the ark." (Carson)

ii. "Prayer was not normally practiced *at the street corners*, but…one who strictly observed the afternoon hour of prayer could deliberately time his movements to bring him to the most public place at the appropriate time." (France)

c. **That they may be seen by men**: These hypocrites prayed not to be heard by God, but to **be seen by men**. This is a common fault in public prayer today, when people pray to impress or teach others instead of genuinely pouring out their hearts before God.

i. Such prayers are an insult to God. When we mouth words towards God while really trying to impress others, we then use God merely as a tool to impress others.

d. **They have their reward**: Again, those praying to be seen of men **have their reward**, and they should enjoy it in full - because that is all they will receive. There is no reward in heaven for such prayers.

e. **But you, when you pray, go into your room**: Rather, we should meet with God in our **room** (or "closet"). The idea is of a private place where we can impress no one except God.

i. The specific ancient Greek word "**room**" was used for a storeroom where treasures were kept. This reminds us that there are treasures waiting for us in our prayer closet.

ii. Jesus certainly did not prohibit public prayer, but our prayers should always be directed to God and not towards man.

4. (7-8) The right way to pray.

"And when you pray, do not use vain repetitions as the heathen *do*. For they think that they will be heard for their many words. Therefore do not be like them. For your Father knows the things you have need of before you ask Him."

a. **When you pray, do not use vain repetitions**: The right kind of prayer does not use **vain repetitions**, which is any and all prayer which is mostly words and no meaning; all lips and no mind or heart.

i. "Rabbi Levi said, 'Whoever is long in prayer is heard.' Another saying has it: 'Whenever the righteous make their prayer long, their prayer is heard.'" (Barclay) One famous Jewish prayer began like this: "Blessed, praised, and glorified, exalted, and honored, magnified and lauded be the name of the Holy One."

ii. One can pray long – but to the wrong god. In 1 Kings 18:26 the prophets of Baal cried out, "O Baal answer us" for half the day. In Acts 19:34 a mob in Ephesus shouted, "Great is Artemis of the Ephesians" for two hours. The true God isn't impressed by the *length* or *eloquence* of our prayers, but the heart. "Prayer requires more of the *heart* than of the *tongue*. The eloquence of prayer consists in the fervency of desire, and the simplicity of faith." (Clarke)

iii. When we try to impress God (or worse, other people) with our many words, we deny that God is a loving, yet holy Father. Instead, we should follow the counsel of Ecclesiastes 5:2: *God is in heaven, and you are on earth; therefore let your words be few.*

iv. "Christians' prayers are measured by weight, and not by length. Many of the most prevailing prayers have been as short as they were strong." (Spurgeon)

v. The NIV translates the phrase **vain repetitions** as "keep on babbling." That may be an accurate sense of the ancient Greek word *battalogeo*, which may be a word that sounds like "babbling" and has the sense of "blah-blah-blah."

b. **Your Father knows the things you have need of before you ask Him**: We don't pray to tell God things that He didn't know before we told Him. We pray to commune with and appeal to a loving God who wants us to bring every need and worry before His throne.

i. "Prayer is not designed to *inform* God, but to give *man* a sight of his misery; to humble his heart, to excite his desire, to inflame his faith, to animate his hope, to raise his soul from earth to heaven, and to put him in mind that THERE is his *Father*, his *country*, and *inheritance*." (Clarke)

ii. In the following verses, Jesus will begin a memorable explanation of the right way to pray with the words, "*In this manner, therefore pray.*" Jesus then gave His disciples a model for prayer, prayer marked by close relationship, reverence, submission, and trust and dependence. Since Luke 11:2-4 has much the same material, it is reasonable to believe that this was not the only time Jesus taught His disciples on this subject.

ii. "In contrast with ostentatious prayer or thoughtless prayer, Jesus gives his disciples a model. But it is only a model: 'This is how [not what] you should pray.'" (Carson)

iii. "We may use the Paternoster, but we are not bound to use it. It is not in turn to become a fetish. Reformers do not arise to break old fetters only in order to forge new ones." (Bruce)

5. (9-13) The model prayer.

In this manner, therefore, pray:

Our Father in heaven,
Hallowed be Your name.
Your kingdom come.
Your will be done
On earth as *it is* in heaven.
Give us this day our daily bread.
And forgive us our debts,
As we forgive our debtors.
And do not lead us into temptation,
But deliver us from the evil one.
For Yours is the kingdom and the power and the glory forever. Amen.

a. **Our Father in heaven**: The right kind of prayer comes to God as a **Father in heaven**. It rightly recognizes whom we pray to, coming with a privileged title that demonstrates a privileged relationship. It was very unusual for the Jews of that day to call God "**Father**" because it was considered too intimate.

i. It is true that God is the mighty sovereign of the universe who created, governs, and will judge all things – but He is also to us a **Father**.

ii. He is our **Father**, but He is our **Father in heaven**. When we say "**in heaven**," we remember God's holiness and glory. He is **our Father**, but our Father **in heaven**.

iii. This is a prayer focused on *community*; Jesus said "**Our Father**" and not "My Father." "The whole prayer is social. The singular pronoun is absent. Man enters the presence of the Father, and then prays as one of the great family." (Morgan)

iv. "There is no evidence of anyone before Jesus using this term to address God." (Carson)

b. **Hallowed be Your name. Your kingdom come. Your will be done on earth as it is in heaven**: The right kind of prayer has a passion for God's glory and agenda. His **name**, **kingdom** and **will** have the top priority.

i. Everyone wants to guard their own name and reputation, but we must resist the tendency to protect and promote ourselves first and instead put God's **name**, **kingdom** and **will** first.

ii. Jesus wanted us to pray with the desire that the **will** of God would **be done on earth as it is in heaven**. In heaven there is no disobedience and no obstacles to God's will; on earth there is disobedience and at least apparent obstacles to His will. The citizens of Jesus' kingdom will want to see His will done as freely **on earth as it is in heaven**.

iii. "He that taught us this prayer used it himself in the most unrestricted sense. When the bloody sweat stood on his face, and all the fear and trembling of a man in anguish were upon him, he did not dispute the decree of the Father, but bowed his head and cried. 'Nevertheless, not as I will, but as thou wilt.'" (Spurgeon)

iv. A man can say, "**Your will be done**" in different ways and moods. He may say it with fatalism and resentment, "You will do your will, and there is nothing I can do about it anyway. Your will wins, but I don't like it" or he may say it with a heart of perfect love and trust, "Do Your will, because I know it is the best. Change me where I don't understand or accept Your will."

v. One might rightly wonder why God wants us to pray that *His* will would be done, as if He were not able to accomplish it Himself. God is more than able to do His will without our prayer or cooperation; yet He invites the participation of our prayers, our heart, and our actions in seeing His **will be done on earth as it is in heaven**.

c. **Give us this day our daily bread. And forgive us our debts, as we forgive our debtors. And do not lead us into temptation, but deliver us from the evil one**: The right kind of prayer will freely bring its own needs to God. This will include needs for daily provision, forgiveness, and strength in the face of temptation.

i. When Jesus spoke of **bread**, He meant real bread, as in the sense of daily provisions. Early theologians allegorized this, because they couldn't imagine Jesus speaking about an everyday thing like bread in such a majestic prayer like this. So they thought bread referred to *communion*, the Lord's Supper. Some have thought it referred to Jesus Himself as the bread of life. Others have thought it speaks of the Word of God as our daily bread. Calvin rightly said of such interpretations which fail to see God's interest in everyday things, "This is exceedingly absurd." God *does* care about everyday things, and we should pray about them.

ii. "The prayer is for our needs, not our greeds. It is for one day at a time, reflecting the precarious lifestyle of many first-century workers who were paid one day at a time and for whom a few days' illness could spell tragedy." (Carson)

iii. "Sin is represented here under the notion of a *debt*, and as our sins are *many*, they are called here *debts*. God made man that he might live to his glory, and gave him a law to walk by; and if, when he does any thing that tends not to glorify God, he contracts a debt with Divine Justice." (Clarke)

iv. **Temptation** literally means a *test*, not always a solicitation to do evil. God has promised to keep us from any testing that is greater than what we can handle (1 Corinthians 10:13).

v. "God, while he does not 'tempt' men to do evil (James 1:13), does allow his children to pass through periods of testing. But disciples, aware of their weakness, should not desire such testing, and should pray to be spared exposure to such situations in which they are vulnerable." (France)

vi. "The man who prays 'Lead us not into temptation,' and then goes into it is a liar before God…'Lead us not into temptation,' is shameful profanity when it comes from the lips of men who resort to places of amusement whose moral tone is bad." (Spurgeon)

vii. If we truly pray, **lead us not into temptation**, it will be lived out in several ways. It will mean:

- Never boast in your own strength.
- Never desire trials.
- Never go into temptation.

- Never lead others into temptation.

d. **For Yours is the kingdom and the power and the glory forever**: The right kind of prayer praises God and credits to Him **the kingdom and the power and the glory**.

> i. There is some dispute as to whether this doxology is in the original manuscript Matthew wrote or was added in later by a scribe. Most modern Biblical scholars believe this line was a later addition.

> ii. "It is *variously* written in several MSS., and omitted by most of the fathers, both Greek and Latin. As the doxology is at least very ancient, and was in use among the Jews, as well as all the other petitions of this excellent prayer, it should not, in my opinion, be left out of the text, merely because some MSS. have omitted it, and it has been variously written in others." (Clarke)

6. (14-15) More on the importance of forgiveness.

"For if you forgive men their trespasses, your heavenly Father will also forgive you. But if you do not forgive men their trespasses, neither will your Father forgive your trespasses."

a. **If you forgive men their trespasses, your heavenly Father will also forgive you**: Forgiveness is required for those who have been forgiven. We are not given the luxury of holding on to our bitterness towards other people.

> i. "Once our eyes have been opened to see the enormity of our offence against God, the injuries which others have done to us appear by comparison extremely trifling. If, on the other hand, we have an exaggerated view of the offences of others, it proves that we have minimized our own." (Stott, cited in Carson)

b. **Neither will your Father forgive your trespasses**: Jesus has much more to say about forgiveness (Matthew 9:2-6, 18:21-35, and Luke 17:3-4). Here, the emphasis is on the *imperative* of forgiveness; on the fact that it is not an option.

7. (16-18) The right way to fast.

"Moreover, when you fast, do not be like the hypocrites, with a sad countenance. For they disfigure their faces that they may appear to men to be fasting. Assuredly, I say to you, they have their reward. But you, when you fast, anoint your head and wash your face, so that you do not appear to men to be fasting, but to your Father who *is* in the secret *place;* and your Father who sees in secret will reward you openly."

a. **When you fast**: Jesus spoke to these fundamental practices of spiritual life in His kingdom: giving, praying, and now fasting. Clearly, Jesus assumed that His followers *would* fast.

i. The Old Testament commanded fasting on the Day of Atonement (Leviticus 16:29-31 and 23:37-32; Numbers 29:7). During the Exile, the Jewish people expanded the practice of fasting (Zechariah 7:3-5 and 8:19).

ii. "A fast is termed by the Greeks νηστις, from νη *not*, and εσθειν *to eat*; hence fast means, a *total abstinence from food for a certain time*. Abstaining from *flesh*, and living on *fish, vegetables*, &c., is no fast, or may be rather considered a burlesque on fasting. Many pretend to take the true definition of a fast from Isa 58:3, and say that it means *a fast from sin*. This is a mistake; there is no such term in the Bible as *fasting from sin*; the very idea is ridiculous and absurd, as if *sin* were a part of our *daily food*." (Clarke)

iii. Fasting is something good that was corrupted by the hypocrisy of the religious people of Jesus' day. Our corrupt natures can corrupt something good into something bad. A modern example of a good thing gone bad is the manner of dressing nice on Sunday. There is nothing wrong with this in itself – it can even be good as an expression of reverence; yet if it is used to compete with others or to draw attention to one's self, something good has become something bad.

iv. "Fasting took a leading place in devotion under the Law, and it might profitably be more practiced even now under the Gospel. The Puritans called it 'soul-fattening fasting,' and so many have found it." (Spurgeon)

b. **When you fast, do not be like the hypocrites**: The hypocritical scribes and Pharisees wanted to make sure that everybody knew they were fasting, so they would have a **sad countenance** and **disfigure their faces** so their agony of fasting would be evident to all.

i. The Pharisees typically fasted twice a week (Luke 18:12). "Twice a week in ordinary Pharasic practice: Thursday and Monday (ascent and descent of Moses on Sinai)." (Bruce)

ii. **Assuredly, I say to you, they have their reward**: When hypocrites receive the admiration of men for these "spiritual" efforts, they receive all the reward they will ever get.

iii. The real problem with the hypocrite is self-interest. "Ultimately, our only reason for pleasing men around us is that we may be pleased." (D. Martin Lloyd-Jones)

c. **When you fast, anoint your head and wash your face, so that you do not appear to men to be fasting**: In contrast, Jesus instructed us to take care of ourselves as usual and to make the fast something of a secret before God.

> i. "Oil does not here symbolize extravagant joy but normal body care." (Carson)

B. The place of material things: a warning against covetousness.

1. (19-21) The choice between two treasures.

"Do not lay up for yourselves treasures on earth, where moth and rust destroy and where thieves break in and steal; but lay up for yourselves treasures in heaven, where neither moth nor rust destroys and where thieves do not break in and steal. For where your treasure is, there your heart will be also."

a. **Do not lay up for yourselves treasures on earth**: The ancient Greek more literally says *do not treasure for yourself treasures on earth*. The idea is that earthly treasure is temporary and fading away (**where moth and rust destroy and where thieves break in and steal**), but heavenly treasure is secure.

> i. The issue isn't that earthly treasures are intrinsically bad, but they are of no ultimate value either. If this is the case, then it is wrong for the disciple of Jesus to dedicate his life to continually expanding his earthly treasures.

> ii. To **lay up for yourselves treasure on earth** is also to doom yourself to a life of frustration and emptiness. Regarding material things the secret to happiness is not *more*, it is *contentment*. In a 1992 survey, people were asked how much money they would have to make to have "the American dream." Those who earn $25,000 or less a year thought they would need around $54,000. Those in the $100,000 annual income bracket said that they could buy the dream for an average of $192,000 a year. These figures indicate that we typically think we would have to have double our income in order to find the good life. But the Apostle Paul had the right idea in 1 Timothy 6:6: *Now godliness with contentment is great gain.*

> iii. "The Master does not say it is wrong to possess earthly treasure. He does say it is wrong to lay it up for self. We are to hold it as stewards." (Morgan)

b. **But lay up for yourselves treasures in heaven**: In contrast, heavenly treasures are everlasting and incorruptible. **Treasures in heaven** give enjoyment *now*, in the contentment and sense of well-being that comes from being a giver. But their ultimate enjoyment comes on the other side of eternity.

i. It has been wisely observed that a moving truck full of possessions never follows a hearse. Everything one might take with them to the world beyond is left behind. The pharaohs of Egypt were buried with gold and treasures to take into the afterlife, but they left it all behind. Even further, though gold is a precious thing on earth, God uses it to pave the streets of heaven.

ii. Our material treasures will not pass from this life to the next; but the good that has been done for the kingdom of God through the use of our treasures lasts for eternity, and the work God does *in us* through faithful giving will last for eternity.

c. **For where your treasure is, there your heart will be also**: Jesus drew the conclusion that you can only have your treasure (and your heart) in one place; we can't store up treasure on earth and on heaven at the same time.

i. "It is not so much the disciple's wealth that Jesus is concerned with as his loyalty. As Matthew 6:24 will make explicit, materialism is in direct conflict with loyalty to God." (France)

2. (22-23) The choice between two visions.

"The lamp of the body is the eye. If therefore your eye is good, your whole body will be full of light. But if your eye is bad, your whole body will be full of darkness. If therefore the light that is in you is darkness, how great *is* that darkness!"

a. **The lamp of the body is the eye**: Simply, the idea is that "light" comes into the body through the eye. If our eyes were blind, we would live in a "dark" world.

b. **If therefore your eye is good, your whole body will be full of light**: The idea behind having a **good** eye is either being *generous* or being *single minded*. Both principles apply to the disciple's attitude towards material things.

i. "There seems to be a deliberate *double-entendre* here, with *haplous* taking up not only the theme of undivided loyalty but also that of detachment from material concern, hence of generosity." (France)

ii. Being *generous* brings light to our lives. We are happier and more content when we have God's heart of generosity. But if we are not generous, it is as if **your whole body will be full of darkness**. Our selfish, miserly ways cast darkness over everything that we think or do.

iii. Being *single minded* brings light to our lives, and we are also happier and more content when we focus on the kingdom of God and His righteousness, knowing that all the material things will be added to us (Matthew 6:33). But when we are double-minded, it is as if **your whole body** is **full of darkness**. We try to live for two masters at the same time, and it puts a dark shadow over everything in our life.

c. **Full of light...full of darkness**: In any case, Jesus tells us that either our eye is directed at heavenly things (and therefore **full of light**) or it is directed at earthly things (and therefore **full of darkness**).

i. "An *evil eye* was a phrase in use, among the ancient Jews, to denote an *envious*, *covetous* man or disposition; a man who repined at his neighbour's prosperity, loved his own money, and would do nothing in the way of charity for God's sake." (Clarke)

d. **How great is that darkness**: Building on the analogy of the eye, Jesus reminds us that if we are blind in our eyes, the whole body is blind. The **darkness** is then **great** in our whole body. In the same way, our attitude towards material treasure will either bring great **light** or great **darkness** to our lives.

i. Often a materialistic, miserly, selfish Christian justifies their sin by saying, "It's just one area of my life." But even as the darkness of the eye affects everything in the body, so a wrong attitude towards material things brings darkness to our whole being.

3. (24) The choice between two masters.

"No one can serve two masters; for either he will hate the one and love the other, or else he will be loyal to the one and despise the other. You cannot serve God and mammon."

a. **No one can serve two masters**: Having **two masters** is not like working two jobs. Jesus had the master and slave relationship in mind, and no slave could serve two masters.

i. Jesus states that serving two masters is a simple impossibility. If you think that you are successfully serving two masters, you are deceived. It can't be done. As ancient Israel struggled with idolatry, they *thought* they could worship the Lord God and Baal. God constantly reminded them that to worship Baal was to forsake the Lord God. To be **loyal to the one** is to **despise the other**.

ii. "In the natural sphere it is impossible for a slave to serve two masters, for each claims him as his property, and the slave must respond to one or other of the claims with entire devotion, either from love or from interest." (Bruce)

iii. It can be simply said: Don't serve your money. Let your money serve the Lord and it will serve you.

b. **You cannot serve God and mammon**: There are different opinions regarding the origin of the term **mammon**. Some think it was the name of a pagan god. Others think the name comes "From the Hebrew *aman*, to *trust, confide*; because men are apt to trust in riches." (Clarke) Whatever its origin, the meaning is clear: **mammon** is materialism, or "wealth personified." (Bruce)

i. According to France, the idea of **mammon** itself was morally neutral. The word was used in some ancient Jewish texts that showed this, translating Proverbs 3:9 as *Honor God with your mammon* and Deuteronomy 6:5 as *You shall love the Lord your God with…all your mammon*. Therefore **mammon** itself represents material things we possess or want, and those things can be used for God's kingdom and glory or as idols.

ii. Certainly, Jesus spoke of the *heart* here. Many *say* they love God, but how they serve money shows that they do not. How can we tell who or what we serve? We may remember this principle: *you will sacrifice for your God*. If you sacrifice for the sake of money, but will not sacrifice for the sake of Jesus, don't deceive yourself: money is your God.

iii. We must remember that we don't have to be rich to serve **mammon** (money and material things); the poor can be just as greedy and covetous as the rich can be.

C. **The place of material things: anxiety over material things.**

1. (25) Therefore: because the Kingdom of God is so greatly superior to earthly pursuits, *it* deserves our attention.

"Therefore I say to you, do not worry about your life, what you will eat or what you will drink; nor about your body, what you will put on. Is not life more than food and the body more than clothing?"

a. **Do not worry about your life**: We should not get tangled up worrying about the things of this world, because our life is more than those things.

i. "You can be as unfaithful to God through care as well as through covetousness." (Bruce)

ii. **What you will eat or what you will drink…what you will put on:** "These three inquiries engross the whole attention of those who are living without God in the world. The belly and back of a worldling are his compound god; and these he worships in the lust of the flesh, in the lust of the eye, and in the pride of life." (Clarke)

iii. Perhaps Adam Clarke would add in our own age, "What you will do to entertain yourself."

b. **Do not worry**: There is a difference between a godly sense of responsibility and an ungodly, untrusting worry. However, an ungodly, untrusting sense of worry usually masquerades as responsibility.

i. "You cannot say that Jesus Christ ever troubled his head about what he should eat, or what he should drink; his meat and his drink consisted in doing his Father's will." (Spurgeon)

ii. We *are* to be concerned with the right things; the ultimate issues of life - and we then leave the management (and the worry) over material things with our heavenly Father.

c. **Is not life more than food**: The worry Jesus spoke of debases man to the level of an animal who is merely concerned with physical needs. Your life is **more**, and you have eternal matters to pursue.

2. (26-30) Example and arguments against worry.

"Look at the birds of the air, for they neither sow nor reap nor gather into barns; yet your heavenly Father feeds them. Are you not of more value than they? Which of you by worrying can add one cubit to his stature? So why do you worry about clothing? Consider the lilies of the field, how they grow: they neither toil nor spin; and yet I say to you that even Solomon in all his glory was not arrayed like one of these. Now if God so clothes the grass of the field, which today is, and tomorrow is thrown into the oven, *will He* not much more *clothe* you, O you of little faith?"

a. **Look at the birds of the air...your heavenly Father feeds them**: God provides for the birds, and He takes care of them. Therefore, we should expect that God would take care of us.

i. Yet take careful note: the birds don't *worry*, but they do *work*. Birds don't just sit with open mouths, expecting God to fill them.

ii. "This argument presupposed a biblical cosmology without which faith makes no sense. God is so sovereign over the universe that even the feeding of a wren falls within his concern." (Carson)

b. **Are you not of more value than they**: The worry many people have over the material things of life is rooted in a low understanding of their **value** before God. They don't comprehend how much He loves and cares for them.

c. **Which of you by worrying can add one cubit to his stature**: Worry accomplishes nothing; we can **add** nothing to our lives by worrying. There may be greater sins than worry, but there are none more self-defeating and useless.

> i. **Can add**: The ancient Greek may mean *adding to life* instead of *adding to height*, but the thought is the same. Indeed, instead of *adding* to our life, we can actually harm ourselves through worry. Stress is one of the great contributors to disease and poor health.

d. **If God so clothes the grass of the field**: God even takes care of the **grass of the field**, so He will certainly take care of you. We are confident of the power and care of a loving heavenly Father.

> i. **You of little faith**: "'*Little faith*' is not a little fault; for it greatly wrongs the Lord, and sadly grieves the fretful mind. To think the Lord who clothes the lilies will leave his own children naked is shameful. O little faith, learn better manners!" (Spurgeon)

3. (31-32) You have a heavenly Father that knows your needs.

"Therefore do not worry, saying, 'What shall we eat?' or 'What shall we drink?' or 'What shall we wear?' For after all these things the Gentiles seek. For your heavenly Father knows that you need all these things."

a. **Therefore do not worry**: We are invited to know a freedom from the worry and anxiety that comes from undue concern about material things. We can reflect the same kind of heart that Matthew Henry showed when he said the following after being robbed:

> *Lord, I thank You:*
> *That I have never been robbed before.*
> *That although they took my money, they spared my life.*
> *That although they took everything, it wasn't very much.*
> *That it was I who was robbed, not I who robbed.*

b. **For after all these things the Gentiles seek**: Jesus contrasted the life of those who do not know God and are separated from Him with those who do know God and receive His loving care. Those who know God should **seek** after other things.

4. (33) Summary: Put God's kingdom first - He will take care of these things!

"But seek first the kingdom of God and His righteousness, and all these things shall be added to you."

a. **But seek first the kingdom of God**: This must be the rule of our life when ordering our priorities. Yet it is wrong to think that this is just another priority to fit onto our list of priorities – and to put at the top. Instead, in everything we do, we **seek first the kingdom of God**.

i. For example, we rarely have to choose between honoring God and loving our wives or being good workers. We honor God and **seek first the kingdom of God** by being good husbands and good workers.

ii. We should also remember this statement in its immediate context. Jesus reminds us that our physical well-being is not a worthy object to devote our lives unto. If you think it is worthy that your god is mammon, then your life is cursed with worry, and you live life too much like an animal, concerned mostly with physical needs.

iii. Jesus didn't just tell them to stop worrying; He told them to *replace* worry with a concern for the kingdom of God. A habit or a passion can only be given up for a greater habit or passion.

iv. "What this verse demands is, therefore, a commitment to find and to do the will of God, to ally oneself totally with his purpose. And this commitment must come *first*." (France)

b. **And all these things shall be added to you**: If you put God's kingdom first, and do not think that your physical well-being is a worthy object to live your life for, you then may enjoy **all these things**. He promises heavenly treasure, rest in divine provision, and fulfillment of God's highest purpose for man - fellowship with Him, and being part of His kingdom.

i. This choice – to **seek first the kingdom of God** – is the fundamental choice everyone makes when they first repent and are converted. Yet every day after that, our Christian life will either reinforce that decision or deny it.

5. (34) A conclusion with common sense.

"Therefore do not worry about tomorrow, for tomorrow will worry about its own things. Sufficient for the day *is* its own trouble."

a. **Do not worry about tomorrow**: If you *must* worry, worry only for the things of today. Most of our worry is over things that we have absolutely no control over anyway, and is therefore foolish as well as harmful.

b. **Sufficient for the day is its own trouble**: Jesus reminds us of the importance of living for the present **day**. It isn't wrong to remember the past or plan for the future; to some degree both of those are good. Yet it is easy to become too focused on either the past or the future and to let **the day** and **its own trouble** be ignored. God wants us to remember the past, plan for the future, but live in the present.

Matthew 7 - The Sermon on the Mount (Continued)

A. Judgment and discernment.

1. (1-2) A summary statement on passing judgment upon others.

"Judge not, that you be not judged. For with what judgment you judge, you will be judged; and with the measure you use, it will be measured back to you."

a. **Judge not, that you be not judged**: Here Jesus moved to another idea in the Sermon on the Mount. He had primarily dealt with themes connected with the *interior* spiritual life (attitudes in giving, prayer, fasting, materialism, and anxiety over material things). Now He touches on an important theme related to the way we think of and treat others.

i. We remember that Jesus called for a righteousness that was greater than that of the scribes and Pharisees (Matthew 5:20). In the way some people think, the way to make one's self more righteous is to be more judgmental of others. Jesus here rebuked that kind of thinking.

b. **Judge not, that you be not judged**: With this command Jesus warned against passing judgment upon others, because when we do so, we will be **judged** in a similar manner.

i. Among those who seem to know nothing of the Bible, this is the verse that seems to be most popular. Yet most the people who quote this verse don't understand what Jesus said. They seem to think (or hope) that Jesus commanded a universal acceptance of any lifestyle or teaching.

ii. Just a little later in this same sermon (Matthew 7:15-16), Jesus commanded us to know ourselves and others by the fruit of their life, and *some* sort of assessment is necessary for that. The Christian is called to show unconditional love, but the Christian is not called to unconditional *approval*. We really *can* love people who do things that should not be approved of.

iii. So while this does not prohibit examining the lives of others, it certainly prohibits doing it in the spirit it is often done. An example of unjust judgment was the disciples' condemnation of the woman who came to anoint the feet of Jesus with oil (Matthew 26:6-13). They thought she was wasting something; Jesus said she had done a good work that would always be remembered. They had a rash, harsh, unjust judgment.

- We break this command when we think the worst of others.
- We break this command when we only speak to others of their faults.
- We break this command when we judge an entire life only by its worst moments.
- We break this command when we judge the hidden motives of others.
- We break this command when we judge others without considering ourselves in their same circumstances.
- We break this command when we judge others without being mindful that we ourselves will be judged.

c. **For with what judgment you judge, you will be judged**: Jesus did not *prohibit* the judgment of others. He only requires that our judgment be completely fair, and that we only judge others by a standard we would also like to be judged by.

i. When our judgment in regard to others is wrong, it is often not because we judge according to a standard, but because we are hypocritical in the application of that standard - we ignore the standard in our own life. It is common to judge others by one standard and ourselves by another standard - being far more generous to ourselves than others.

d. **With the measure you use, it will be measured back to you**: This is the principle upon which Jesus built the command, "**Judge not, that you be not judged**." God will measure unto us according to the same measure we use for others. This is a powerful motivation for us to be generous with love, forgiveness, and goodness to others. If we want more of those things from God, we should give more of them to others.

i. According to the teaching of some rabbis in Jesus' time, God had two measures that He used to judge people. One was a **measure** of *justice* and the other was a **measure** of *mercy*. Whichever **measure** you want God to use with you, you should use that same **measure** with others.

ii. We should only judge another's behavior when we are mindful of the fact that *we ourselves will be judged*, and we should consider how we would want to be judged.

2. (3-5) An illustration of Jesus' principle regarding judging.

"And why do you look at the speck in your brother's eye, but do not consider the plank in your own eye? Or how can you say to your brother, 'Let me remove the speck from your eye'; and look, a plank *is* in your own eye? Hypocrite! First remove the plank from your own eye, and then you will see clearly to remove the speck from your brother's eye."

a. **Why do you look at the speck in your brother's eye, but do not consider the plank in your own eye?** The figures of a **speck** and a **plank** are real figures, yet used humorously. Jesus shows how we are generally far more tolerant to our own sin than we are to the sin of others.

i. Though there might be a literal **speck** in one's eye, there obviously would not be a literal **plank** or board in an eye. Jesus used these exaggerated, humorous pictures to make His message easier to understand and more memorable.

ii. It is a humorous picture: A man with a board in his eye trying to help a friend remove a speck from the friend's eye. You can't think of the picture without smiling and being amused by it.

iii. An example of looking for a speck in the eye of another while ignoring the plank in one's own is when the religious leaders brought the woman taken in adultery to Jesus. She had certainly sinned; but their sin was much worse and Jesus exposed it as such with the statement, *He who is without sin among you, let him throw a stone at her first* (John 8:7).

b. **Look, a plank is in your own eye**: Jesus indicates that the one with the **plank in** his **own eye** would not immediately be aware of it. He is blind to his obvious fault. It is the attempt to correct the fault of someone else when we ourselves have the same (or greater fault) that earns the accusation, "**Hypocrite!**"

i. "Jesus is gentle, but he calls that man a '*hypocrite*' who fusses about small things in others, and pays no attention to great matters at home in his own person." (Spurgeon)

ii. Our hypocrisy in these matters is almost always more evident to others than to ourselves. We may find a way to ignore the plank in our own eye, but others notice it immediately. A good example of this kind of hypocrisy was David's reaction to Nathan's story about a man who unjustly stole and killed another man's lamb. David quickly condemned the man, but was blind to his own sin, which was much greater (2 Samuel 12).

c. **First remove the plank from your own eye, and then you will see clearly to remove the speck from your brother's eye**: Jesus didn't say that it was wrong for us to help our brother with the speck in his eye. It is a good thing to help your brother with his speck, *but not before* dealing with the plank in your own eye.

3. (6) Balancing love with discernment.

"Do not give what is holy to the dogs; nor cast your pearls before swine, lest they trample them under their feet, and turn and tear you in pieces."

a. **Do not give what is holy to the dogs**: After He warned us against judgmental attitudes and self-blind criticism, Jesus here reminded us that He did not mean to imply that the people of His Kingdom suspend all discernment. They must discern that there are some good, precious things that should not be given to those who will receive them with contempt.

i. We might say that Jesus means, "Don't be judgmental, but don't throw out all discernment either."

ii. The **dogs** and **swine** here are often understood as those who are hostile to the Kingdom of God and the message that announces it. Our love for others must not blind us to their hardened rejection of the good news of the kingdom.

iii. Yet we may also see this in the context of the previous words against hypocrites. It may be that in Jesus' mind, the **dogs** and **swine** represent hypocritical, judgmental believers. These sinning hypocrites should not be offered the **pearls** that belong to the community of the saints.

iv. "The *Didache*, or, to give it its full name, *The Teaching of the Twelve Apostles*, which dates back to A.D.; 100 and which is the first service order book of the Christian Church, lays it down: "Let no one eat or drink of your Eucharist except those baptized into the name of the Lord; for as regards this, the Lord has said, 'Give not that which is holy unto dogs.'" (Barclay)

v. Jesus also spoke in the context of *correcting another brother or sister*. Godly correction is a pearl (though it may sting for a moment) that must not be cast before swine (those who are determined not to receive it).

b. **Nor cast your pearls before swine**: Our **pearls** of the precious gospel may only confuse those who do not believe, who are blinded to the truth by the god of this age (2 Corinthians 4:4) and may only expose the gospel to their ridicule.

i. "The gospel is to be preached *to every creature*, Mark 16:15. But when the Jews *were hardened*, and *spoke evil of that way before the multitude*, Acts 19:9, the apostles left preaching them." (Poole)

ii. Of course, Jesus did not say this to discourage us from sharing the gospel. Previously in this very sermon Jesus told us to let our lights shine before the world (Matthew 5:13-16). Jesus said this to call us to discernment, and to encourage us to look for prepared hearts that are ready to receive. When we find such open hearts, we can trust that God has already been working upon them.

B. More instructions for prayer.

1. (7-8) Jesus invites us to keep on asking, seeking and knocking.

"Ask, and it will be given to you; seek, and you will find; knock, and it will be opened to you. For everyone who asks receives, and he who seeks finds, and to him who knocks it will be opened."

a. **Ask...seek...knock**: We see a progressive intensity, going from **ask** to **seek** to **knock**. Jesus told us to have intensity, passion, and persistence in prayer. The fact that Jesus came back to the subject of prayer – already dealt with in some depth in Matthew 6:5-15 – shows the importance of prayer.

i. In this three-fold description of prayer as *asking*, *seeking*, and *knocking* we see different aspects of prayer and different aspects of its reward.

- Prayer is like asking in that we simply make our requests known to God, and **everyone who asks receives**. Receiving is the reward of asking.

- Prayer is like seeking in that we search after God, His word, and His will; and **he who seeks finds**. Finding is the reward of seeking.

- Prayer is like knocking until the door is opened, and we seek entrance into the great heavenly palace of our Great King. Entering through the **opened** door into His palace is the reward of knocking, and the best reward of all.

ii. "*Ask* with confidence and humility. *Seek* with care and application. *Knock* with earnestness and perseverance." (Clarke)

iii. The idea of *knocking* also implies that we sense resistance. After all, if the door were already open, there would be no need to knock. Yet

Jesus encouraged us, "Even when you sense that the door is closed and you must knock, then do so and continue to do so, and you will be answered."

iv. Yet the image of knocking also implies that there is a door that *can* be opened. "His doors are meant to open: they were made on purpose for entrance; and so the blessed gospel of God is made on purpose for you to enter into life and peace. It would be of no use to knock at a wall, but you may wisely knock at a door, for it is arranged for opening." (Spurgeon)

v. We come to God's door and all we must do is **knock**. If it were locked against us we would need a burglar's tools to break in, but that isn't necessary; all we must do is **knock**, and even if I don't have a burglar's skills I can still **knock** – I know enough to do that!

vi. "Any uneducated man can knock if that is all, which is required of him…A man can knock though he may be no philosopher A dumb man can knock. A blind man can knock. With a palsied hand a man may knock…The way to open heaven's gate is wonderfully simplified to those who are lowly enough to follow the Holy Spirit's guidance, and ask, seek, and knock believingly. God has not provided a salvation which can only be understood by learned men…it is intended for the ignorant, the short-witted, and the dying, as well as for others, and hence it must be as plain as knocking at a door." (Spurgeon)

b. **Ask and it will be given to you**: God promises an answer to the one who diligently seeks Him. Many of our passionless prayers are not answered for good reason, because it is almost as if we ask God to care about something we care little or nothing about.

i. God values persistence and passion in prayer because they show that we share His heart. It shows that we care about the things He cares about. Persistent prayer does not overcome God's stubborn reluctance; it gives glory to Him, expresses dependence upon Him, and aligns our heart more with His.

ii. "No soul can pray in vain that prays as directed above. The truth and faithfulness of the Lord Jesus are pledged for its success.- Ye SHALL receive - ye SHALL find – it SHALL be opened. These words are as strongly binding on the side of God, as *thou shalt do no murder* is on the side of man. Bring Christ's *word*, and Christ's *sacrifice* with thee, and not one of Heaven's blessings can be denied thee." (Clarke)

2. (9-11) Jesus illustrates the giving nature of God.

"Or what man is there among you who, if his son asks for bread, will give him a stone? Or if he asks for a fish, will he give him a serpent? If you then, being evil, know how to give good gifts to your children, how much more will your Father who is in heaven give good things to those who ask Him!"

a. **Or what man is there among you who, if his son asks for bread, will give him a stone**: Jesus made it clear that God doesn't have to be persuaded or appeased in prayer. He wants to give us not just bread, but even *more* than what we ask for.

i. Thankfully, the times we ask for something as bad as **a serpent** without knowing, like a loving parent God often mercifully spares us the just penalty of our ignorance.

b. **If you then, being evil, know how to give good gifts to your children, how much more will your Father who is in heaven**: It is blasphemous to deny God's answer to the seeking heart. We then imply that God is even worse than an evil man is.

i. Instead, in comparison to even the best human father, **how much more** is God a good and loving father. "*How much more!* says our Lord, and he does not say how much more, but leaves *that* to our meditations." (Spurgeon)

ii. "What a picture is here given of the goodness of God! Reader, ask thy soul, could this heavenly Father *reprobate* to *unconditional* eternal damnation any creature he has made? He who can believe that he has, may believe any thing: but still GOD IS LOVE." (Clarke)

C. Conclusion to the Sermon on the Mount: A partial summary and a repeated call to decision.

1. (12) A summation of Jesus' ethical teaching regarding our treatment of others: the Golden Rule.

"Therefore, whatever you want men to do to you, do also to them, for this is the Law and the Prophets."

a. **Whatever you want men to do to you, do also to them**: The negative way of stating this command was known long before Jesus. It had long been said, "You should *not* do to your neighbor what you would *not* want him to do to you." But it is a significant advance for Jesus to put it in the positive, to say that we should *do unto others* what we want them to *do unto us*.

i. "The Golden Rule was not invented by Jesus; it is found in many forms in highly diverse settings. About a.d. 20, Rabbi Hillel, challenged by a Gentile to summarize the law in the short time the Gentile could stand on one leg, reportedly responded, 'What is hateful to you, do not do to anyone else. This is the whole law; all the rest is commentary. Go and learn it.' (b. *Shabbath* 31a). Apparently only Jesus phrased the rule positively." (Carson)

ii. In so doing, Jesus makes the command much broader. It is the difference between *not* breaking traffic laws and in *doing* something positive like helping a stranded motorist. Under the negative form of the rule, the goats of Matthew 25:31-46 are found "not guilty." Yet under the positive form of the Golden Rule – Jesus' form – they are indeed found guilty.

iii. This especially applies to Christian fellowship. If we would experience love and have people reach out to us, we must love and reach out to others.

iv. "None but he whose heart is filled with love to God and all mankind can keep this precept, either in its *spirit* or *letter*…It seems as if God had written it upon the hearts of all men, for sayings of this kind may be found among all nations, Jewish, Christian, and Heathen." (Clarke)

b. **For this is the Law and the Prophets**: Jesus shows that this simple principle - the *Golden Rule* - summarizes all **the Law and the Prophets** say about how we should treat others. If we would simply treat others the way we would want to be treated, we would naturally obey all the law says about our relationships with others.

i. "Oh, that all men acted on it, and there would be no slavery, no war, no swearing, no striking, no lying, no robbing; but all would be justice and love! What a kingdom is this which has such a law!" (Spurgeon)

ii. This makes the law easier to understand, but it doesn't make it any easier to obey. No one has ever consistently done unto others as they would like others to do unto themselves.

2. (13-14) The decision between two ways and one of two destinations.

"Enter by the narrow gate; for wide *is* the gate and broad *is* the way that leads to destruction, and there are many who go in by it. Because narrow *is* the gate and difficult *is* the way which leads to life, and there are few who find it."

a. **Enter by the narrow gate**: Jesus did not speak of this gate as our destiny, but as the entrance to a path. There is a right way and a wrong way, and Jesus appealed to His listeners to decide to go the more difficult way, **which leads to life.**

i. He understood and taught that not all ways and not all destinations are equally good. One leads to **destruction**, the other to **life**.

ii. "The strait gate signifies literally what we call a *wicket*, i.e. a little door in a large gate." (Clarke)

iii. "Jesus is not encouraging committed disciples, 'Christians,' to press on along the narrow way and be rewarded in the end. He is rather commanding his disciples to enter the way marked by persecution and rewarded in the end." (Carson)

b. **Narrow is the gate and difficult is the way which leads to life**: The true gate is both *narrow* and *difficult*. If your road has a gate that is easy and well-traveled, you do well to watch out.

i. "You must not therefore wonder if my precepts be hard to your carnal apprehensions, nor be scandalized though you see but few going in the right road to the kingdom of heaven." (Poole)

3. (15-20) The danger of false prophets and the decision between two trees with their fruit.

"Beware of false prophets, who come to you in sheep's clothing, but inwardly they are ravenous wolves. You will know them by their fruits. Do men gather grapes from thornbushes or figs from thistles? Even so, every good tree bears good fruit, but a bad tree bears bad fruit. A good tree cannot bear bad fruit, nor *can* a bad tree bear good fruit. Every tree that does not bear good fruit is cut down and thrown into the fire. Therefore by their fruits you will know them."

a. **Beware of false prophets**: Jesus just warned us of a path that leads to destruction. Now He reminds us that there are many who would try to guide us along the broad path that leads to destruction. The first step to combating these **false prophets** is to simply **beware** of them.

i. "Warnings against false prophets are necessarily based on the conviction that not all prophets are true, that truth can be violated, and that the gospel's enemies usually conceal their hostility and try to pass themselves off as fellow believers." (Carson)

b. **Who come to you in sheep's clothing, but inwardly they are ravenous wolves**: It is in the nature of these **false prophets** to deceive and deny their true character. Often they deceive even themselves, believing themselves to be sheep when in fact they are **ravenous wolves**.

i. "The basic fault of the false prophet is *self interest*." (Barclay) It can be expressed by a desire for gain or an easy life, a desire for prestige, or the desire to advance one's own ideas and not God's ideas.

c. **You will know them by their fruits**: We guard ourselves against false prophets by taking heed to their **fruits**. This means paying attention to several aspects of their life and ministry.

i. We should pay attention to the *manner of living* a teacher shows. Do they show righteousness, humility and faithfulness in the way they live?

ii. We should pay attention to the *content* of their teaching. Is it true fruit from God's Word, or is it man-centered, appealing to ears that want to be tickled?

iii. We should pay attention to the *effect* of their teaching. Are people growing in Jesus or merely being entertained, and eventually falling away?

d. **Even so, every good tree bears good fruit, but a bad tree bears bad fruit**: This **fruit** is the inevitable result of who we *are*. Eventually - though it may take a time for the harvest to come - the good or bad fruit is evident, revealing what sort of "tree" we are.

i. **Every tree that does not bear good fruit**: "Not to have *good fruit* is to have *evil*: there can be no innocent sterility in the invisible tree of the heart. He that brings forth *no* fruit, and he that brings forth *bad* fruit, are both only fit for the *fire*." (Clarke)

ii. "It is not merely the wicked, the bearer of poison berries, that will be cut down; but the neutral, the man who bears no fruit of positive virtue must also be cast into the fire." (Spurgeon)

iii. Earlier in the chapter Jesus warned us to judge ourselves first, to look for the speck in our own eye before turning our attention to the beam in our neighbor's eye, therefore, before asking it of anyone else, we should first ask: "Do I bear fruit unto God's glory?"

4. (21-23) The decision between two claims of Jesus' Lordship, one false and one true.

"Not everyone who says to Me, 'Lord, Lord,' shall enter the kingdom of heaven, but he who does the will of My Father in heaven. Many will say to Me in that day, 'Lord, Lord, have we not prophesied in Your name, cast out demons in Your name, and done many wonders in Your name?' And then I will declare to them, 'I never knew you; depart from Me, you who practice lawlessness!'"

a. **Not everyone who says to Me, "Lord, Lord," shall enter the kingdom of heaven**: Jesus spoke here of a proper verbal confession, where these ones called Jesus **Lord**. This is vital, but never enough by itself.

i. We must use the language of "Lord, Lord" – we cannot be saved if we do not. Though hypocrites may say it, we should not be ashamed to say it. Yet it alone is not enough.

ii. This warning of Jesus applies to people who speak or say things to Jesus or about Jesus, but don't really mean it. It isn't that they believe Jesus is a devil; they simply say the words very superficially. Their mind is elsewhere, but they believe there is value in the bare words and fulfilling some kind of religious duty with no heart, no soul, not spirit – only bare words and passing thoughts.

iii. This warning of Jesus applies to people who say "Lord, Lord," and yet their spiritual life has nothing to do with their daily life. They go to church, perhaps fulfill some daily religious duties, yet sin against God and man just as any other might. "There are those that speak like angels, live like devils; that have Jacob's smooth tongue, but Esau's rough hands." (Trapp)

b. **Who says to Me…will say to Me in that day**: It is staggering that Jesus claimed *He* is the one that people must stand before on that final day of judgment, and *He* is the one rightly called **Lord**. This obscure teacher in a backwater part of the world claimed to be the judge of all men **in that day**.

i. By saying "**in that day**" Jesus drew our attention to a coming day of judgment for all men. "What is the chief object of your life? Will you think as much of it "in that day" as you do now? Will you then count yourself wise to have so earnestly pursued it? You fancy that you can defend it now, but will you be able to defend it then, when all things of earth and time will have melted into nothingness?" (Spurgeon)

c. **Lord, Lord, have we not**: The people Jesus speaks of here had impressive spiritual accomplishments. They **prophesied**, **cast out demons**, and had **done many wonders**. These are wonderful things, but they meant nothing without true fellowship, true connection with Jesus.

i. Jesus did not seem to doubt their claims of doing the miraculous. He didn't say, "You didn't really prophesy or cast out demons or do miracles." This leads us to understand that sometimes miracles are granted through pretended believers, reminding us that in the final analysis, miracles *prove* nothing.

ii. Significantly, they even did these things *in the name of Jesus*. Yet, they never really had a relationship of love and fellowship with Jesus. "Through my love to the souls of men, I blessed your preaching; but yourselves I could never esteem, because you were destitute of the spirit of my Gospel, unholy in your hearts, and unrighteous in your conduct." (Clarke)

iii. "If preaching could save a man, Judas would not have been damned. If prophesying could save a man, Balaam would not have been a castaway." (Spurgeon)

d. **I never knew you; depart from Me, you who practice lawlessness**: In the end, there is one basis of salvation; it isn't mere verbal confession, not "spiritual works," but knowing Jesus and being known by Him. It is our connection to Him – by the gift of faith that He gives to us – that secures our salvation. Connected to Jesus we are secure; without connection to Him all the miracles and great works prove nothing.

i. "What a terrible word! What a dreadful separation! Depart from ME! From the very Jesus whom you have proclaimed in *union* with whom alone eternal life is to be found. For, united to Christ, all is *heaven*; separated from him, all is *hell*." (Clarke)

ii. In addition, these are not people who *lost* their salvation. Instead, they never truly had it (**I *never* knew you**).

5. (24-27) The decision between two builders and their destiny.

"Therefore whoever hears these sayings of Mine, and does them, I will liken him to a wise man who built his house on the rock: and the rain descended, the floods came, and the winds blew and beat on that house; and it did not fall, for it was founded on the rock. But everyone who hears these sayings of Mine, and does not do them, will be like a foolish man who built his house on the sand: and the rain descended, the floods came, and the winds blew and beat on that house; and it fell. And great was its fall."

a. **I will liken him to a wise man who built his house on the rock**: In Jesus' illustration of the two builders, each house looked the same from the outside. The real foundation of our life is usually hidden and is only proven in the storm, and we could say that the storms come from both heaven (**rain**) and earth (**floods**).

i. "The article used to denote not an individual rock, but a category – a rocky foundation." (Bruce)

ii. "The wise and the foolish man were both engaged in precisely the same avocations, and to a considerable extent achieved the same design; both of them undertook to build houses, both of them persevered in building, both of them finished their houses. The likeness between them is very considerable." (Spurgeon)

b. **And the rain descended, the floods came, and the winds blew and beat on the house**: A storm (**rain, floods, wind**) was the ultimate in power to generations that didn't have nuclear weapons. Jesus warns us that the foundations of our lives will be shaken at some time or another, both now (in trials) and in the ultimate judgment before God.

> i. Time and the storms of life will prove the strength of one's foundation, even when it is hidden. We may be surprised when we see who has truly built upon the good foundation. "At last, when Judas betrayed Christ in the night, Nicodemus faithfully professed him in the day." (Trapp)

> ii. It is better that we test the foundation of our life *now* rather than later, at our judgment before God when it is too late to change our destiny.

> iii. Jesus may have had in mind an Old Testament passage: *When the whirlwind passes by, the wicked is no more, but the righteous has an everlasting foundation.* (Proverbs 10:25)

c. **Everyone who hears these sayings of Mine, and does not do them**: Merely *hearing* God's Word isn't enough to provide a secure foundation. It is necessary that we are also *doers* of His Word. If we are not, we commit the sin that will surely find us out, the sin of doing nothing (Numbers 32:23) - and **great** will be *our* **fall**.

> i. "Wherein lay the second builder's folly? Not in deliberately seeking a bad foundation, but in taking no thought of foundation…His fault was not an error in judgment, but inconsiderateness. It is not, as is commonly supposed, a question of two foundations, but of looking to, and neglecting to look to, the foundation." (Bruce)

> ii. "Their misery and calamity shall be the greater, by how much their hopes have been the stronger, the disappointment of their expectations adding to their misery." (Poole)

> iii. Yet no one can read this without seeing that they have not, do not, and will not ever completely **do them**. Even if we **do them** in a general sense (in which we should), the revelation of the Kingdom of God in the Sermon on the Mount drives us back again and again as needy sinners upon our Savior. "The Mount of ethical enunciation reveals the need for the Mount of the Cross." (Morgan)

6. (28-29) The effect of Jesus' sermon on those who heard Him.

And so it was, when Jesus had ended these sayings, that the people were astonished at His teaching, for He taught them as one having authority, and not as the scribes.

a. **For He taught them as one having authority, and not as the scribes**: His audience could not but notice that Jesus taught with an authority lacking in the other teachers in His day, who often only quoted other rabbis. Jesus spoke with inherent authority, and the authority of God's revealed Word.

i. "The scribes spoke *by* authority, resting all they said on traditions of what had been said before. Jesus spake *with* authority, out of His own soul." (Bruce)

ii. "Two things surprised them: the substance of his teaching, and the manner of it. They had never heard such *doctrine* before; the precepts which he had given were quite new to their thoughts. But their main astonishment was at his manner: there was a certainty, a power, a weight about it, such as they had never seen." (Spurgeon)

b. **The people were astonished at His teachings**: Whenever God's Word is presented as it truly is, with its inherent power, it will astonish people and set itself apart from the mere opinions of man.

i. When we really understand Jesus in this Sermon on the Mount, we should be **astonished** also. If we are not **astonished**, then we probably haven't really heard or understood what Jesus has said.

ii. To have the hearers astonished was a good thing; but it was not good if that was the extent of the effect. A good preacher always wants to do far more than astonish his listeners.

Matthew 8 - Healing, Teaching, and Miracles

A. Jesus cleanses a leper.

1. (1-2) The leper makes his request of Jesus.

When He had come down from the mountain, great multitudes followed Him. And behold, a leper came and worshiped Him, saying, "Lord, if You are willing, You can make me clean."

> a. **When He had come down from the mountain, great multitudes followed Him**: The miracles of Jesus attracted much attention; but so did His teaching ministry. Matthew demonstrated this by his mention of the **great multitudes** that followed Him after coming down from the Mount of Beatitudes.

>> i. When we compare the events of this chapter with the record of Mark or Luke, we find different order and chronology. Carson, along with others, claims that Matthew arranged his material here according to topics and themes, not according to chronology. "Matthew does not purport to follow anything other than a topical arrangement, and most of his 'time' indicators are very loose." (Carson)

>> ii. We remember an important foundational verse for Matthew's Gospel: *Now Jesus went about all Galilee, teaching in their synagogues, preaching the gospel of the kingdom, and healing all kinds of sickness and disease among the people* (Matthew 4:23). Matthew went on to tell us about the teaching ministry of Jesus (Matthew 5-7); now he tells us more about the healing ministry of Jesus, and how His works confirmed His words.

> b. **Behold, a leper came and worshipped Him**: In the ancient world, leprosy was a terrible, destructive disease – and still is in some parts of the world. The ancient leper had no hope of improvement, so this **leper came** to Jesus with a great sense of need and desperation.

i. "Leprosy might begin with the loss of all sensation in some part of the body; the nerve trunks are affected; the muscles waste away; the tendons contract until the hands are like claws. There follows ulceration of the hands and feet. Then comes the progressive loss of fingers and toes, until in the end a whole hand or a whole foot may drop off. The duration of that kind of leprosy is anything from twenty to thirty years. It is a kind of terrible progressive death in which a man dies by inches." (Barclay)

ii. According to Jewish law and customs, one had to keep 6 feet (2 meters) from a leper. If the wind was blowing toward a person from a leper, they had to keep 150 feet (45 meters) away. The only thing *more* defiling than contact with a leper was contact with a dead body.

iii. "In the middle ages, if a man became a leper, the priest donned his stole and took his crucifix, and brought the man into the church, and read the burial service over him. For all human purposes the man was dead." (Barclay)

iv. For all these reasons, the condition of leprosy is a model of sin and its effects. It is a contagious, debilitating disease that corrupts its victim and makes him essentially dead while alive; and it followed that almost universally, society and religious people scorned lepers. Rabbis especially despised lepers, and saw them as people under the special judgment of God, deserving no pity or mercy.

v. In Jesus' time, rabbis sometimes boasted about how badly they treated lepers. One bragged that he refused to buy even an egg on a street where he saw a leper; another boasted that he threw rocks at lepers upon seeing them.

vi. Nevertheless, the leper came to Jesus by himself and despite many discouragements.

- He knew how terrible his problem was.
- He knew that other people gave up on him as having a hopeless condition.
- He had no one who would or could take him to Jesus.
- He had no previous example of Jesus healing a leper to give him hope.
- He had no promise that Jesus would heal him.
- He had no invitation from Jesus or the disciples.
- He must have felt ashamed and alone in the crowd.

c. **A leper came and worshipped Him**: Despite his desperate condition, this man not only begged Jesus – he also **worshipped Him**.

i. "The Greek verb is *proskenein*, and that word is never used of anything but *worship of the gods*; it always describes a man's feeling and action in presence of the divine." (Barclay)

ii. How did the leper worship Jesus?

- He **worshipped** Jesus by coming to Him, honoring Him as the One who could meet His otherwise impossible need.

- He **worshipped** Jesus with his posture, probably bowing or kneeling before Jesus.

- He **worshipped** Jesus with the word "**Lord**," honoring Him as master and God.

- He **worshipped** Jesus with his humility, by not demanding but leaving the request up to the will of Jesus.

- He **worshipped** Jesus with his respect of the power of Jesus, saying that all that was necessary was the will of Jesus, and he would be healed.

- He **worshipped** Jesus with his confidence that Jesus could make him more than healthy; Jesus could make him **clean**.

iii. "The leper rendered to Christ divine homage; and if Jesus had been merely a good man, and nothing more, he would have refused the worship with holy indignation." (Spurgeon)

iv. "Those who call Jesus '*Lord*,' and do not worship him, are more diseased than the leper was." (Spurgeon)

d. **Lord, if You are willing**: The leper had no doubt whatsoever about the *ability* of Jesus to heal. His only question was if Jesus was **willing** to heal.

i. He believed in the *power* of Jesus. When a Syrian commander named Naaman was afflicted with leprosy, he came to Jehoram, the king of Israel because he heard there was a prophet in Israel whom God used to do miraculous things. When Naaman came to Jehoram, Jehoram knew that *he* had no power to help him, and he said: "*Am I God, to kill and make alive, that this man sends a man to heal me of his leprosy?*" (2 Kings 5:7) Leprosy was so hopeless in the ancient world that healing a leper was compared to raising the dead; yet this leper knew that all Jesus needed was to be **willing**.

ii. Yet this leper was sure that Jesus was **willing** to use His power for the leper's benefit. "Men more easily believe in miraculous power than in miraculous love." (Bruce)

e. **Lord, if You are willing, You can make me clean**: This leper sought more than healing. He wanted *cleansing*; not only from the leprosy, but also from all its terrible effects on his life and his soul.

i. In addition, this is the first place in the gospel where Jesus is called **Lord**. This title that was particularly meaningful in light of the fact that the word **Lord** was used to translate the Hebrew word *Yahweh*, and Matthew wrote his gospel to those who would be familiar with the Jewish context of that word.

2. (3) Jesus touches the leper and he is cleansed.

Then Jesus put out *His* hand and touched him, saying, "I am willing; be cleansed." Immediately his leprosy was cleansed.

a. **Jesus put out His hand and touched him**: This was a bold and compassionate touch from Jesus. The idea is that the leper kept his distance from Jesus, but He **put out His hand and touched him**. It was against the ceremonial law to touch a leper, which made the touch all the more meaningful to the afflicted man. Of course, as soon as Jesus touched him, he was no longer a leper!

i. **Touched him**: Jesus did not have to touch the leper in order to heal him. He could have healed him with a word or even a thought. Yet He healed the leper with a touch because that is what the leper needed.

ii. Jesus often varied the *manner* of healing, and usually He chose a particular manner that would be meaningful to the afflicted individual.

iii. Mark 1:41 says when Jesus looked, He was *moved with compassion*. It had been a long time since this leper had seen a face of compassion.

b. **I am willing**: Jesus' assurance that **I am willing** simply answered the man's question, and gives us a starting point for the times we wonder if Jesus is willing to heal. We should assume Jesus is willing to heal unless He shows us differently.

i. How can we know if Jesus is willing to heal us? By assuming that He is willing, but listening to Him if He should tell us that He does not. This is how it happened with the Apostle Paul in 2 Corinthians 12:7-10; it seems that Paul assumed that Jesus would heal his thorn in the flesh until word came to him that He would not.

c. **Immediately his leprosy was cleansed**: The former leper's life was changed forever. He was not only healed, but as he requested he **was**

cleansed. Jesus had recently said, *ask and it will be given to you* (Matthew 7:7). This was certainly true for the now **cleansed** former leper.

> i. This is the first individual healing described by Matthew. Previously, we were told of Jesus' healing ministry in a general sense (Matthew 4:23-24), but here in a specific case.

3. (4) Jesus commands the healed man to give testimony of his healing to the priests only.

And Jesus said to him, "See that you tell no one; but go your way, show yourself to the priest, and offer the gift that Moses commanded, as a testimony to them."

> a. **See that you tell no one**: Jesus often commanded people to be quiet about their healing or some miraculous work that He had done for them. He did this because He wanted to keep down the excitement of the crowds until the proper time for His formal revelation to Israel, which was an exact date as prophesied in Daniel 9.
>
> > i. In addition, Jesus' miracles were not primarily calculated to make Him famous or a celebrity (though they certainly did give testimony to His ministry). More so, Jesus healed to meet the needs of specific individuals and to demonstrate the evident power of the Messiah in the setting of love and care for the personal needs of humble people.
> >
> > ii. Therefore, Jesus was cautious about how the multitudes saw Him and why they followed Him. "This motif of secrecy...is better understood as reflecting a real danger that Jesus could achieve unwanted popularity merely as a wonder-worker, or worse still as a nationalistic liberator, and so foster a serious misunderstanding of the true nature of his mission." (France)
> >
> > iii. Mark tells us that the leper did not obey Jesus and instead *he went out and began to proclaim it freely* (Mark 1:44-45).
>
> b. **Show yourself to the priest**: Jesus commanded the man to give **a testimony** to the priests, and what a testimony it was! The Mosaic Law prescribed specific sacrifices to be conducted upon the healing of a leper, and when the man reported it to the priests, they no doubt had to perform ceremonies that were rarely (if ever) done (Leviticus 14).
>
> > i. Going to the priest would also bring the former leper back into society. Jesus wanted the healing of the man's disease to have as much benefit as possible.
> >
> > ii. "This gift was *two living, clean birds, some cedar wood, with scarlet and hyssop*, Leviticus 14:4, which were to be brought *for* his cleansing;

and, *when* clean, *two he lambs, one ewe lamb, three tenth deals of flour, and one log of oil,* Leviticus 14:10; but if the person was *poor,* then he was to bring *one lamb, one tenth deal of flour, one log of oil and two turtle doves, or young pigeons,* Leviticus 14:21, 22." (Clarke)

B. Jesus heals a centurion's servant.

1. (5-6) Jesus is approached by a Roman centurion.

Now when Jesus had entered Capernaum, a centurion came to Him, pleading with Him, saying, "Lord, my servant is lying at home paralyzed, dreadfully tormented."

a. **When Jesus had entered Capernaum**: Matthew 4:13 tells us this is where Jesus lived; *He came and dwelt in Capernaum.*

b. **A centurion came to Him**: The centurion was obviously a Gentile, because a **centurion** was an officer in the Roman army. Most every Jew under Roman occupation felt a reason to hate this **centurion**, yet he came to a Jewish teacher for help. Significantly, he came not for a selfish reason, but on behalf of his **servant**.

i. Whenever the New Testament mentions a centurion (there are at least seven), it presents them as honorable, good men.

ii. This centurion had an unusual attitude towards his slave. Under Roman law a master had the right to kill his slave, and it was expected that he would do so if the slave became ill or injured to the point where he could no longer work.

c. **Pleading with Him**: This shows that the centurion did not make a casual request. Matthew describes him as **pleading with** Jesus on behalf of his **servant**.

i. "He seeks a cure, but does not prescribe to the Lord how or where he shall work it; in fact, he does not put his request into words, but pleads the case, and lets the sorrow speak." (Spurgeon)

2. (7-9) The centurion's understanding of Jesus' spiritual authority.

And Jesus said to him, "I will come and heal him." The centurion answered and said, "Lord, I am not worthy that You should come under my roof. But only speak a word, and my servant will be healed. For I also am a man under authority, having soldiers under me. And I say to this *one,* 'Go,' and he goes; and to another, 'Come,' and he comes; and to my servant, 'Do this,' and he does *it.*"

a. **I will come and heal him**: Jesus did not hesitate to go to the centurion's house, and we half wish the centurion would have allowed Him. It was completely against Jewish custom for a Jew to enter a Gentiles' house; yet it was not against God's law.

i. The centurion sensed this when he said, "**Lord, I am not worthy that You should come under my roof**"; most Jews believed that a Gentile home was not worthy of them, and the centurion supposed that a great rabbi and teacher like Jesus would consider his home unworthy.

ii. The centurion also showed great sensitivity to Jesus, in that he wanted to spare Jesus the awkward challenge of whether or not to enter a Gentile's house - as well as the time and trouble of travel. He didn't know Jesus well enough to know that He would not feel awkward in the least; but his *consideration* of Jesus in this situation was impressive. In his concern for both his servant and for Jesus, this centurion was an others-centered person.

b. **But only speak a word, and my servant will be healed**: The centurion fully understood that Jesus' healing power was not some sort of magic trick that required the magician's presence. Instead he knew Jesus had true *authority*, and could command things to be done and completed outside His immediate presence.

i. The centurion showed great faith in Jesus' **word**. He understood that Jesus can heal with His **word** just as easily as with a touch.

ii. "This means that the centurion's words presuppose an understanding of the Roman military system... A footsoldier who disobeyed would not be defying a mere centurion but the emperor, Rome itself, with all its imperial majesty and might." (Carson)

c. **For I also am a man under authority, having soldiers under me**: The centurion also knew about the military chain of command, and how the orders of one in authority were unquestioningly obeyed. He saw that Jesus had *at least* that much authority.

i. "As the authority of the Caesars flowed through his own yielded life, so the authority of God over diseases, demons, and all else would flow through Christ's." (Meyer)

3. (10-13) Jesus praises the centurion's faith and heals his servant

When Jesus heard *it*, He marveled, and said to those who followed, "Assuredly, I say to you, I have not found such great faith, not even in Israel! And I say to you that many will come from east and west, and sit down with Abraham, Isaac, and Jacob in the kingdom of heaven. But the sons of the kingdom will be cast out into outer darkness. There will be weeping and gnashing of teeth." Then Jesus said to the centurion,

"Go your way; and as you have believed, *so* let it be done for you." And his servant was healed that same hour.

a. **When Jesus heard it, He marveled**: The man's understanding of Jesus' spiritual authority made Jesus marvel. His simple confidence in the ability of Jesus' mere word to heal showed a faith that was free of any superstitious reliance on merely external things. This was truly **great faith**, worthy of praise.

b. **Assuredly, I say to you, I have not found such great faith, not even in Israel**: Jesus considered the faith of this Gentile centurion – a living symbol of Jewish oppression – and thought it greater than any faith He had seen among the people of **Israel**.

   i. As a political entity, there was no **Israel**; there was only a covenant people descended from Abraham, Isaac, and Jacob. Yet Jesus still called them **Israel**.

c. **Many will come from east and west, and sit down with Abraham**: The fact that such faith was present in a Gentile caused Jesus to announce that there would be Gentiles in the **kingdom of heaven**. They will even sit down to dinner with **Abraham, Isaac, and Jacob**!

   i. This was a radical idea to many of the Jewish people in Jesus' day; they assumed that this great Messianic Banquet would have no Gentiles, and that all Jews would be there. Jesus corrected both mistaken ideas.

   ii. These few words of Jesus tell us a little something of what heaven is like.

   • It is a place of rest; we **sit down** in heaven.

   • It is a place of good company to sit with; we enjoy the friendship of **Abraham, Isaac, and Jacob** in heaven.

   • It is a place with **many** people; Jesus said that **many** will come into heaven.

   • It is a place with people from all over the earth; **from east and west** they will come to heaven.

   • It is a certain place; Jesus said **many will come**, and when Jesus says it **will** happen, it will happen.

   iii. "But ye shall hear those loved voices again; ye shall hear those sweet voices once more, ye shall yet know that those whom ye loved have been loved by God. Would not that be a dreary heaven for us to inhabit, where we should be alike unknowing and unknown? I would not care to go to such a heaven as that. I believe that heaven is a fellowship of the saints, and that we shall know one another there." (Spurgeon)

d. **But the sons of the kingdom will be cast out into outer darkness**: As well, Jesus reminded his Jewish listeners that just as the Gentile's racial identity was no automatic barrier to the kingdom, *their* racial identity was no guarantee of the kingdom. Though Jews were **sons of the kingdom**, they might end up in hell.

i. "There could hardly be a more radical statement of the change in God's plan of salvation inaugurated by the mission of Jesus." (France)

ii. Trapp on **outer darkness**: "Into a darkness beyond a darkness; into a dungeon beyond and beneath the prison."

iii. "The definite articles with 'weeping' and 'gnashing' (cf. Greek) emphasize the horror of the scene: *the* weeping and *the* gnashing… Weeping suggests suffering and gnashing of teeth despair." (Carson)

iv. "What is it that the lost are doing? They are 'weeping and gnashing their teeth.' Do you gnash your teeth now? You would not do it except you were in pain and agony. Well, in hell there is always gnashing of teeth." (Spurgeon)

v. We see that Jesus was unafraid to speak of hell, and in fact did so more than any other in the Bible. "There are some ministers who never mention anything about hell. I heard of a minister who once said to his congregation - 'If you do not love the Lord Jesus Christ you will be sent to that place which it is not polite to mention.' He ought not to have been allowed to preach again, I am sure, if he could not use plain words." (Spurgeon)

C. More suffering people are healed.

1. (14-15) Jesus heals Peter's mother-in-law.

Now when Jesus had come into Peter's house, He saw his wife's mother lying sick with a fever. So He touched her hand, and the fever left her. And she arose and served them.

a. **He saw his wife's mother lying sick**: This clearly establishes the fact that Peter was married. The Roman Catholic Church teaches that all priests must be celibate and unmarried, but the man they would call the first and greatest Pope was certainly married.

i. "St. Ambrose saith that all the apostles were married men, save John and Paul. And those pope-holy hypocrites that will not hear of priests' marriage, but hold it far better for them to have and keep at home many harlots than one wife." (Trapp)

ii. "Learn hence, says Theophylact, that *marriage* is no hinderance to *virtue*, since the chief of the apostles had his wife. Marriage is one of

the first of Divine institutions, and is a positive command of God."
(Clarke)

iii. "This mother-in-law was a specially good woman, for she was
allowed to live with her son-in-law, and he was anxious to have her
restored to health." (Spurgeon)

b. **He touched her hand, and the fever left her**: Jesus healed this woman
with a gentle touch of His hand. Her sickness was much less severe than
the leper, yet Jesus still cared for her. Jesus cares for smaller problems also.

i. "The miracle here was not in the cure of an incurable disease, but in
the way of the cure, by a touch of his hand." (Poole)

c. **And she arose and served them**: Peter's mother-in-law showed a
fitting response for those who have been touched by Jesus' power - she
immediately began to serve. Serving Jesus is a wonderful evidence of being
restored to spiritual health.

i. "With gratitude beaming from her face, she placed each dish upon
the table, and brought forth water with which her guests might wash
their feet. The moment the Lord Jesus Christ saves a soul he gives that
soul strength for its appointed service." (Spurgeon)

2. (16-17) Jesus, in fulfillment of prophecy, delivers many from sickness and
demonic possession.

**When evening had come, they brought to Him many who were demon-
possessed. And He cast out the spirits with a word, and healed all who
were sick, that it might be fulfilled which was spoken by Isaiah the
prophet, saying:**

"He Himself took our infirmities
And bore *our* sicknesses."

a. **They brought to Him many**: Jesus' care for the individual is shown by
the implication that Jesus dealt with each person individually, not in some
cold, "assembly line" procedure.

i. **Many who were demon possessed**: "Dr. Lightfoot gives two sound
reasons why Judea, in our Lord's time, abounded with *demoniacs*. First,
because they were then advanced to the very height of impiety. See
what Josephus, their own historian, says of them: There was not (said
he) a nation under heaven more wicked than they were. Secondly,
because they were then strongly addicted to *magic*, and so, as it were,
invited evil spirits to be familiar with them." (Clarke)

b. **That it might be fulfilled which was spoken by Isaiah**: Matthew
rightly understood this as a partial fulfillment of Isaiah's prophecy in Isaiah

53, which primarily refers to spiritual healing, but also definitely includes physical healing. In this, Matthew showed Jesus as the true Messiah in delivering people from the bondage of sin and the effects of a fallen world.

c. **He Himself took our infirmities and bore our sicknesses**: The provision for our healing (both physically and spiritually) was made by the sufferings (the *stripes*) of Jesus. The physical dimension of our healing is partially realized now, but finally only in resurrection.

i. This healing work of our Savior *cost* Jesus something; it wasn't as if He had a magic bag of healing power that He drew from and cast about to the needy. It came at the cost of His own agony. "If His word and touch brought instant deliverance to men, it was because in a great mystery of grace He suffered in order to save." (Morgan)

ii. "The prophet speaketh of spiritual infirmities, the evangelist applieth it to corporal. And not unfitly; for these are the proper effects of those." (Trapp)

d. **He Himself took our infirmities and bore our sicknesses**: This section of Matthew's Gospel shows four different people being healed, each one different from the other.

i. Different people were healed.

- A Jew with no social or religious privileges.
- A Gentile officer of the army occupying and oppressing Israel.
- A woman related to one of Jesus' devoted followers.
- Unnamed multitudes.

ii. Their requests were made in different ways.

- A direct request from the sufferer, made in his own faith.
- A request from one man for another, made in faith on behalf of a suffering man.
- No request was made because Jesus came to the sufferer, so there was no evidence of faith from the healed.
- Sufferers that were brought to Jesus, with different kinds of faith.

iii. Jesus used different methods to heal.

- Jesus used a touch that was forbidden.
- Jesus used a word spoken from afar.
- Jesus used a tender touch.
- Jesus used a variety of unnamed methods.

iv. From all this, we understand that physical healing is an area where God especially shows His sovereignty, and He does things as He pleases, not necessarily as men might expect.

E. Jesus teaches on discipleship.

1. (18-20) Jesus speaks to an over-enthusiastic follower about the need to appreciate the cost in following Jesus.

And when Jesus saw great multitudes about Him, He gave a command to depart to the other side. Then a certain scribe came and said to Him, "Teacher, I will follow You wherever You go." And Jesus said to him, "Foxes have holes and birds of the air *have* nests, but the Son of Man has nowhere to lay *His* head."

a. **When Jesus saw great multitudes about Him, He gave a command to depart to the other side**: Jesus increased in popularity, yet He did not follow the crowds or even seek to make them bigger. In some ways he seemed to avoid the **great multitudes about Him**.

b. **Teacher, I will follow You wherever You go**: With the miracles associated with the ministry of Jesus, following Him might have seemed more glamorous than it really was. Jesus perhaps received many spontaneous offers like this.

i. "I wonder if this man thought, 'Well, now, I am a scribe. If I join that company, I shall be a leader. I perceive that they are only fishermen, the bulk of them; and if I come in amongst them, I shall be a great acquisition to that little band. I shall no doubt be the secretary.' Perhaps he may have thought that there was something to be made out of such a position; there was one who thought so." (Spurgeon)

c. **Foxes have holes and birds of the air have nests, but the Son of Man has nowhere to lay His head**: Jesus didn't tell the man "No, you can't follow Me." But He told him the truth, without painting a glamorized version of what it was like to follow Him. This is the *opposite* of techniques used by many evangelists today, but Jesus wanted the man to know what it would really be like.

i. "In the immediate context of Jesus' ministry, the saying does not mean that Jesus was penniless but homeless; the nature of his mission kept him on the move and would keep his followers on the move." (Carson)

ii. "Many homes, like Peter's, were open to him, but he had none of his own." (France)

iii. The reason this man turned away from Jesus was because Jesus lived a very simple life by faith, trusting His Father for every need and without reserves of material resources. *This is just the kind of thing that would make Jesus more attractive to a truly spiritual man.* "Here is a man who lives completely by faith and is satisfied with few material things; I should follow Him and learn from Him."

d. **The Son of Man**: The phrase "Son of Man" is used 81 times in the gospels; every time it is either something Jesus said of Himself, or the words of someone quoting Jesus. It is an important phrase He used to describe Himself. He used it as a title that reflected both the glory (Daniel 7:13-14) and the humility (Psalm 8:4) of the Messiah.

i. Especially, its connection to the Daniel passage means that it was an image of power and glory, yet without the unwanted associations of other titles. By using it often, Jesus told His listeners: "I'm the Messiah of power and glory, but not the one you were expecting."

2. (21-22) Jesus speaks to a hesitant follower about the surpassing importance of following Him.

Then another of His disciples said to Him, "Lord, let me first go and bury my father." But Jesus said to him, "Follow Me, and let the dead bury their own dead."

a. **Lord, let me first go and bury my father**: Actually, this man did not ask for permission to dig a grave for his deceased father. He wanted to remain in his father's house and care for him until the father died. This was obviously an indefinite period, which could drag on and on.

i. This man was **another of His disciples**; yet he did not follow Jesus as he should have, nor as the 12 disciples did. This shows us that the term **disciples** has a somewhat broad meaning in the Gospel of Matthew, and must be understood in its context.

ii. The man wanted to follow Jesus, *but not just yet*. He knew it was good and that he should do it, but he felt there was a good reason why he could not do it *now*. "If the scribe was too quick in promising, this 'disciple' was too slow in performing." (Carson)

b. **Follow Me, and let the dead bury their own dead**: Jesus pressed the man to follow Him *now*, and clearly stated the principle that family obligations – or any other obligation – must not be put ahead of following Jesus. Jesus must come first.

i. Jesus was not afraid to discourage potential disciples. Unlike many modern evangelists, He was interested more in *quality* than in *quantity*. "Nothing has done more harm to Christianity than the practice of filling the ranks of Christ's army with every volunteer who is willing to make a little profession, and to talk fluently of experience." (Ryle, cited in Carson)

ii. In addition, Jesus was merely being *honest*. This is what it meant to follow Him, and He wanted people to know it at the beginning.

iii. "Much of the concerns of politics, party tactics, committee meetings, social reforms, innocent amusements, and so forth, may be very fitly described as burying the dead. Much of this is very needful, proper, and commendable work; but still only such a form of business as unregenerate men can do as well as disciples of Jesus. Let them do it; but if we are called to preach the Gospel, let us give ourselves wholly to our sacred calling." (Spurgeon)

F. Jesus shows His power over the wind and the waves.

1. (23-25) A storm arises on the Sea of Galilee.

Now when He got into a boat, His disciples followed Him. And suddenly a great tempest arose on the sea, so that the boat was covered with the waves. But He was asleep. Then His disciples came to *Him* and awoke Him, saying, "Lord, save us! We are perishing!"

a. **Now when He got into a boat**: The village of Capernaum was right on the shore of the Sea of Galilee. Jesus, like many Galileans, was familiar with boats and life near this fairly large lake.

b. **Suddenly a great tempest arose on the sea**: The Sea of Galilee is well known for its sudden, violent storms. The severity of this storm was evident in the fact that the disciples (many of who were experienced fishermen on this lake) were terrified, crying out "**Lord, save us! We are perishing!**"

i. Bruce on **the boat was covered with waves**: "Was covered, hidden, the waves rising high above the boat, breaking on it, and gradually filling with water."

c. **But He was asleep**: Though the disciples were desperate, Jesus **was asleep**. It must have seemed strange to them that He could sleep in the midst of such a **great tempest**.

i. Bruce says that the grammar of the phrase "**But He was asleep**" conveys a "dramatic contrast"; the storm raged, the disciples panicked, **but He was asleep**.

ii. We are impressed by the fact that He *needed to sleep*, showing His true humanity. He became tired and would sometimes need to catch sleep wherever He was able to, even in unlikely places. "It was the sleep of one worn by an intense life, involving constant strain on body and mind." (Bruce)

iii. We are impressed by the fact that He *could sleep*. His mind and heart were peaceful enough, trusting in the love and care of His Father in heaven, that He could sleep in the storm.

2. (26-27) Jesus displays authority over the creation.

But He said to them, "Why are you fearful, O you of little faith?" Then He arose and rebuked the winds and the sea, and there was a great calm. So the men marveled, saying, "Who can this be, that even the winds and the sea obey Him?"

a. **Why are you fearful, O you of little faith?** Jesus rebuked their fear and unbelief, not their request or waking Him. We shouldn't think that Jesus was in a bad mood from being awakened. He was upset at their fear, because fear and unbelief go together. When we trust God as we should trust Him, there is little room left for fear.

i. "He spoke to the men first, for they were the most difficult to deal with: wind and sea could be rebuked afterwards." (Spurgeon)

ii. "He does not chide them for disturbing him with their prayers, but for disturbing themselves with their fears." (Henry, cited in Carson)

iii. They actually had many reasons to have faith, even great faith.

- They had just seen Jesus do significant miracles, showing great power and authority.
- They had seen an example of great faith with the centurion who trusted Jesus to heal his servant.
- They had Jesus with them in the boat. And, they saw Jesus sleep; His peace should have given them peace.

b. **Then He arose and rebuked the winds and the sea**: Jesus didn't merely *quiet* the wind and the sea; He **rebuked the winds and the sea**. This, together with the disciples' great fear and what Jesus would encounter at His destination, leads some to believe that there was some type of spiritual attack in the storm.

i. Adam Clarke supposed that the storm was "Probably excited by Satan, the prince of the power of the air, who, having got the author and all the preachers of the Gospel together in a small vessel, thought by drowning it, to defeat the purposes of God, and thus to prevent the salvation of a ruined world. What a noble opportunity must this have appeared to the enemy of the human race!"

c. **So the men marveled**: The disciples were amazed. Such a powerful display over creation led them to ask, "**Who can this be?**" It could only be the LORD, Jehovah, who only has this power and authority: *O LORD God of hosts, who is mighty like You, O LORD? Your faithfulness surrounds You. You rule the raging of the sea; when waves rise, You still them.* (Psalm 89:8-9)

> i. In the span of a few moments, the disciples saw both the complete humanity of Jesus (in His tired sleep) and the fullness of His deity. They saw Jesus for who He is: truly man and truly God.

G. Jesus' power over demonic spirits.

1. (28-29) Jesus meets two demon-possessed men.

When He had come to the other side, to the country of the Gergesenes, there met Him two demon-possessed *men*, coming out of the tombs, exceedingly fierce, so that no one could pass that way. And suddenly they cried out, saying, "What have we to do with You, Jesus, You Son of God? Have You come here to torment us before the time?"

a. **There met Him two demon-possessed men**: The other gospel accounts mention only one of these men. This must be because there was one that was far more severe in his state of demonic possession, having many demons.

b. **Coming out of the tombs, exceedingly fierce**: These two unfortunates were unclean because of their contact with the dead, and they displayed **fierce**, uncontrollable behavior. The demons drove these men to live among the **tombs**.

- Because graveyards and the dead were terribly unclean and offensive to the Jewish people.
- Because demons love death.
- Because it was no proper place for men to live.
- Because it made the men more frightening to others.
- Because it encouraged superstition in others, fearing that the men were actually possessed with the spirits of the dead in the graveyard.

c. **What have we to do with You**: The demons tormenting these poor men wanted to be *left alone*. They didn't want Jesus to interfere with their horrible work.

> i. "This is the old cry, 'Mind your own business! Do not interfere with our trade! Let us alone, and go elsewhere!' Devils never like to be interfered with. But if the devils have nothing to do with Jesus, he has something to do with them." (Spurgeon)

d. **What have we to do with You, Jesus, You Son of God?** The demons knew who Jesus was even if the disciples didn't. We can contrast the two statements:

- *Who can this be?* (Matthew 8:27)
- **Jesus, You Son of God** (Matthew 8:29)

e. **Have You come here to torment us before the time**: These demons also knew of both their immediate destiny (to be cast out) and their ultimate destiny (to suffer everlasting **torment**). They wanted the freedom to do as much damage as they could **before the time**, their destiny of torment.

i. They also understood that they had *limited* time, so they worked as hard as they could up until they could not work anymore. This is one of the few admirable things we can say about Satan and his demons.

2. (30-32) Jesus casts the demons into a herd of swine.

Now a good way off from them there was a herd of many swine feeding. So the demons begged Him, saying, "If You cast us out, permit us to go away into the herd of swine." And He said to them, "Go." So when they had come out, they went into the herd of swine. And suddenly the whole herd of swine ran violently down the steep place into the sea, and perished in the water.

a. **There was a herd of many swine**: Both Jews and Gentiles populated the region of Galilee, so this may have been a herd of pigs owned by Gentiles. But most commentators believe that since the pigs were unclean for Jews, they should not have been there, even if a Gentile man owned them.

b. **If You cast us out, permit us to go away into the herd of swine**: The demons wanted to enter the **swine** because these evil spirits are bent on destruction and *hate to be idle*. "The devil is so fond of doing mischief, that he will rather play at a small game than stand out." (Poole)

i. Yet we also notice that the demons can't even afflict *pigs* without the permission of God. "And if a legion of devils had not power over a herd of hogs, much less have they over Christ's flock of sheep, saith Tertullian." (Trapp)

c. **When they had come out, they went into the herd of swine...the whole herd of swine ran violently...and perished in the water**: There is nothing really comparable to this in the Bible, the casting of demons from a human into animals. Yet Jesus had a good reason to allow this.

i. The fact that the demons immediately drove the swine to destruction helps explain *why* Jesus allowed the demons to enter the pigs - because He wanted everyone to know what the real intention of these demons was. They wanted to destroy the men just as they destroyed the pigs. Because men are made in the image of God, they could not have their way as easily with the men, but their intention was just the same - to kill and destroy.

ii. Another reason why the devils were sent into the pigs was to conclusively show that they had been indeed cast out of the men.

iii. Some protest that this was unfair to the owner of the pigs. "'But the owners of the swine lost their property.' Yes, and learn from this how small value temporal riches are in the estimation of God." (Clarke)

iv. Spurgeon had several wise comments on the way the demons affected the swine:

- "*Swine* prefer death to devilry; and if men were not worse than swine, they would be of the same opinion."
- "They run hard whom the devil drives."
- "The devil drives his hogs to a bad market."

3. (33-34) The people ask Jesus to leave the region.

Then those who kept *them* fled; and they went away into the city and told everything, including what *had happened* to the demon-possessed men. And behold, the whole city came out to meet Jesus. And when they saw Him, they begged *Him* to depart from their region.

a. **Told everything... the whole city came out to meet Jesus**: Since Jesus knew human nature, He knew what to expect from this crowd coming from the city. Yet His disciples probably thought that these people would be pleased that Jesus had delivered these formerly **demon-possessed men**.

i. The work of Jesus had unified the **whole city**, and they had all come out to meet with and to talk to Jesus; but it was not in a good way. "Here was a whole city at a prayer meeting, praying against their own blessing...Horrible was their prayer; *but it was heard*, and Jesus *departed out of their coasts*." (Spurgeon)

b. **They begged Him to depart from their region**: We would think that the people of the region would be happy that these two demon-possessed men had been delivered. Perhaps they were more interested in their pigs than in people. Certainly, the delivering power of Jesus did not make all men feel comfortable.

i. This may explain another reason why the demons wanted to enter the swine. The idea is that the demons wanted to stir up hatred and rejection of Jesus, so they drove the swine to destruction hoping it would be blamed on Jesus, and He would then be unwelcome there.

Matthew 9 - Jesus Ministers and Heals

A. A paralyzed man is healed and forgiven.

1. (1-2) A paralytic is brought to Jesus.

So He got into a boat, crossed over, and came to His own city. Then behold, they brought to Him a paralytic lying on a bed. When Jesus saw their faith, He said to the paralytic, "Son, be of good cheer; your sins are forgiven you."

> a. **His own city**: This must mean Capernaum, as previously noted (Matthew 4:13).

> b. **They brought to Him a paralytic lying on a bed**: Other Gospels (in Mark 2 and Luke 5) explain how the man was brought to Jesus. Because of the crowds, his friends lowered him down to Jesus through the roof.

>> i. This will be another example of Jesus healing the sick and diseased, and the Messiah's role as healer was clearly prophesied in passages like Isaiah 35:5-6: *Then the eyes of the blind shall be opened, and the ears of the deaf shall be unstopped. Then the lame shall leap like a deer, and the tongue of the dumb sing. For waters shall burst forth in the wilderness, and streams in the desert.* Thus, Jesus' miracles were a testimony not only to the fact that He was sent by God, but that also He was the anticipated Messiah.

>> ii. However, as noted earlier, Jesus' miracles were not primarily calculated for crowd effect. Instead they were primarily done to minister to the humble needs of humble people. For the most part, most Jewish people of that time would have preferred much more spectacular signs - like calling down fire from heaven upon a Roman Legion.

>> iii. We also note that the presence of so much sickness among Israel was evidence of their unfaithfulness to the covenant and their low spiritual condition. God gave them the opposite of what He promised

under Exodus 15:26: *If you diligently heed the voice of the LORD your God and do what is right in His sight, give ear to His commandments and keep all His statutes, I will put none of the diseases on you which I have brought on the Egyptians. For I am the LORD who heals you.*

c. **When Jesus saw their faith**: Jesus saw the faith of his friends, not of the paralyzed man himself. It was evident that they had the faith to bring the their paralyzed friend to Jesus and their faith was active enough to take apart a roof and lower the man down before Jesus.

i. We also can assume that the paralyzed man himself had little faith; Jesus noted the faith of his friends, not his. Therefore Jesus wanted to encourage this man's faith by His next words.

ii. "With swift sure diagnosis Jesus sees in the man not in faith but deep depression…and uttering first a kindly hope-inspiring word, such as a physician might address to a patient: cheer up, child!" (Bruce)

d. **Son, be of good cheer; your sins are forgiven you**: The faith of the paralyzed man's friends *did* something - they brought this man to Jesus. Yet they only thought of bringing him to Jesus for the healing of his body. They certainly didn't think that Jesus would forgive His **sins**.

i. But Jesus addressed the man's greater problem. As bad as it is to be paralyzed, it is infinitely worse to be bound and lost in your sin.

ii. We need not infer that the man was paralyzed as the direct result of some sin that needed forgiving. This did not seem to be Jesus' point in saying, "**your sins are forgiven you**."

iii. Matthew Poole saw six reasons why Jesus dealt with the man's sin first. To paraphrase Poole's reasons why the sin was dealt with first:

- Because sin is the root from which all our evils come.
- To show that forgiveness is more important than bodily healing.
- To show that the most important thing Jesus came to do was to deal with sin.
- To show that when a man's sins are forgiven, he becomes a son of God.
- To show that the response to faith is the forgiveness of sin.
- To begin an important conversation with the scribes and Pharisees.

2. (3) The reaction of the religious leaders.

And at once some of the scribes said within themselves, "This *Man* blasphemes!"

a. **And at once some of the scribes said within themselves**: We notice that they objected immediately yet privately, saying it **within themselves**. Jesus will address what they said **within themselves**, showing that our thoughts and opinions are open to God and of interest to Him.

b. **This Man blasphemes**: The scribes correctly understood that Jesus claimed to do something that only God can do. But they were incorrect in assuming that Jesus was not God Himself, and that Jesus blasphemed by considering Himself God.

i. "Here the teachers of the law, in their whispered consultation, expanded blasphemy to include Jesus' claim to do something only God could do." (Carson)

ii. "They did not call him '*man*'; the word is in italics in our version. They did not know what to call him even in their hearts; they meant 'this' – this upstart, this nobody, this strange being." (Spurgeon)

iii. "This is the first mention of opposition to Jesus, which will be a recurrent theme." (France)

3. (4-5) Jesus reads the evil hearts of the scribes and presents a question.

But Jesus, knowing their thoughts, said, "Why do you think evil in your hearts? For which is easier, to say, '*Your* sins are forgiven you,' or to say, 'Arise and walk'?"

a. **But Jesus, knowing their thoughts**: This alone should have been enough for Jesus to prove His deity, demonstrating that He could know their evil hearts. Yet He would also offer a greater proof of His deity.

b. **For which is easier, to say**: Both healing and forgiveness are impossible with man. Yet only the promise of healing could be immediately proven, because though you can't see someone's sin being forgiven, you can *see* that they are healed.

i. "This appears to have been founded on Psalm 103:3. *Who forgiveth all thine iniquities, and healeth all thy diseases.* Here *pardon* precedes *health*." (Clarke)

4. (6-8) Jesus asserts His authority over both sin and disease.

"But that you may know that the Son of Man has power on earth to forgive sins"; then He said to the paralytic, "Arise, take up your bed, and go to your house." And he arose and departed to his house. Now when the multitudes saw *it*, they marveled and glorified God, who had given such power to men.

a. **But that you may know that the Son of Man has power on earth to forgive sins**: Jesus answered His own question before the religious leaders did. Since He could make good on His claim to heal the man, it gave proof of His claim to also have the authority to forgive sins.

b. **And he arose and departed to his house**: The man was instantly healed, proving that Jesus did have the power of God both to heal and forgive.

> i. "He did not go to the temple with the sacramentarian, nor to the theater with the man of the world: he went to his home…A man's restoration by grace is best seen in his own house." (Spurgeon)

> ii. "A man gives proof of his conversion from sin to God who imitates this paralytic person. He who does not *rise* and *stand upright*, but either continues *grovelling* on the earth, or *falls back* as soon as he is *got up*, is not yet cured of his spiritual palsy." (Clarke)

c. **When the multitudes saw it, they marveled and glorified God**: At the man's healing, the crowd properly gave God the glory for this miracle. Jesus obviously did not draw attention to Himself by the manner in which the healing was done.

B. The call of Matthew the tax collector.

1. (9) Matthew obeys Jesus' call to come follow Him.

As Jesus passed on from there, He saw a man named Matthew sitting at the tax office. And He said to him, "Follow Me." So he arose and followed Him.

a. **A man named Matthew**: Mark 2:14 says that this man was also named *Levi the son of Alphaeus*. Matthew 10:3 mentions that there was another disciple who was a son of Alphaeus (James, often called *James the Less* to distinguish him from James the brother of John). So it seems that both this **Matthew** and his brother James were among the 12.

b. **A man named Matthew sitting at the tax office**: Tax collectors were not only notorious sinners; they were also properly regarded as collaborators with the Romans against their fellow Jews. Nobody liked the man who sat **at the tax office**.

> i. The Jewish people rightly thought of them as *traitors* because they worked for the Roman government, and they had the force of Roman soldiers behind them to make people pay taxes. They were the most visible Jewish collaborators with Rome.

> ii. The Jewish people rightly considered them *extortioners* because they were allowed to keep whatever they over-collected. A tax collector bid among others for the tax-collecting contract. For example, many tax collectors might want to have the tax contract for a city like Capernaum. The Romans awarded the contract to the highest bidder.

The man collected taxes, paid the Romans what he promised, and kept the remainder. Therefore, there was a lot of incentive for tax collectors to over-charge and cheat any way they could. It was pure profit for them. "He was at this time busy *taking*, but he was called to a work that was essentially *giving*." (Spurgeon)

iii. "When a Jew entered the customs service he was regarded as an outcast from society: he was disqualified as a judge or a witness in a court session, was excommunicated from the synagogue, and in the eyes of the community his disgrace extended to his family." (Lane, Commentary on Mark)

iv. The old King James Version uses the word *publican* for a tax-collector. "The *publicani* were tax-gatherers, and were so called because they dealt with public money and with public funds." (Barclay)

v. "A faithful publican was so rare that Rome itself, that one Sabinus, for his honest managing of that office, in an honourable remembrance thereof, had certain images erected with this superscription, For the honest publican." (Trapp)

c. **And He said to him, "Follow Me"**: Understanding how almost everyone hated tax collectors, it is remarkable to see how Jesus loved and called Matthew. It proved to be a well-placed love; Matthew responded to Jesus' invitation by leaving his tax collecting business and following Jesus - and eventually writing this same gospel account.

i. "He left his tax-collector's table; but took from it one thing – his pen…this man, whose trade had taught him to use a pen, used that skill to compose the first handbook of the teaching of Jesus." (Barclay)

ii. In one way this was more of a sacrifice than some of the other disciples made. Peter, James, and John could more easily go back to their fishing business, but it would be hard for Levi to go back to tax collecting.

iii. There is archaeological evidence that fish taken from the Sea of Galilee were taxed. So Jesus took as His disciple the taxman that may have taken money from Peter, James, and John and the other fishermen among the disciples. This might have made for some awkward introductions.

2. (10-13) Jesus eats with tax collectors and sinners.

Now it happened, as Jesus sat at the table in the house, *that* behold, many tax collectors and sinners came and sat down with Him and His disciples. And when the Pharisees saw *it*, they said to His disciples, "Why does your Teacher eat with tax collectors and sinners?" When

Jesus heard *that*, He said to them, "Those who are well have no need of a physician, but those who are sick. But go and learn what *this* means: 'I desire mercy and not sacrifice.' For I did not come to call the righteous, but sinners, to repentance."

a. **Many tax collectors and sinners came and sat down with Him**: The context suggests that this was a gathering of Matthew's friends and former business associates. We might say that Jesus took advantage of Matthew's decision to also reach those whom he knew.

i. "Jesus aims at a mission among the reprobated classes, and His first step is the call of Matthew to discipleship, and His second the gathering together through him, of a large number of these classes to a social entertainment." (Bruce)

ii. In noting that there were **many tax collectors and sinners**, Bruce estimates that this was held not in a private home, but in a public hall, and that "In any case it was a great affair – scores, possibly hundreds, present, too large for a room in a house."

b. **Why does your Teacher eat with tax collectors and sinners**: The answer to this question was simple: Because Jesus is the friend of sinners. *But God demonstrates His own love toward us, in that while we were still sinners, Christ died for us* (Romans 5:8).

i. "'Sinners' may include common folk who did not share all the scruples of the Pharisees." (Carson)

c. **Those who are well have no need of a physician, but those who are sick**: This was the principle that the criticizing Pharisees did not understand. The Pharisees were like doctors who wanted to avoid all contact with sick people. Of course they wished that sick people would become healthy, but they wouldn't risk getting infected themselves.

i. We are fortunate that God calls sinners and not just saintly people. Jesus came to benefit those who understood their inherent need for Him (**those who are sick** and the *poor in spirit* of Matthew 5:3). Yet the proud who see no need for Jesus (**those who are well**) benefit nothing from Jesus.

ii. "Lord, grant that if ever I am found in the company of sinners, it may be with the design of healing them, and may I never become myself infected with their disease!" (Spurgeon)

d. **Go and learn what this means: "I desire mercy and not sacrifice"**: Here Jesus quoted Hosea 6:6. In Hosea's day, God's people were still good at bringing sacrifice (Hosea 5:6), but they had forsaken **mercy**, and they abandoned **mercy** because they gave up the knowledge of God and truth

(Hosea 4:1). God would rather have right hearts, full of truth and mercy than sacrifice.

> i. "These words are the more arresting when we remember that they were addressed to the teachers of men...The rebuke of Christ showed that they did not know God, and He bade them go and learn the meaning of their own Scriptures." (Morgan)

> ii. "This would be distasteful to men who thought they knew everything already." (Spurgeon)

C. The new and old covenants and their difference.

1. (14) The disciples of John ask a question: why don't Jesus' disciples fast as they and the Pharisees do?

Then the disciples of John came to Him, saying, "Why do we and the Pharisees fast often, but Your disciples do not fast?"

> a. **Why do we and the Pharisees fast often**: The ministry of John the Baptist was strict in its character and had an emphasis on humble repentance (Matthew 3:1-4). John's disciples imitated this, and showed their own proper humility in light of their own sin and that of their people.

> b. **The Pharisees fast often**: Pharisees were also known for their practice of fasting (often twice a week, according to Luke 18:12), but they did not do it out of a spirit of humble repentance. They often fasted wanting to impress themselves and others with their spirituality (Matthew 6:16-18).

> c. **But Your disciples do not fast**: Apparently the disciples of Jesus did not fast as either of these two groups did. Jesus will next explain why.

2. (15-17) The principle: things are different now that the Messiah is here.

And Jesus said to them, "Can the friends of the bridegroom mourn as long as the bridegroom is with them? But the days will come when the bridegroom will be taken away from them, and then they will fast. No one puts a piece of unshrunk cloth on an old garment; for the patch pulls away from the garment, and the tear is made worse. Nor do they put new wine into old wineskins, or else the wineskins break, the wine is spilled, and the wineskins are ruined. But they put new wine into new wineskins, and both are preserved."

> a. **Can the friends of the bridegroom mourn as long as the bridegroom is with them?** It wasn't right for Jesus' disciples to imitate the Pharisees in their hypocritical shows. Nor was it right for them to imitate John's disciples in their ministry of humble preparation, because the disciples lived in the experience that John tried to prepare people for.

b. **But the days will come**: There would come a day when fasting would be appropriate for Jesus' followers, but at the present time when Jesus was among them, it was not that day.

    i. The old Puritan commentator John Trapp drew three points from this: "1. That fasting is not abolished with the ceremonial law, but still to be used as a duty of the gospel. 2. That times of heaviness are times of humiliation. 3. That our halcyons here are but as marriage-feasts, for continuance; they last not long."

    ii. There is a slight dark note in the words, "**the days will come when the bridegroom will be taken away from them.**" It was as if Jesus said, "They are going to take Me away; I threaten their system." It is the first slight hint of His coming rejection.

c. **Nor do they put new wine into old wineskins, or else the wineskins break**: With this illustration of the **wineskins**, Jesus explained that He did not come to repair or reform the old institutions of Judaism, but to institute a new covenant altogether. The new covenant doesn't just improve the old; it replaces it and goes beyond it.

d. **But they put new wine into new wineskins, and both are preserved**: Jesus' reference to the wineskins was His announcement that the present institutions of Judaism could not and would not contain His **new wine**. He would form a new institution – the church – that would bring Jew and Gentile together into a completely new body (Ephesians 2:16).

    i. Jesus reminds us that what is old and stagnant often cannot be renewed or reformed. God will often look for new vessels to contain His new work, until those vessels eventually make themselves unusable. This reminds us that the religious establishment of any age is not necessarily pleasing to Jesus. Sometimes it is in direct opposition to, or at least resisting His work.

    ii. Jesus came to introduce something new, not to patch up something old. This is what salvation is all about. In doing this, Jesus doesn't destroy the old (the law), but He fulfills it, just as an acorn is fulfilled when it grows into an oak tree. There is a sense in which the acorn is gone, but its purpose is fulfilled in greatness.

E. Two people are healed: A little girl and a woman with an issue of blood.

1. (18-19) A ruler among the Jews asks Jesus to heal his daughter.

While He spoke these things to them, behold, a ruler came and worshiped Him, saying, "My daughter has just died, but come and lay Your hand on her and she will live." So Jesus arose and followed him, and so *did* His disciples.

a. **A ruler came and worshiped Him**: Note that this man **worshiped Him,** and Jesus received this worship - which would have been blasphemous if Jesus had not Himself been God.

i. In other instances in the New Testament where such worship is offered to a human (Acts 10:25-26) or to an angel (Revelation 22:8-9), it is always immediately refused.

b. **My daughter has just died, but come and lay Your hand on her and she will live**: This **ruler** did the right thing in coming to Jesus, but his faith is small in comparison to the centurion of Matthew 8. The **ruler** thought it is essential that Jesus personally come touch the little girl, while the centurion understood Jesus had the authority to heal with a word, even at a great distance.

2. (20-22) A woman is healed by her faith and her touch of Jesus.

And suddenly, a woman who had a flow of blood for twelve years came from behind and touched the hem of His garment. For she said to herself, "If only I may touch His garment, I shall be made well." But Jesus turned around, and when He saw her He said, "Be of good cheer, daughter; your faith has made you well." And the woman was made well from that hour.

a. **And suddenly, a woman**: Mark 5:21-43 and Luke 8:43-48 give a much fuller account of this miracle, but Matthew's account is enough to show the compassion of Jesus and the fact that His power was not magical. Here we simply see the power of God responding to the faith of those who seek Him.

i. "Matthew relates this story shortly, as he doth many others, being only intent upon recording the miracle." (Poole)

b. **If only I may touch His garment, I shall be made well**: Because this woman's condition was embarrassing, and because she was ceremonially unclean and would be condemned for touching Jesus or even being in a pressing crowd, she wanted to do this secretly. She would not openly ask Jesus to be healed, but she thought "**If only I may touch His garment, I shall be made well.**"

i. "These fringes were four tassels of hyacinth blue worn by a Jew on the corners of his outer garment...It was meant to identify a Jew as a Jew, and as member of the chosen people, no matter where he was; and it was meant to remind a Jew every time he put on and took off his clothes that he belonged to God." (Barclay)

ii. This also shows us that Jesus dressed like other people of His time. He felt no need to distinguish Himself by the clothes He wore. "In dress Jesus was not noncomformist." (Bruce)

iii. To the best of our knowledge, there was no promise or pattern that touching the garment of Jesus would bring healing. It seems that the woman believed this in a somewhat superstitious way. Yet even though her faith had elements of error and superstition, she believed in the healing power of Jesus and His garment served as a point of contact for that faith. There are many things that we could find wrong with this woman's faith. Yet her faith was in *Jesus*; and the object of faith is much more important than the quality or even quantity of faith.

iv. "She was ignorant enough to think that healing went from him unconsciously; yet her faith lived despite her ignorance, and triumphed despite her bashfulness." (Spurgeon)

c. **And the woman was made well**: Her faith, though imperfect, was enough to receive what Jesus wanted to give her. Her 12-year disease was immediately cured.

d. **When He saw her, He said**: This woman hoped to receive something from Jesus without drawing any attention to herself or her embarrassing problem. Jesus insisted on making public notice of her, and He did this for good reasons.

- He did it so she would know that she was healed, having heard an official declaration of it from Jesus.

- He did it so others would know she was healed, because her ailment was private in nature.

- He did it so she would know why she was healed, that it was by her **faith** and not because of a superstitious touch in and of itself.

- He did it so that she would not think she had stolen a blessing from Jesus, and so she would never feel that she needed to hide from Him.

- He did it so that the ruler of the synagogue would see the power of Jesus at work and therefore have more faith himself for his ill daughter.

- He did it so that He could bless her in a special way, giving her an honored title that we never see Jesus give to any other: **daughter**.

3. (23-26) Jesus, despite scorn, raises the little girl from the dead.

When Jesus came into the ruler's house, and saw the flute players and the noisy crowd wailing, He said to them, "Make room, for the girl is not dead, but sleeping." And they ridiculed Him. But when the crowd

was put outside, He went in and took her by the hand, and the girl arose. And the report of this went out into all that land.

a. **The flute players and the noisy crowd**: These were probably paid mourners, who in the custom of the day offered an ostentatious display of mourning for a price, and not out of sincere sorrow. When we notice how quickly they moved from **wailing** to ridiculing Jesus, it showed their lack of sincerity.

i. "Professional mourners were hired even by the poorest families (Mishnah *Ketuboth* 4:4 specifies 'not less than two flutes and one wailing woman')." (France)

ii. "Mourning, like everything else, had been reduced to a system, two flutes and one mourning woman at the burial of a wife incumbent on the poorest man." (Bruce)

b. **When the crowd was put outside, He went in and took her by the hand, and the girl arose**: Jesus endured the scorn from the crowd and raised the girl to life. He certainly would not let the criticism or mocking of the crowd keep Him from doing God's will.

i. Jesus didn't raise every dead child He encountered, but Jesus did so here in a simple act of mercy and compassion to the grieving father. In addition, Jesus must have hated death and its cause, and enjoyed the opportunity to hand death a small defeat before He would defeat it altogether at the cross and the empty tomb.

F. Three more accounts of healing.

1. (27-31) Jesus heals two blind men.

When Jesus departed from there, two blind men followed Him, crying out and saying, "Son of David, have mercy on us!" And when He had come into the house, the blind men came to Him. And Jesus said to them, "Do you believe that I am able to do this?" They said to Him, "Yes, Lord." Then He touched their eyes, saying, "According to your faith let it be to you." And their eyes were opened. And Jesus sternly warned them, saying, "See *that* no one knows *it*." But when they had departed, they spread the news about Him in all that country.

a. **Two blind men followed Him**: It was not easy for these blind men to follow Jesus, but they did. They had to ask others where Jesus was going, and they had to listen to every sound that might guide them. Yet they were determined to follow Him to the best of their ability.

i. "Blindness was a distressingly common disease in Palestine. It came partly from the glare of the eastern sun on unprotected eyes, and partly because people knew nothing of the importance of cleanliness and hygiene. In particular the clouds of unclean flies carried infections which led to loss of sight." (Barclay)

b. **Son of David, have mercy on us**: The two blind men followed Jesus and shouted this open recognition of Jesus as Messiah, because **Son of David** was a rich Messianic title. They asked Jesus for the best thing they could ask for: **mercy**.

> i. "Their sole appeal was to mercy. There was no talk about merit, no pleading of their past sufferings, or their persevering endeavors, or their resolves for the future; but, 'Have mercy on us.' He will never win a blessing from God who demands it as if he had a right to it." (Spurgeon)

> ii. "This is the first time Jesus is called 'Son of David' and there can be no doubt that the blind men were confessing Jesus as Messiah." (Carson)

> iii. John 9:22 tells us that the Pharisees judged that anyone who proclaimed Jesus as the Christ, the Messiah, would be removed from the synagogue. Though the occasion in John seems to have been after this healing of the blind men, we can still believe that there was a price to pay for calling Jesus "**Son of David**."

> iv. **When He had come into the house, the blind men came to Him**: "Jesus did not deal with the blind men until they were indoors. This may have been to dampen messianic expectations on a day marked by two highly public and dramatic miracles." (Carson)

c. **Do you believe that I am able to do this**: Again, Jesus healed the blind men in response to their faith. Faith does not *guarantee* healing for every individual, yet there are undoubtedly multitudes that are *not* healed because they lack faith. These men simply proclaimed their faith by saying, "**Yes, Lord**."

> i. "He touched *them* with his hand; but they must also touch him with their faith." (Spurgeon)

d. **According to your faith let it be so to you**: Here again Matthew emphasized the proper **faith** that men should have in Jesus, and the blessings that come to men through that faith.

- The leper of Matthew 8:1-4 showed faith because he absolutely knew that Jesus was able to heal his leprosy.

- The centurion of Matthew 8:5-13 had such great faith that Jesus openly praised it as *great faith*, that He had not found among the people of Israel.

- The disciples failed in faith when in the storm on the Sea of Galilee (Matthew 8:23-27)

- The woman with the issue of blood was healed by her faith (Matthew 9:18-26).

i. In many ways, God says the same to men and women today: "**According to your faith let it be so to you**." There is much to have by faith, and much that is never received because it is never grasped with faith. "'According to your faith' does not mean 'in proportion to your faith' (so much faith, so much sight) but rather 'since you believe, your request is granted'." (Carson)

ii. "The word of power in the last sentence is one upon which he acts so continually, that we may call it, as to many blessings, a rule of the kingdom. We have the measuring of our own mercies; our faith obtains less or more according to its own capacity to receive." (Spurgeon)

iii. The faith of these two blind men is worthy of notice.

- They had the faith to *follow* Jesus; this meant forsaking other paths, other directions and deciding to follow Him.

- They had the faith to *cry out*, willing to put words to their desire.

- They had the faith to make some noise, and to be unafraid of embarrassment.

- They had the faith to identify Jesus as the **Son of David**, recognizing Him as the Messiah.

- They had the faith to ask Jesus for **mercy**, knowing they didn't deserve healing.

- They had the faith to believe that Jesus was able heal them.

- They had the faith to say, "**Yes, Lord**."

e. **See that no one knows it**: Despite Jesus' warning, they couldn't resist telling others. Though we do not admire their well-intentioned disobedience, we admire their excitement over the work of God. This was their only area of unbelief – they didn't have the faith to obey Jesus as they should have.

2. (32-34) A mute man healed.

As they went out, behold, they brought to Him a man, mute and demon-possessed. And when the demon was cast out, the mute spoke. And the

multitudes marveled, saying, "It was never seen like this in Israel!" But the Pharisees said, "He casts out demons by the ruler of the demons."

a. **A man, mute and demon-possessed**: In the Jewish understanding of demon possession, this man could not be helped. This was because most rabbis of that day thought that the essential first step in exorcism was to compel or trick the demon into telling you its name. The name was then thought of as a handle by which the demon could then be removed.

i. Therefore, a demon that made a man **mute** had cleverly prevented the revelation of the name of the demon inhabiting the victim, and therefore prevented the exorcism.

ii. Yet Jesus had no problem, **the demon was cast out** and **the mute spoke**.

b. **It was never seen like this in Israel**: For these reasons this miracle was particularly amazing to the multitudes. It showed not only the complete authority of Jesus over the demonic realm, but also the weakness of the rabbis' traditions.

c. **But the Pharisees said, "He casts out demons by the ruler of the demons"**: In attributing this work of Jesus to the power of Satan, we see in this gospel the Pharisees and other religious leaders continuing their rejection of Jesus and His work.

i. "Nothing was too bad for them to say of Jesus…Surely this was going very near to the unpardonable sin." (Spurgeon)

ii. Carson on Matthew 9:34: "This verse is missing from the Western textual tradition…But the external evidence is strong; and the verse seems presupposed in Matthew 10:25."

3. (35-38) Jesus' compassion on the multitudes.

Then Jesus went about all the cities and villages, teaching in their synagogues, preaching the gospel of the kingdom, and healing every sickness and every disease among the people. But when He saw the multitudes, He was moved with compassion for them, because they were weary and scattered, like sheep having no shepherd. Then He said to His disciples, "The harvest truly *is* plentiful, but the laborers *are* few. Therefore pray the Lord of the harvest to send out laborers into His harvest."

a. **Jesus went about all the cities and villages**: As Jesus encountered the depth of human need **He was moved with compassion for them**. Jesus was not unfeeling or stoic in the face of people and their problems.

i. Matthew 9:35 shows us that what happened in Matthew 8 and 9, though mostly located in Capernaum, was an example of what Jesus did all over the Galilee region.

ii. In the previous verses Jesus was terribly and unfairly criticized, yet it did not make Him stop His work. He didn't say, "Oh, they are saying terrible things about Me! What can I do? How can I make them stop?" Jesus simply ignored terrible and unfair criticism and got about His Father's business.

iii. "The word which is used for *moved with compassion* (*splagchnistheis*) is the strongest word for pity in the Greek language…it describes the compassion which moves a man to the deepest depths of his being." (Barclay)

iv. "The original word is a very remarkable one. It is not found in classic Greek. It is not found in the Septuagint. The fact is, it was a word coined by the evangelists themselves. They did not find one in the whole Greek language that suited their purpose, and therefore they had to make one." (Spurgeon)

b. **They were weary and scattered, like sheep having no shepherd**: Jesus here described what man is apart from God; that we are **like sheep having no shepherd**. This means that we are in a lot of trouble until we come under the care of our Shepherd.

i. "This troubled our Saviour more than their bodily bondage to the Romans, which yet was very grievous." (Trapp)

ii. Sadly, one could say that the Jewish people of that day did indeed have some kind of spiritual guides and shepherds, namely the scribes, priests, Levites, and Pharisees. Yet for the most part they were worthless. "Christ accounts those people to have no ministers who have no good ones." (Poole)

iii. "The state of things suggested two pictures to His mind: a neglected flock of sheep, and a harvest going to waste for lack of reapers. Both imply, not only a pitiful plight of the people, but a blameworthy neglect of duty on the part of their religious guides…The Pharisaic comments on the Capernaum mission festival (Matthew 9:11) were sufficient to justify the adverse judgment." (Bruce)

c. **The harvest truly is plentiful, but the laborers are few**: Jesus saw the greatness of human need as an opportunity, as a **harvest** that was **plentiful**. A harvest is a good thing, and this was a **plentiful** harvest.

i. But it was also a harvest that needed **laborers**. The good of a harvest can go to waste if there are no **laborers** to take advantage of the bounty. Jesus warned us that opportunities to meet human need and bring people into His kingdom may be wasted because of a shortage of **laborers**.

ii. Jesus described the workers in His kingdom as **laborers** – that is, those who work hard. "The householder hath somewhat to do, the magistrate more, but the minister most of all. He labours more in a day many times, than the husbandman does in a month. The sweat of the brow is nothing to that of the brain; the former furthers health, the latter impairs it, wearying and wearing out the body, wasting the vitals, and hastening old age and untimely death." (Luther, cited in Trapp)

iii. "Pretenders were many, but real '*laborers*' in the harvest were few… Man-made ministers are useless. Still are the fields encumbered with gentlemen who cannot use the sickle. Still the real ingatherers are few and far between. Where are the instructive, soul-winning ministries?" (Spurgeon)

d. **Therefore pray the Lord of the harvest to send out laborers into His harvest**: Since the harvest belongs to the **Lord of the harvest**, we are commanded to **pray** that He would compel workers to reap His harvest.

i. "He also believed that the Lord would work by means, and that many laborers were required to gather in a plenteous harvest, and therefore he told us to pray for them." (Spurgeon)

ii. We are to pray that the Lord would **send out laborers**: "Now the Greek is much more forcible, it is that he would push them forward, and thrust them out; it is the same word which is used for the expulsion of a devil from a man possessed. It takes great power to drive a devil out, it will need equal power from God to drive a minister out to his work." (Spurgeon)

iii. This is a prayer we must pray, but we can only pray it honestly if we pray with an ear open to hearing Him tell us, "*You* go into the harvest."

iv. In this chapter Jesus faced many accusations:

- He was accused of blasphemy.
- He was accused of low morals.
- He was accused of ungodliness.
- He was accused of being in league with the devil.

v. Though Matthew has fully established Jesus' credentials as the Messiah, Jesus is beginning to be rejected and criticized by the religious authorities. These conflicts with the religious leaders will become more frequent and intense.

Matthew 10 - The Sending of the Twelve

A. Twelve disciples chosen and commissioned.

1. (1-4) The twelve disciples are listed.

And when He had called His twelve disciples to *Him*, He gave them power *over* unclean spirits, to cast them out, and to heal all kinds of sickness and all kinds of disease. Now the names of the twelve apostles are these: first, Simon, who is called Peter, and Andrew his brother; James the *son* of Zebedee, and John his brother; Philip and Bartholomew; Thomas and Matthew the tax collector; James the *son* of Alphaeus, and Lebbaeus, whose surname was Thaddaeus; Simon the Canaanite, and Judas Iscariot, who also betrayed Him.

a. **When He had called His twelve disciples to Him**: The main feature of this list is its *diversity*. Jesus chose His disciples from a variety of backgrounds and life experiences. About all they had in common was it seems that none of them were privileged or from backgrounds of high status. This is very much in the spirit of 1 Corinthians 1:26-29.

b. **He gave them power over unclean spirits, to cast them out, and to heal all kinds of sickness and all kinds of disease**: Jesus did not only *call* the twelve; He also gave them *power* to do what He had called them to do. The same principle holds true today: whom God calls, God equips. The equipping may not be completely evident before the ministry begins, but it will be evident along the way.

c. **Now the names of the twelve apostles are these**: These twelve (excepting Judas), have an important place in God's plan of redemption, including some particular role in the future judgment (Matthew 19:28), and in the founding of the church (Ephesians 2:20). The Bible promises that their position and work will be remembered through eternity (Revelation 21:14).

i. This is the first and only time in Matthew that **the twelve** are called **apostles**. "The word apostle literally means *one who is sent out*; it is the word for an *envoy* or an *ambassador.*" (Barclay) "Called here for the first and last time *apostoloi*, with reference at once to the immediate minor mission and to the later great one." (Bruce)

- The word *apostle* can mean a mere messenger, as in John 13:16, referring to *he who is sent.*

- Jesus is called an apostle in Hebrews 3:1: *consider the Apostle and High Priest of our confession.*

- Paul sometimes used the word in the sense of messengers or representatives, as in 2 Corinthians 8:23: *they are messengers* [apostles] *of the churches*; possibly also in Romans 16:7.

- Yet Paul also used the term in a more narrow sense, referring to the Twelve and himself by special dispensation (1 Corinthians 9:1-5 and 15:7-10; Galatians 1:17 and 1:19 following).

ii. There are four different lists of **the twelve** in the New Testament. Here in Matthew 10:2-4, and also in Mark 3:16-19, Luke 6:13-16, and Acts 1:13. In these lists, Peter is always listed first and Judas is always last. The two pairs of brothers (Peter and Andrew; James and John) are always listed first. In the lists they are arranged in a way that suggests that they were arranged in three groups of four, each with a leader.

- In each list Peter is first mentioned, followed by Andrew, James, and John.

- In each list Philip is fifth mentioned, followed by Bartholomew, Thomas, and Matthew.

- In each list James the son of Alphaeus is ninth mentioned, followed by Thaddaeus/Judas brother of James, Simon the Zealot, and Judas.

iii. "The apostolic number fitly represents the twelve tribes of Israel; and for practical purposes the twelve form a workable band of leaders, a sufficient jury, and a competent company of witnesses." (Spurgeon)

iv. **Bartholomew** is often identified with Nathanael of John 1:43-51 and John 21:2. "Many are of opinion that this was *Nathanael...* whose name was probably *Nathanael bar Talmai*, Nathanael, the son of *Talmai*: here, his own name is repressed, and he is called *Bar Talmai*, or *Bartholomew*, from his *father.*" (Clarke)

v. "Bartholomew is never mentioned without an *and*: he was a kind of man to work with other people." (Spurgeon)

vi. "We must not understand by *Canaanite* a pagan, (for Christ sent out none but Jews,) but one of Cana." (Poole)

vii. "*Iscariot* is usually thought to mean 'man of Kerioth' (a city in southern Judaea), but has also been explained as meaning 'traitor', 'assassin', 'carrier of the leather bag', or 'redhead'!" (France)

viii. They are called **disciples** in Matthew 10:1 and **apostles** in Matthew 10:2. "It is worthy of notice, that those who were Christ's *apostles* were first his *disciples*; to intimate, that men must be first *taught* of God, before they be *sent* of God." (Clarke)

2. (5-6) Where they are to go: unto Israel (the Jewish people) only.

These twelve Jesus sent out and commanded them, saying: "Do not go into the way of the Gentiles, and do not enter a city of the Samaritans. But go rather to the lost sheep of the house of Israel."

a. **These twelve Jesus sent out**: Jesus was touring around the region of Galilee teaching, preaching, and helping needy people with miraculous power (Matthew 4:23). The sending of **these twelve** was a conscious expanding of that work. Now the work of Jesus was being done by many more than simply Jesus Himself.

i. **And commanded them**: "This word in Greek has four special usages. (i) It is the regular word of military command...(ii) It is the word used of calling one's friends to one's help...(iii) It is the word which is used of a teacher giving rules and precepts to his students...(iv) It is the word which is regularly used for an imperial command." (Barclay)

b. **Do not go into the way of the Gentiles**: This is the pattern of the gospel - it is *for the Jew first and also for the Greek* (Romans 1:16). Later, the gospel would go to both the **Samaritans** and the **Gentiles**, but it had to begin with **the lost sheep of the house of Israel**.

i. "That Jesus felt it necessary to mention the Samaritans at all presupposes John 4. The disciples, happy in the exercise of their ability to perform miracles, might have been tempted to evangelize the Samaritans because they remembered Jesus' success there." (Carson)

ii. "The emphasis of the saying lies not primarily on the prohibition of a wider mission, but on the priority of the mission to Israel." (France)

c. **But go rather to the lost sheep of the house of Israel**: God's intention was to reach the whole world, but beginning with **Israel**. There was certainly enough work to do among the **lost sheep of the house of Israel** to keep the twelve busy until God directly commanded them to expand their ministry.

i. Significantly, Jesus still called the Jewish people "**the house of Israel**" even though they had lost their Jewish state many decades before this time. *God* still saw them as "**Israel**," even when there was not a political entity known as "Israel."

ii. Who were the **lost sheep of Israel**? In a sense, all of them were. *All we like sheep have gone astray; we have turned, every one, to his own way.* (Isaiah 53:6). Yet in another sense, there were also **lost sheep** that were abused and neglected by their spiritual shepherds, the scribes, priests, and Pharisees. This is the sense of Jeremiah 50:6: *My people have been lost sheep. Their shepherds have led them astray.*

iii. Because so many were so spiritually neglected, Jesus sent these apostles out. "The beginnings of the mission to the neglected 'lost' sheep of Israel may be found in the Capernaum feast (Matthew 9:10). As time went on Jesus felt increasingly the pressure of the problem and the need for extended effort." (Bruce)

iv. "Like sheep, that silly creature, than the which as none is more apt to wander, so neither any more unable to return." (Trapp)

3. (7-8a) What they are to do: go out preaching and healing.

"And as you go, preach, saying, 'The kingdom of heaven is at hand.' Heal the sick, cleanse the lepers, raise the dead, cast out demons."

a. **As you go, preach, saying, "The kingdom of heaven is at hand"**: Earlier (Matthew 4:17) we were told that Jesus' message was, "*Repent, for the kingdom of heaven is at hand.*" The disciples brought the same message Jesus preached, simply bringing it over a much broader area than Jesus could just by Himself.

i. We may also surmise that they were to repeat many of the themes found in the Sermon on the Mount (Matthew 5-7), because that message tells what life in the **kingdom of heaven** should be like.

ii. "Men will do much for a kingdom. And nothing less than a kingdom, and that of heaven, can buy men out of their sweet sins." (Trapp)

iii. There is no mention of them *preaching* in the synagogues, only being scourged in them (Matthew 10:17). This was a house-to-house, open field, street preaching ministry.

b. **Heal the sick, cleanse the lepers, raise the dead, cast out demons**: The disciples both had a message to preach and a power to display. In this, they were truly followers of their Master.

i. The authority for these disciples to **raise the dead** is remarkable; yet the later fulfillment of it was recorded in both Acts 9 and 20, and there were no doubt other unrecorded instances. We have no evidence that either such a thing was common, or that this authority has been permanently withdrawn. It is wise for Christians today to both believe in God's power to do such miracles through His people, and to not be too quick to believe unsubstantiated reports of such miracles.

4. (8b-15) How they were to provide for themselves.

"Freely you have received, freely give. Provide neither gold nor silver nor copper in your money belts, nor bag for *your* journey, nor two tunics, nor sandals, nor staffs; for a worker is worthy of his food. Now whatever city or town you enter, inquire who in it is worthy, and stay there till you go out. And when you go into a household, greet it. If the household is worthy, let your peace come upon it. But if it is not worthy, let your peace return to you. And whoever will not receive you nor hear your words, when you depart from that house or city, shake off the dust from your feet. Assuredly, I say to you, it will be more tolerable for the land of Sodom and Gomorrah in the day of judgment than for that city!"

a. **Freely you have received, freely give**: Jesus charged His disciples nothing, and He expected them to give ministry unto others without charge. This is the foundational principle for the commands that follow.

i. "What a scandal is it for a man to traffic with gifts which he pretends, at least, to have received from the Holy Ghost, of which he is not the master, but the dispenser. He who preaches to get a *living*, or to make a *fortune*, is guilty of the most infamous *sacrilege*." (Clarke)

b. **Provide neither gold nor silver nor copper in your money belts**: They should expect *God* to meet their needs, without taking undue concern for their own needs. Furthermore, they should expect that God would normally meet their needs through the inspired hospitality of others.

i. "Our Saviour designed to give them an experience of the providence of God, and to teach them to trust in it." (Poole)

ii. "He was once again speaking words which were very familiar to a Jew. The *Talmud* tells us that: 'No one is to go to the Temple Mount with staff, shoes, girdle of money, or dusty feet.' The idea was that when a man entered the temple, he must make it quite clear that he had left everything which had to do with trade and business and worldly affairs behind." (Barclay)

iii. "*Take* [**Provide**] is literally 'obtain'...The saying in its Matthaean form thus does not so much specify the appropriate equipment for traveling, but rather assures the disciples that no previous fund-raising is necessary, nor need special equipment be acquired. They can go just as they are, and the mission is urgent." (France)

iv. "The well-known discrepancy over the *staff* (Mark 6:8 specifically allows them to carry one) may arise from the difference in the verbs: the Matthaean version forbids the acquisition of a staff for the journey, while the Marcan allows them to take (only) the one they already possess." (France)

v. "See Luke 22:36: 'He that hath a purse, let him take it...' Different modes of procedure are to be adopted at different times. Oh, that some of our very spiritual brethren had a little common sense! We offer the prayer with a very faint heart." (Spurgeon)

c. **For a worker is worthy of his food**: When they came among others, they were to be *workers* among them. They would work among them in both spiritual work and practical work. We can imagine them preaching the Word of God, praying for and with people, and helping with the farm work.

i. Even though the twelve could expect their needs to be met through the people they served, they should never require their needs to be met as payment. The foundational principle was **freely you have received, freely give**.

d. **If the household is worthy... if it is not worthy**: Those who did receive these disciples can expect to be blessed (**let your peace come upon it**); but those places that refused them could expect to be treated as Gentile cities (**shake off the dust from your feet**), and as such, were in serious danger of judgment.

i. "To settle in the house of a 'worthy' person implies that the disciples were not to shop around for the most comfortable quarters." (Carson)

ii. "Easy to perform, not easy to perform in a right spirit; too apt to be the outcome of irritation, disappointment, and wounded vanity - they did not appreciate *me*, I abandon them to their fate. Christ meant the act to symbolize the responsibility of the inhabitants for the result." (Bruce)

iii. "Two sure signs of reprobate goats: 1. Not to receive Christ's ministers to house and harbour, accounting themselves happy in such entertainment. 2. Not to hear their words." (Trapp)

B. Jesus prepares the disciples for persecution.

1. (16-18) Persecution will come.

"Behold, I send you out as sheep in the midst of wolves. Therefore be wise as serpents and harmless as doves. But beware of men, for they will deliver you up to councils and scourge you in their synagogues. You will be brought before governors and kings for My sake, as a testimony to them and to the Gentiles."

a. **I send you out as sheep in the midst of wolves**: Jesus honestly warned His disciples that they would face persecution. As they went with no police or military protection, He sent them **as sheep in the midst of wolves**.

i. "Here you see sheep sent forth among the wolves, as if they were the attacking party, and were bent upon putting down their terrible enemies. It is a novel sight, such as nature can never show, but grace is full of marvels." (Spurgeon)

ii. "After all, the mission of sheep to wolves is a hopeful one, since we see in the natural world that the sheep, though so feeble, by far outnumber the wolves who are so fierce." (Spurgeon)

b. **Therefore be wise as serpents and harmless as doves**: Despite their vulnerable position, Jesus' followers were not to defend themselves with worldly forms of power. They were to remain **harmless as doves**, though **wise as serpents**.

i. Wisdom would keep them from attracting trouble unnecessarily or show them how to avoid it without compromise. **Serpents** are attacked by everyone, and must use creativity and wisdom to survive.

ii. Remaining harmless would keep them from giving in to the temptation of retaliation.

iii. "The Christian missionary will need to be wary, to avoid receiving harm; but he must be of a guileless mind, that he do no harm." (Spurgeon)

c. **But beware of men, for they will deliver you up**: Jesus also warned them that men would persecute them in the civic arena (**councils**) and the religious arena (**synagogues**). They could expect opposition from both city hall and the halls of religion.

d. **You will be brought before governors and kings for My sake**: This was a remarkable statement, recognizing the great influence the gospel and its preachers would have. **Governors and kings** would notice them – and arrest them, bringing them to trial.

i. "This affords a striking proof of the prescience of Christ. Who could have thought, at *that time*, that these *despised* and *illiterate* men could excite so much attention, and be called upon to apologize for the profession of their faith before the tribunals of the most illustrious personages of the earth?" (*Wakefield*, cited in Clarke)

e. **For My sake, as a testimony to them and to the Gentiles**: Because they were persecuted for Jesus' **sake**, they could be a **testimony** to both religious and civic persecutors.

i. "The specific mention of the *Gentiles* suggests that the wider mission of the post-resurrection period is already in view." (France)

2. (19-20) When Jesus' disciples are brought before rulers, God will help them.

"But when they deliver you up, do not worry about how or what you should speak. For it will be given to you in that hour what you should speak; for it is not you who speak, but the Spirit of your Father who speaks in you."

a. **Do not worry about how or what you should speak**: Jesus' disciples could have perfect trust in God in that moment, knowing that He would speak through them even if they were unprepared.

i. "It was not the humiliation which early Christians dreaded, not even the cruel pain and the agony. But many of them feared that their own unskilfulness in words and defence might injure rather than commend the truth. It is the promise of God that when a man is on trial for his faith, the words will come to him." (Barclay)

b. **For it will be given to you in that hour what you should speak**: This gave them confidence that the **Spirit of the Father** would speak to and through them at the necessary moment, even if they were not prepared with a statement.

i. This isn't a justification of poor preparation in teaching and preaching God's Word, but it is a promise of strength and guidance for the persecuted that have an opportunity to testify of Jesus.

3. (21-23) The extent of persecution: even among families, from city to city.

"Now brother will deliver up brother to death, and a father *his* child; and children will rise up against parents and cause them to be put to death. And you will be hated by all for My name's sake. But he who endures to the end will be saved. When they persecute you in this city, flee to another. For assuredly, I say to you, you will not have gone through the cities of Israel before the Son of Man comes."

a. **Now brother will deliver up brother to death**: Jesus knew that in some cases the gospel would divide family members, and that some of the most bitter persecution would take place among families.

b. **And cause them to be put to death**: Jesus plainly said that persecution would sometimes result in **death**. Though most Christians have endured persecution in economic or social arenas, through the centuries, literally millions have given their lives in faithfulness to Jesus.

c. **You will be hated by all for My name's sake**: At times this has been true; when entire cultures have **hated** the followers of Jesus. It seems strange that people who live by the kingdom expectations of Matthew 5-7 should be so greatly hated, but it is the same paradox that inspired the world to condemn and crucify the only sinless man ever to live.

i. It must be painfully admitted that there are times when Christians, because of great unfaithfulness or false profession of faith, have been **hated** for good reason. Yet no one who is filled with the presence of Jesus and lives like He did can be hated for good reason.

d. **But he who endures to the end will be saved**: A commitment to *endure to the end* is required for those who will weather the storms of persecution. We who face little real persecution have little understanding of just how difficult it is to endure under it.

i. "Why, if every man would be saved who began to follow Christ, who would be damned? In such a country as this, the most of men have at least one religious spasm in their lives." (Spurgeon)

e. **When they persecute you in this city, flee to another**: In this, Jesus taught His disciples that it was wrong for them to *court* martyrdom. They were not to run at persecution, or even remain if they had the chance for an honorable escape. If they could **flee to another** place, they were to do it.

f. **You will not have gone through the cities of Israel before the Son of Man comes**: This is one of the hardest-to-understand statements of Jesus in Matthew. Could Jesus really mean that He would return to this earth before the disciples would make it through all the cities of Israel? If so, this would make Jesus plainly wrong in this prediction. Instead, it is better to see His "coming" in *this* passage as His *coming in judgment* upon Judea in AD 70 which did happen before the gospel came to *every* city in Israel.

i. This is the fulfillment of *the day of judgment* warned of in Matthew 10:15. In many ways, the judgment poured out by God upon Judea through the Roman armies in AD 70 was worse than the judgment that came upon Sodom and Gomorrah.

ii. "When they face persecution, they must take it as no more than a signal for strategic withdrawal to the next city where witness must continue, for the time is short. They will not have finished evangelizing the cities of Israel before the Son of Man comes in judgment on Israel." (Carson)

4. (24-25) Why Jesus' disciples must expect persecution.

"A disciple is not above *his* teacher, nor a servant above his master. It is enough for a disciple that he be like his teacher, and a servant like his master. If they have called the master of the house Beelzebub, how much more *will they call* those of his household!"

a. **A disciple is not above his teacher**: Simply put, the disciples should not expect to be treated *better* than Jesus was treated. If they called Jesus Himself Satan (**Beelzebub**), the disciples of Jesus should expect worse.

> i. This already is the second reference in Matthew we have to Jesus being associated with Satan by His enemies. "Matthew 9:34 suggests that it was a frequent slur." (Carson)

> ii. "Thank God, they may *call* us what they like, but they cannot make us evil…God was slandered in Paradise, and Christ on Calvary; how can we hope to escape?" (Spurgeon)

b. **It is enough for a disciple that he be like his teacher, and a servant like his master**: This is the goal of both the **disciple** and **servant** of Jesus. We simply want to be **like** our **teacher** and **master**, as we are *conformed to the image of His Son, that He might be the firstborn among many brethren* (Romans 8:29).

5. (26-31) Even in the midst of persecution, Jesus' disciples should not fear, but be bold in their proclamation of the gospel.

"Therefore do not fear them. For there is nothing covered that will not be revealed, and hidden that will not be known. Whatever I tell you in the dark, speak in the light; and what you hear in the ear, preach on the housetops. And do not fear those who kill the body but cannot kill the soul. But rather fear Him who is able to destroy both soul and body in hell. Are not two sparrows sold for a copper coin? And not one of them falls to the ground apart from your Father's will. But the very hairs of your head are all numbered. Do not fear therefore; you are of more value than many sparrows."

a. **Therefore do not fear them**: Jesus' disciples could have confidence that the truth *would* prevail, so they should go out and preach it with boldness, despite the danger of persecution.

> i. If persecution or the threat of persecution makes us draw back from speaking and preaching God's word, then in some measure Satan has won a victory. His threat of persecution may not have succeeded in harming us, but in holding back the work of the Word of God.

> ii. "Fear not what cannot be avoided if you would be of any use. Fear suits not an apostle any more than a soldier or a sailor, who both take coolly the risks of their calling." (Bruce)

b. **For there is nothing covered that will not be revealed, and hidden that will not be known**: Jesus promised His persecuted followers that the truth of their honorable sacrifice would be known, even if the persecutors did their best to hide it among the pages of history. God would reveal all and justify His servants and reveal the crime of those who thought they had hidden it.

i. The judgment of eternity gives us great confidence in God's ultimate justice. Those who seem to cheat justice on earth will never cheat it in eternity.

c. **Whatever I tell you in the dark, speak in the light; and what you hear in the ear, preach on the housetops**: The message of Jesus was gloriously *public*. It was not for a secret few and was not to be hidden in any way. There isn't one message for the inner circle and another for those on the outside. Those on the outside may not understand the message, but they can hear it and it is not to be hidden from them.

d. **And do not fear those who kill the body but cannot kill the soul. But rather fear Him who is able to destroy both soul and body in hell**: God is the one to fear, not the men who persecute the followers of Jesus. The worst they can do is to destroy the body, but being a coward before God can have eternal consequences.

i. "There is no cure for the fear of man like the fear of God." (Spurgeon)

ii. "Hence we find that the body and the soul are distinct principles, for the *body* may be slain and the *soul* escape; and, secondly, that the soul is immaterial, for the murderers of the body are not able, have it not in their power, to injure it." (Clarke)

e. **Do not fear therefore; you are of more value than many sparrows**: Jesus' disciples didn't need to be afraid, because God really did care for them, even down to the most minute detail. If God cares for the **sparrows**, and numbers the very hairs of our head, then He will also pay careful attention to our needs. The persecuted easily feel that God forgets them, but He has not.

i. God knows us better than our friends know us; better than our husband or wife knows us; He knows us better than we know ourselves. We don't know how many hairs are numbered on our head. The God who knows us so well will take care of us.

ii. The emphasis in this short section is clearly "**do not fear**." "This is the third time, in six verses, that they and we are bid to banish this cowardly base passion, this causeless, fruitless, harmful, sinful fear of men. He that fears God need fear none else." (Trapp)

6. (32-39) The attitude Jesus' disciples must be equipped with.

"Therefore whoever confesses Me before men, him I will also confess before My Father who is in heaven. But whoever denies Me before men,

him I will also deny before My Father who is in heaven. Do not think
that I came to bring peace on earth. I did not come to bring peace but
a sword. For I have come to 'set a man against his father, a daughter
against her mother, and a daughter-in-law against her mother-in-law';
and 'a man's enemies will be those of his *own* household.' He who loves
father or mother more than Me is not worthy of Me. And he who loves
son or daughter more than Me is not worthy of Me. And he who does not
take his cross and follow after Me is not worthy of Me. He who finds his
life will lose it, and he who loses his life for My sake will find it."

a. **Whoever confesses Me before men, him I will also confess before My
Father who is in heaven**: The disciple must confess Jesus *publicly* – **before
men**. If we will not be public about our allegiance to Him, we cannot
expect Him to be public about His allegiance to us.

> i. Everyone Jesus called He called publicly. There is really no such thing
> as a "secret" Christian, at least not in a permanent sense. This is a
> contradiction in terms - an oxymoron.

> ii. Each individual Christian life should supply enough evidence
> – evidence that can be seen by the world – that they are indeed
> Christians. It is to be feared that many modern Christians, if arrested
> for the crime of following Jesus and tried in a court, would have the
> charges dismissed for a lack of evidence.

> iii. "What Christ is to you on earth, that you will be to Christ in
> heaven. I shall repeat that truth. Whatever Jesus Christ is to you on
> earth, you will be to him in the day of judgment. If he be dear and
> precious to you, you will be precious and dear to him. If you thought
> everything of him, he will think everything of you." (Spurgeon)

> iv. Yet we dare not miss that Jesus here claimed that one's eternal
> destiny depended upon their response to *Him*. "This 'egocentricity' is
> a striking characteristic of the teaching of Jesus. 'It is without parallel
> in the world of Jesus' (Jeremias, *NTT*, pp. 250-255). Even more
> remarkably, the saying is patterned on 1 Samuel 2:30, where the one
> honoured or despised is God himself." (France)

b. **Do not think that I came to bring peace on earth. I did not come
to bring peace but a sword**: The message of Jesus – as reflected in the
Sermon on the Mount – is indeed a message of peace. Yet since it calls
the individual to a radical commitment to Jesus Himself, it is a message
of peace that *divides* between those who choose it and those who reject it.
The division between these two choices explains how Jesus **did not come
to bring peace but a sword**.

c. **For I have come to "set a man against his father"…and "a man's enemies will be those of his own household"**: The dividing line between those who accept Jesus and those who reject Him would even run through families. The **sword** Jesus spoke of would sometimes cut through families.

d. **He who loves father or mother more than Me is not worthy of Me**: In strong terms, Jesus explained that the disciple must love and follow Jesus supremely. Our devotion to Jesus must come above even our **own household**.

> i. We should expect that normally, following Jesus makes us *better* husbands, fathers, wives, mothers, sons, daughters and so forth. Yet there are times when the presence of Jesus divides rather than unifies.

> ii. The greatest danger of idolatry comes not from what is bad, but from what is *good* - like love in family relationships. The greatest danger to the *best* comes from *second best*.

e. **Take his cross and follow after Me**: The disciple must follow Jesus even to the place of taking **his cross**. When a person took a cross in Jesus' day, it was for one reason: to die. The ancient Roman cross did not negotiate, did not compromise, and did not make deals. There was no looking back when you took up your cross, and your only hope was in *resurrection* life.

> i. **His cross**: Your **cross** isn't really your particular trial or trouble. The cross means one thing: *death* - death to self, but resurrection life unto God.

> ii. This is the first mention of the **cross** in Matthew's Gospel, and it is not directly associated with Jesus' own crucifixion. Such an extreme statement – likening discipleship with the horror of crucifixion, something too terrible to be mentioned in polite company – must have jarred the disciples.

> iii. Yet they knew what the **cross** was all about. "Crucifixion itself was not an uncommon sight in Roman Palestine; 'cross-bearing' language would have a clear enough meaning, even before they realized how literally he himself was to exemplify it." (France)

> iv. "When the Roman general, Varus, had broken the revolt of Judas in Galilee [4 BC], he crucified two thousand Jews, and placed the crosses by the wayside along the roads to Galilee." (Barclay)

f. **He who finds his life will lose it, and he who loses his life for My sake will find it**: The disciple lives in a paradox. He can only find life by losing it, and he can only live by dying. Resurrection life can only come after we take up our cross to follow Jesus.

i. "Bearing the cross, we are to *follow after* Jesus: to bear a cross without following Christ is a poor affair. A Christian who shuns the cross is no Christian; but a crossbearer who does not follow Jesus equally misses the mark." (Spurgeon)

7. (40-42) The reward due to those who, in contrast to the persecutors, receive the disciples of Jesus.

"He who receives you receives Me, and he who receives Me receives Him who sent Me. He who receives a prophet in the name of a prophet shall receive a prophet's reward. And he who receives a righteous man in the name of a righteous man shall receive a righteous man's reward. And whoever gives one of these little ones only a cup of cold *water* in the name of a disciple, assuredly, I say to you, he shall by no means lose his reward."

a. **He who receives you receives Me**: The good done to Jesus' disciples is as if it were good done to Jesus Himself, because they are His representatives, carrying on His ministry.

b. **He who receives a prophet in the name of a prophet shall receive a prophet's reward**: We can share in the reward of God's servants by supporting them in their work. Even seemingly insignificant works of kindness (**a cup of cold water**) performed for God's people are meaningful in God's eyes.

i. What could seem more insignificant than giving a person **a cup of cold water**? In a short time, they will be thirsty again. Yet even such a small gesture will always be remembered and rewarded by God. They **shall by no means lose** their **reward**.

ii. "Of Midas it is fabled, that whatever he touched turned into gold. Sure it is that whatsoever the hand of charity touch, be it but a cup of cold water, it turns the same, not into gold, but into heaven itself." (Trapp)

iii. "Again it is not philanthropy which is in view, but reception of a disciple *because he is a disciple* (again literally 'in the name of')." (France) The promise is that those who are His disciples really do represent Him, with both the cost and the reward.

iv. "'These little ones' surely includes all the apostles, prophets, and righteous men; they are all 'little ones' because they are all targets of the world's enmity." (Carson)

Matthew 11 – Not the Messiah they Expected Him to Be

A. Jesus and John the Baptist.

1. (1-3) John the Baptist's disciples ask a question on behalf of John to Jesus: are You really the Messiah (**the Coming One**)?

Now it came to pass, when Jesus finished commanding His twelve disciples, that He departed from there to teach and to preach in their cities. And when John had heard in prison about the works of Christ, he sent two of his disciples and said to Him, "Are You the Coming One, or do we look for another?"

a. **When Jesus finished commanding His twelve disciples**: According to Bruce, **to preach in their cities** does not refer to the cities of the disciples, but the cities of Galilee. In this way Jesus gave His commissioned disciples room to do their work.

b. **He sent two of his disciples**: It is also possible – but perhaps less likely – that John did not ask this question for his own sake, but for the sake of his disciples - he wanted them to go to Jesus and ask the question for themselves, causing them to focus their attention on Jesus.

i. "John's arrest was mentioned in Matthew 4:12; the full story of his imprisonment will wait until Matthew 14:3-12." (France)

ii. "Herod Antipas of Galilee had paid a visit to his brother in Rome. During that visit he seduced his brother's wife. He came home again, dismissed his own wife, and married the sister-in-law whom he had lured away from her husband. Publicly and sternly John rebuked Herod. It was never safe to rebuke an eastern despot and Herod took his revenge; John was thrown into the dungeons of the fortress of Machaerus in the mountains near the Dead Sea." (Barclay)

c. **Are You the Coming One, or do we look for another**: John 1:29-36 and other passages indicated that before this, John clearly recognized Jesus as the Messiah. His present doubt may be explained because perhaps he himself had misunderstood the ministry of the Messiah. Perhaps he thought that if Jesus were really the Messiah, He would perform works connected with a political deliverance of Israel - or at least the deliverance of John, who was in prison.

> i. It is possible that John made a mistaken distinction between **the Coming One** and the Christ, the Messiah. There is some indication that some Jews of that time distinguished between a prophet to come promised by Moses (Deuteronomy 18:15) and the Messiah. The dominant note here is one of *confusion*; John's long trial in prison has confused him.

2. (4-6) Jesus' answer to John the Baptist's disciples: tell John that prophecy regarding the Messiah is being fulfilled.

Jesus answered and said to them, "Go and tell John the things which you hear and see: *The* blind see and *the* lame walk; *the* lepers are cleansed and *the* deaf hear; *the* dead are raised up and *the* poor have the gospel preached to them. And blessed is he who is not offended because of Me."

> a. **Go and tell John the things which you hear and see**: Jesus wanted to assure both John and his disciples that He was the Messiah. But He also reminded them that His power would be displayed mostly in humble acts of service, meeting individual needs, and not in spectacular displays of political deliverance.

> > i. We might phrase John's question like this: "Jesus, why aren't You doing more?" Morgan answered this: "To all such restless impatience, He utters the same warning…For the most part, the way of the Lord's service is the way of plodding perseverance in the doing of apparently small things. The history of the Church shows that this is one of the lessons most difficult to learn."

> > ii. "Why is it that, in these days, it is said that the miracles are rather a trial of faith than a support of it? An unbelieving generation turns even food into poison." (Spurgeon)

> b. **Blessed is he who is not offended because of Me**: Jesus knew that the focus of His ministry was offensive to the expectation of the Jewish people, who longed for political deliverance from Roman domination. But there was a blessing for those who were **not offended** because of the Messiah who came against the expectation of the people.

i. "A friend has turned these words into another beatitude – The blessedness of the unoffended." (Meyer)

ii. "Blessed is he who can be left in prison, can be silenced in his testimony, can seem to be deserted of his Lord, and yet can shut out every doubt. John speedily regained this blessedness, and fully recovered his serenity." (Spurgeon)

3. (7-15) Jesus speaks about John.

As they departed, Jesus began to say to the multitudes concerning John: "What did you go out into the wilderness to see? A reed shaken by the wind? But what did you go out to see? A man clothed in soft garments? Indeed, those who wear soft *clothing* are in kings' houses. But what did you go out to see? A prophet? Yes, I say to you, and more than a prophet. For this is *he* of whom it is written: 'Behold, I send My messenger before Your face, who will prepare Your way before You.' Assuredly, I say to you, among those born of women there has not risen one greater than John the Baptist; but he who is least in the kingdom of heaven is greater than he. And from the days of John the Baptist until now the kingdom of heaven suffers violence, and the violent take it by force. For all the prophets and the law prophesied until John. And if you are willing to receive *it*, he is Elijah who is to come. He who has ears to hear, let him hear!"

a. **A prophet...and more than a prophet**: Jesus reminded them that John was God's chosen herald of the Messiah, not a man-pleaser or a self-pleaser. He was in fact **more than a prophet**, because he alone had the ministry of serving as the Messiah's herald. For that, he was the greatest of prophets and the greatest of men (**among those born of women there has not risen one greater than John the Baptist**).

i. **This is he of whom it is written**: Matthew noted that this ministry of the Messiah's herald was prophesied in Isaiah 40:3 and Malachi 3:1.

ii. Though some might put John in a bad light because of his seeming doubts regarding Jesus, Jesus Himself spoke quite highly of John. "John had often borne witness to Jesus; now Jesus bears witness of John." (Carson)

- John was *steady*, not shaken easily like a reed.
- John was *sober*, in that he lived a disciplined life, not in love with the luxuries and comforts of this world.
- John was a *servant*, a prophet of God.
- John was *sent*, as the special messenger of the Lord.

- John was *special*, in that he could be considered the greatest under the Old Covenant.

- John was *second* to even the least in the kingdom under the New Covenant.

b. **He who is least in the kingdom of heaven is greater than he**: Though John was great, he was not born again under the New Covenant. This is because he lived and died before the completion of Jesus' work at the cross and empty tomb. Therefore, he did not enjoy the benefits of the New Covenant (1 Corinthians 11:25, 2 Corinthians 3:6, Hebrews 8:6-13).

i. "As we may say, as a rule, that the darkest day is lighter than the brightest night; so John, though first of his own order, is behind the last of the new or Gospel order. The least in the Gospel stands on higher ground than the greatest under the law." (Spurgeon)

c. **The kingdom of heaven suffers violence, and the violent take it by force**: Jesus' reference to **violence** refers to both the intensity of spiritual warfare surrounding the ministry of Jesus and His herald, and also to the intensity required to persevere in following God and His kingdom.

i. The exact sense of this has been greatly debated, and is made more difficult by complicated grammar. Carson probably gives the best sense of both expressions. "The kingdom has come with holy power and magnificent energy that has been pushing back the frontiers of darkness. This is especially manifest in Jesus' miracles and ties in with Jesus' response to the Baptist…The kingdom is making great strides; now is the time for courageous souls, forceful people, to take hold of it." (Carson)

ii. The kingdom will never be received *passively*. It is always founded on God's work on our behalf, but God's work will always produce a response in us. "They are not lazy wishes or cold endeavours that will bring men to heaven." (Poole)

iii. "Frequently complaints are made and surprise expressed by individuals who have never found a blessing rest upon anything they have attempted to do in the service of God. 'I have been a Sunday-school teacher for years,' says one, 'and I have never seen any of my girls or boys converted.' No, and the reason most likely is you have never been violent about it; you have never been compelled by the Divine Spirit to make up your mind that converted they should be, and no stone should be left unturned until they were. You have never been brought by the Spirit to such a passion, that you have said, 'I cannot live unless God bless me. I cannot exist unless I see some of these children saved.' Then, falling on your knees in agony of prayer, and putting forth afterwards your trust with the same intensity towards heaven, you would never have been disappointed, 'for the violent take it by force.'" (Spurgeon)

d. **For all the prophets and the law prophesied until John**: Jesus saw an era ending with John; **all the prophets and the law** anticipated John and his ministry as a herald. There is a sense in which John spoke for every prophet who heralded Jesus' coming.

i. Under the Old Covenant, every other prophet announced, "The Messiah is coming." John alone had the privilege of saying, "The Messiah is here."

e. **And if you are willing to receive it, he is Elijah who is to come**: John may also be seen as Elijah, in a partial fulfillment of Malachi 4:5. John was not *actually* Elijah, but he served in the same spirit and power of Elijah, thus fulfilling his "office" (Luke 1:17). Because John was Elijah in this symbolic sense, Jesus added "**if you are willing to receive it.**"

i. Elijah did come in fact during Jesus' ministry, during the transfiguration (Matthew 17:3). But in further fulfillment of the Malachi 4:5 promise, Elijah will come again before the Second Coming of Jesus, likely as one of the two prophets of Revelation 11:3-12.

ii. If John the Baptist's ministry was like that of Elijah, we remember that Elijah became depressed and discouraged also.

iii. **He who has ears to hear, let him hear!** "A proverbial form of speech often used by Jesus after important utterances, here for the first time in Matthew." (Bruce)

4. (16-19) Jesus rebukes those who refuse to be pleased by either John the Baptist's or Jesus' ministry.

"But to what shall I liken this generation? It is like children sitting in the marketplaces and calling to their companions, and saying:

**'We played the flute for you,
And you did not dance;
We mourned to you,
And you did not lament.'**

For John came neither eating nor drinking, and they say, 'He has a demon.' The Son of Man came eating and drinking, and they say, 'Look, a glutton and a winebibber, a friend of tax collectors and sinners!' But wisdom is justified by her children."

a. **But to what shall I liken this generation**: Jesus here considered the nature of His current **generation**, and how they were choosy and uncertain in receiving God's message and His messengers.

b. **We played the flute for you, and you did not dance; we mourned to you, and you did not lament**: The idea is that those who have a heart to criticize will find something to criticize. Many people wouldn't be pleased with *either* John or Jesus.

i. "They refused to hear God's voice in either form, the somber or the joyful, in judgment or in mercy, if it did not accord with their conventions. There was no pleasing them." (France)

c. **A friend of tax collectors and sinners**: Jesus quoted the criticisms of others against Him. Though these words were meant to condemn, they have become wonderful. Jesus really is **a friend of...sinners**.

i. "A malicious nick-name at first, it is now a name of honour: the sinner's lover." (Bruce)

d. **But wisdom is justified by her children**: However, the wise man is proved to be wise by his wise actions (**her children**). Jesus had especially in mind the wisdom to accept *both* Jesus and John for what they were and what they were called to be.

i. People might criticize John, but look at what he *did* – he led thousands of people into repentance, preparing the way for the Messiah. People might criticize Jesus, but look at what He *did* – taught and worked and loved and died like no one ever has.

B. The condemned and the accepted.

1. (20-24) Jesus rebukes the cities that did not repent in light of both John the Baptist's ministry and Jesus' own ministry.

Then He began to rebuke the cities in which most of His mighty works had been done, because they did not repent: "Woe to you, Chorazin! Woe to you, Bethsaida! For if the mighty works which were done in you had been done in Tyre and Sidon, they would have repented long ago in sackcloth and ashes. But I say to you, it will be more tolerable for Tyre and Sidon in the day of judgment than for you. And you, Capernaum, who are exalted to heaven, will be brought down to Hades; for if the mighty works which were done in you had been done in Sodom, it would have remained until this day. But I say to you that it shall be more tolerable for the land of Sodom in the day of judgment than for you."

a. **He began to rebuke the cities in which most of His mighty works had been done, because they did not repent**: Because **most of His mighty**

works were done in these cities, they experienced a greater light, which also required a greater accountability.

i. This principle – greater light means greater responsibility – means that the western world has a tremendous accountability before God. The west has had an access to the gospel that no other society has, yet remains in desperate need of repentance.

ii. "Unresponsiveness to the voice of God is the characteristic of *this generation*, and will be its downfall." (France)

b. **It will be more tolerable**: When Jesus said that **it will be more tolerable** for certain cities in the day of judgment, He implied that there are in fact different degrees of judgment. Some will be punished more severely in the final judgment than others.

i. "There are degrees of felicity in paradise and degrees of torment in hell (Matthew 12:41; 23:13; cf. Luke 12:47-48), a point Paul well understood (Romans 1:20-2:16). The implications for Western, English speaking Christendom today are sobering." (Carson)

ii. "If Turks and Tartars shall be damned, debauched Christians shall be double-damned." (Trapp)

c. **Chorazin… Bethsaida… Capernaum**: God's judgment was fulfilled against these cities. Each one of them was destroyed long ago and has been desolate for generations upon generations.

i. We don't read in the gospels of the great works Jesus did in Chorazin or Bethsaida, but we are told something in John 21:25: *And there are also many other things that Jesus did, which if they were written one by one, I suppose that even the world itself could not contain the books that would be written*. What Jesus did in Chorazin and Bethsaida are among those unwritten works. This is a good reminder that the gospels are a true account of Jesus' life, but He did much that was not included in the gospel records.

ii. "Capernaum, his own city, the headquarters of the army of salvation, had seen and heard the Son of God…therefore he mourned to see Capernaum remain as hardened as ever." (Spurgeon)

iii. "These cities did not attack Jesus Christ; they did not drive him from their gates; they did not seek to crucify him; they simply disregarded him. Neglect can kill as much as persecution can." (Barclay)

2. (25-27) Jesus praises those who do receive His message.

At that time Jesus answered and said, "I thank You, Father, Lord of heaven and earth, that You have hidden these things from *the* wise and

prudent and have revealed them to babes. Even so, Father, for so it seemed good in Your sight. All things have been delivered to Me by My Father, and no one knows the Son except the Father. Nor does anyone know the Father except the Son, and *the one* to whom the Son wills to reveal *Him*."

a. **I thank You, Father, Lord of heaven and earth**: We sense a strong note of *joy* in Jesus' communication with His Father. The persons of the Trinity speak and commune with each other with joy.

i. "The use of the word 'answered' is suggestive, revealing the perpetual fact of communion existing between Christ and God. The note of praise was the response of Christ's heart to the secret of Jehovah." (Morgan)

b. **You have hidden these things from the wise and prudent and have revealed them to babes**: Jesus was happy that God had chosen the unlikely – seen by the world as **babes** – to respond to His message of the kingdom. This should be seen in the larger context of the rising rejection of Jesus and His messengers starting in Matthew 9.

i. It also reminds us that if we do respond to Jesus, it is because the Father has **revealed** these things to **babes** like us.

c. **Nor does anyone know the Father except the Son, and the one to whom the Son wills to reveal Him**: Since Jesus referred to Himself as **the Son**, we have another staggering self-focused statement from Jesus. Here He proclaimed that only *He* had a true relationship with God the **Father**, and that the Father could only be known through the Son (**to whom the Son wills to reveal Him**). These are astonishing self-claims.

i. Matthew 11:27 reveals much to us about the relationship between God the Father and God the Son.

- There are no secrets between the Father and the Son.
- There is no one who knows the Son as well as the Father does.
- There is no one who knows the Father as well as the Son does.
- The Son chooses to reveal the Father to some.

ii. There is an important difference in the way that the Son knows the Father, and the way we may know Him. We know God the Father because He stoops low to us to make Himself known. God the Son knows God the Father because they are equal in nature, completely compatible with one another.

3. (28-30) Jesus' invitation.

"Come to Me, all *you* who labor and are heavy laden, and I will give you rest. Take My yoke upon you and learn from Me, for I am gentle and lowly in heart, and you will find rest for your souls. For My yoke *is* easy and My burden is light."

a. **Come unto Me**: Jesus showed His authority when He says **come unto Me**. This invitation is unthinkable in the mouth of anyone else but God, and woe to the men who call people to themselves instead of to Jesus!

> i. "'*Come*'; he drives none away; he calls them to himself. His favorite word is 'Come.' Not, go to Moses – 'Come *unto me*.' To Jesus himself we must come, by a personal trust. Not to doctrine, ordinance, nor ministry are we to come first; but to the personal Saviour." (Spurgeon)

b. **All you who labor and are heavy laden**: Jesus directed His call to those who were burdened. He called those who sensed they must come to Him to relieve their need instead of living in self-sufficiency.

> i. According to Carson, **labor** implies the burdens we take upon ourselves, and **heavy laden** implies the burdens others put upon us.

> ii. **Heavy laden** suggests the same thought as Matthew 23:4, where Jesus spoke against the religious leaders of His day as those who *bind heavy burdens, hard to bear, and lay them on men's shoulders.*

c. **Take My yoke upon you and learn from Me**: Jesus made a wonderful offer, inviting us to **take My yoke upon you and learn from Me**. We must come as disciples to learn, willing to be guided by His yoke - not merely to receive something.

> i. According to Adam Clarke, the ancient Jews commonly used the idea of **yoke** to express someone's obligation to God. There was the yoke of the kingdom, the yoke of the law, the yoke of the command, the yoke of repentance, the yoke of faith, and the general yoke of God. In this context, it is easy to see Jesus simplifying and saying, "Forget about all those other yokes. **Take My yoke upon you and learn from Me.**"

> ii. When someone looks at the yoke of Jesus from a distance, it is easy to get all kinds of wrong ideas about it. But if we would just listen to what Jesus said – "**take My yoke upon you**" – we would take it, and see what kind of yoke it is.

> - The yoke of Jesus is easy and light as compared with the yoke of others.

> - The yoke of Jesus is easy and light as long as we do not rebel against it.

- The yoke of Jesus has nothing to do with worries that are forbidden to us.

- The yoke of Jesus does not include the burdens we choose to add to it.

d. **For I am gentle and lowly in heart**: Jesus revealed His nature when He described Himself as **gentle and lowly of heart**. It is His servant's heart, displayed throughout His ministry, making Him qualified to be the one who bears our burdens.

e. **And you will find rest for your souls**: Jesus described His gift to His followers as **rest for your soul**. This unmatchable gift – both powerful and profound – should be considered the birthright of those who come to Jesus and are His followers. They should believe that something is wrong if they don't experience **rest for your souls**.

   i. "*You will find rest for your souls* is an echo of the Hebrew text of Jeremiah 6:16, where it is the offer of God to those who follow his way; Jesus now issues the invitation in his own name!" (France)

f. **My yoke is easy and My burden is light**: Jesus summarized this wonderful call with this assurance. The **yoke is easy** and the **burden is light** because *He bears it with us*. Borne alone, it might be unbearable; but with Jesus it can be **easy** and **light**.

   i. When training a new animal (such as an ox) to plow, ancient farmers often yoked it to an older, stronger, more experienced animal who bore the burden and guided the young animal through the learning process.

   ii. "The word *easy* is in Greek *chrestos*, which can mean *well-fitting*. In Palestine ox-yokes were made of wood…The yoke was carefully adjusted, so that it would fit well, and not gall the neck of the patient beast. The yoke was tailor-made to fit the ox." (Barclay)

   iii. This isn't a call to a lazy or indulgent life. There is still a **yoke** to bear and **burden** to carry. Yet with and in Jesus, they are easy and light. "Jesus' yoke is *easy*, not because it makes lighter demands, but because it represents entering into a disciple-relationship." (France)

   iv. If your yoke is *hard* and your burden is *heavy*, then we can say that it isn't *His* yoke or burden, and you aren't letting Him bear it with you. Jesus said it plainly: **My yoke is easy and My burden is light**.

Matthew 12 - The Religious Leaders Continue to Reject Jesus

A. Sabbath controversies.

1. (1-2) The Pharisees condemn the disciples of Jesus for supposedly harvesting grain on the Sabbath.

At that time Jesus went through the grainfields on the Sabbath. And His disciples were hungry, and began to pluck heads of grain and to eat. And when the Pharisees saw *it*, they said to Him, "Look, Your disciples are doing what is not lawful to do on the Sabbath!"

a. **His disciples were hungry, and began to pluck the heads of grain and to eat**: There was nothing wrong with *what they did*, because their gleaning was not considered stealing according to Deuteronomy 23:25. The issue was only *the day* on which they did it. The rabbis made an elaborate list of "do" and "don't" items relevant to the Sabbath, and this violated several items on this list.

i. "We incidentally learn from this story that our Lord and his disciples were poor, and that he who fed the multitudes did not use his miraculous power to feed his own followers, but left them till they did what poor men are forced to do to supply a little stay for their stomachs." (Spurgeon)

ii. The law of Israel allowed people traveling through an area to glean enough grain for a small meal from fields in the area (Deuteronomy 23:25). Farmers were commanded to not completely harvest their crops to leave a little behind for the sake of travelers and the poor.

iii. Matthew just quoted Jesus offering us an easy yoke and a light burden. Now he shows us the kind of heavy burdens and hard yokes the religious leaders put upon the people. When the **disciples began**

to pluck the heads of grain, in the eyes of the religious leaders they were guilty of:

- Reaping.
- Threshing.
- Winnowing.
- Preparing food.

This represented four violations of the Sabbath in one mouthful!

iv. At this time, many rabbis filled Judaism with elaborate rituals related to the Sabbath and observance of other laws. Ancient rabbis taught that on the Sabbath a man could not carry something in his right hand or in his left hand, across his chest or on his shoulder; but he could carry something with the back of his hand, with his foot, elbow, or in the ear, on the hair, in the hem of his shirt, or in his shoe or sandal. On the Sabbath one was forbidden to tie a knot - except a woman could tie a knot in her girdle. So if a bucket of water had to be raised from a well, one could not tie a rope to the bucket, but a woman could tie her girdle to the bucket and then to the rope.

v. "The Jews were so superstitious, concerning the observance of the Sabbath, that in their wars with *Antiochus Epiphanes*, and the *Romans*, they thought it a crime even to attempt to defend themselves on the Sabbath: when their enemies observed this, they deterred their operations to that day. It was through this, that *Pompey* was enabled to take Jerusalem." (Clarke)

b. **Look, Your disciples are doing what is not lawful to do on the Sabbath**: Jesus never violated God's command to observe the Sabbath or approved of His disciples violating God's Sabbath command, but He often broke man's legalistic additions to that law and He sometimes seems to have *deliberately* broken those human additions.

i. Even some Jewish people in Jesus' day recognized that the rules about the Sabbath were mostly human additions to the law. Carson quotes an ancient Jewish writing that said, "The rules about the Sabbath…are as mountains hanging by a hair, for Scripture is scanty and the rules are many."

ii. The Pharisees here seem hard at work supervising and accusing the disciples. This was a greater violation of the Sabbath. "Did they not break the Sabbath by setting a watch over them?" (Spurgeon)

2. (3-8) Jesus defends His disciples.

But He said to them, "Have you not read what David did when he was hungry, he and those who were with him: how he entered the house of God and ate the showbread which was not lawful for him to eat, nor for those who were with him, but only for the priests? Or have you not read in the law that on the Sabbath the priests in the temple profane the Sabbath, and are blameless? Yet I say to you that in this place there is *One* greater than the temple. But if you had known what *this* means, 'I desire mercy and not sacrifice,' you would not have condemned the guiltless. For the Son of Man is Lord even of the Sabbath."

a. **Have you not read what David did when he was hungry**: The first principle Jesus presented is simple and illustrated by David's experience with the priests and the showbread (1 Samuel 21). Jesus reminded them that human need is more important than observing ceremonial rituals.

i. The incident with David was a valid defense, because:

- It was a case of eating.
- It probably happened on the Sabbath (1 Samuel 21:6).
- It concerned not only David, but also his followers.

ii. The *context* of David's taking the bread in 1 Samuel 21 shows that it was justified for him to do it. "To have eaten the holy bread out of profanity, or bravado, or levity, might have involved the offender in the judgment of death; but to do so in urgent need was not blameworthy in the case of David." (Spurgeon)

b. **The priests in the temple profane the Sabbath, and are blameless**: The second principle Jesus presented is also simple. **The priests** themselves break the Sabbath all the time. Perhaps the Pharisees didn't understand as much about Sabbath observance as they thought they did.

i. "The Temple ritual always involved work – the kindling of fires, the slaughter and the preparation of animals, the lifting of them on to the altar, and a host of other things. This work was actually doubled on the Sabbath, for on the Sabbath the offerings were doubled (cp. e.g. *Numbers* 28:9)." (Barclay)

ii. The reference to the passage **I desire mercy and not sacrifice** (Hosea 6:6), and the Pharisees' lack of understanding of this principle was also a way that Jesus questioned the confidence the Pharisees had in their man-made traditions. They used those traditions to justify lifting principles like **sacrifice** above principles like **mercy**, when God would have them do just the opposite.

iii. "Where two laws in respect of some circumstance seem to clash one with another, so as we cannot obey both, our obedience is due to that which is the more excellent law." (Poole)

c. **For the Son of Man is Lord even of the Sabbath**: The third principle was the most dramatic, based on who Jesus is. He is **greater than the temple**, even as much as they honored and valued the temple. Even more so, He **is Lord even of the Sabbath**.

i. This was a direct claim to Deity. Jesus said that He had the authority to know if His disciples broke the Sabbath law, because He is the **Lord even of the Sabbath**.

ii. Jesus was indeed **greater than the temple**. Considering how highly the temple was regarded in the days of Jesus, this was a shocking statement. Yet the temple as it stood in Jesus' day did not have the ark of the covenant, that important demonstration of the throne and presence of God. Yet Jesus was a much greater demonstration of the presence of God – He was God made flesh! The temple also lacked the *Shekinah*, the Urim and Thummim, and the sacred fire from heaven. Yet Jesus is all these things to us; He is surely greater than the temple.

iii. Since Jesus is **greater than the temple**, we should regard Him as so.

- The temple was admired with love and wonder; we should admire Jesus even more.

- The temple was joyfully visited; we should come to Jesus with even more joy.

- The temple was honored as a holy place; we should honor Jesus even more so.

- The temple was a place of sacrifice and service; we should do even more for Jesus.

- The temple was a place for worship; we should worship Jesus even more.

3. (9-14) A controversy regarding healing on the Sabbath.

Now when He had departed from there, He went into their synagogue. And behold, there was a man who had a withered hand. And they asked Him, saying, "Is it lawful to heal on the Sabbath?"; that they might accuse Him. Then He said to them, "What man is there among you who has one sheep, and if it falls into a pit on the Sabbath, will not lay hold of it and lift *it* out? Of how much more value then is a man than a sheep? Therefore it is lawful to do good on the Sabbath." Then He said to the man, "Stretch out your hand." And he stretched *it* out, and it was

restored as whole as the other. Then the Pharisees went out and plotted against Him, how they might destroy Him.

a. **He went into their synagogue**: A general theme through this section of Matthew is the rising opposition against Jesus. Sometimes this opposition is expressed against Him directly and sometimes attacks on His disciples. Yet we see that Jesus, as a faithful Jewish man, continued to go to **synagogue** normally. We might say that Jesus was a faithful church-going man, even when He had reason not to be.

i. "Jesus set the example of attending public worship. The synagogues had no divine appointment to authorize them, but in the nature of things it must be right and good to meet for the worship of God on his own day, and therefore Jesus was there. He had nothing to learn, yet he went up to the assembly on the day which the Lord God had hallowed." (Spurgeon)

b. **A man who had a withered hand**: At best, the religious leaders saw the man with the **withered hand** as an interesting test case. It is more likely that they saw the man as bait for a Sabbath controversy trap for Jesus. In contrast, Jesus looked at the man through eyes of compassion.

i. These accusers also *knew* Jesus would do something when He saw this man in need. In this sense, these critics had more faith than many of us. We sometimes seem to doubt that Jesus wants to really or miraculously meet the needs of others.

c. **Is it lawful to heal on the Sabbath**: Jesus exposed their hypocrisy by showing their greater concern for their own possessions than for a man in need, arguing persuasively that it can't be wrong to do good on the Sabbath. Then Jesus compassionately healed the man.

i. "The *withered hand* was literally 'dry', *i.e.* lifeless, perhaps paralysed; the man was thus not in imminent danger of death, which alone justified treatment on the sabbath according to Mishnah *Yoma* 8:6. He could just as well be healed the next day." (France)

d. **Stretch out your hand**: When Jesus commanded the man "**stretch out your hand**," He commanded the man to do something impossible in his current condition. But Jesus gave both the command and the ability to fulfill it, and the man put forth the effort and was healed.

i. "The man's hand was withered; but God's mercy had still preserved to him the use of his feet: He uses them to bring him to the public worship of God, and Jesus meets and heals him there." (Clarke)

ii. "He stretched out his restored hand, assuming that not till restored could the hand be stretched out. The healing and the outstretching may be conceived as contemporaneous." (Bruce)

iii. "Christ sometimes used the ceremony of laying on his hand; here he doth not, to let us know that that was but a sign of what was done by his power." (Poole)

e. **Then the Pharisees went out and plotted against Him, how they might destroy Him**: In response to this display of compassion, power, and wisdom the Pharisees, in the hardness of their hearts, did not respond in reverent worship and submission but in hardened, murderous rejection.

i. This is a significant development in the opposition against Jesus from the religious leaders. "Hitherto, they had been content with finding fault; now it is come to plotting against His life – a tribute to His power...Such is the evil fruit of Sabbath controversies." (Bruce)

ii. Luke 6:11 says that the critics of Jesus were *filled with rage* when Jesus healed this man. Which was more a violation of the Sabbath: When Jesus healed a man, or when these hate-filled men **plotted** the murder of a godly Man who never sinned against anybody?

4. (15-21) In spite of the rejection of the religious leaders, the common people still follow Jesus, and He remains God's chosen servant.

But when Jesus knew *it*, He withdrew from there. And great multitudes followed Him, and He healed them all. Yet He warned them not to make Him known, that it might be fulfilled which was spoken by Isaiah the prophet, saying:

"Behold! My Servant whom I have chosen,
My Beloved in whom My soul is well pleased!
I will put My Spirit upon Him,
And He will declare justice to the Gentiles.
He will not quarrel nor cry out,
Nor will anyone hear His voice in the streets.
A bruised reed He will not break,
And smoking flax He will not quench,
Till He sends forth justice to victory;
And in His name Gentiles will trust."

a. **But when Jesus knew it, He withdrew from there**: For a time, Jesus withdrew somewhat from public ministry as the opposition rose against Him. This was not out of cowardice, but in respect to God the Father's timing for the course and culmination of His ministry. It could not be allowed to peak too soon.

b. **And great multitudes followed Him, and He healed them all**: Jesus did what He could to escape the press of the crowds, but the crowds simply followed Him. Nevertheless, He responded with compassion and **He healed them all**.

i. This is one of the few references in the gospels of Jesus healing **all** on a specific occasion, yet it is important and appropriate here. Matthew wants us to know that the press of the crowd did not make Jesus impatient or angry. He also wants us to know that the determination of this crowd was evidence of their faith; therefore, **all** were healed.

c. **Behold! My Servant whom I have chosen**: The quotation from Isaiah 42:1-5 speaks of the gentle character of the Messiah, who is the **Servant** of Yahweh. This was a common and important designation of Jesus.

i. Jesus described Himself as a servant in Matthew 20:25-28, Matthew 23:11, Mark 9:35, Mark 10:43-45. Peter, in his Acts 3 sermon, gives our Savior the title *His Servant Jesus* (Acts 3:13 and 3:26). In Acts 4, the praying people of God spoke of *Your holy Servant Jesus* (Acts 4:27, 4:30). But Jesus isn't just *a* servant. He is *The Servant*, and everyone should **behold**, as the LORD says, **My Servant**.

ii. Jesus the **Servant** is an *example* to us as servants, but He is so much *more* than that. He is our **Servant**. He serves us; not only in what He did in the past, but also He serves us every day through His constant love, care, guidance, and intercession. Jesus did not stop serving when He went to heaven; He serves all His people *more effectively than ever* from heaven.

d. **He will not quarrel nor cry out, nor will anyone hear His voice in the streets**: This doesn't mean that Jesus never spoke loudly. It refers to His gentle, lowly heart and actions. Jesus didn't make His way by an overpowering personality and loud, overwhelming talk. Instead, Jesus made an impression upon others by the Spirit of God upon Him.

e. **A bruised reed He will not break, and smoking flax He will not quench**: This is another reference to the gentle character of Jesus. A reed is a fairly fragile plant, yet if a reed is **bruised** the Servant will handle it so gently that **He will not break** it. And if flax, used as a wick for an oil lamp, does not flame but only smokes, He will not **quench** it into extinguishing. Instead, the Servant will gently nourish the **smoking flax**, fanning it into flame again.

i. Often we feel that God deals roughly with our weaknesses and failures. Just the opposite is true. He deals with them gently, tenderly, helping them along until the **bruised reed** is strong and the **smoking flax** is in proper flame.

ii. Jesus sees the value in a **bruised reed**, even when no one else can. He can make beautiful music come from a **bruised reed**, as He puts His strength in it! Though a **smoking flax** is good for nothing, Jesus knows it is valuable for what it can be when it is refreshed with oil. Many of us are like the **bruised reed**, and we need to *be strengthened with might through His Spirit in the inner man* (Ephesians 3:16). Others are like the **smoking flax**, and can only burn brightly for the LORD again when we are drenched in oil, with a constant supply coming, as we are filled with the Holy Spirit.

f. **In His name Gentiles will trust**: Finally, the quotation from Isaiah 42 also speaks of the ultimate ministry of Jesus to the Gentiles. This was something surprising - and perhaps even offensive - to Matthew's Jewish readers, but it is obviously Scriptural, according to Isaiah 42.

B. Continuing rejection by the religious leaders.

1. (22-24) Jesus delivers a man possessed by a demon.

Then one was brought to Him who was demon-possessed, blind and mute; and He healed him, so that the blind and mute man both spoke and saw. And all the multitudes were amazed and said, "Could this be the Son of David?" Now when the Pharisees heard *it* they said, "This *fellow* does not cast out demons except by Beelzebub, the ruler of the demons."

a. **He healed him, so that the blind and mute man both spoke and saw**: Again, Jesus displayed His complete power and authority over demons, casting out demonic powers that the traditions of the day considered impossible.

b. **Could this be the Son of David**: The crowds reacted with Messianic expectation, but the religious leaders responded by attributing Jesus' power to the prince of demons (**This fellow does not cast out demons except by Beelzebub**).

i. "The Pharisees' accusation amounts to a charge of sorcery, one which continued to be leveled against Jesus in later Jewish polemic." (France)

ii. "Let others censure with the Pharisees; let us wonder with the multitudes." (Trapp)

2. (25-29) Jesus answers the accusation that He works by Satan's power.

But Jesus knew their thoughts, and said to them: "Every kingdom divided against itself is brought to desolation, and every city or house

divided against itself will not stand. If Satan casts out Satan, he is divided against himself. How then will his kingdom stand? And if I cast out demons by Beelzebub, by whom do your sons cast *them* out? Therefore they shall be your judges. But if I cast out demons by the Spirit of God, surely the kingdom of God has come upon you. Or how can one enter a strong man's house and plunder his goods, unless he first binds the strong man? And then he will plunder his house.

a. **But Jesus knew their thoughts**: This was remarkable, but not necessarily a mark of the divinity of Jesus. The Holy Spirit can give the gift of supernatural knowledge to an individual (the *word of knowledge* mentioned in 1 Corinthians 12:8).

b. **Every kingdom divided against itself is brought to desolation**: Jesus logically observed that it makes no sense for Satan to cast out Satan. The Pharisees needed to explain how *Satan* benefited by the work Jesus had just done.

i. "One devil may yield and give place to another, to gain a greater advantage for the whole society, but one never quarrelleth with another." (Poole)

ii. "Satan may be wicked, He says in effect, but he is not a fool." (Bruce) "Whatever fault the devils have, they are not at strife with each other; that fault is reserved for the servants of a better Master." (Spurgeon)

c. **By whom do your sons cast them out**: Jesus asked a question based on their (wrong) premise that He operated by Satan's power. If that were true, then how did their own Jewish exorcists cast them out?

i. "The Jewish exorcists operated in conventional fashion by use of herbs and magical formulae, and the results were probably insignificant. The practice was sanctioned by custom, and harmless. But in casting out devils, as in all other things, Jesus was original, and His method was *too effectual*. His power, manifest to all, was His offence." (Bruce)

ii. "Envy causes persons often to *condemn* in *one*, what they *approve* in *another*." (Spurgeon)

iii. **I cast out demons by the Spirit of God**: "Though our Lord had power all his own, he honored the Spirit of God, and worked by his energy, and mentioned the fact that he did so." (Spurgeon)

d. **And then he will plunder his house**: Using an analogy, Jesus explained His authority to bind Satan's power. He is stronger than the **strong man** is. In so doing, Jesus presented a valuable principle in spiritual warfare as we remember that Jesus gives us the permission to use His name and authority, giving us the strength we need in binding the **strong man**.

i. Jesus also made it clear that He was the *stronger man* who was not captive under the **strong man**. His message was, "I'm not under Satan's power. Instead, I'm proving that I am stronger than he is by casting him out of those he has possessed." "The very fact that I have been able so successfully to invade Satan's territory is proof that he is bound and powerless to resist." (Barclay)

ii. Jesus looks at every life delivered from Satan's domination and says, "I'm plundering the kingdom of Satan one life at a time." There is *nothing* in our life that *must* stay under Satan's domination. The One who binds the strong man and **will plunder his goods** is our risen Lord.

3. (30-32) Jesus reveals the desperate place of those who could be hardened enough to attribute His workings to Satanic power.

"He who is not with Me is against Me, and he who does not gather with Me scatters abroad. Therefore I say to you, every sin and blasphemy will be forgiven men, but the blasphemy *against* the Spirit will not be forgiven men. Anyone who speaks a word against the Son of Man, it will be forgiven him; but whoever speaks against the Holy Spirit, it will not be forgiven him, either in this age or in the *age* to come."

a. **He who is not with Me is against Me**: Jesus first removed illusions about any neutral response to Him or His work. If one is not for Him, then that one is against Him. If one does not work with Jesus, by either active opposition or passive disregard, that one works against Jesus (**he who does not gather with Me scatters abroad**).

i. "Only two forces are at work in the world, the gathering and the scattering. Whoever does the one contradicts the other." (Morgan)

b. **Blasphemy against the Spirit will not be forgiven**: Jesus solemnly warned the religious leaders against rejecting Him. Their rejection of Jesus – especially considered what they had seen of Jesus and His work – showed that they were *completely* rejecting the Holy Spirit's ministry. That ministry is to testify to Jesus, hence the warning of committing the unforgivable sin.

i. The Holy Spirit's main ministry is to testify of Jesus (*He will testify of Me*, John 15:26). When that testimony of Jesus is fully and finally rejected, one has truly blasphemed the Holy Spirit and essentially called Him a liar in respect to His testimony about Jesus. The religious leaders were close to this.

ii. To reject Jesus from a distance or with little information is bad; to reject the *testimony of the Holy Spirit about Jesus* is fatal.

c. **It will not be forgiven him, either in this age or in the age to come**: The eternal consequences of this sin force us to regard it seriously. Therefore, how can one know if they have in fact blasphemed the Holy Spirit? The fact that one desires Jesus *at all* shows that they are not guilty of this sin. Yet continued rejection of Jesus makes us more hardened against Him and puts us on the path of a full and final rejection of Him.

i. Some people – as a joke or a dare – *intentionally* say words they suppose commit the sin of **blasphemy against the Spirit**. They think it a light thing to joke with eternity. Yet true **blasphemy against the Spirit** is more than a formula of words; it is a settled disposition of life that rejects the testimony of the Holy Spirit regarding Jesus. Even if someone has intentionally said such things, they can still repent and prevent a *settled* rejection of Jesus.

ii. "Many sincere people have been grievously troubled with apprehensions that they had committed the unpardonable sin; but let it be observed that no man who believes the Divine mission of Jesus Christ, ever can commit this sin: therefore let no man's heart fail because of it, from henceforth and for ever, Amen." (Clarke)

4. (33-37) The words of the religious leaders betray the depravity of their hearts.

"Either make the tree good and its fruit good, or else make the tree bad and its fruit bad; for a tree is known by *its* fruit. Brood of vipers! How can you, being evil, speak good things? For out of the abundance of the heart the mouth speaks. A good man out of the good treasure of his heart brings forth good things, and an evil man out of the evil treasure brings forth evil things. But I say to you that for every idle word men may speak, they will give account of it in the day of judgment. For by your words you will be justified, and by your words you will be condemned."

a. **A tree is known by its fruit**: The bad fruit of their words (when they condemned Jesus) betrayed the bad root growing in their hearts. If they got their hearts right with God, their words about Jesus would also be right.

b. **Brood of vipers!** With these words, Jesus essentially called the religious leaders "sons of Satan." They were a generation associated with the serpent, not with God. It was this evil nature that made them speak evil of Jesus (**How can you, being evil, speak good things**).

c. **Out of the abundance of the heart the mouth speaks**: Our words reveal our heart. If there were **good treasure** in the heart of these religious leaders, it would show itself in **good things**.

i. **For every idle word men may speak, they will give account of it in the day of judgment**: "Idle and wasted words are to be accounted for; what then of evil and wicked?" (Trapp)

ii. Adam Clarke said that the sense of the ancient Greek word used for an **idle word** is "a word that *does nothing*, that neither ministers *grace* nor *instruction* to them who hear it." If this is true, many preachers might find themselves guilty of this sin.

d. **By your words you will be justified and by your words you will be condemned**: By this Jesus answered an anticipated objection – that He made too much of mere words. Instead, because words reflect the heart, one can be rightly judged by their words.

i. Paul also wrote about the importance of our words: *That if you confess with your mouth the Lord Jesus and believe in your heart that God has raised Him from the dead, you will be saved.* (Romans 10:9)

C. The scribes and Pharisees request a sign from Jesus.

1. (38-40) Jesus responds to the request from the scribes and Pharisees.

Then some of the scribes and Pharisees answered, saying, "Teacher, we want to see a sign from You." But He answered and said to them, "An evil and adulterous generation seeks after a sign, and no sign will be given to it except the sign of the prophet Jonah. For as Jonah was three days and three nights in the belly of the great fish, so will the Son of Man be three days and three nights in the heart of the earth."

a. **Teacher, we want to see a sign from You**: Their desire to see a sign really expressed another way in which they hoped to reject Him. If Jesus *did* provide a sign, they would find some way to speak against it, thus proving to themselves that Jesus was who they already thought He was - an emissary of Satan (Matthew 12:24).

i. "The apparent respect and earnestness of the request are feigned: 'teacher, we desire from *you* (emphatic position) to see a sign'. It reminds one of the mock homage of the soldiers at the Passion (Matthew 27:27-31)." (Bruce)

ii. "Had not Christ shown them signs enough? What were all the miracles he had wrought in their sight? They either speak this out of a further idle curiosity...or else they speak it in direct opposition." (Poole)

b. **An evil and adulterous generation seeks after a sign**: Jesus condemned their seeking after a sign, especially when countless signs had already happened before their eyes. It is easy to overestimate the power of miraculous signs to change the heart of doubters and skeptics.

c. **The sign of the prophet Jonah**: Jesus assured them of a sign, but the great sign He would show was the sign of a resurrected Jesus. **Jonah** was a **prophet** in the sense beyond his preaching to Nineveh; also his life was a prophecy of the death and resurrection of Jesus.

d. **As Jonah was three days and three nights in the belly of the great fish**: Jonah was indeed a picture of the work of Jesus. Jonah gave his life to appease the wrath of God coming upon others. But death did not hold him; after three days and nights of imprisonment, he was alive and free. This is a glorious picture of Jesus in an unexpected place.

> i. Because Jesus here refers to **three days and three nights**, some think that Jesus had to spend at least 72 hours in the grave. This upsets most chronologies of the death and resurrection of Jesus, and is unnecessary - because it doesn't take into account the use of ancient figures of speech. Rabbi Eleazar ben Azariah (around the year AD 100; cited in Clarke and other sources) explained this way of speaking when he wrote: "A day and a night make a whole day, and a portion of a whole day is reckoned as a whole day." This demonstrates how in Jesus' day, the phrase **three days and three nights** did not necessarily mean a full 72-hour period, but a period including at least the portions of three days and three nights. There may be other good reasons for challenging the traditional chronology of Jesus' death and resurrection, but it is not necessary in order to fulfill the words of Jesus here.

> ii. If Jesus rose from the dead on the first day or on the fifth day, we could say "Jesus was a liar and a false prophet. He said He would rise again on the third day, but He got it wrong." But Jesus didn't get it wrong. He never does.

> iii. Yet we should not miss the central point here. "You are asking for a sign – *I am God's sign*. You have failed to recognize me. The Ninevites recognized God's warning in Jonah; the Queen of Sheba recognized God's wisdom in Solomon." (Barclay)

2. (41-42) Jesus announces the condemnation of the religious leaders at the hands of the Ninevites and the queen of the South.

"The men of Nineveh will rise up in the judgment with this generation and condemn it, because they repented at the preaching of Jonah; and indeed a greater than Jonah *is* here. The queen of the South will rise up in the judgment with this generation and condemn it, for she came

from the ends of the earth to hear the wisdom of Solomon; and indeed a greater than Solomon *is* here."

a. **The men of Nineveh will rise up in the judgment with this generation and condemn it**: Simply put, greater light requires greater judgment. Both **Nineveh** and **the queen of the South** repented even though they had a lesser light shining in their midst. The rejection of the greater light by the religious leaders was indefensible.

i. Adam Clarke described several ways that the witness of Jesus was **greater than Jonah**.

- "Christ, who preached to the Jews, was infinitely greater than Jonah, in his nature, person, and mission."

- "Jonah preached repentance in Nineveh only *forty* days, and Christ preached among the Jews for several years."

- "Jonah wrought no miracles to authorize his preaching; but Christ wrought miracles every day, in every place where he went, and of every kind."

- "Notwithstanding all this, the people of Judea did not repent, though the people of Nineveh did."

b. **A greater than Solomon is here**: Solomon was the son of David, and one of the great messianic titles of Jesus is "Son of David." Jesus was a much **greater** Son of David than Solomon was.

i. We again are impressed by the greatness of Jesus' self-claim. To stand in front of these religious leaders and claim to be **greater** than Israel's richest and wisest king was audacious. Yet the seeming audacity of Jesus was well justified.

3. (43-45) The dangerous consequences of their rejection of Jesus.

"When an unclean spirit goes out of a man, he goes through dry places, seeking rest, and finds none. Then he says, 'I will return to my house from which I came.' And when he comes, he finds *it* empty, swept, and put in order. Then he goes and takes with him seven other spirits more wicked than himself, and they enter and dwell there; and the last *state* of that man is worse than the first. So shall it also be with this wicked generation."

a. **When an unclean spirit goes out of a man**: In context, the main point of Jesus was not upon principles of demon possession. He explained the seriousness of rejecting Him as completely as the religious leaders had.

i. This rejection and opposition of Jesus would leave them much worse off than ever before. **This wicked generation** – exemplified by the

religious leaders who were rejecting Jesus – would find their **last state…
worse than the first**. In large measure they rejected Jesus because He
wasn't messianic *enough* for their taste, in the sense of being a political
and military messiah. Yet their thirst for this kind of messiah would
lead them to ruin by AD 70.

ii. Yet the use of the illustration shows us some interesting principles
of demon possession, and shows us that Jesus regarded it as a real
phenomenon and not just a contemporary superstition. "If there
had been no reality in demoniacal possessions, our Lord would have
scarcely appealed to a case of this kind here, to point out the real state
of the Jewish people, and the desolation which was coming upon
them." (Clarke)

b. **When an unclean spirit goes out of a man, he goes through dry
places, seeking rest, and finds none**: Apparently demons (or at least some
of them) desire a human host and look for a place among the empty, seeing
it as an invitation.

i. "The devil cannot be at rest where he hath no mischief to do to
men." (Poole)

ii. **I will return to my house**: "The foul fiend calls the man, '*My
house.*' His audacity is amazing. He did not build or buy that house,
and he has no right to it." (Spurgeon)

iii. A demon can only inhabit someone if **he finds it empty** – that is,
without the indwelling Spirit of Jesus Christ. If it is **empty**, it does not
matter to the demon if it is also **swept, and put in order**. "The devil
has no objection to his house being swept and garnished; for a moralist
may be as truly his slave as the man of debauched habits. So long as
the heart is not occupied by his great foe, and he can use the man for
his own purposes, the adversary of souls will let him reform as much
as he pleases." (Spurgeon)

iv. If we are filled with Jesus – being born again by the Spirit of God –
then we cannot be empty and therefore inhabited by demons. "Though
he shake his chain at us, he cannot fasten his fangs in us." (Trapp)

c. **And the last state of that man is worse than the first**: This presses the
urgency of being filled with the Spirit of Jesus Christ. There is something
worse than being simply demon possessed; one can be possessed in a greater
measure unto great misery. The answer to such misery is to be filled with
the Spirit of Jesus Christ.

4. (46-50) Jesus identifies His true family.

While He was still talking to the multitudes, behold, His mother and brothers stood outside, seeking to speak with Him. Then one said to Him, "Look, Your mother and Your brothers are standing outside, seeking to speak with You." But He answered and said to the one who told Him, "Who is My mother and who are My brothers?" And He stretched out His hand toward His disciples and said, "Here are My mother and My brothers! For whoever does the will of My Father in heaven is My brother and sister and mother."

a. **His mother and brothers stood outside, seeking to speak with Him**: Considering the general context of opposition to Jesus, it may well be that the family of Jesus wanted to appeal to Him to not be so controversial in His ministry.

i. "The members of his family had come to take him, because they thought him beside himself. No doubt the Pharisees had so represented his ministry to his relatives that they thought they had better restrain him." (Spurgeon)

b. **Who is My mother and who are My brothers**: We might have expected that Jesus' family would have special privileges before Him. It almost surprises us that they did not have such special privileges.

i. **Who is My mother**: Mary, the mother of Jesus, had no special favor with Jesus either then or now. She stands as a wonderful example of one who was privileged by God and stood by Jesus, but she is not on a higher level than anyone who **does the will of My Father in heaven**.

ii. **Who are My brothers**: Jesus plainly had **brothers**. The Roman Catholic idea of the perpetual virginity of Mary is in contradiction to the plain meaning of the Bible. But the brothers of Jesus never seemed to be supportive of His ministry before His death and resurrection (John 7:5).

iii. "The most natural way to understand 'brothers' is that the term refers to sons of Mary and Joseph and thus to brothers of Jesus on his mother's side." Efforts to make brothers mean something else are "nothing less than farfetched exegesis in support of a dogma that originated much later than the New Testament." (Carson)

c. **For whoever does the will of My Father in heaven is My brother and sister and mother**: These beloved ones who do the will of God stand in contrast to the *evil and adulterous generation* represented by the Pharisees (Matthew 12:39).

i. "He is not ashamed to call them brethren." (Spurgeon)

ii. We can see this as a gracious invitation – even to these religious leaders who deepened their hostility against Jesus and plotted against Him. They could still come and be part of His family.

iii. "Those are the best acknowledged relatives of Christ who are united to him by spiritual ties, and who are become *one* with him by the indwelling of his Spirit. We generally suppose that Christ's relatives must have shared much of his affectionate attention; and doubtless they did: but here we find that whosoever does the will of God is equally esteemed by Christ, as his *brother, sister,* or even his *virgin mother.*" (Clarke)

iv. "The only thing to be further learned from this paragraph is, how dear believers and holy persons are to Christ; he counts them as dear as mother, brethren, or sisters, and thereby teacheth us the esteem we ought to have for such." (Poole)

Matthew 13 - The Kingdom Parables

A. The parable of the soils.

1. (1-3a) Jesus teaches with parables.

On the same day Jesus went out of the house and sat by the sea. And great multitudes were gathered together to Him, so that He got into a boat and sat; and the whole multitude stood on the shore. Then He spoke many things to them in parables,

a. **He got into a boat and sat**: Jesus sometimes used a boat as His "pulpit" (Mark 4:1). It gave Him a place to speak, away from the press of the crowds, provided good acoustics, and probably a nice backdrop.

i. When Jesus taught from **a boat**, surely that was a new thing. We can imagine some critic saying, "You can't do that! Teaching belongs in the synagogue or in some other appropriate place." It would be easy to come up with objections: "The damp air might make people sick" or "There are a lot of mosquitoes down at the shore" or "Someone might drown." But Jesus knew that teaching from a boat suited His purposes well enough.

ii. "When the doors of the synagogue were closed against him, he took to the temple of the open air, and taught men in the village streets, and on the roads, and by the lake-side, and in their own homes." (Barclay)

iii. "The teacher *sat*, and the people *stood*: we should have less sleeping in congregations if this arrangement still prevailed." (Spurgeon)

b. **Then He spoke many things to them in parables**: The idea behind the word *parable* is "to throw alongside of." It is a story thrown alongside the truth intended to teach. Parables have been called "earthly stories with a heavenly meaning."

i. "The Greek *parabole* is wider than our 'parable'; in the LXX it translates *masal*, which includes proverbs, riddles and wise sayings as well as parables. Matthew uses it for instance for Jesus' cryptic saying about defilement (Matthew 15:10-11, 15), and in Matthew 24:32 ('lesson') it indicates a comparison." (France)

ii. "It had a double advantage upon their hearers: first, upon their memory, we being very apt to remember stories. Second, upon their minds, to put them upon studying the meaning of what they heard so delivered." (Poole)

iii. Parables generally teach *one main point* or principle. We can get into trouble by expecting that they be intricate systems of theology, with the smallest detail revealing hidden truths. "A parable is not an allegory; an allegory is a story in which every possible detail has an inner meaning; but an allegory has to be *read and studied*; a parable is *heard*. We must be very careful not to make allegories of the parables." (Barclay)

2. (3b-9) A simple story about a farmer and sowing seeds.

"Behold, a sower went out to sow. And as he sowed, some *seed* fell by the wayside; and the birds came and devoured them. Some fell on stony places, where they did not have much earth; and they immediately sprang up because they had no depth of earth. But when the sun was up they were scorched, and because they had no root they withered away. And some fell among thorns, and the thorns sprang up and choked them. But others fell on good ground and yielded a crop: some a hundredfold, some sixty, some thirty. He who has ears to hear, let him hear!"

a. **A sower went out to sow**: Jesus spoke according to the agricultural customs of His day. In those days, seed was scattered first and then it was plowed into the ground.

i. Before one can be a sower, he must be an eater and a receiver. This one came out of the granary – the place where seed is stored – and from his Bible the **sower** brought forth seed.

b. **As he sowed, some seed fell by the wayside...on stony places... among thorns...on good ground**: In this parable the seed fell on four different types of soil.

i. **The wayside** was the path where people walked and nothing could grow because the ground was too hard.

ii. **Stony places** were where the soil was thin, lying upon a rocky shelf. On this ground the seed springs up quickly because of the warmth of the soil, but the seed is unable to take root because of the rocky shelf.

iii. **Among thorns** describes soil that is fertile - perhaps too fertile, because **thorns** grow there as well as grain.

iv. **Good ground** describes soil that is both fertile and weed-free. A good, productive crop grows in the **good ground**.

c. **He who has ears to hear, let him hear**: This was not a call for all to listen. Rather, it was a call for those who were spiritually sensitive to take special note. This was especially true in light of the next few verses, in which Jesus explained the purpose of parables.

3. (10-17) Why did Jesus use parables? In this context, to *hide* the truth from those who would not listen to the Holy Spirit.

And the disciples came and said to Him, "Why do You speak to them in parables?" He answered and said to them, "Because it has been given to you to know the mysteries of the kingdom of heaven, but to them it has not been given. For whoever has, to him more will be given, and he will have abundance; but whoever does not have, even what he has will be taken away from him. Therefore I speak to them in parables, because seeing they do not see, and hearing they do not hear, nor do they understand. And in them the prophecy of Isaiah is fulfilled, which says:

'Hearing you will hear and shall not understand,
And seeing you will see and not perceive;
For the hearts of this people have grown dull.
***Their* ears are hard of hearing,**
And their eyes they have closed,
Lest they should see with *their* eyes and hear with *their* ears,
Lest they should understand with *their* hearts and turn,
So that I should heal them.'

But blessed *are* your eyes for they see, and your ears for they hear; for assuredly, I say to you that many prophets and righteous *men* desired to see what you see, and did not see *it*, and to hear what you hear, and did not hear *it*."

a. **Why do You speak to them in parables?** The way Jesus used parables prompted the disciples to ask this. Apparently, Jesus' use of parables wasn't as easy as simple illustrations of spiritual truth.

b. **Because it has been given to you to know the mysteries of the kingdom of heaven, but to them it has not been given**: Jesus explained that He used parables so that the hearts of those rejecting would not be hardened further.

i. The same sun that softens the wax hardens the clay; and so the very same gospel message that humbles the honest heart and leads to repentance may also harden the heart of the dishonest listener and confirm that one in their path of disobedience.

ii. "The parable *conceals truth from those who are either too lazy to think or too blinded by prejudice to see*. It puts the responsibility fairly and squarely on the individual. It *reveals* truth to him who desires truth; it *conceals* truth from him who does not wish to see the truth." (Barclay)

iii. "Thus the parables spoke to the crowds do not simply convey information, nor mask it, but challenge the hearers." (Carson)

c. **For whoever has, to him more will be given…but whoever does not have, even what he has will be taken away from him**: The idea is that those who are open and sensitive to spiritual truth **more will be given** through the parables. Yet to those who are not open – who do **not have**, these ones will end up in an even worse condition.

i. "Life is always a process of gaining more or losing more…For weakness, like strength, is an increasing thing." (Barclay)

d. **Therefore I speak to them in parables, because seeing they do not see, and hearing they do not hear, nor do they understand**: In this sense, the parables of Jesus were not illustrations making difficult things clear to all. They presented God's message so the spiritually sensitive could understand, but the hardened would merely hear a story without heaping up additional condemnation for rejecting God's Word.

i. Parables are an example of God's mercy towards the hardened. The parables were given in the context of the Jewish leaders' building rejection of Jesus and His work. In this sense they were examples of mercy given to the undeserving.

e. **And in them the prophecy of Isaiah is fulfilled**: By speaking in parables Jesus also fulfilled the prophecy of Isaiah, speaking in a way that the hardened would hear but not hear and see but not see.

i. **The heart of this people has grown dull** is more literally "fat" instead of **dull**. "A fat heart is a fearful plague…None can delight in God's law that are fat-hearted." (Trapp)

ii. "They did not really see what they saw, nor hear what they heard. The plainer the teaching, the more they were puzzled by it." (Spurgeon)

f. **But blessed are your eyes for they see, and your ears for they hear**: In light of this, those who *do* understand the parables of Jesus are genuinely

blessed. Not only do they gain the benefit of the spiritual truth illustrated, but they also display some measure of responsiveness to the Holy Spirit.

i. "You under the Gospel are made to know what the greatest and best of men under the law could not discover. The shortest day of summer is longer than the longest day in winter." (Spurgeon)

4. (18-23) The parable of the sower explained: each soil represents one of four responses to the word of the kingdom.

"Therefore hear the parable of the sower: When anyone hears the word of the kingdom, and does not understand *it*, then the wicked *one* comes and snatches away what was sown in his heart. This is he who received seed by the wayside. But he who received the seed on stony places, this is he who hears the word and immediately receives it with joy; yet he has no root in himself, but endures only for a while. For when tribulation or persecution arises because of the word, immediately he stumbles. Now he who received seed among the thorns is he who hears the word, and the cares of this world and the deceitfulness of riches choke the word, and he becomes unfruitful. But he who received seed on the good ground is he who hears the word and understands *it*, who indeed bears fruit and produces: some a hundredfold, some sixty, some thirty."

a. **This is he who received seed by the wayside**: As the birds devoured the seed on the wayside (Matthew 13:4), so some receive the word with hardened hearts and **the wicked one** quickly **snatches away** the sown word. The word has no effect because it never penetrates and is quickly taken away.

i. The **wayside** soil represents those who never really hear the word with understanding. The Word of God must be understood before it can truly bear fruit. One of Satan's chief works is to keep men in darkness regarding their understanding of the gospel (2 Corinthians 4:3-4).

ii. "Satan is always on the watch to hinder the Word...He is always afraid to leave the truth even in hard and dry contact with a mind." (Spurgeon)

iii. "People are now so sermon-trodden many of them, that their hearts, like footpaths, grow hard by the word, which takes no more impression than rain doth upon a rock: they have brawny breasts, horny heart-strings, dead and dedolent dispositions." (Trapp)

b. **On stony places**: As seed falling on the thin soil on top of the stony places quickly springs up and then quickly withers and dies (Matthew

13:5-6), so some respond to the word with immediate enthusiasm yet soon wither away.

i. This soil represents those who receive the word enthusiastically, but their life is short-lived, because they are not willing to endure **tribulation or persecution... because of the word**.

ii. Spurgeon made a good point: "I want you clearly to understand that the fault did not lie in the suddenness of their supposed conversion. Many sudden conversions have been among the best that have ever happened." The problem was not their sudden growth, but their lack of depth.

iii. "*Tribulation* is a general term for suffering which comes from outside; *persecution* is deliberately inflicted, and usually implies a religious motive. *Falls away* is literally 'is tripped up'; it is not a gradual loss of interest, but a collapse under pressure." (France)

c. **Among the thorns**: As seed falling among thorns grew, the stalks of grain were soon choked out (Matthew 13:7), so some respond to the word and grow for a while, but are choked and stopped in their spiritual growth by competition from unspiritual things.

i. This soil represents fertile ground for the word; but their soil is *too* fertile, because it also grows all sorts of other things that choke out the Word of God; namely, it is **the cares of this world and the deceitfulness of riches** that **choke the word**.

d. **Good ground**: As seed falling on good ground brings a good crop of grain (Matthew 13:8), so some respond rightly to the word and bear fruit.

i. This soil represents those who receive the word, and it bears fruit in their soil - in differing proportions (**some hundredfold, some sixty, some thirty**), though each has a generous harvest.

e. **Therefore, hear the parable of the sower**: We benefit from seeing bits of ourselves in all four soils.

- Like the **wayside**, sometimes we allow the Word no room at all in our lives.

- Like the **stony places**, we sometimes have flashes of enthusiasm in receiving the Word that quickly burn out.

- Like the soil **among thorns**, the cares of this world and the deceitfulness of riches are constantly threatening to choke out God's Word and our fruitfulness.

- Like the **good ground**, the Word bears fruit in our lives.

i. We notice that the difference in each category was with the soil itself. The same seed was cast by the same sower. You could not blame the differences in results on the sower or on the seed, but only on the soil. "O my dear hearers, you undergo a test today! Peradventure you will be judging the preacher, but a greater than the preacher will be judging you, for the Word itself shall judge you." (Spurgeon)

ii. The parable was also an encouragement to the disciples. Even though it might seem that few respond, God is in control and the harvest will certainly come. This was especially meaningful in light of the rising opposition to Jesus. "Not all will respond, but there will be some who do, and the harvest will be rich." (France)

iii. "Who knoweth, O teacher, when thou labourest even among the infants, what the result of thy teaching may be? Good corn may grow in very small fields." (Spurgeon)

iv. Even more than describing the mixed progress of the gospel message, the parable of the sower compels the listener to ask, "What kind of soil am I? How can I prepare my heart and mind to be the *right* kind of soil?" This parable invites *action* so that we would receive the Word of God to full benefit.

B. Parables of corruption among the kingdom community.

1. (24-30) The parable of the wheat and the tares.

Another parable He put forth to them, saying: "The kingdom of heaven is like a man who sowed good seed in his field; but while men slept, his enemy came and sowed tares among the wheat and went his way. But when the grain had sprouted and produced a crop, then the tares also appeared. So the servants of the owner came and said to him, 'Sir, did you not sow good seed in your field? How then does it have tares?' He said to them, 'An enemy has done this.' The servants said to him, 'Do you want us then to go and gather them up?' But he said, 'No, lest while you gather up the tares you also uproot the wheat with them. Let both grow together until the harvest, and at the time of harvest I will say to the reapers, "First gather together the tares and bind them in bundles to burn them, but gather the wheat into my barn."'"

a. **His enemy came and sowed tares among the wheat**: This parable describes the work of an **enemy** who tried to destroy the work of the **man who sowed good seed in his field**. The enemy's purpose in sowing **tares among the wheat** was to destroy the wheat. But the wise farmer would not allow the enemy to succeed. Instead, the farmer decided to sort it out at harvest time.

i. We note that this parable *clearly describes corruption among the people of God*. Just as in the previous parable, the wheat represents the people of God. Some corrupting influence is brought, and an influence that may look genuine even as tares may resemble real wheat.

ii. "The *weeds* are probably darnel, a poisonous plant related to wheat and virtually indistinguishable from it until the ears form." (France)

b. **Lest while you gather up the tares you also uproot the wheat with them**: In the interest of preserving and protecting the wheat, the wise farmer did not separate the **tares** from the **wheat** until the time of harvest.

i. The wise farmer recognized that the ultimate answer to tares among the wheat would only come at the final harvest.

ii. Knowing the explanation of this parable as explained in Matthew 13:36-43, we understand why Jesus said it right after explaining the parable of the sower, especially with the seed that grew up among the thorns. "But one might ask whether the Messiah's people should immediately separate the crop from the weeds; and this next parable answers the question negatively: there will be a delay in separation until the harvest." (Carson)

2. (31-32) The parable of the mustard seed.

Another parable He put forth to them, saying: "The kingdom of heaven is like a mustard seed, which a man took and sowed in his field, which indeed is the least of all the seeds; but when it is grown it is greater than the herbs and becomes a tree, so that the birds of the air come and nest in its branches."

a. **The kingdom of heaven is like a mustard seed...when it is grown it is greater than the herbs and becomes a tree**: Some, or even most, regard this as a description of the growth and eventual dominance of the church, the kingdom community. Yet in light of both the parable itself and the context of the parables both before and after, this should be regarded as another description of *corruption* in the kingdom community, just as the previous parable of the wheat and the tares described (Matthew 13:24-30).

i. Adam Clarke is a good example of the majority opinion on the meaning of this parable and the one following: "Both these parables are *prophetic*, and were intended to show, principally, how, from very small beginnings, the Gospel of Christ should pervade all the nations of the world, and fill them with righteousness and true holiness."

b. **When it is grown it is greater than the herbs and becomes a tree, so that the birds of the air come and nest in its branches**: Again many, or even most, regard this as a beautiful picture of the church growing so large that it provides refuge for all of the world. But this **mustard seed** plant grew unnaturally large, and it harbored **birds**, which, in the previous parables were emissaries of Satan (Matthew 13:4, 13:19).

i. **Becomes a tree**: The mustard plant customarily never grows beyond what one would call a bush, and at its normal size would be an unlikely place for bird's nests. The **tree**-like growth from this **mustard seed** describes something unnatural.

ii. "The language suggests that Jesus was thinking of the Old Testament use of the tree as an image for a great empire (see especially Ezekiel 17:23; 31:3-9; Daniel 4:10-12)." (France)

iii. This was a **tree**, "Not in nature but in size; an excusable exaggeration in a popular discourse…it serves admirably to express the thought of a growth *beyond expectation*. Who would expect so tiny a seed to produce such a large herb, a monster in the garden?" (Bruce)

iv. This parable accurately describes what the kingdom community became in the decades and centuries after the Christianization of the Roman Empire. In those centuries the church grew abnormally large in influence and dominion, and was a nest for much corruption. "Birds lodging in the branches most probably refers to elements of corruption which take refuge in the very shadow of Christianity." (Morgan)

v. "Close study of birds as symbols in the Old Testament and especially in the literature of later Judaism shows that birds regularly symbolize evil and even demons or Satan (cf. b. *Sanhedrin*, 107a; cf. Revelation 18:2)." (Carson)

3. (33) Another illustration of corruption in the kingdom community: the parable of the leaven in the meal.

Another parable He spoke to them: "The kingdom of heaven is like leaven, which a woman took and hid in three measures of meal till it was all leavened."

a. **The kingdom of heaven is like leaven**: Jesus used a surprising picture here. Many, if not most, regard this as a beautiful picture of the kingdom of God working its way through the whole world. Yet **leaven** is consistently used as a picture of sin and corruption (especially in the Passover narrative of Exodus 12:8, 12:15-20). Again, both the content and the context point towards this being a description of corruption in the kingdom community.

i. "There would be a certain shock in hearing the Kingdom of God compared to leaven." (Barclay)

b. **Leaven, which a woman took and hid in three measures of meal till it was all leavened**: This was an unusually large amount of meal. It was much more than any normal woman would prepare, and again suggests the idea of massive or unnatural size.

> i. "*Three measures of meal* would be about 40 litres, which would make enough bread for a meal for 100 people, a remarkable baking for an ordinary *woman*." (France)

c. **Hid in it**: The idea of hiding leaven in **three measures of meal** would have offended any observant Jew. This certainly isn't a picture of the church gradually influencing the whole world for *good*. Rather, in the context of increasing opposition to His work, Jesus announced that His kingdom community would also be threatened by corruption and impurity.

> i. G. Campbell Morgan wrote that the leaven represents "paganizing influences" brought into the church.

4. (34-35) Jesus' teaching in parables as a fulfillment of prophecy.

All these things Jesus spoke to the multitude in parables; and without a parable He did not speak to them, that it might be fulfilled which was spoken by the prophet, saying:

"I will open My mouth in parables;
I will utter things kept secret from the foundation of the world."

a. **Without a parable He did not speak to them**: This does not mean that Jesus never, in His entire teaching and preaching ministry, spoke in anything other than **a parable**. It describes this particular season of Jesus' ministry, again in the context of increasing opposition from the Jewish leaders.

> i. "Implying that this was Jesus' constant custom...In short parables were an essential part of his spoken ministry." (Carson)

b. **I will open My mouth in parables**: Another reason Jesus taught about the kingdom community in parables is because the church itself was part of the **things which have been kept secret from the foundation of the world**, and would not be revealed in fullness until later.

c. **Kept secret from the foundation of the world**: Later, Paul expresses this same idea about the church in Ephesians 3:4-11.

5. (36-43) Jesus explains the parable of the wheat and the tares.

Then Jesus sent the multitude away and went into the house. And His disciples came to Him, saying, "Explain to us the parable of the tares of the field." He answered and said to them: "He who sows the good seed is the Son of Man. The field is the world, the good seeds are the sons of

the kingdom, but the tares are the sons of the wicked *one*. The enemy who sowed them is the devil, the harvest is the end of the age, and the reapers are the angels. Therefore as the tares are gathered and burned in the fire, so it will be at the end of this age. The Son of Man will send out His angels, and they will gather out of His kingdom all things that offend, and those who practice lawlessness, and will cast them into the furnace of fire. There will be wailing and gnashing of teeth. Then the righteous will shine forth as the sun in the kingdom of their Father. He who has ears to hear, let him hear!"

a. **Explain to us the parable of the tares of the field**: In His explanation, Jesus made it clear what the different figures in the parable represent.

- The **field** represents the **world**.

- The **good seeds** represent God's true people, the **sons of the kingdom**.

- The **tares** represent false believers in the world, **the sons of the wicked one**, who (like tares among wheat) may superficially look like God's true people.

i. In this we see that the parable of the tares changes the figures slightly from the parable of the soils (Matthew 13:3-9; 13:18-23). In the parable of the soils, the seed represented the Word of God; here it represents true believers. The point of the parables is completely different; the parable of the soils shows how men receive and respond to the Word of God, and the parable of the tares of the field shows how God will divide His true people from false believers at the **end of this age**.

ii. "Satan has a shoot of iniquity for every shoot of grace; and, when God revives his work, Satan revives his also." (Clarke)

iii. This parable powerfully teaches that it is *God's* job to divide in judgment. "Magistrates and churches may remove the openly wicked from their society; the outwardly good who are inwardly worthless they must leave; for the judging of hearts is beyond their sphere." (Spurgeon)

iv. "Jesus announced God's kingdom, and this would lead many of his hearers to expect a cataclysmic disruption of society, an immediate and absolute division between the 'sons of light' and the 'sons of darkness'...It was to this impatience that the parable was primarily directed." (France)

b. **The field is the world**: Significantly, this parable illustrates not necessarily that there will be false believers among true believers in the church (though that is also true to some extent); otherwise Jesus would have explained that the **field is the** *church*. Yet He carefully said that **the field is the world**.

> i. "Of greater importance in the history of the church has been the view that this actually means that the field is the church. The view was largely assumed by the early church fathers, and the tendency to interpret the parable that way was reinforced by the Constantinian settlement. Augustine made the interpretation official struggling against the Donatists...Most Reformers followed the same line." (Carson)

> ii. Yet the point is clear, both in the world and in the kingdom community. Ultimately it is not the job of the church to weed out those who appear to be Christians but actually are not; that is God's job at the **end of this age**.

> iii. As long as God's people are still in this **world** (the **field**), there will be unbelievers among them; but it should not be because God's people receive unbelievers as if they were believers, ignoring either the belief or conduct of professed believers.

> iv. There is additional significance in saying, "**The field is the world**" instead of "The field is Israel." "This brief statement presupposes a mission beyond Israel." (Carson)

c. **The enemy who sowed them is the devil**: Clearly, the enemy plants counterfeits in the world and in the kingdom community, and this is why merely being a member of the Christian community isn't enough.

d. **The reapers are angels... The Son of Man will send out His angels**: We often don't consider that the **angels** of God have a special role in the judgment of the world. Yet they do, and are worthy of respect because of that role.

> i. "This casts special scorn upon the great evil angel. He sows the tares, and tries to destroy the harvest; and, therefore, the good angels are brought in to celebrate his defeat, and to rejoice together with their Lord in the success of the divine husbandry." (Spurgeon)

e. **Will cast them into the furnace of fire...the righteous will shine forth as the sun in the kingdom of their Father**: Jesus used this parable to clearly illustrate the truth that there are two different paths and eternal destinies. A **furnace of fire** represents one destiny and radiant glory (**shine forth as the sun**) the other destiny.

> i. "The fate of these ungodly ones will be *fire*, the most terrible of punishments; but this will not annihilate them; for they shall exhibit

the surest tokens of a living woe – *'wailing and gnashing of teeth.'"* (Spurgeon)

ii. The wheat comes into God's barn from all over the world, from all ranks of society, from all ages of God's church. The one thing they have in common is that they were sown of the Lord, and from the good seed of His Word.

C. More parables about the kingdom.

1. (44) The parable of the hidden treasure.

"Again, the kingdom of heaven is like treasure hidden in a field, which a man found and hid; and for joy over it he goes and sells all that he has and buys that field."

a. **The kingdom of heaven is like treasure hidden in a field**: The field is the world, but the **man** does not represent the believer, because we have nothing to buy this treasure with. Instead, Jesus is the **man** who gave all that He had to buy the field.

i. "Under rabbinic law if a workman came on a treasure in a field and lifted it out, it would belong to his master, the field's owner; but here the man is careful not to lift the treasure out till he has bought the field." (Carson)

ii. This parable and the one following are different in character than the previous three. The previous three parables (the wheat and the tares, the mustard seed, and the leaven) each spoke of corruption in the kingdom community. These two parables speak of how highly the King values the people of His kingdom.

b. **And for joy over it he goes and sells all that he has and buys that field**: The **treasure** so wonderful that Jesus would give all to purchase is *the individual believer*. This powerfully shows how Jesus gave everything to redeem the whole world to preserve a treasure in it, and the treasure is His people.

i. "Finding the treasure appears to be by chance. In a land as frequently ravaged as Palestine, many people doubtless buried their treasures; but…to actually find a treasure would happen once in a thousand lifetimes. Thus the extravagance of the parable dramatizes the supreme importance of the kingdom." (Carson)

ii. "So did Jesus himself, at the utmost cost, buy the world to gain his church, which was the treasure which he desired." (Spurgeon)

2. (45-46) The parable of the costly pearl.

"Again, the kingdom of heaven is like a merchant seeking beautiful pearls, who, when he had found one pearl of great price, went and sold all that he had and bought it."

a. **The kingdom of heaven is like a merchant seeking beautiful pearls**: Again, Jesus is the buyer and the individual believer is the pearl that He sees as so valuable that He would happily give all to have it forever.

i. "To the ancient peoples, as we have just seen, a pearl was the loveliest of all possessions; that means that the Kingdom of Heaven is the loveliest thing in the world." (Barclay)

b. **One pearl of great price**: It seems crazy for a merchant to sell **all that he had** for one pearl, but for this merchant it was well worth it. That shows how much he valued this **pearl of great price**, and how much Jesus values His people.

3. (47-50) The parable of the dragnet.

"Again, the kingdom of heaven is like a dragnet that was cast into the sea and gathered some of every kind, which, when it was full, they drew to shore; and they sat down and gathered the good into vessels, but threw the bad away. So it will be at the end of the age. The angels will come forth, separate the wicked from among the just, and cast them into the furnace of fire. There will be wailing and gnashing of teeth."

a. **The kingdom of heaven is like a dragnet**: Jesus shows that the world will remain divided right up until the end, and the Church will not reform the world, ushering in the kingdom.

b. **So it will be at the end of the age**: There will be both the **wicked** and the **just** until the end of the age (as also demonstrated in the previous parable of the wheat and the tares). At that time **the angels will come forth** and assist the King in the work of judgment, sending some **into the furnace of fire** for final judgment.

i. "The reference, as in the weeds, is not primarily to a mixed church, but to the division among mankind in general which the last judgment will bring to light." (France)

4. (51-52) The disciples claim to understand Jesus' parables.

Jesus said to them, "Have you understood all these things?" They said to Him, "Yes, Lord." Then He said to them, "Therefore every scribe instructed concerning the kingdom of heaven is like a householder who brings out of his treasure *things* new and old."

a. **They said to Him, "Yes, Lord."** We wonder if the disciples really did understand Jesus here. However, Jesus did not deny their claim to understand.

> i. Assuming that the disciples did understand, they had an advantage over many among the multitudes. "The multitude went away (as most people do from sermons) never the wiser, understanding nothing of what they heard, nor caring to understand it." (Poole)

b. **Every scribe instructed concerning the kingdom**: Jesus said that everyone who really knows God's Word both will know the **old** and learn the **new** of the kingdom. "He is not weary of the *old*; he is not afraid of the *new*." (Spurgeon)

> i. **Every scribe**: Jesus used the term here simply to describe a teacher. "The scribes amongst the Jews were not only clerks, that were employed in writing, but teachers of the law; such a one was Ezra (Ezra 7:6)." (Poole)

> ii. The main idea is that the disciples – who had just claimed to understand what Jesus taught – are now responsible to bring forth their understanding to others, as if they were distributing from the storehouse of their wisdom and understanding. This storehouse contains **things new and old**.

> iii. "After you have been instructed by me, you have the knowledge, not only of the things you used to know, but of things you never knew before, and even the knowledge which you had before is illuminated by what I have told to you." (Barclay)

> iv. "A small degree of knowledge is not sufficient for a preacher of the Gospel. The sacred writings should be his *treasure*, and he should properly understand them... his knowledge consists in being *well instructed* in the things concerning the kingdom of heaven, and the art of conducting men thither." (Clarke)

> v. "Ministers of the gospel should not be novices, 1 Timothy 3:6, raw and ignorant men; but men mighty in the Scriptures, well acquainted with the writings of the Old and New Testament, and the sense of them; men that have a stock of spiritual knowledge, able readily to speak a word to the weary, and to speak to men and women's particular cases and questions." (Poole)

D. Further rejection: Jesus is rejected at Nazareth.

1. (53-56) The people of Nazareth are surprised that one of their own could grow up to do such spectacular things.

Now it came to pass, when Jesus had finished these parables, that He departed from there. And when He had come to His own country, He taught them in their synagogue, so that they were astonished and said, "Where did this *Man* get this wisdom and *these* mighty works? "Is this not the carpenter's son? Is not His mother called Mary? And His brothers James, Joses, Simon, and Judas? And His sisters, are they not all with us? Where then did this *Man* get all these things?"

a. **Where did this Man get this wisdom and these mighty works? Is this not the carpenter's son**: Because these villagers were familiar with Jesus as a boy and accustomed to unspectacular things from Him, we may conclude that Jesus must have grown up a very normal boy unlike the fantastic stories told in apocryphal books like *The Infancy of Jesus*.

i. **Is this not the carpenter's son**: This question was asked out of ignorant prejudice. Yet it can also be asked out of deep appreciation of the fact that the Son of God took such a noble, lowly place.

ii. "Justin Martyr, an ancient writer, testifieth, that our Saviour, ere he entered upon the ministry, made ploughs, yokes, and so forth. But was not that an honest occupation?" (Trapp)

iii. "Julian the apostate, as he is called, once asked a certain Christian, 'What do you think the carpenter's son is doing now?' 'Making coffins for you and for all his enemies,' was the prompt reply." (Spurgeon)

b. **His brothers James, Joses, Simon, and Judas**: Jesus plainly had many brothers and sisters; the Roman Catholic idea of the perpetual virginity of Mary is in contradiction to the plain meaning of the Bible.

i. "It is the very ordinariness of Jesus' home background that causes the astonishment (*cf.* John 6:42)." (France)

ii. "This insulting question seems to intimate that our Lord's family was a very *obscure one*; and that they were of small *repute* among their neighbours, except for their *piety*." Clarke)

iii. People bring the same charge against Jesus today; "I see those associated with Him, and they seem lowly or very normal; Jesus must also not be special."

c. **Where then did this Man get all these things**: Their reception of Jesus was not welcoming or friendly. They speak skeptically and will refer to Him only as "**this Man**."

2. (57-58) A prophet without honor.

So they were offended at Him. But Jesus said to them, "A prophet is not without honor except in his own country and in his own house." Now He did not do many mighty works there because of their unbelief.

a. **So they were offended at Him**: When we think of how strongly Jesus is identified with Nazareth (see at Matthew 2:23), it is even more surprising to note that the people of Nazareth did not appreciate it. The success and glory of Jesus seemed only to make them more resentful towards Him.

b. **A prophet is not without honor except in his own country, and in his own house**: We often have wrong ideas about what it means to be spiritual. We often think that spiritual people will be much more strange than normal. Therefore, those closest to truly spiritual people see just how normal they are and sometimes think that they *aren't* spiritual because they *are* normal.

c. **He did not do many mighty works there because of their unbelief**: It is truly remarkable that Jesus was, in some manner, limited by their unbelief. As long as God chooses to work in concert with human agency, developing our ability to partner with Him, our unbelief can and may hinder the work of God.

   i. The old Puritan commentator John Trapp here remarked that **unbelief** was "A sin of that venomous nature, that it transfuseth, as it were, a dead palsy into the hands of omnipotency."

Matthew 14 - Jesus Displays Authority over Nature

A. Herod and John the Baptist.

1. (1-2) Herod fears that Jesus is John the Baptist raised from the dead.

At that time Herod the tetrarch heard the report about Jesus and said to his servants, "This is John the Baptist; he is risen from the dead, and therefore these powers are at work in him."

a. **At that time Herod the tetrarch heard the report about Jesus**: The fame and **report** of Jesus spread around the region. This Herod was known as *Herod Antipas* and was one of the sons of Herod the Great who reigned when Jesus was born.

i. "*Tetrarch* literally means *the ruler of a fourth part*; but it came to be used quite generally, as here, of any subordinate ruler of a section of a country." (Barclay) A **tetrarch** was lower than a *king*. Herod Antipas wanted to be recognized as a king, and later asked the Emperor Caligula for this title, but Caligula refused. This humiliation was part of what later sent Herod to exile in Gaul.

ii. This **Herod the tetrarch** – also known as Herod Antipas – ruled over Galilee and therefore heard much about Jesus. His brother Archelaus ruled to the south, and his brother Philip ruled to the north.

b. **This is John the Baptist; he is risen from the dead**: Though this may seem unreasonable in retrospect, Herod's guilt and superstition led him to this fear.

i. "He imagined still that he saw and heard that holy head shouting and crying out against him, staring him also in the face at every turn… God hath laid upon evil-doers the cross of their own consciences, that thereon they may suffer afore they suffer; and their greatest enemies need not wish them a greater mischief." (Trapp)

ii. Barclay cites the ancient Christian writer Origen, who said that Jesus and John the Baptist closely resembled each other in appearance. If this were true, it would give more reason for Herod Antipas to believe that Jesus was John come back from the dead.

2. (3-12) Herod's cruel treatment of John the Baptist.

For Herod had laid hold of John and bound him, and put *him* in prison for the sake of Herodias, his brother Philip's wife. Because John had said to him, "It is not lawful for you to have her." And although he wanted to put him to death, he feared the multitude, because they counted him as a prophet. But when Herod's birthday was celebrated, the daughter of Herodias danced before them and pleased Herod. Therefore he promised with an oath to give her whatever she might ask. So she, having been prompted by her mother, said, "Give me John the Baptist's head here on a platter." And the king was sorry; nevertheless, because of the oaths and because of those who sat with him, he commanded *it* to be given to *her*. So he sent and had John beheaded in prison. And his head was brought on a platter and given to the girl, and she brought *it* to her mother. Then his disciples came and took away the body and buried it, and went and told Jesus.

a. **Because John had said to him, "It is not lawful for you to have her"**: Having told us of the death of John the Baptist, Matthew will now explain to us how he died. It began when Herod imprisoned John for the bold rebuke of the king's sin. Yet he did not immediately kill him because **he feared the multitude**.

i. John spoke out against Herod's marriage because he had illegally divorced his previous wife and then seduced and married his brother Philip's wife named **Herodias**. The father of Herod's first wife was the King of Petra, and he later made successful war against Herod Antipas because of how he had disgraced the King of Petra's daughter.

ii. Adam Clarke on **Herodias**: "This infamous woman was the daughter of *Aristobulus* and *Bernice*, and grand-daughter of Herod the Great. Her first marriage was with Herod Philip, her *uncle*, by whom she had *Salome*: some time after, she left her husband, and lived publicly with Herod Antipas."

iii. In speaking out against Herod and Herodias, there is the suggestion that John did this repeatedly. "It was, moreover, perhaps more than a passing remark: *said* is in the imperfect tense, which may indicate a continuing 'campaign'." (France)

iv. In that he **feared the multitude**, Herod is like many people today. They fear the opinion of people before fearing God. The only thing that kept Herod from even greater wickedness was the fear of man.

v. Yet one must say that Herod seemed to fear his wife Herodias more than he feared the multitude, because he imprisoned John **for the sake of Herodias**. "She ruled him at her pleasure, as Jezebel did Ahab...But it never goes well when the hen crows." (Trapp)

b. **The daughter of Herodias danced before them and pleased Herod**: Herodias' daughter shamelessly danced before Herod and friends, winning favor and a special request.

i. This **daughter Herodias** is described as a **girl** (Matthew 14:11). This means that she was not a cute little girl; "*Girl* is a term which can be used of those of marriageable age; she was at least a teenager." (France)

ii. "The dancing of a mere girl would have been no entertainment to the sensual revelers. The treat lay in the indecency." (Bruce)

iii. "The dances which these girls danced were suggestive and immoral. For a royal princess to dance in public at all was an amazing thing." (Barclay)

iv. "In these days mothers too often encourage their daughters in dress which is scarcely decent and introduce them to dances which are not commendable for purity. No good can come of this; it may please the Herods, but it displeases God." (Spurgeon)

c. **Having been prompted by her mother, said, "Give me John the Baptist's head here on a platter"**: The request of Herodias shows that the mother had this planned for some time. She knew her husband and she knew the situation, and knew she could get what she wanted this way.

i. She was shrewd enough to demand that it be done *immediately*, while the guests were still at the party. "That was an essential part of the request. No time must be left for repentance. If not done at once under the influence of wine and the momentary gratification given by the voluptuous dance, it might never be done at all." (Bruce)

ii. "It would have been bad enough if she herself had sought ways of taking vengeance on the man of God who confronted her with her shame. It was infinitely worse that she used her daughter for her nefarious purposes and made her as great a sinner as herself." (Barclay)

d. **And the king was sorry; nevertheless, because of the oaths and because of those who sat with him, he commanded it to be given to**

her: Because Herod was afraid to go against his wife or to lose face before his friends, he did something that he knew was wrong.

i. "Rash promises, and even oaths, are no excuse for doing wrong. The promise was in itself null and void, because no man has a right to promise to do wrong." (Spurgeon) "Like most weak men, Herod feared to be thought weak." (Plumptre, cited in Carson)

ii. "All points to immediate production of the head on a platter in the banqueting hall before the guests; gruesome sight!" (Bruce)

iii. "The HEAD was in the possession of *Herodias*, who, 'tis probable, took a diabolic pleasure in viewing that speechless mouth which had often been the cause of planting thorns in her criminal bed; and in offering indignities to that *tongue* from which she could no longer dread a reproof." (Clarke)

iv. Herod had a terrible end. In order to take his brother's wife Herodias, he put away his first wife, a princess from a neighboring kingdom to the east. Her father was offended and came against Herod with an army, defeating him in battle. Then his brother Agrippa accused him of treason against Rome, and he was banished into the distant Roman province of Gaul. In Gaul, Herod and Herodias committed suicide.

e. **Then his disciples came and took away the body and buried it**: The disciples of John the Baptist honored his life and memory the best they could. He had lived and died as a great and righteous man.

i. "It is not said by the Evangelist that they buried John, but '*they took up his body, and buried it,*' not *him*. The real John no man could bury, and Herod soon found that, being dead, he yet spoke." (Spurgeon)

3. (13) Jesus departs, not wishing to run afoul of Herod.

When Jesus heard *it*, He departed from there by boat to a deserted place by Himself. But when the multitudes heard it, they followed Him on foot from the cities.

a. **When Jesus heard it, He departed from there**: Again, this was not from cowardice but from an understanding of the Father's timing, and also of prophetic timing.

b. **When the multitudes heard it, they followed Him on foot**: Jesus could escape the potential violence of Herod, but He could not escape the attention of **the multitudes**. Though both the religious and now the political leaders opposed Jesus, He was still popular with **the multitudes**.

i. The Puritan commentator John Trapp admired the diligence of these multitudes: "Whose diligence and devotion is check to our dullness and devotion: if Christ would set up a pulpit at the alehouse door, some would hear him oftener." (Trapp)

B. Jesus feeds the five thousand.

1. (14-16) Jesus' compassion for the multitude.

And when Jesus went out He saw a great multitude; and He was moved with compassion for them, and healed their sick. When it was evening, His disciples came to Him, saying, "This is a deserted place, and the hour is already late. Send the multitudes away, that they may go into the villages and buy themselves food." But Jesus said to them, "They do not need to go away. You give them something to eat."

a. **He was moved with compassion for them**: The great compassion of Jesus for the multitude moved Him to heal the sick and to teach them (Mark 6:34). Jesus did this all the way until **evening**. His gracious compassion for the demanding crowds was remarkable.

i. "Jesus had come to find peace and quiet and loneliness; instead he found a vast crowd eagerly demanding what he could give. He might so easily have resented them. What right had they to invade his privacy with their continual demands?" (Barclay)

ii. Jesus and the disciples could have made many legitimate excuses. "This isn't the right place." "This isn't the right time." "The people can take care of themselves." Indeed, there was no physical necessity to feed this multitude. These were people who were used to skipping meals, and they certainly expected nothing. Yet Jesus had **compassion** on them nonetheless.

iii. His **compassion** was great: "The original word is very expressive; his whole being was stirred to its lowest depth, and therefore he proceeded at once to work miracles of mercy among them." (Spurgeon)

b. **You give them something to eat**: With this, Jesus challenged both the *compassion* and the *faith* of the disciples. Yet He did not ask them to do anything to meet the need without also guiding them through the work.

i. "If they remembered the miracle of the wine in Cana (John 2:1-11), they should have asked Jesus to meet the need, not send the people away." (Carson)

ii. Both Jesus and the disciples were aware of the **great multitude** and aware of their needs. Yet it was the **compassion** of Jesus and His awareness of the power of God that led Him to go about feeding the multitude.

- The people are hungry, and the empty religionist offers them some ceremony or empty words that can never satisfy.

- The people are hungry, and the atheists and skeptics try to convince them that they aren't hungry at all.

- The people are hungry, and the religious showman gives them video and special lighting and cutting-edge music.

- The people are hungry, and the entertainer gives them loud, fast action, so loud and fast that they don't have a moment to think.

- The people are hungry – who will give them the bread of life?

iii. Spurgeon used the words, **they do not need to go away** (*they need not depart* in the KJV) as the basis of a sermon. The theme of the sermon was that if there was no need for these mostly casual hearers of Jesus to depart, there is even less reason for the follower of Jesus to **go away** from continual communion and fellowship with Jesus.

- Circumstances don't need to make you **go away**. You won't have things so hard or so easy that you don't need Jesus.

- There is nothing in Jesus that would make you want to **go away**.

- There is nothing in the future that will make you need to **go away**.

2. (17-19) Jesus distributes bread to the multitude.

And they said to Him, "We have here only five loaves and two fish." He said, "Bring them here to Me." Then He commanded the multitudes to sit down on the grass. And He took the five loaves and the two fish, and looking up to heaven, He blessed and broke and gave the loaves to the disciples; and the disciples gave to the multitudes.

a. **We have here only five loaves and two fish**: These were obtained from a little boy among the crowd (John 6:9). It is much to the credit of the disciples that they themselves traveled light, without carrying a lot of food for themselves. They trusted Jesus to make sure they were provided for.

b. **He commanded the multitudes to sit down on the grass**: This command suggests that this was more than just putting food in their stomachs; that could be done standing up. The idea was that there was a bit of a banquet-like atmosphere of enjoyment.

i. "What a feast this was! Christ for the Master of the feast; apostles for butlers; thousands for numbers; and miracles for supplies!" (Spurgeon)

c. **Looking up to heaven, He blessed**: Jesus blessed the Father for the food that He *did* have. He may have prayed a familiar Jewish prayer before a meal: "Blessed art Thou, Jehovah our God, King of the universe, who bringest forth bread from the earth."

d. **He blessed and broke and gave the loaves to the disciples; and the disciples gave to the multitudes**: This miracle displays Jesus' total authority over creation. Yet He insisted on doing this miracle *through* the hands of the disciples. He could have done it directly, but He wanted to use the disciples.

i. No one knew where this bread actually came from. Jesus showed us that God can provide out of resources that we cannot see or perceive in any way. It is easier to have faith when we think we know *how* God might provide, but God often provides in unexpected and undiscoverable ways.

3. (20-21) The multitudes are fed.

So they all ate and were filled, and they took up twelve baskets full of the fragments that remained. Now those who had eaten were about five thousand men, besides women and children.

a. **They all ate and were filled**: Not only was God's provision abundant, but God also did not want the leftovers to go to waste. Therefore they took measures to preserve what was left over (**and they took up twelve baskets full of the fragments that remained**).

i. "God's generous giving and our wise using must go hand in hand." (Barclay)

b. **Now those who had eaten were about five thousand men, besides women and children**: The number of 5,000 men suggests a total perhaps of 15,000 to 20,000 people when women and children are included in the count.

i. The prominence of this story – recorded in all four gospels – shows that both the Holy Spirit and the early church thought this story was important, and important as more than an example of the miraculous power of Jesus.

• It shows that Jesus could feed the people of God, even as Israel was fed in the wilderness. There was a common expectation that the Messiah would restore the provision of manna, and this adds to the messianic credentials of Jesus.

• It shows that Jesus had compassion and care for the people of God, even when we might have expected His patience would be exhausted.

- It shows that Jesus chose to work through the hands of the disciples, even when it was not essential to the immediate result.

- It shows a preview example of the great messianic banquet that the Messiah will enjoy with His people.

ii. The feeding of the 5,000 also gives us three principles regarding God's provision.

- Thank God for and wisely use what you have.

- Trust God's unlimited resources.

- Don't waste what He gives you.

C. Jesus walks on the water and comforts His disciples.

1. (22-24) Another storm on the Sea of Galilee.

Immediately Jesus made His disciples get into the boat and go before Him to the other side, while He sent the multitudes away. And when He had sent the multitudes away, He went up on the mountain by Himself to pray. Now when evening came, He was alone there. But the boat was now in the middle of the sea, tossed by the waves, for the wind was contrary.

a. **Immediately Jesus made His disciples get into the boat**: Jesus felt it was important for He and His followers to leave the area quickly. Perhaps this was to avoid the multitudes clinging to Him as a potential source of constant bread. Therefore, Jesus *compelled* (**made**) the disciples get into the boat.

i. Actually, there were several reasons why Jesus did this. He did this because He wanted to be alone to pray; because He wanted to escape the crowd and get some rest; and because He wanted the crowd to disperse so as to avoid a messianic uproar (John 6:15).

ii. John 6:14-15 tells us that the crowd responded to the miraculous feeding with a rush of messianic expectation. If the disciples shared this enthusiasm – perhaps sensing that *now was the time* to openly promote Jesus as Messiah the King – then it was more important than ever for Jesus to get the disciples away from the excited crowd.

b. **He went up on the mountain by Himself to pray**: Jesus was jealous for time spent alone with His Father. In the midst of His great ministry to others, He did not - He could not - neglect prayer.

i. "Secret prayer fats the soul, as secret morsels feed the body." (Trapp)

ii. "Whilst the disciples were periling, and well-nigh perishing, Christ was praying for them: so he still is for us, at the right hand of the Majesty on high." (Trapp)

c. **The boat was now in the middle of the sea, tossed by the waves, for the wind was contrary**: The Sea of Galilee is well known for its sudden storms, and during this storm Jesus wasn't in the boat with the disciples.

2. (25-27) Jesus comes to both help and comfort His disciples.

Now in the fourth watch of the night Jesus went to them, walking on the sea. And when the disciples saw Him walking on the sea, they were troubled, saying, "It is a ghost!" And they cried out for fear. But immediately Jesus spoke to them, saying, "Be of good cheer! It is I; do not be afraid."

a. **In the fourth watch of the night**: This was somewhere between 3 a.m. and 6 a.m. According to Mark (Mark 6:47-52), Jesus came to the disciples when the boat was in the middle of the sea and after they had exhausted themselves rowing against the waves and windy storm.

b. **Jesus went to them, walking on the sea**: This walk on the water must have been quite a shock to the disciples; they were indeed **troubled** and **they cried out for fear**.

c. **Be of good cheer! It is I; do not be afraid**: Jesus didn't come to the disciples to trouble them or make them afraid. Therefore, He **immediately** spoke to them these comforting words.

i. There are two good reasons to put away fear. One reason may be that the problem is not nearly as bad as one had thought; perhaps you are afraid because you exaggerate the danger. The other reason is that even though the problem may be real, there is an even greater solution and help at hand.

3. (28-33) Peter's bold move and subsequent lack of faith.

And Peter answered Him and said, "Lord, if it is You, command me to come to You on the water." So He said, "Come." And when Peter had come down out of the boat, he walked on the water to go to Jesus. But when he saw that the wind *was* boisterous, he was afraid; and beginning to sink he cried out, saying, "Lord, save me!" And immediately Jesus stretched out *His* hand and caught him, and said to him, "O you of little faith, why did you doubt?" And when they got into the boat, the wind ceased. Then those who were in the boat came and worshiped Him, saying, "Truly You are the Son of God."

a. **Lord, if it is You, command me to come to You on the water**: We have no idea what prompted Peter to ask such a question, but his faith in Jesus was remarkable. He really responded to Jesus' invitation and got out of the boat.

i. "Peter's protasis ('if it's you') is a real condition, almost 'since it's you.' The request is bold, but the disciples had been trained for some time and given power to do exactly the sort of miracles Jesus was doing (Matthew 10:1). What is more natural than for a fisherman who knew and respected the dangers of Galilee to want to follow Jesus in this new demonstration of supernatural power?" (Carson)

b. **He walked on the water to go to Jesus. But when he saw that the wind was boisterous, he was afraid; and beginning to sink**: This is a wonderful picture of walking in faith, showing that Peter was able to do the miraculous as long as he looked to Jesus. When **he saw that the wind was boisterous**, he was troubled by fear and began to **sink**.

i. "Peter walked on the *water* but feared the *wind*: such is human nature, often achieving great things, and at fault in little things." (Bruce)

c. **Beginning to sink he cried out, saying, "Lord, save me"**: Even when Peter failed, Jesus was there to save him. Peter knew who to call out to at the moment of crisis. Jesus then brought Peter back to the boat.

i. "What a sight! Jesus and Peter, hand in hand, walking upon the sea!" (Spurgeon)

d. **O you of little faith**: Once Jesus rescued Peter, He spoke to Peter about his **little faith**. This **little faith** led to the doubt and distraction that made Peter sink under the wind and the waves.

i. "It was not the violence of the winds, nor the raging of the waves, which endangered his life, but his *littleness of faith*." (Clarke)

ii. "THERE is only one word in the original for the phrase, 'O thou of little faith.' The Lord Jesus virtually addresses Peter by the name of 'Little-faith,' in one word." (Spurgeon)

iii. Peter here shows us the weakness of **little faith**.

- Little faith is often found in places where we might expect great faith.
- Little faith is far too eager for signs.
- Little faith is apt to have too high an opinion of its own power.
- Little faith is too much affected by it surroundings.
- Little faith is too quick to exaggerate the peril.

iv. Yet Peter also shows us some of the strengths of **little faith**.

- Little faith is true faith.
- Little faith will obey the word of Jesus.

- Little faith struggles to come to Jesus.
- Little faith will accomplish great things for a time.
- Little faith will pray when it is in trouble.
- Little faith is safe, because Jesus is near.

v. "You do believe, and if you believe, why doubt? If faith, why *little* faith? If you doubt, why believe? And if you believe, why doubt?" (Spurgeon)

e. **Why did you doubt**: Jesus only asked this question once Peter was safe and in the boat again. Yet at that point it was an entirely reasonable question to ask. Why *did* Peter doubt?

i. "*Doubt* is literally 'be divided in two'; true faith is single-mindedly focused on Jesus." (France)

ii. "If you believe a thing you want evidence, and before you doubt a thing you ought to have evidence too. To believe without evidence is to be credulous, and to doubt without evidence is to be foolish. We should have ground for our doubts as well as a basis for our faith." (Spurgeon)

iii. We can say that in theory, there might be reasons for doubting Jesus and His promises.

- If on former occasions, you have found God unfaithful to His promise.
- If some old follower of Jesus has solemnly told you that God cannot be trusted.
- If your problem is a new one and so extremely difficult that it is certain that God cannot help you.
- If God has abolished His promises, and made them no longer valid.
- If God has changed.

iv. "Our doubts are unreasonable: '*Wherefore didst though doubt?*' If there be reason for little faith, there is evidently reason for great confidence. If it be right to trust Jesus at all, why not trust him altogether?" (Spurgeon)

v. It is useful for us to confront our doubts.

- Was there good reason for your doubt?
- Was there any good excuse for it?
- Did any good come from your doubt?

f. **Those who were in the boat came and worshiped Him**: They moved quickly from fearing the storm to worshipping Jesus. This was a logical reaction considering the power Jesus showed in walking on the water, and the love He showed in taking care of a sinking Peter.

> i. "This is the first time we meet with so plain and open an acknowledgement of his being *the Son of God*." (Poole)

4. (34-36) Multitudes are healed as they touch Jesus.

When they had crossed over, they came to the land of Gennesaret. And when the men of that place recognized Him, they sent out into all that surrounding region, brought to Him all who were sick, and begged Him that they might only touch the hem of His garment. And as many as touched *it* were made perfectly well.

a. **When they had crossed over, they came to the land of Gennesaret**: The Gospel of John tells us that this crossing over was miraculous. As Jesus got into the boat with them, miraculously the boat was instantly carried over to the other side (John 6:21).

> i. "*Gennesaret* was a region (not just a town) on the western shore south of Capernaum. [This was a] surprising return to Antipas' territory." (France)

b. **Begged Him that they might only touch the hem of His garment**: Even the hem of Jesus' garment provides an important point of contact for their faith. Like Paul's sweatbands (Acts 19:11-12) and Peter's shadow (Acts 5:15), Jesus' hem provided a physical object that helped them to believe God for healing at that moment.

> i. "The stricter groups, such as the Pharisees and the Essenes, counted it an abomination to rub shoulders in a crowd – one never knew what ceremonial uncleanness one might contract." (Carson)

Matthew 15 - Jesus Corrects the Pharisees and Ministers to Gentiles

A. Jesus denounces religious externalism.

1. (1-2) Leaders from Jerusalem question Jesus.

Then the scribes and Pharisees who were from Jerusalem came to Jesus, saying, "Why do Your disciples transgress the tradition of the elders? For they do not wash their hands when they eat bread."

a. **Scribes and Pharisees who were from Jerusalem came to Jesus**: Up to this point, most of Jesus' ministry had been in the region of Galilee. Galilee was north of Judea, where Jerusalem is. These **scribes and Pharisees** were an official delegation from Jerusalem, coming to investigate and assess the words and work of this man Jesus.

   i. "They are genuinely bewildered; and in a very short time they are going to be genuinely outraged and shocked." (Barclay)

b. **Why do Your disciples transgress the tradition of the elders?** These washings were commanded by **tradition**, not by Scripture. They leaders said so by referring to **the tradition of the elders** not God's commandment.

   i. "The 'elders' here are not the living rulers of the people, but the past bearers of religious authority, the more remote the more venerable." (Bruce)

c. **They do not wash their hands when they eat bread**: The matter in question had nothing to do with good hygiene. The religious officials were offended that the disciples did not observe the rigid, extensive rituals for washing before meals.

   i. Many ancient Jews took this **tradition of the elders** very seriously. "The Jewish Rabbi Jose saith, *He sinneth as much who eateth with unwashen hands, as he that lieth with a harlot.*" (Poole)

ii. "In what estimation these are held by the Jews, the following examples will prove: 'The words of the scribes are lovely beyond the words of the law: for the words of the law are *weighty* and *light*, but the words of the scribes are *all* weighty.' *Hierus. Berac.* fol. 3." (Clarke)

2. (3) Jesus answers with a question setting man's tradition against God's will.

He answered and said to them, "Why do you also transgress the commandment of God because of your tradition?"

a. **Why do you also transgress the commandment of God**: When the disciples were accused of sin, Jesus answered with an accusation. Jesus was strong in His reply because these leaders were far too concerned with these ceremonial trivialities. When they declared people unclean because of their **tradition**, they denied the people access to God.

i. This was a strong reply from Jesus. Ultimately, these conflicts with the religious leaders became the outward reason why Jesus was delivered to the Romans for death.

b. **Because of your tradition**: Jesus repeated what the scribes and Pharisees had already mentioned – that this accusation was based on **tradition**. The religious leaders demanded these ceremonial washings based on **tradition**, not the Scriptures.

3. (4-6) An example of how their traditions dishonored God: the practice of not helping your parents with resources said to be devoted to God.

"For God commanded, saying, 'Honor your father and your mother'; and, 'He who curses father or mother, let him be put to death.' But you say, 'Whoever says to his father or mother, "Whatever profit you might have received from me *is* a gift *to God*"; then he need not honor his father or mother.' Thus you have made the commandment of God of no effect by your tradition."

a. **Honor your father and mother**: The clear command of God said that everyone should give **honor** to their **father and mother** – even stating a penalty for extreme disobedience to this command. When we are adults and no longer in our parents' household or under their authority, we no longer have to *obey* our father and mother. Yet we are still commanded to **honor** them; that command endures.

b. **Whatever profit you might have received from me is a gift to God**: Some Jewish people of Jesus' day had a way to get around the command to **honor your father and mother**. If they declared that all their possessions or savings were **a gift to God** that were especially dedicated to Him, they could then say that their resources were unavailable to help their parents.

i. "This convenient declaration apparently left the property actually still at the disposal of the one who made the vow, but deprived his parents of any right to it." (France)

ii. "Our Saviour here also let us know, that the fifth commandment obligeth children to relieve their parents in their necessity, and this is the sense of the term *honour* in other texts of Scripture." (Poole)

c. **Thus you have made the commandment of God of no effect by your tradition**: Through this trick one could completely disobey the command to **honor his father or mother**, and do it while being ultra-religious.

4. (7-9) Jesus condemns their hollow tradition as hypocrisy.

"Hypocrites! Well did Isaiah prophesy about you, saying:

'These people draw near to Me with their mouth,
And honor Me with *their* lips,
But their heart is far from Me.
And in vain they worship Me,
Teaching *as* doctrines the commandments of men.'"

a. **Honor Me with their lips, but their heart is far from Me**: This was true of the religious leaders Jesus confronted and quoted the passage from Isaiah to. Yet it may also be true of us. We can *appear* to draw near to God, all the while having our **heart far from** Him. It is easy to want and be impressed by the *image* of being near to God without really doing it with our **heart**.

i. God is interested in the internal and the real. We are far more interested in the merely external and image. One must take care that their relationship with God is not merely external and image.

b. **Teaching as doctrines the commandments of men**: The quotation from Isaiah accurately described the real problem with these religious leaders. They elevated man's tradition to an equal level with God's revealed Word.

i. Jesus didn't say, "All traditions are bad." He didn't say, "All traditions are good." He compared traditions to the Word of God, and put them at a much lower priority than what *God* has said.

5. (10-11) Jesus speaks to the multitude about religious externalism.

When He had called the multitude to *Himself,* He said to them, "Hear and understand: Not what goes into the mouth defiles a man; but what comes out of the mouth, this defiles a man."

a. **When He had called the multitude to Himself**: Having dealt with the religious leaders, Jesus now instructed the common people about authentic godliness.

b. **Not what goes into the mouth defiles a man; but what comes out of the mouth, this defiles a man**: Jesus stated a fundamental principle. Eating with "unclean hands" or any other such thing that we put into us is not defiling; rather, what **comes out** is what defiles and reveals if we have unclean (defiled) hearts.

> i. This is not to say that there are not defiling things that we can take into ourselves; one example of this might be pornography. But in this specific context, Jesus spoke about ceremonial cleanliness in regard to food, and He anticipated that under the New Covenant all food would be declared kosher (Acts 10:15).

> ii. "The principles set out by Jesus' words in Matthew 15:11 and 17-20 made the ultimate abandonment of the Old Testament food-laws by the church inevitable." (France)

6. (12-14) Jesus then warns His disciples that only what is of God and of truth will last and be secure.

Then His disciples came and said to Him, "Do You know that the Pharisees were offended when they heard this saying?" But He answered and said, "Every plant which My heavenly Father has not planted will be uprooted. Let them alone. They are blind leaders of the blind. And if the blind leads the blind, both will fall into a ditch."

a. **Do You know that the Pharisees were offended when they heard this saying?** This is a humorous scene. The disciples came to Jesus, saying something like this: "Jesus - did you know that you offended those guys?" Of course Jesus knew that He offended them! He *intended* to offend them and the way they valued man's tradition too highly.

b. **Every plant which My heavenly Father has not planted will be uprooted**: This applied directly to the religious leaders and all like them. Their *commandments of men* will not last, because they are not rooted either in God or truth.

> i. "There was no need for the disciples to combat the Pharisees, they would be uprooted in the natural order of things by the inevitable consequences of their own course." (Spurgeon)

> ii. Yet this principle should make us examine ourselves to see if we imitate the Pharisees by making our traditions into commandments. "By this test we need ever to try our traditions, customs, habits, rules, regulations." (Morgan)

c. **Let them alone**: Jesus did not organize a focused "Anti-Scribe and Pharisee" committee. He knew that their efforts would fail under the weight of its own legalism.

d. **They are blind leaders of the blind...both will fall into a ditch**: We sense that Jesus said this with sadness, and perhaps with more sadness for those who are led by the blind than the **blind leaders of the blind**.

> i. "Though the Pharisees and teachers of the law had scrolls and interpreted them in the synagogues, this does not mean that they really understood them...The Pharisees did not follow Jesus; so they did not understand and follow the Scriptures." (Carson)

> ii. "I pity the poor people, for whilst the blind lead the blind they both fall into a ditch. An ignorant and unfaithful ministry is the greatest plague God can send amongst a people." (Poole)

> iii. In these words of Jesus, we see the *guilt* of those who are **blind leaders of the blind**. We also see the *responsibility* of followers to make sure their leaders are not blind.

7. (15-20) The condition of the heart is what really defiles a person.

Then Peter answered and said to Him, "Explain this parable to us." So Jesus said, "Are you also still without understanding? Do you not yet understand that whatever enters the mouth goes into the stomach and is eliminated? But those things which proceed out of the mouth come from the heart, and they defile a man. For out of the heart proceed evil thoughts, murders, adulteries, fornications, thefts, false witness, blasphemies. These are *the things* which defile a man, but to eat with unwashed hands does not defile a man."

a. **Explain this parable to us**: In Matthew 15:12-14 Jesus didn't really speak in a **parable** (except for the brief illustration of the blind leading the blind). Yet because the disciples did not understand Him, they asked for an explanation (**Are you also still without understanding?**).

b. **Those things which proceed out of the mouth come from the heart, and they defile a man**: Jesus amplified the point first made in Matthew 15:11. We are defiled from the *inside out* rather than from the *outside in*, and this is particularly true of ceremonial things like foods.

> i. Jesus boldly said that these evil things come from our innermost nature. They aren't accidents or mere "mistakes"; they reveal how corrupt we are in our fallen nature. "*The heart* is the source of man's true character, and therefore of his purity or impurity...the true person as he really is, not just as he appears outwardly." (France)

> ii. "'*Murders*' begin not with the dagger, but with the malice of the soul. '*Adulteries and fornications*' are first gloated over in the heart before they are enacted by the body. The heart is the cage from whence these unclean birds fly forth." (Spurgeon)

iii. Said plainly, many people who worry about external habits (what they eat and drink and other such things) should care more about what words come out of their mouth. They do more against God and His people by what they say than by what they eat or drink.

iv. **And is eliminated**: "A vulgar word and a vulgar subject which Jesus would gladly have avoided, but He forces Himself to speak of it for the sake of His disciples.... Doubtless Jesus said this, otherwise no one would have put it into His mouth." (Bruce)

c. **But to eat with unwashed hands does not defile a man**: Unfortunately, the emphasis of the religious leaders in Jesus' day – and often in our own – is often only on these external things, not the internal things that make for true righteousness.

B. Jesus answers a Gentile's request.

1. (21-22) Jesus is met with a request from a Gentile woman.

Then Jesus went out from there and departed to the region of Tyre and Sidon. And behold, a woman of Canaan came from that region and cried out to Him, saying, "Have mercy on me, O Lord, Son of David! My daughter is severely demon-possessed."

a. **To the region of Tyre and Sidon**: Tyre and Sidon were Gentile cities, located some 50 miles (80 kilometers) away. Jesus went all this way to meet this one Gentile woman's need. This shows remarkable and unexpected love from Jesus to this **woman of Canaan**.

i. "Matthew's used of the old term 'Canaanite' shows that he cannot forget her ancestry: now a descendant of Israel's ancient enemies comes to the Jewish Messiah for blessing." (Carson)

ii. It was unlikely for Jesus to go to the **region of Tyre and Sidon**. "At that time, or not much later, Josephus could write: 'Of the Phoenicians, the Tyrians have the most ill-feeling towards us.'" (Barclay)

iii. "Let us always plow to the very end of the field, and serve our day and generation to the extreme limits of our sphere." (Spurgeon)

b. **Have mercy on me...My daughter is severely demon-possessed**: This woman came to intercede for her daughter, and she provided a picture of an effective intercessor – her great need taught her how to pray. When she came to Jesus, she made her *daughter's* needs her *own*.

c. **Have mercy on me, O Lord, Son of David!** This Gentile woman also understood who Jesus was. Many of Jesus' own countrymen didn't know who Jesus was, but this **woman of Canaan** knew.

i. Perhaps this woman knew that Jesus had healed Gentiles before (Matthew 4:24-25; 8:5-13). Yet what made this encounter unique is that Jesus did those miracles as Gentiles came *to Him* in Jewish territory. Here, Jesus came to Gentile territory and met this woman.

2. (23-24) Jesus' cold response to the request of the Gentile woman.

But He answered her not a word. And His disciples came and urged Him, saying, "Send her away, for she cries out after us." But He answered and said, "I was not sent except to the lost sheep of the house of Israel."

a. **But He answered her not a word**: Though the Gentile mother interceded for her daughter, Jesus did not immediately give her an encouraging reply. His reticence drew a more energetic and faith-filled response from the Gentile woman.

i. "As Augustine says, 'The Word spoke not a word,' and that was so unlike him. He who was always so ready with responses to the cry of grief had no response for her." (Spurgeon)

b. **Send her away, for she cries out after us**: It is likely that the disciples meant, "Send her away by giving her what she wants." The easiest way for her to go away was for Jesus to fix her problem.

i. **Send her away**: "The same verb in Luke 2:29 applies to a dismissal with desire satisfied." (France)

c. **I was not sent except to the lost sheep of the house of Israel**: Jesus defined the focus of His mission to His irritated disciples and to the Gentile woman. He made it clear that He was *not* sent to Gentiles like her.

i. It is fair to ask whether Jesus meant the **lost sheep** *among* the house of Israel, or meant Israel as a whole. Matthew 10:6 ("*go rather to the lost sheep of the house of Israel*") would seem to imply the latter.

3. (25-27) The Gentile woman's persistent appeal to Jesus.

Then she came and worshiped Him, saying, "Lord, help me!" But He answered and said, "It is not good to take the children's bread and throw *it* to the little dogs." And she said, "Yes, Lord, yet even the little dogs eat the crumbs which fall from their masters' table."

a. **Then she came and worshiped Him, saying, "Lord, help me!"** She responded to the rebuff from Jesus with increased dedication to prevail with her request. In so doing, the Gentile woman continued to show what a dedicated intercessor does.

i. "She could not solve the problems of the destiny of her race, and of the Lord's commission; but she could pray...If, as a Shepherd, he may not gather her, yet, as Lord, he may *help* her." (Spurgeon)

ii. "I urge you who seek the conversion of others to follow her example. Notice, she did not pray, 'Lord, help my daughter;' but, 'Lord, help *me.*'" (Spurgeon)

iii. "I commend this prayer to you because it is *such a handy prayer.* You can use it when you are in a hurry, you can use it when you are in a fright, you can use it when you have not time to bow your knee. You can use it in the pulpit if you are going to preach, you can use it when you are opening your shop, you can use it when you are rising in the morning. It is such a handy prayer that I hardly know any position in which you could not pray it: 'Lord, help me.'" (Spurgeon)

b. **It is not good to take the children's bread and throw it to the little dogs**: Jesus continued to say discouraging things to the woman, yet this was not quite as severe as it might first sound. When Jesus called her one of the **little dogs**, He used **little** as a way to soften the harshness of calling her a dog. This softened the traditional Jewish slur towards Gentiles, which called them **dogs** in the most derogatory sense.

i. We are at the great disadvantage of not hearing the tone of Jesus' voice as He spoke to this woman. We suspect that His tone was not harsh; we rather suspect that it was winsome with the effect of inviting greater faith from the woman. It is possible to speak harsh words in a playful or winsome manner.

ii. "Its harshest word [**dogs**] contains a loophole. [**Dogs**] does not compare Gentiles to the dogs without, in the street, but to the household dogs belonging to the family, which have their portion though not the children's." (Bruce)

c. **Yes, Lord, yet even the little dogs eat the crumbs which fall from their masters' table**: The woman responded with great faith. She admitted her low estate, and did not debate the issue when Jesus called her one of the **little dogs**. She did not demand to be seen as a child; but only to be blessed as a dog.

i. It was as if she said, "Jesus, I understand that the focus of Your ministry is to the Jews – that they have a special place in God's redemptive plan. Yet I also understand that Your ministry extends beyond the Jewish people, and I want to be part of that extended blessing."

ii. Her response is especially meaningful in light of the increasing rejection of Jesus by the Jewish religious leaders. It was as if the woman said, "I'm not asking for the portion that belongs to the children, just the **crumbs** that they don't want." In the flow of Matthew's gospel, there was more and more that the Jewish religious establishment did not want to receive.

iii. These were two faith-filled words: **Yet even**. She accepted Jesus' description and asked for mercy despite it – or perhaps because of it. "She would not give over, though he gave her three repulses. So as she said, like Jacob, *I will not thee go, until thou bless me*. And as he, like a prince, so she, like a princess, prevailed with God and obtained the thing which she desired." (Poole)

iv. "Dear friend, possibly someone has whispered in your ear, 'Suppose you are not one of the elect.' Well, that was very much what our Lord's expression meant to her...Notice that this woman does not battle with that truth at all, she does not raise any question about it; she wisely waives it, and she just goes on praying, 'Lord, help me! Lord, have mercy upon me!' I invite you, dear friend, to do just the same." (Spurgeon)

4. (28) Jesus rewards the great faith of the Gentile woman.

Then Jesus answered and said to her, "O woman, great *is* your faith! Let it be to you as you desire." And her daughter was healed from that very hour.

a. **Then Jesus answered**: Finally, the woman will receive an encouraging word from Jesus.

b. **O woman, great is your faith!** Jesus never said this to another person. He complimented the great faith of the Roman centurion who asked Jesus to heal his servant (Matthew 8:10), but He said it to the crowd, not to the centurion directly. This Gentile woman heard it from Jesus directly.

i. Significantly, the only two people to receive this compliment from Jesus were these Gentiles. This shows us that:

- Great faith may be found in unexpected places – not merely Gentiles, but a *centurion* and a *woman*!

- Great faith is sometimes measured from its disadvantages. Their faith was great because it did not have the advantage of being nourished by the institutions of Judaism.

- Faith is often greatest when it is expressed on behalf of someone else's need.

ii. **Great is your faith!** "No-one else receives from Jesus the accolade." (France)

c. **O woman, great is your faith! Let it be to you as you desire**: Her faith was **great** enough to receive her request – what she desired from Jesus.

- Her faith was great, even *compared to her other virtues*. She was humble, she was patient, she was persevering, she cared for her child.

Yet Jesus didn't compliment any of these good things, but only her *faith*.

- Her faith was great because it was *unlikely*. No one might have expected a Gentile to trust Jesus so much.

- Her faith was great because she *worshipped* Jesus even before she had an answer from Him.

- Her faith was great because it had been *tested so severely*. It's hard to think of a greater test than a demon-possessed child; but her faith was also tried by the seeming indifference or coldness of Jesus.

- Her faith was great because it was *clever*. She turned Jesus' word inside-out and made what might have been taken as an insult as a door open for faith.

- Her faith was great because it concerned *a need right in front of her, and a real need at that*. Many people have faith for everything except those things that are right in front of them.

- Her faith was great because it *would not give up*. She did not stop until she got what she needed from Jesus.

- You could say that *her faith conquered Jesus*. He not only healed her daughter but He did so immediately, something that she had not even asked for.

  i. We read of *nothing else* that Jesus did during this time in Tyre and Sidon. It would seem that His only divine appointment was to meet the need of this woman of faith and her afflicted daughter.

C. The feeding of the 4,000.

1. (29-31) Jesus ministers healing to the multitude.

Jesus departed from there, skirted the Sea of Galilee, and went up on the mountain and sat down there. Then great multitudes came to Him, having with them *the* lame, blind, mute, maimed, and many others; and they laid them down at Jesus' feet, and He healed them. So the multitude marveled when they saw *the* mute speaking, *the* maimed made whole, *the* lame walking, and *the* blind seeing; and they glorified the God of Israel.

a. **Then great multitudes came to Him**: Though Jesus briefly withdrew from the **multitudes**, He did not do so permanently. He still had work to do among the **great multitudes**.

  i. Most commentators believe this marks a unique period in the ministry of Jesus, when He did His healing and providing work in the predominately Gentile region of Galilee. Especially correlating this with Mark 7:31-37, we see that this happened on the *eastern* side of the Sea of Galilee, the region known as the *Decapolis*. As well, the remoteness of the place (*in the wilderness*, Mathew 15:33) fits better with the eastern side.

ii. "These people were most probably heathen or semi-heathen, gathered from the region of the Decapolis (Mark 7:31)." (Morgan)

iii. As Jesus healed and provided for this mixed or predominately Gentile multitude, it showed that the Gentiles in fact were getting more than just a few crumbs from the table.

b. **They laid them down at Jesus' feet, and He healed them**: In this incident we read nothing about any faith on the part of those who were healed, except for the fact that they came to Jesus for help.

i. "Among those brought were certain classed as *kullous* [**maimed**], which is usually interpreted 'bent,' as with rheumatism. But in Matthew 18:8 it seems to mean 'mutilated'...Grotius argues for this sense, and infers that among Christ's works of healing were the restoration of lost limbs, though we do not read of such anywhere else." (Bruce)

c. **They glorified the God of Israel**: Even in something as potentially self-promoting as ministry of healing, Jesus always drew attention to God the Father, **the God of Israel**. This multitude – most likely predominately Gentile – learned to praise **the God of Israel**.

i. "The expression suggests a non-Israelite crowd and seems to hint that after all for our evangelist Jesus is on the east side and in heathen territory." (Bruce)

2. (32-39) The feeding of the 4,000.

Now Jesus called His disciples to *Himself* and said, "I have compassion on the multitude, because they have now continued with Me three days and have nothing to eat. And I do not want to send them away hungry, lest they faint on the way." Then His disciples said to Him, "Where could we get enough bread in the wilderness to fill such a great multitude?" Jesus said to them, "How many loaves do you have?" And they said, "Seven, and a few little fish." So He commanded the multitude to sit down on the ground. And He took the seven loaves and the fish and gave thanks, broke *them* and gave *them* to His disciples; and the disciples *gave* to the multitude. So they all ate and were filled, and they took up seven large baskets full of the fragments that were left. Now those who ate were four thousand men, besides women and children. And He

sent away the multitude, got into the boat, and came to the region of Magdala.

a. **I do not want to send them away hungry, lest they faint on the way**: This miracle follows the same basic pattern as the feeding of the 5,000, except that it reveals that the disciples were generally as slow to believe as we are (**where could we get enough bread in the wilderness to fill such a great multitude?**).

i. Perhaps the disciples had not "expected Jesus to use his Messianic power, when the crowd was a Gentile one." (France)

ii. It is important to see that this is not just a retelling of the previous feeding of the 5,000. There are many differences distinguishing this from the prior feeding of the 5,000:

* Different numbers of those being fed.
* Different locales (on the western and the eastern shores of the Sea of Galilee).
* Different seasons of the year, indicated by no mention of grass in the second account.
* Different supply of food at the beginning.
* Different number of baskets holding the leftovers, and even a different word for "baskets" in the second account.
* Different period of time of waiting for the people (Matthew 15:32).

b. **The disciples gave to the multitude**: Jesus did what only He could do (the creative miracle), but left to the disciples what they could do (the distribution of the meal).

c. **So they all ate and were filled, and they took up seven large baskets full of the fragments that were left**: At the end of the meal they gather more, not less. The **seven large baskets** show that God provided out of His abundance.

i. **And were filled**: "The Greek word here is, in its proper signification, used of fattening cattle." (Trapp)

ii. **Those who ate were four thousand men**: "Here there is no desire to swell the number, to make the wonder greater." (Spurgeon)

iii. The way that the Messiah miraculously fed both Jews and Gentiles was a preview of the great Messianic banquet. This was greatly anticipated among the Jews of Jesus' day, but they were offended by the idea that Gentiles would also attend.

Matthew 16 - Revealing Who Jesus Is and What He Came to Do

A. Warnings against the Sadducees and the Pharisees.

1. (1-4) The Sadducees and the Pharisees seek a sign from Jesus.

Then the Pharisees and Sadducees came, and testing Him asked that He would show them a sign from heaven. He answered and said to them, "When it is evening you say, *'It will be* fair weather, for the sky is red'; and in the morning, *'It will be* foul weather today, for the sky is red and threatening.' Hypocrites! You know how to discern the face of the sky, but you cannot *discern* the signs of the times. A wicked and adulterous generation seeks after a sign, and no sign shall be given to it except the sign of the prophet Jonah." And He left them and departed.

a. **Then the Pharisees and Sadducees**: Their working together showed a deep fear among the religious leaders. The Sadducees and Pharisees were long-standing enemies, and the fact that they came together against Jesus shows they regarded Him as a serious threat.

    i. "It is an extraordinary phenomenon to find a combination of the Pharisees and Sadducees. They stood for both beliefs and policies which were diametrically opposed." (Barclay)

- The Pharisees lived according to the smallest points of the oral and scribal law; the Sadducees received only the written words of the Hebrew Scriptures.

- The Pharisees believed in angels and the resurrection; the Sadducees did not (Paul used this division in Acts 23:6-10).

- The Pharisees were not a political party and were prepared to live under any government that would leave them alone to practice their religion the way they wanted to; the Sadducees

238

were aristocrats and collaborated with the Romans to keep their wealth and power.

- The Pharisees looked for and longed for the Messiah; the Sadducees did not.

ii. Yet for all these differences, Jesus brought them together. Not in a good way – they came together in *opposition* to Jesus, but they came together nonetheless.

b. **And testing Him asked that He would show them a sign from heaven**: Jesus *had* done many signs and they remained unconvinced. They looked for **a sign from heaven** such as calling down fire from heaven, preferably against a Roman legion. They said they were not convinced by the signs "on earth" Jesus had already done.

i. Jesus had already been asked for a sign in Matthew 12:38, and in response He had already pointed them to the sign of Jonah. Tradition held that a sign done on earth could be a counterfeit from Satan, but signs done **from heaven** (coming in or from the sky) were assumed to be from God.

ii. "The immediate demand of the Jewish leaders for a *sign from heaven* contrasts sharply with the Gentile crowd's response to Jesus' miracles (Matthew 15:31)." (France)

c. **Hypocrites! You know how to discern the face of the sky, but you cannot discern the signs of the times**: Jesus condemned their hypocrisy. They felt confident about predicting the weather from the signs they saw around them, but were blind to the signs regarding Jesus' Messianic credentials right before their eyes.

i. "The proof that they cannot discern the 'signs' is that they ask for a sign!" (Carson)

ii. Jesus wasn't the only one to notice hypocrisy in His day. There was a proverb in that day saying that if all the hypocrites in the world were divided into ten parts, Jerusalem would contain nine of the ten parts.

iii. **You cannot discern the signs of the times**: Jesus said this of the religious leaders of His own day regarding the signs of His *first coming*. There were prophecies, circumstances, and evidences that should have made it clear to them as **signs of the times** that the Messiah and come. Many people today are just as blind to the **signs of the times** regarding the *second coming* of Jesus.

d. **A wicked and adulterous generation seeks after a sign**: This statement of Jesus reminds us that signs alone convert no one. It is easy to place far too much confidence in signs and wonders as tools to bring people to faith in Jesus.

i. The problem isn't that the signs are themselves weak, but that **a wicked and adulterous generation seeks after** them. The Bible gives repeated examples of those who saw remarkable signs, yet did not believe.

e. **No sign shall be given to it except the sign of the prophet Jonah**: Jesus promised a sign that *would* have power to bring people to faith - His resurrection. He had previously mentioned **the sign of the prophet Jonah** in Matthew 12:39-41, clearly explaining it as His coming resurrection.

i. We remember some of the similarities between Jonah and Jesus:

- Jonah sacrificed himself that others would be saved.
- Jonah disappeared from all human view in doing this.
- Jonah was sustained the days when he could not be seen.
- Jonah came back after three days, as back from the dead.
- Jonah preached repentance.

2. (5-12) Jesus cautions the disciples against false teaching.

Now when His disciples had come to the other side, they had forgotten to take bread. Then Jesus said to them, "Take heed and beware of the leaven of the Pharisees and the Sadducees." And they reasoned among themselves, saying, *"It is* because we have taken no bread." But Jesus, being aware of *it,* said to them, "O you of little faith, why do you reason among yourselves because you have brought no bread? Do you not yet understand, or remember the five loaves of the five thousand and how many baskets you took up? Nor the seven loaves of the four thousand and how many large baskets you took up? How is it you do not understand that I did not speak to you concerning bread?; *but* to beware of the leaven of the Pharisees and Sadducees." Then they understood that He did not tell *them* to beware of the leaven of bread, but of the doctrine of the Pharisees and Sadducees.

a. **Take heed and beware of the leaven of the Pharisees and Sadducees**: After the preceding conflict with the religious leaders, Jesus gave this warning to His disciples, using the metaphor of **leaven**.

i. As noted previously in the parable of the leaven (Matthew 13:33), **leaven** is consistently used as a picture of sin and corruption (especially in the Passover narrative of Exodus 12:8, 12:15-20).

ii. "It was the Jewish metaphorical expression for an *evil influence*. To the Jewish mind leaven was always symbolic of evil...leaven stood for an evil influence liable to spread through life and to corrupt it." (Barclay) "False doctrine; which is fitly called leaven, because it soureth, swelleth, spreadeth, corrupteth the whole lump, and all this secretly." (Trapp)

b. **It is because we have taken no bread**: This was a strange concern after Jesus had, in the recent past, miraculously fed both crowds exceeding 5,000 and 4,000 people. The disciples didn't understand Jesus at all here and His use of **leaven** as a metaphor.

 i. "Our memories are naturally like hour-glasses, no sooner filled with good instructions and experiments than running out again. It must be our prayer to God that he would put his finger upon the hole, and so make our memories like the pot of manna, preserving holy truths in the ark of the soul." (Trapp)

c. **Then they understood that He did not tell them to beware of the leaven of bread, but of the doctrine of the Pharisees and Sadducees**: Jesus impressed the importance of being on guard against false teaching, especially that in the service of religious hypocrisy.

 i. Jesus charged His disciples with three things:

 • *Ignorance*, because they didn't understand that He was using material things (leaven) to illustrate spiritual things (the dangerous teachings and practices of the Sadducees and Pharisees).

 • *Unbelief*, because they were overly concerned with the supply of bread, when they had seen Jesus miraculously provide bread on several previous occasions.

 • *Forgetfulness*, because they seemed to forget what Jesus had done before in regard to providing bread.

B. Peter proclaims Jesus as Messiah.

1. (13) Jesus asks the disciples to tell Him who others say He is.

When Jesus came into the region of Caesarea Philippi, He asked His disciples, saying, "Who do men say that I, the Son of Man, am?"

a. **When Jesus came into the region of Caesarea Philippi**: Jesus again withdrew from the mainly Jewish region of Galilee and came to a place more populated by Gentiles. This was likely a retreat from the pressing crowds.

 i. "Caesarea Philippi lies about twenty-five miles [46 kilometers] northeast of the Sea of Galilee...The population was mainly non-Jewish, and there Jesus would have peace to teach the Twelve." (Barclay)

b. **Who do men say that I, the Son of Man, am?** Jesus did not ask this question because He didn't know who He was, or because He had an unfortunate dependence on the opinion of others. He asked this question as an introduction to a more important follow-up question.

i. Caesarea Philippi was an area associated with idols and rival deities. "The area was scattered with temples of the ancient Syrian Baal worship...Hard by Caesarea Philippi there rose a great hill, in which was a deep cavern; and that cavern was said to be the birthplace of the great god Pan, the god of nature...In Caesarea Philippi there was a great temple of white marble built to the godhead of Caesar...It is as if Jesus deliberately set himself against the background of the world's religions in all their history and splendour, and demanded to be compared to them and to have the verdict given in his favour." (Barclay)

2. (14-16) A pointed question and a pointed answer.

So they said, "Some *say* John the Baptist, some Elijah, and others Jeremiah or one of the prophets." He said to them, "But who do you say that I am?" Simon Peter answered and said, "You are the Christ, the Son of the living God."

a. **Some say John the Baptist, some Elijah, and others Jeremiah or one of the prophets**: People who thought that Jesus was **John the Baptist**, didn't know much about Him, and they didn't know that Jesus and John had ministered at the same time. Yet John, **Elijah**, and **Jeremiah** (along with other **prophets**) were national reformers who stood up to the corrupt rulers of their day.

i. Some thought Jesus was a herald of national repentance, like **John the Baptist** and some thought Jesus was a famous worker of miracles, like **Elijah**. Some thought Jesus was someone who spoke the words of God, like **Jeremiah** and the **prophets**.

ii. Perhaps in seeing Jesus in these roles, people hoped for a political messiah who would overthrow the corrupt powers oppressing Israel.

iii. The general tendency in all these answers was to *underestimate* Jesus; to give Him a measure of respect and honor, but to fall far short of honoring Him for who He really is.

b. **Who do you say that I am?** It was fine for the disciples to know what *others* thought about Jesus. But Jesus had to ask them, as individuals, what *they* believed about Him.

i. This is the question placed before all who hear of Jesus; and it is we, not He, who are judged by our answer. In fact, we answer this question every day by what we believe and do. If we really believe Jesus is who He says He is, it will affect the way that we live.

ii. "Our Lord presupposes that his disciples would not have the same thoughts as '*men*' had. They would not follow the spirit of the age, and shape their views by those of the 'cultured' persons of the period." (Spurgeon)

c. **You are the Christ, the Son of the living God**: Peter knew the opinion of the crowd - while it was complimentary towards Jesus - wasn't accurate. Jesus was much more than John the Baptist or Elijah or a prophet. He was more than a national reformer, more than a miracle worker, more than a prophet. Jesus is **the Christ**, the Messiah.

i. We can surmise that this was an understanding that Peter and the other disciples came to over time. In the beginning, they were attracted to Jesus as a remarkable and unusual rabbi. They committed themselves to Him as His disciples or students, as was practiced in that day. Yet over time Peter – and presumably other of the disciples by this point – understood that Jesus was in fact not only the Messiah (**the Christ**), but also **the Son of the living God**.

ii. Peter understood that Jesus was not only God's Messiah, but also God Himself. The Jews properly thought that to receive the title "**the Son of the living God**," in a unique sense, was to make a claim to deity itself.

iii. "The adjective *living* may perhaps have been included to contrast the one true God with the local deities (Caesarea Philippi was a centre of the worship of Pan)." (France)

3. (17-20) Jesus compliments Peter for His bold and correct declaration.

Jesus answered and said to him, "Blessed are you, Simon Bar-Jonah, for flesh and blood has not revealed *this* to you, but My Father who is in heaven. And I also say to you that you are Peter, and on this rock I will build My church, and the gates of Hades shall not prevail against it. And I will give you the keys of the kingdom of heaven, and whatever you bind on earth will be bound in heaven, and whatever you loose on earth will be loosed in heaven." Then He commanded His disciples that they should tell no one that He was Jesus the Christ.

a. **Flesh and blood has not revealed this to you, but My Father who is in heaven**: Jesus reveals to Peter that he spoke by divine inspiration, even if he didn't even know it at the time. In this, Peter was genuinely **blessed** – both by the insight itself and how it came to him.

i. We too often expect God to speak in strange and unnatural ways. Here God spoke through Peter so naturally that he didn't even realize it was the **Father who is in heaven** that revealed it to him.

ii. This also speaks to us of our need for a supernatural revelation of Jesus. "If you know no more of Jesus than flesh and blood has revealed to you, it has brought you no more blessing than the conjectures of their age brought to the Pharisees and Sadducees, who remained an adulterous and unbelieving generation." (Spurgeon)

b. **I also say to you that you are Peter**: This was not only recognition of Peter's more Roman name; it was also a promise of God's work in Peter. The name Peter means "Rock." Though perhaps unlikely, Peter *was* a rock, and *would become* a rock. God was and would transform his naturally extreme character into something solid and reliable.

c. **On this rock I will build My church**: The words **this rock** have been the source of much controversy. It is best to see them as referring to either Jesus Himself (perhaps Jesus gesturing to Himself as He said this), or as referring to Peter's confession of who Jesus is.

i. Peter, by His own testimony, did not see *himself* as the rock on which the church was founded. He wrote that we are living stones, but Jesus is the cornerstone. We could say that Peter was the "first believer"; that he was the "first rock" among "many rocks."

ii. Peter said as much in 1 Peter 2:4-5: *Coming to Him as to a living stone, rejected indeed by men, but chosen by God and precious, you also, as living stones, are being built up a spiritual house, a holy priesthood, to offer up spiritual sacrifices acceptable to God through Jesus Christ.*

d. **I will build My church**: This is the first use of the word **church** in the New Testament (or the Bible for that matter), using the ancient Greek word *ekklesia*. Significantly, this was well before the beginnings of what we normally think of as the church on the Day of Pentecost in Acts 2.

i. This shows that Jesus was *anticipating* or *prophesying* what would come from these disciples/apostles and those who would believe in their message that Jesus is **the Christ, the Son of the living God**.

ii. The ancient Greek word *ekklesia* was not primarily a religious word at all; it just meant, "group" or "called-out group." In describing the later group of His followers and disciples, Jesus deliberately chose a word without a distinctly religious meaning.

iii. Furthermore, this statement of Jesus was a clear claim of ownership (**My church**). *The church belongs to Jesus.* This was also a claim to deity:

"What is striking is…the boldness of Jesus' description of it as *my* community, rather than God's." (France)

iv. Taken together, the promise is wonderful:

- He brings His people together in common: **I will build**.
- He builds on a firm foundation: **On this rock I will build**.
- He builds something that belongs to Him: **My church**.
- He builds it into a stronghold: **the gates of Hades shall not prevail against it**.

e. **And the gates of Hades shall not prevail against it**: Jesus also offered a promise – that the forces of death and darkness can't prevail against or conquer the church. This is a valuable promise in dark or discouraging times for the church.

i. The Puritan commentator John Trapp explained **the gates of Hades** this way: "All the power and policy of hell combined."

ii. "Neither doth *hell* signify here the place of the damned…but either death, or the graves, or the state of the dead: yet the devil is also understood here, as he *that hath the power of death*, Hebrews 2:14." (Poole)

iii. "*The gates of hell*, i.e., the *machinations* and *powers* of the invisible world. In ancient times the gates of fortified cities were used to hold councils in, and were usually places of great strength. Our Lord's expression means, that neither the *plots, stratagems*, nor *strength* of Satan and his angels, should ever so far prevail as to destroy the sacred truths in the above confession." (Clarke)

iv. A slightly different view: "Is thus to say that it will not die, and be shut in by the 'gates of death.'" (France)

f. **And I will give you the keys of the kingdom of heaven**: This idea of Peter holding the **keys of the kingdom of heaven** has captured the imagination (and theology) of many Christians throughout the centuries. In artistic representation, Peter is almost always shown with **keys**.

i. Some people think that this means that Peter has the authority to admit people to heaven, or to keep people out of heaven. This is the basis for the popular image of Peter at the Pearly Gates of Heaven, allowing people to enter or turning them away.

ii. Some people think that it also means that Peter was the first Pope, and that his supposed successors have the keys that were first given to Peter. Indeed, the Papal insignia of the Roman Catholic Church is made up of two prominent keys crossed together.

iii. There is no doubt that Peter had a special place among all the disciples, and that he had some special privileges:

- He is always listed first in the listings of the disciples.

- He opened doors of the kingdom to the Jews in Acts 2:38-39.

- He opened doors of the kingdom to the Gentiles in Acts 10:34-44.

iv. Yet there is no Biblical argument whatsoever that Peter's privilege or authority was passed on. To put it one way; one might say that Jesus gave Peter the keys, but didn't give him the authority to pass them on to further generations, and there is not a *whisper* in the Scriptures that Peter's authority was to be passed on.

v. The idea that apostolic authority comes from Jesus, who gave it to Peter, who set his hands on the heads of approved and ordained men, who in turn set their hands on the heads of approved and ordained men, and so on and so on through the generations until today is *nonsense*. It is exactly what Spurgeon said it was: *the laying of empty hands on empty heads.*

g. **And whatever you bind on earth will be bound in heaven, and whatever you loose on earth will be loosed in heaven**: The power for binding and loosing is something that the Jewish rabbis of that day used. They **bound** or **loosed** an individual in the application of a particular point of the law. Jesus promises that Peter - and the other apostles - would be able to set the boundaries authoritatively for the New Covenant community. This was the authority given to the *apostles and prophets* to build a *foundation* (Ephesians 2:20).

i. We should understand this as Jesus giving both the permission and the authority to the first-generation apostles to make the rules for the early church – and indirectly, the inspired writings that would guide all generations of Christians. The authority that Peter carries is "not an authority which he alone carries, as may be seen from the repetition of the latter part of the verse in Matthew 18:18 with reference to the disciple group as a whole." (France)

ii. "Binding" and "loosing" were administrative terms in daily Jewish life; whenever a Jew came up against the Law of Moses, that Jewish person was either "bound" or "loosed" in regard to that law. To loose was to permit; to bind was to prohibit. To loose was to free from the law, to bind was to put under the law. "Their regular sense, which any Jew would recognize was *to allow* and *to forbid. To bind* something was *to declare it forbidden; to loose* was *to declare it allowed.* These were the regular phrases for taking decisions in regard to the law." (Barclay)

iii. In daily Jewish life, this could be rather complicated. Here is one example from ancient rabbinical writings, cited by teacher Mike Russ:

- If your dog dies in your house, is your house clean or unclean? *Unclean.*

- If your dog dies outside your house, is your house clean or unclean? *Clean.*

- If your dog dies on the doorstep, is your house clean or unclean? Ancient rabbinical writings took the issue on and decided that if the dog died with his nose pointing into the house, the house was *unclean*; if the dog died with his nose pointing away from the house, the house was *clean.*

iv. As their rabbi, Jesus did this binding and loosing for His own disciples. Without using the same words, this is what Jesus did when He allowed them to take the grains of wheat in the field (Matthew 12:1-8).

v. Significantly, when it came time to understand the dietary laws of the Old Covenant in light of the new work of Jesus, God spoke to Peter *first*. He and the other apostles, guided by the Spirit of God, would bind and loose Christians regarding such parts of the Old Covenant.

vi. In a lesser, secondary sense, this power is with the Church today. "The words of his sent servants, spoken in his name, shall be confirmed of the Lord, and shall not be, either as to promise or threatening, a mere piece of rhetoric." (Spurgeon)

h. **He commanded His disciples that they should tell no one that He was Jesus the Christ**: Jesus was pleased that His disciples were coming to know who He was in truth, but He still didn't want His identity popularly known before the proper time.

i. "Before they could preach that Jesus was the Messiah, they had to learn what that meant." (Barclay)

4. (21) Jesus begins to reveal the full extent of His mission.

From that time Jesus began to show to His disciples that He must go to Jerusalem, and suffer many things from the elders and chief priests and scribes, and be killed, and be raised the third day.

a. **He must go to Jerusalem, and suffer many things…and be killed**: This must have come as quite a shock to His disciples. After fully understanding that Jesus was the Messiah, the last thing they expected was the Messiah would **suffer many things** and **be killed**.

i. Yet this was the predicted work of the Messiah (Isaiah 53:3-12). He **must** die, and He **must** after His death **be raised the third day**.

ii. The suffering and death of Jesus was a **must** because of two great facts: the *man's sin* and *God's love*. While His death was the ultimate example of man's sin against God, it was also the supreme expression of God's love to man.

iii. "The 'must' of Jesus' suffering lies, not in unqualified determinism, nor in heroic determination (though some of both is present), but in willing submission to his Father's will." (Carson)

iv. "*The elders and chief priests and scribes* were the three groups who together made up the Sanhedrin, Israel's highest court; Jesus is to be officially executed. The estrangement between Jesus and the official Jewish leadership is thus already irrevocable." (France)

b. **And be raised the third day**: The disciples were probably so shocked that Jesus said He would be killed in Jerusalem that these words didn't sink in. Later, an angel reminded them of these words (Luke 24:6-8).

5. (22-23) Peter's unwitting opposition of Jesus.

Then Peter took Him aside and began to rebuke Him, saying, "Far be it from You, Lord; this shall not happen to You!" But He turned and said to Peter, "Get behind Me, Satan! You are an offense to Me, for you are not mindful of the things of God, but the things of men."

a. **Far be it from You, Lord; this shall not happen to You!** At this moment Peter had the remarkable boldness to **rebuke** Jesus. Peter did it privately (**took Him aside**), yet was confident enough to tell Jesus that He was wrong to consider going to Jerusalem to be killed.

i. It's not hard to see Peter following these steps:

- Peter confesses Jesus as the Messiah.

- Jesus compliments Peter, telling him that God revealed this to him.

- Jesus tells of His impending suffering, death, and resurrection.

- Peter feels this isn't right, and he feels that he hears from God and therefore has some authority or right to speak.

- Peter begins to rebuke Jesus. "'Began' suggests that Peter gets only so far before Jesus cuts him off." (Carson)

ii. We can infer that if Peter was bold enough to **rebuke** Jesus, he was confident that God told him that he was right and that Jesus was wrong at this point. Where it all broke down was that Peter was far too confident in his ability to hear from God.

- What Peter said didn't line up with the Scriptures.
- What Peter said was in contradiction to the spiritual authority over him.

b. **Get behind Me, Satan!** This was a strong rebuke from Jesus, yet entirely appropriate. Though a moment before, Peter spoke as a messenger of God, he then spoke as a messenger of **Satan**. Jesus knew there was a satanic purpose in discouraging Him from His ministry on the cross, and Jesus would not allow that purpose to succeed.

i. We can be sure that Peter *was not aware* that he spoke for Satan, just as a moment before he was not aware that he spoke for God. It is often much easier to be a tool of God or of the devil than we want to believe.

c. **You are not mindful of the things of God, but the things of men**: Jesus exposed how Peter came into this satanic way of thinking. He didn't make a deliberate choice to reject God and embrace Satan; he simply let his mind settle on **the things of men** instead of **the things of God**, and Satan took advantage of it.

i. Peter is a perfect example of how a sincere heart coupled with man's thinking can often lead to disaster.

ii. Peter's rebuke of Jesus is an evidence of the *leaven* mentioned in Matthew 16:6. With his mind on **the things of men**, Peter only saw the Messiah as the embodiment of power and strength, instead of as a suffering servant. Because Peter couldn't handle a suffering Messiah, he rebuked Jesus.

C. Jesus' call to disciples.

1. (24) Jesus declares His expectation that His followers would follow Him by dying to self.

Then Jesus said to His disciples, "If anyone desires to come after Me, let him deny himself, and take up his cross, and follow Me."

a. **Said to His disciples, "If anyone desires to come after Me"**: This was a word spoken to the **disciples** of Jesus; to those who genuinely wanted to follow (**come after**) Him.

b. **Let him deny himself, and take up his cross**: It was bad enough for the disciples to hear that Jesus would suffer, be rejected, and die on a cross. Now Jesus told them that they must do the same thing.

c. **Deny himself, and take up his cross**: Everybody knew what Jesus meant when He said this. Everyone knew that the cross was an unrelenting instrument of death. The **cross** had no other purpose.

i. The **cross** wasn't about religious ceremonies; it wasn't about traditions and spiritual feelings. The cross was a way to execute people.

ii. In these twenty centuries after Jesus, we have done a pretty good job in sanitizing and ritualizing the cross. Yet Jesus said something much like this: "Walk down death row daily and follow Me." Taking up your cross wasn't a journey; it was a one-way trip. There was no return ticketing; it was never a round trip.

iii. "Cross bearing does not refer to some irritation in life. Rather, it involves the way of the cross. The picture is of a man, already condemned, required to carry his cross on the way to the place of execution, as Jesus was required to do." (Wessel, commentary on Mark)

iv. "Every Christian must be a Crucian, said Luther, and do somewhat more than those monks that made themselves wooden crosses, and carried them on their back continually, making all the world laugh at them." (Trapp, commentary on Mark)

d. **Deny himself, and take up his cross**: Jesus made **deny himself** equal with **take up his cross**. The two express the same idea. The cross wasn't about self-promotion or self-affirmation. The person carrying a cross knew they couldn't save themselves.

i. "Denying self is not the same as self-denial. We practice self-denial when, for a good purpose, we occasionally give up things or activities. But we deny self when we surrender ourselves to Christ and determine to obey His will." (Wiersbe, commentary on Mark)

ii. Denying self means to live as an others-centered person. Jesus was the only person to do this perfectly, but we are to follow in His steps (**and follow Me**). This is following Jesus at its simplest: He carried a cross, He walked down death row; so must those who follow Him.

iii. Human nature wants to indulge self, not **deny** self. Death to self is always terrible, and if we expect it to be a pleasant or mild experience, we will often be disillusioned. Death to self is the radical command of the Christian life. To **take up** your cross meant one thing: you were going to a certain death, and your only hope was in resurrection power.

2. (25-27) The paradox of the cross: finding life by losing it.

"For whoever desires to save his life will lose it, but whoever loses his life for My sake will find it. For what profit is it to a man if he gains

the whole world, and loses his own soul? Or what will a man give in exchange for his soul? For the Son of Man will come in the glory of His Father with His angels, and then He will reward each according to his works."

a. **Whoever desires to save his life will lose it, but whoever loses his life for My sake will find it**: We must follow Jesus this way, because it is the only way that we will ever find life. It sounds strange to say, "You will never live until you first walk to your death with Jesus," but that is the idea. You can't gain resurrection life without dying first.

i. You don't lose a seed when you plant it, though it seems dead and buried. Instead, you set the seed free to be what it was always intended to be.

b. **What profit is it to a man if he gains the whole world, and loses his own soul?** Avoiding the walk to death with Jesus means that we may gain the **whole world**, and end up losing everything.

i. Jesus Himself had the opportunity to gain all the world by worshipping Satan (Luke 4:5-8), but He found life and victory in obedience instead.

ii. Amazingly, the people who live this way before Jesus are the ones who are really, genuinely happy. Giving our lives to Jesus all the way, and living as an others-centered person does not take away from our lives, it adds to it.

c. **He will reward each according to his works**: This ultimate gain is given on this day. If we live life blind to this truth, we really will lose our **own soul**.

i. "Not only Jesus' example, but the judgment he will exercise is an incentive to take up one's cross and follow him." (Carson)

ii. **With His angels**: "They are *his* angels: he stands so far above them that he owns them and uses them." (Carson)

3. (28) A promise to **see the Son of Man coming in His kingdom**.

"Assuredly, I say to you, there are some standing here who shall not taste death till they see the Son of Man coming in His kingdom."

a. **Some standing here… shall not taste death till they see the Son of Man coming in His kingdom**: Jesus said this at this moment to emphasize an important truth. Walking with Jesus doesn't just mean a life of death and crosses. It also means a life of the power and glory of the kingdom of God. Jesus promised some of His disciples would see glimpses of that power and glory.

Matthew 17 - Jesus Transfigured, Triumphant, and Taxed

A. Jesus is transfigured.

1. (1-2) The transformation of Jesus before His disciples.

Now after six days Jesus took Peter, James, and John his brother, led them up on a high mountain by themselves; and He was transfigured before them. His face shone like the sun, and His clothes became as white as the light.

a. **Jesus took Peter, James, and John**: Jesus did not invite all the disciples, but only these three. Perhaps Jesus did this to prevent the account of this amazing miracle being told of before the time was right (Matthew 17:9). Others have suggested that He did it because these three needed closer supervision than the others.

i. **Six days**: "Luke's 'about eight days after Jesus said this' (Luke 9:28) is based on a Greek way of speaking and means 'about a week later'." (Carson)

b. **Led them up on a high mountain**: There have been several suggestions for the location of the Mount of Transfiguration.

- Mount Tabor (about 1,900 feet, 580 meters); but it isn't **high**, and isn't on the way from Caesearea Philippi to Capernaum.

- Mount Hermon (about 9,300 feet, 2,835 meters) is **high**; but perhaps too high and too cold on its summit, where they seem to have spent the night. It also would not be close to the Jewish crowds that met Jesus immediately on His descent from the mountain (Matthew 17:14, Luke 9:37).

- Mount Miron (about 3,900 feet, 1,190 meters) was the highest mountain in a Jewish area, and is on the way between Caesearea Philippi and Capernaum. Carson favors this location.

    i. "The name of the '*high mountain*' can never be known; for those who knew the locality have left no information. Tabor, if you please; Hermon, if you prefer it. No one can decide." (Spurgeon)

c. **He was transfigured before them**: The word **transfigured** speaks of a *transformation*, not merely a change in outward appearance. The effect was extremely striking; Jesus became so bright in appearance that He was even difficult to look at (**like the sun**).

    i. "The verb *metamorphoo* ('transfigure,' 'transform,' 'change in form') suggests a change of inmost nature that may be outwardly visible." (Carson) It may be that this glory shone forth in Gethsemane, when those who arrested Him fell back when Jesus said, "I am."

    ii. Essentially this was not a *new* miracle, but the temporary cessation of an ongoing one. The real miracle was that Jesus, most of the time, could keep from displaying this glory. Yet John said, *We beheld His glory*. Peter wrote, *We were eyewitnesses of His majesty*.

    iii. "For Christ to be glorious was almost a less matter than for him to restrain or hide his glory. It is forever his glory that he concealed his glory; and that, though he was rich, for our sakes he became poor." (Spurgeon)

    iv. This happened as a fulfillment of Jesus' promise in Matthew 16:28. We should remember that chapter and verse divisions were certainly not in the original writings of the apostles, and did not come until the 16th Century.

d. **His face shone like the sun, and His clothes became as white as the light**: It was **His face** that did shine as the sun. He wasn't transformed into another being with another body; it was **His** own **face** that shone.

    i. Jesus has His disciples with Him when He shines in His glory. He is not glorified apart from them, because they share in His glory. *Father, I desire that they also whom You gave Me may be with Me where I am, that they may behold My glory which You have given Me.* (John 17:24)

    ii. "We are scarcely aware of the glory of which the human body is capable." (Spurgeon)

2. (3) Moses and Elijah appear with Jesus.

And behold, Moses and Elijah appeared to them, talking with Him.

a. **Moses and Elijah**: Remarkably, these two Old Testament persons **appeared** and spoke with the transfigured Jesus. Moses had lived some 1400 years before; Elijah some 900 years before; yet they were alive and in some sort of resurrected, glorified state.

  i. It is fair to think that these two particular persons from the Old Testament appeared because they represent the Law (**Moses**) and the Prophets (**Elijah**). The sum of Old Testament revelation came to meet with Jesus at the Mount of Transfiguration.

  ii. We can also say that **Moses and Elijah** represent those who are caught up to God (**Moses** at Jude 9 and **Elijah** at 2 Kings 2:11). More specifically, Moses represents those who die and go to glory, and Elijah represents those who are caught up to heaven without death (as in the rapture described in 1 Thessalonians 4:13-18).

  iii. "Saints long departed still alive; live in their personality; are known by their names; and enjoy near access to Christ." (Spurgeon)

b. **Talking with Him**: Luke 9:31 tells us the theme of their conversation; they *spoke of His decease which He was about to accomplish at Jerusalem.* They spoke of the upcoming work of the cross, and presumably of the resurrection to follow.

  i. "And where could there have been found greater subjects than this wondrous death, and his glorious resurrection?" (Meyer)

  ii. "They 'appeared unto *them*' but they 'talked with *him*': the object of the two holy ones was not to converse with the apostles, but with their Master. Although saints are seen of men, their fellowship is with Jesus." (Spurgeon)

3. (4-5) Peter equates Jesus with Moses and Elijah and is dramatically rebuked by a voice from the cloud of God's glory.

Then Peter answered and said to Jesus, "Lord, it is good for us to be here; if You wish, let us make here three tabernacles: one for You, one for Moses, and one for Elijah." While he was still speaking, behold, a bright cloud overshadowed them; and suddenly a voice came out of the cloud, saying, "This is My beloved Son, in whom I am well pleased. Hear Him!"

a. **Lord, it is good for us to be here; if You wish, let us make here three tabernacles: one for You, one for Moses, and one for Elijah**: Mark 9:6 and Luke 9:33 point out that Peter didn't know what he was saying when he said this. Though said without careful thought, the effect of his words put Jesus on an equal level with Moses and Elijah, building equal shrines for each of them.

i. "Peter suggested the retention of the three in association: Moses, the law-giver; Elijah, the reformer; and Jesus, the Messiah." (Morgan)

ii. "The *booths* [**tabernacles**] (the word normally means 'tents') would be temporary shelters of branches, such as were erected for the Feast of Tabernacles." (France)

iii. "How selfish the one thought, '*It is good for us!*' What was to be done for the rest of the twelve, and for the other disciples, and for the wide, wide world?" (Spurgeon)

b. **A bright cloud overshadowed them**: This is the cloud of God's glory, called the *shekinah* in the Old Testament. From this cloud of glory, God the Father spoke.

i. "When God draws near to man it is absolutely necessary that his glory should be veiled. No man can see his face and live. Hence the cloud, in this instance, and in other cases." (Spurgeon)

c. **This is My beloved Son, in whom I am well pleased. Hear Him!** The Father, from heaven, rebuked Peter's attempt to put Jesus on an equal footing with Moses and Elijah – and **while he was still speaking**. It was important to interrupt Peter, so that all would know that Jesus is unique and the **beloved Son** - He deserves our special attention, so **Hear Him!**

i. One might say that everything that the Father said came from the Scriptures.

- In Psalm 2:7, the Father says to the Son: *You are my Son.*

- In Isaiah 42:1, the Father says to the Son that He is *One in whom My soul delights.* Or as Matthew 12:18 quotes the passage: *in whom My soul is well pleased!*

- In Deuteronomy 18:15, God the Father says through Moses the prophet about the coming Jesus, *Him you shall hear.*

ii. "The occasion was most august, yet no better words are needed by the Lord himself concerning his own Son than those recorded in former ages in the pages of Holy Writ...So that this voice of the Lord utters three Bible words, and surely if the Lord speaks in the language of Scripture, how much more should his servants? We preach best when we preach the word of God." (Spurgeon)

iii. This is another development of the significant theme in Matthew of the conflict between Jesus and the religious leaders. With these words from heaven, God the Father clearly set Jesus above the Law and the Prophets. He is not merely *another* or even a *better* lawgiver or prophet. Jesus is the **only begotten Son**.

iv. "If the Father says, 'This is my Son,' observe the graciousness of our adoption! With such a Son the Lord had no need of children. He did not make us his children because he needed sons, but because we needed a father." (Spurgeon)

d. **Hear Him!** If we should listen to anyone, we should listen to Jesus. One would think that a voice from heaven would say, "Listen to me!" But the Father said, "**Hear Him!**" Everything points us to Jesus.

i. "If Peter be our master, let us call him so; if Calvin be our master, let us call him so; and if Wesley be our master, let us call him so; but if we be disciples of Jesus, then let us follow Jesus, and follow him with other men only so far as we perceive they followed Christ." (Spurgeon)

4. (6-8) The disciples react with a holy fear.

And when the disciples heard *it*, they fell on their faces and were greatly afraid. But Jesus came and touched them and said, "Arise, and do not be afraid." When they had lifted up their eyes, they saw no one but Jesus only.

a. **They fell on their faces and were greatly afraid**: They didn't fall on their faces when they saw Jesus transfigured; not when His face shone like the sun; not when His clothes became as white as the light; not when Moses and Elijah appeared with Him; not when Moses and Elijah spoke with Jesus; and not even when the cloud of glory appeared and overshadowed them. But **when the disciples heard** the voice from heaven, **they fell on their faces and were greatly afraid**.

i. "They were in the immediate presence of God, and listening to their Father's voice: well might they lie and prostrate and tremble. Too clear a manifestation of God, even though it related to Jesus, would rather overpower than empower us." (Spurgeon)

b. **Arise, and do not be afraid**: The disciples were once again uniquely in awe of Jesus. This helps explain the purpose of the Transfiguration: to reassure the disciples that Jesus was the Messiah, even if He would indeed be crucified as He had so surprisingly revealed.

i. Note the context: Jesus just revealed His humiliation and sufferings to them. It makes sense that they receive another divine testimony to Jesus' status as the Son of God at this time.

c. **When they had lifted up their eyes, they saw no one but Jesus only**: It is significant that their entire focus was forced upon Jesus once again. The cloud was gone; Moses had left, and Elijah had disappeared.

i. It might have been that after the events of the transfiguration, *no one remained for the disciples*. Theoretically, when the experience was over, there would have been no Moses, no Elijah, and no Jesus. This is exactly the experience of many. They have some spiritual experience, or receive some ministry from the Holy Spirit of God; but when it is over, it is over – done and gone. Nothing remains.

ii. It might have been that after the events of the transfiguration, *only Moses remained for the disciples*. Theoretically, when the experience was over, there would have been only Moses. Though Moses was a great man, compared to Jesus he was like the moon is to the sun. It would be sad to exchange the grace and truth that came by Jesus for the law that came by Moses; but there are those sad ones who see Moses and his law only.

iii. It might have been that after the events of the transfiguration, *only Elijah remained for the disciples*. Theoretically, when the experience was over, there would have been only Elijah. Elijah was a man great for the power of his word and the boldness of his national reforms. Yet all this doesn't compare to the person and work of Jesus only.

iv. It might have been that after the events of the transfiguration, *all three remained*. At first, this might have seemed to be the best – why not all three? Yet now that Jesus has come, Moses and Elijah can fade into their supportive roles, and never be put on the same level as Jesus.

v. "Though the apostles saw 'Jesus only,' they saw quite sufficient, for Jesus is enough for time and eternity, enough to live by and enough to die by…O look to him, and though it be Jesus only, though Moses should condemn you, and Elias should alarm you, yet 'Jesus only' shall be enough to comfort and enough to save you." (Spurgeon)

vi. "At this day, my brethren, we have no Master but Christ; we submit ourselves to no vicar of God; we bow down ourselves before no great leader of a sect, neither to Calvin, nor to Arminius, to Wesley, or Whitfield. 'One is our Master,' and that one is enough, for we have learned to see the wisdom of God and the power of God in Jesus only." (Spurgeon)

5. (9-13) The problem of Elijah coming first.

Now as they came down from the mountain, Jesus commanded them, saying, "Tell the vision to no one until the Son of Man is risen from the dead." And His disciples asked Him, saying, "Why then do the scribes say that Elijah must come first?" Jesus answered and said to them, "Indeed, Elijah is coming first and will restore all things. But I say to

you that Elijah has come already, and they did not know him but did
to him whatever they wished. Likewise the Son of Man is also about to
suffer at their hands." Then the disciples understood that He spoke to
them of John the Baptist.

a. **Tell the vision to no one until the Son of Man is risen from the dead**:
Wisely, Jesus told the disciples to not speak of the transfiguration until
after His resurrection. The resurrection of Jesus was the final confirmation
of His ministry and glory; until then, reports of the transfiguration would
be more likely to *test* the faith of those who did not see it rather than
strengthen their faith.

b. **Why then do the scribes say that Elijah must come first?** The disciples
had heard that **Elijah must come**, according to the promise of Malachi
4:5: *Behold, I will send you Elijah the prophet before the coming of the great
and dreadful day of the LORD.*

i. Their question may go like this: "Jesus, we know that Elijah comes
first before the Messiah. We know You are the Messiah, yet we just saw
Elijah, and it seems that he came *after* You."

c. **Indeed, Elijah is coming first and will restore all things**: Jesus
reassured the disciples that Elijah would indeed come first. But the first
coming of Jesus did not bring the *great and dreadful day of the LORD*.
Instead, the Malachi 4:5 coming of Elijah is probably best identified with
the appearance of the two witnesses of Revelation 11:3-13, and then the
Second Coming of Jesus.

d. **But I say to you that Elijah has come already**: Yet there was also a sense
in which Jesus could rightly say **"Elijah has come already."** Elijah had
arrived in the work of John the Baptist, who ministered in Elijah's *spirit
and power* (Luke 1:17).

i. This is evident from a comparison of the life and work of both Elijah
and John the Baptist.

- Elijah was noted as being full of zeal for God; so was John.
- Elijah boldly rebuked sin in high places; so did John the Baptist.
- Elijah called sinners and compromisers to a decision of
repentance; so did John the Baptist.
- Elijah attracted multitudes in his ministry; so did John.
- Elijah attracted the attention and fury of a king and his wife; so
did John the Baptist.
- Elijah was an austere man; so was John the Baptist.

- Elijah fled to the wilderness; John the Baptist also lived there.

- Elijah lived in a corrupt time and was used to restore failing spiritual life; so was it true of John the Baptist.

B. Jesus casts out a difficult demon from a boy.

1. (14-16) A demon too tough for the disciples to handle.

And when they had come to the multitude, a man came to Him, kneeling down to Him and saying, "Lord, have mercy on my son, for he is an epileptic and suffers severely; for he often falls into the fire and often into the water. So I brought him to Your disciples, but they could not cure him."

a. **Have mercy on my son, for he is an epileptic**: This particular boy's epileptic symptoms were demonic in origin (Matthew 17:18), though this certainly could not be said about every case of epileptic symptoms, either then or today. The narrative in Mark 9:14-29 tells us that the boy was made deaf and dumb by this demon.

i. "Matthew describes the boy by the verb *seleniazesthai*, which literally means *to be moonstruck*." (Barclay)

ii. "When Moses came down from the mountain he was confronted by Israel's apostasy (Exodus 32); so on Jesus' return from the mountain he enters a scene of spiritual conflict and unbelief." (France)

iii. "There the mountain; now the valley. There glorified saints; here the lunatic. There the King in His heavenly glory; here the representatives of baffled and beaten faith." (Morgan)

iv. "It is easy to feel Christian in the moment of prayer and meditation; it is easy to feel close to God when the world is shut out. But that is not religion – that is escapism. Real religion is to rise from our knees before God to meet men and the problems of the human situation." (Barclay)

b. **So I brought him to Your disciples, but they could not cure him**: Sometimes Jesus' followers fail, but Jesus never does. The man was wise for going straight to Jesus when His followers failed.

i. On previous occasions, the disciples did cast out demons (Luke 10:17). Yet here **they could not cure him**. This is because there are ranks of demonic powers (Ephesians 6:12), and evidently some demons are stronger (more stubborn, resistant) than others. Since the disciples had been given the authority to cast out demons before (Matthew 10:8), apparently this demon was more difficult than most.

ii. Their failure was in fact good for them. Their failure taught them.

- It taught them not to get into a rut of mechanical ministry.

- It taught them the great superiority of Jesus.

- It taught them to wish for the presence of Jesus.

- It taught them to come to Jesus with the problem.

iii. "They were confounded at their want of success-but not at their want of faith, which was the cause of their miscarriage!" (Clarke)

2. (17-21) Jesus easily casts the demon out.

Then Jesus answered and said, "O faithless and perverse generation, how long shall I be with you? How long shall I bear with you? Bring him here to Me." And Jesus rebuked the demon, and it came out of him; and the child was cured from that very hour. Then the disciples came to Jesus privately and said, "Why could we not cast it out?" So Jesus said to them, "Because of your unbelief; for assuredly, I say to you, if you have faith as a mustard seed, you will say to this mountain, 'Move from here to there,' and it will move; and nothing will be impossible for you. However, this kind does not go out except by prayer and fasting."

a. **O faithless and perverse generation, how long shall I be with you?** There is a sense that Jesus is frustrated with His disciples. His season of ministry before the cross was coming to an end, and perhaps He felt frustration that the disciples did not have more faith.

b. **Jesus rebuked the demon and it came out of him**: Jesus delivered the demon-possessed boy instantly. What was too hard for the disciples was not too hard for Jesus.

c. **Because of your unbelief**: Jesus laid the inability of the disciples to cast out the demon at their **unbelief**. To be successful in a battle against demons, there must be trust in the Lord GOD who has complete authority over the demons.

i. "There are some things which are obtained by a stronger faith, and by more fervent and importunate prayers, than others are. A mercy sometimes seems to come to out of the hand of God with more difficulty, and wrestling for it." (Poole)

ii. There was no point in blaming the boy or his father or the demon, though the demon was strong and had been there long. The fault lay in the disciples. "When the ministers of the Gospel find their endeavours, with respect to some places or persons, ineffectual, they should come, by *private* prayer, to Christ, humble themselves before him, and beg to be informed whether some evil in *themselves* have not been the cause of the unfruitfulness of their labours." (Clarke)

d. **If you have faith as a mustard seed**: The faith that we must have has more to do with what *kind* of faith it is than with *how much* faith there is. A small amount of faith, as small **as a mustard seed** (a very small seed), can accomplish great things if that small amount of faith is placed in the great and mighty God.

i. Little faith can accomplish great things; but great faith can accomplish even greater things. What matters most is what our faith is in, the *object* of our faith. "The eye cannot see itself. Did you ever see your own eye? In a mirror you may have done so, but that was only a reflection of it. And you may, in like manner, see the evidence of your faith, but you cannot look at the faith itself. Faith looks away to itself to the object of faith, even to Christ." (Spurgeon)

ii. **You will say to this mountain, "Move from here to there"**: "Jesus here in effect calls faith an 'uprooter of mountains,' a phrase current in the Jewish schools for a Rabbi distinguished by legal lore or personal experience." (Bruce)

e. **This kind does not go out except by prayer and fasting**: We show our faith in and reliance on God through prayer and fasting. It displays an occupation with and dependence on Jesus.

i. Great prayer and fasting also display earnestness before God that brings answer to prayer. We often pray dispassionately, almost asking God to care about things we care little or nothing about.

ii. **Prayer and fasting** demonstrate:

- Great willingness to identify with the afflicted person.
- Great appreciation of the strength of the demonic world.
- Great dependence upon God.
- Great desire to fight and sacrifice for the sake of deliverance.

iii. "He that would overcome the devil in certain instances must first overcome heaven by prayer, and conquer himself by self-denial." (Spurgeon)

D. Look forward to the death and resurrection of Jesus.

1. (22-23) Jesus reminds His disciples about His future sufferings.

Now while they were staying in Galilee, Jesus said to them, "The Son of Man is about to be betrayed into the hands of men, and they will kill Him, and the third day He will be raised up." And they were exceedingly sorrowful.

a. **The Son of Man is about to be betrayed**: Though they were frequent, these reminders about Jesus' suffering and resurrection were disbelieved and forgotten by the disciples until after His resurrection (Luke 24:6-8).

b. **And the third day He will be raised up**: Jesus rarely told His disciples about His coming death without also telling of His coming resurrection. We know that the disciples didn't really comprehend the glorious triumph of the resurrection, because they were **exceedingly sorrowful**.

2. (24-26) Time to pay the temple tax.

When they had come to Capernaum, those who received the *temple* tax came to Peter and said, "Does your Teacher not pay the *temple* tax?" He said, "Yes." And when he had come into the house, Jesus anticipated him, saying, "What do you think, Simon? From whom do the kings of the earth take customs or taxes, from their sons or from strangers?" Peter said to Him, "From strangers." Jesus said to him, "Then the sons are free."

a. **Does your Teacher not pay the temple tax?** This was a normal tax or fee applied to every Jewish man. Faithful Jewish men paid this obligation; others sought to escape the responsibility.

i. "It was, however, also a matter of controversy, as the Sadducees disapproved of the tax, and the men of Qumran paid it only once in a lifetime." (France)

ii. "Payment could be made in person at the Passover festival in Jerusalem…but collections were made in other areas of Palestine and abroad a month earlier. This incident therefore takes place about a month before Passover." (France)

iii. "After AD 70, when the temple was destroyed, the Romans diverted this tax to the temple of Jupiter in Rome, after which it ceased to be a matter of patriotism and became a symbol of their subjection to a pagan power; the fact that the story is nonetheless recorded is one of the incidental indications that Matthew's Gospel should be dated before AD 70." (France)

b. **From whom do the kings of the earth take customs or taxes, from their sons or from strangers?** Peter gave the quick and natural answer to this question. But then Jesus explained that He is not liable to pay this tax, because the Father doesn't require it of His own Son.

i. "Rabbis were exempt from paying this tax, and so were the priests in Jerusalem; would Jesus claim a similar exemption? The question assumes that he does pay regularly, and Peter agrees." (France)

3. (27) Jesus pays the tax anyway, and by miraculous provision.

"Nevertheless, lest we offend them, go to the sea, cast in a hook, and take the fish that comes up first. And when you have opened its mouth, you will find a piece of money; take that and give it to them for Me and you."

a. **Nevertheless, lest we offend them**: Jesus was not obligated to pay this tax under the principle He had just discussed with Peter; that as a son, not a servant, He did not have to pay this temple tax. Yet Jesus also recognized the importance of avoiding needless controversy, and so was willing to pay the tax so as to not **offend** those who questioned.

i. The use of the Greek word *skandalizein* leads Barclay to write: "Therefore Jesus is saying: 'We must pay so as not to set a bad example to others. We must not only do our duty, we must go beyond duty, in order that we may show others what they ought to do.'"

b. **Cast in a hook**: Peter was a professional fisherman who used *nets*, not **a hook** and a line. It must have humbled Peter to fish in this manner, and we can imagine that he hoped none of his other fishermen friends saw him trying to catch one fish at a time.

i. "How this money came into the mouth of the fish is a very idle dispute, considering that he that speaks was the Creator of all things." (Poole)

c. **Take that and give it to them for Me and you**: Jesus trusted in the miraculous provision of God. It's not every day – or any day – that someone catches a fish and takes a coin out of its mouth. But Jesus used God's provision to pay His taxes.

i. "Thus the great Son pays the tax levied for his Father's house; but he exercises his royal prerogative in the act, and takes the shekel out of the royal treasury. As man he pays, but first as God he causes the fish to bring him the shekel in its mouth." (Spurgeon)

ii. We don't know why Jesus did not tell Peter to provide enough to pay for all the disciples. Perhaps it was implied or understood. Matthew Poole argued that this tribute at this time was only required of Jesus and Peter because it was the collection from the city of Capernaum, and only Peter and Jesus were at this time residents of Capernaum.

iii. Yet He did pay for Peter; as a foreshadow of the work of redemption for all men. Jesus, who did not actually owe the price, paid it nevertheless – and at the same time, with the same price, paid for Peter as well.

Matthew 18 – Qualities and Attitudes of Kingdom Citizens

Among the separatist community at Qumran – those who kept the Dead Sea Scrolls, later discovered in the 20ᵗʰ Century – there was a "Manual of Discipline" (known as 1QS by scholars). Some people think Matthew 18 is an early church version of a "Manual of Disciple." Yet there is a great difference between Matthew 18 and what the Essenes of Qumran had. Their Manual of Disciple dealt with many specific rules; here Jesus deals with principles *and* attitudes *that should mark His people as they get along with each other.*

A. The heart of a child and care for God's little ones.

1. (1) The disciples ask a question.

At that time the disciples came to Jesus, saying, "Who then is greatest in the kingdom of heaven?"

> a. **Who then is greatest**: The disciples were often concerned about the question of greatness. They seem to ask this question thinking that Jesus has already chosen one of them as **greatest**, or as if they wanted Jesus to decide among them.

> > i. We can imagine the disciples arguing amongst themselves about which one was the greatest (as they did in Luke 22:46 and other places), and then saying, "Let's let Jesus settle this."

> > ii. "He spoke of his abasement, they thought of their own advancement; and that '*at the same time*'." (Spurgeon)

> b. **Is greatest in the kingdom of heaven**: The disciples wanted to know who would hold the highest position in the administration Jesus would soon establish.

> > i. "They doubtless fancied a temporal kingdom of the Messiah, in which places would be bestowed." (Poole) "They dreamt of a distribution of

honours and offices, a worldly monarchy, like the kingdoms of the earth." (Trapp)

2. (2-4) Jesus sets a child as an example of humility.

Then Jesus called a little child to Him, set him in the midst of them, and said, "Assuredly, I say to you, unless you are converted and become as little children, you will by no means enter the kingdom of heaven. Therefore whoever humbles himself as this little child is the greatest in the kingdom of heaven."

a. **Jesus called a little child to Him**: Jesus might have answered the question, "who is the greatest?" by pointing to Himself. Instead, Jesus drew their attention to His *nature* by having them look at a child as an example.

i. The fact that the child came when **Jesus called** says something about Jesus. He was the sort of man that children would come to willingly.

ii. It also tells us something about Peter. If Peter really was to be regarded as the first pope in the way Popes are regarded by Roman Catholic theology and history, Jesus should have declared that *Peter* was **the greatest in the kingdom of heaven**.

iii. "There is a tradition that the child grew to be Ignatius of Antioch, who in later days became a great servant of the Church, a great writer, and finally a martyr for Christ." (Barclay) Clarke indicates that this tradition comes from the Christian writer Nicephorus, who says that Ignatius was killed by Trajan in AD 107. Yet Clarke also writes of Nicephorus, that he "is not much to be depended on, being both weak and credulous."

b. **Unless you are converted and become as little children, you will by no means enter the kingdom of heaven**: This was probably a great disappointment to the disciples. They knew that in that day, children were regarded more as property than individuals. It was understood that they were to be seen and not heard. Jesus said we have to take this kind of humble place to **enter the kingdom**, much less be the **greatest** in the kingdom.

i. "A *child* was a person of no importance in Jewish society, subject to the authority of his elders, not taken seriously except as a responsibility, one to be looked after, not one to be looked up to." (France)

ii. Children are not threatening; we aren't afraid of meeting a five-year-old in a dark alley. When we have a tough, intimidating presence, we aren't like Jesus.

iii. Children are not good at deceiving; they are pretty miserable failures at fooling their parents. When we are good at hiding ourselves and deceiving others, we aren't like Jesus.

iv. "The child is held up as an ideal, not of innocence, purity, or faith, but of humility and unconcern for social status." (Carson)

v. Jesus knew that we must be **converted** to be like little children. It isn't in our nature to take the low place and to humble ourselves.

c. **Whoever humbles himself as this little child is the greatest in the kingdom**: Jesus then addressed the issue of *greatness*. When we most fulfill the humble place a child had in that culture, we are then on our way to greatness in His **kingdom**.

i. "*Humbles himself* does not refer to arbitrary asceticism or a phoney false modesty…but the acceptance of an inferior position (as Jesus did, Philippians 2:8, where the same phrase is used)." (France)

ii. "Children do not try to be humble, but they are so; and the same is the case with really gracious persons. The imitation of humility is sickening; the reality is attractive." (Spurgeon)

iii. We know that one Man was actually the **greatest in the kingdom**: Jesus Christ. This means that Jesus Himself was humble like a little child. He wasn't concerned about his own status. He didn't have to be the center of attention. He could not deceive, and He didn't have an intimidating presence.

3. (5-6) Woe to the one who causes one of these to stumble!

"Whoever receives one little child like this in My name receives Me. But whoever causes one of these little ones who believe in Me to sin, it would be better for him if a millstone were hung around his neck, and he were drowned in the depth of the sea."

a. **Whoever receives one little child like this in My name receives Me**: Since the nature of Jesus is like one of these little children, how we treat those who are humble like children shows what we think of the nature of Jesus.

i. "They are not welcomed because they are great, wise, or mighty, but because they come in Jesus' name – i.e., they belong to him." (Carson) "The essential fact in the transformation Christ works is that He changes the great ones into little children." (Morgan)

ii. It is easy to actually *despise* the humble. They are the losers; the kind who will never make it in our competitive and aggressive and get-ahead world. Yet when we despise humble people, we also despise Jesus.

b. **Whoever causes one of these little ones who believe in Me to sin**: Jesus takes it seriously when one of His **little ones** is led into sin. "**Little ones**" does not only mean children, but those who humble themselves as children in the manner Jesus described.

> i. It is a wicked thing to sin, and it is a far greater evil to lead others into sin. But leading one of Jesus' **little ones** into sin is far worse, because you then *initiate* someone into an instance or a pattern of sin that corrupts whatever innocence they had.

c. **It would be better for him if a millstone were hung around his neck, and he were drowned in the depth of the sea**: A severe punishment is described here. It would be **better** for the offending one to receive this punishment of the millstone.

> i. The stone, and anyone attached to it, was sure to sink and never come up again. And, this was a *big* millstone. "Most millstones were hand tools for domestic use…here it is the heavy stone pulled around by a donkey." (Carson)

> ii. "In the deep part of the sea." (Bruce) "Moreover, the very picture of drowning had its terror for the Jew. Drowning was sometimes a Roman punishment, but never Jewish." (Barclay)

4. (7) Offenses are inevitable, but we are to have no part in offending.

"Woe to the world because of offenses! For offenses must come, but woe to that man by whom the offense comes!"

a. **Woe to the world because of offenses!** The first **woe** is a cry of pity for a world in danger of offenses. The second **woe** is a warning to the one who brings or introduces evil to others.

> i. "God hath so ordered it in the wisdom of his providence, that he will not restrain the lusts of all men's hearts, but suffer some to walk in their own ways." (Poole)

b. **Woe to that man by whom the offense comes**: We live in a fallen world, and it is inevitable that sin and hurt and **offenses** come. Yet the person who brings the **offense** is guilty before God, and has no excuse.

> i. This teaches us that we can *let go* of the anger and the bitterness for what people have done against us. God promised to deal with those **by whom the offense comes**.

> ii. If God promises to deal with those who offend His own, it shows that He defends and protects His own. This teaches us that in Jesus Christ, *no other person can wreck our life*. If they bring offense in our life, God will deal with them, but not forsake us in time or eternity.

5. (8-9) In light of the judgment awaiting those who cause others to sin, it is worth it to sacrifice in the battle against sin.

"If your hand or foot causes you to sin, cut it off and cast *it* from you. It is better for you to enter into life lame or maimed, rather than having two hands or two feet, to be cast into the everlasting fire. And if your eye causes you to sin, pluck it out and cast *it* from you. It is better for you to enter into life with one eye, rather than having two eyes, to be cast into hell fire."

a. **If your hand or foot causes you to sin, cut it off and cast it from you**: Some people only keep from sin if it is easy or convenient to do it. Jesus warns us that we must be willing to *sacrifice* in fighting against sin, that nothing is worse than facing the wrath of a righteous God. It really is **better** to sacrifice in the battle against sin *now* than to face the punishment of eternity later.

b. **If your eye causes you to sin, pluck it out and cast it from you**: There are significant problems in taking these words as literal instruction instead of conveying an attitude. The problem is not only from the obvious physical harm that one might bring upon themselves, but more so in the problem that bodily mutilation does not go *far enough* in controlling sin. We need to be transformed from the inside out.

i. If I cut off my right hand, I can still sin with my left. If my left eye is gouged out, my right eye can still sin - and if all such members are gone, I can still sin in my heart and mind. God calls us to a far more radical transformation than any sort of bodily mutilation can address.

6. (10) Another reference to our responsibility to guard God's **little ones**.

"Take heed that you do not despise one of these little ones, for I say to you that in heaven their angels always see the face of My Father who is in heaven."

a. **Do not despise one of these little ones**: Because God's mind and eye is always on His **little ones**, we do well to treat them with love and respect. God protects the humble.

b. **Their angels**: This is often taken as a reference to "guardian angels." We certainly do have angels watching over us and ministering to us (Hebrews 1:14), but there is no need to limit it to only one specific "guardian angel."

7. (11-14) Disciples must share Jesus' heart and care for individuals.

"For the Son of Man has come to save that which was lost. What do you think? If a man has a hundred sheep, and one of them goes astray, does he not leave the ninety-nine and go to the mountains to seek the

one that is straying? And if he should find it, assuredly, I say to you, he rejoices more over that *sheep* than over the ninety-nine that did not go astray. Even so it is not the will of your Father who is in heaven that one of these little ones should perish."

a. **Does he not leave the ninety-nine and go to the mountains to seek the one that is straying?** This story demonstrates the value God places on individuals. Jesus exhorts us to reflect the same care.

i. This parable is similar, yet different to the parable of the Lost Sheep recorded in Luke 15:3-7. "The evidence suggests that these are two similar parables, both taught by Jesus, but with very different aims." (Carson)

ii. Here, Jesus emphasized the love and care we should have for *all* in the Christian community. "The first temptation is to despise one, because only one; the next is to despise one, because that one is so little; the next, and perhaps the most dangerous, form of the temptation, is to despise one, because that one has gone astray." (Spurgeon)

iii. **The one that is straying**: "Oh, how we ought to love sinners, since Jesus loved us, and died for us while we were yet sinners! We must care for drunkards while they still pass round the cup; swearers even while we hear them swear...We must not wait till we see some better thing in them, but feel an intense interest for them as what they are – straying and lost." (Spurgeon)

b. **If he should find it, assuredly, I say to you, he rejoices more over that sheep**: The shepherd was *happy* when he found the sheep. He wasn't angry or bitter over his hard work or lost time. His joy was overflowing.

i. Barclay points out that this parable shows us the character of God's love, being like the care a shepherd gives for a lost sheep.

- It is individual love.
- It is patient love.
- It is seeking love.
- It is rejoicing love.
- It is protecting love.

c. **Even so it is not the will of your Father who is in heaven that one of these little ones should perish**: Some take this as an assurance that before an age of accountability, children are saved. But this is absolutely certain only of the children of believers (1 Corinthians 7:14). For the rest, we must trust in God's mercy and the knowledge that the Judge of all the earth will do right (Genesis 18:25).

B. Dealing with sin in the Kingdom Community.

1. (15) If you are sinned against, go and confront the guilty party directly.

"Moreover if your brother sins against you, go and tell him his fault between you and him alone. If he hears you, you have gained your brother."

a. **Go and tell him his fault between you and him alone**: It is essential that we go to the offending brother first - not griping and gossiping to others, especially under the guise of sharing a prayer request or seeking counsel. Instead, speak to the party directly.

i. It would be wrong for anyone to take Jesus' word here as a *command* to confront **your brother** with *every* sin they commit against you. The Bible says we should bear with one another and be longsuffering towards each other. Yet clearly, there are some things that we cannot suffer long with and must address.

ii. We can say that Jesus gives us two options when **your brother sins against you**. You can go to him directly and deal with it; or you can drop the matter under Christian longsuffering and bearing with one another. Other options – holding onto bitterness, retaliation, gossiping to others about the problem – are not allowed.

iii. "We must not let trespass rankle in our bosom, by maintaining a sullen silence, nor may we go and publish the matter abroad. We must seek out the offender, and tell him his fault as if he were not aware of it; as perhaps he may not be." (Spurgeon)

b. **If he hears you, you have gained your brother**: You have **gained** him in two ways. First, the problem has been cleared up. Perhaps you realized that he was right in some ways and he realized you were right in some ways, but the problem is resolved. Second, you have **gained** him because you have not *wronged* your brother by going to others with gossip and half the side of a dispute.

i. Importantly, Jesus did not say that your brother must agree with you or immediately repent before you. At first, it is enough if **he hears you**.

2. (16-18) If one among the church is adamantly unrepentant, they are to be removed from fellowship.

"But if he will not hear, take with you one or two more, that 'by the mouth of two or three witnesses every word may be established.' And if he refuses to hear them, tell *it* to the church. But if he refuses even to hear the church, let him be to you like a heathen and a tax collector.

Assuredly, I say to you, whatever you bind on earth will be bound in heaven, and whatever you loose on earth will be loosed in heaven."

a. **If he will not hear, take with you one or two more**: The circle of people in the situation only becomes wider as the offending party refuses to listen. If the stubborn, unrepentant attitude remains, they are to be refused fellowship (**let him be to you like a heathen**).

i. It is also true that the **one or two more**, after hearing both sides of the story, may resolve the issue by assigning responsibility differently than the first offended person had thought. *The first one to plead his cause seems right, until his neighbor comes and examines him.* (Proverbs 18:17) The goal must be the restoration of relationship more than proving one's self right.

ii. "Although it is a very unwise thing to interfere in quarrels, yet from this text it is clear that we should be willing to be one of the two or three who are to assist in settling a difference." (Spurgeon)

b. **Like a heathen and a tax collector**: The unrepentant one must be treated just as we should treat a **heathen and a tax collector** - with great love, with the goal of bringing about a full repentance and reconciliation.

i. So if the matter cannot be resolved, then one is to be regarded **like a heathen and a tax collector**. This sense of being refused full standing and participation in the body of Christ is what Paul meant when he said to *deliver such a one to Satan* (1 Corinthians 5:1-8). There is a sense in which the unrepentant one is chastened by their being placed outside of the blessing and protection of fellowship.

ii. "There is, of course, no indication in this verse of how, or by what agency, this authority of the congregation is to be exercised; no church leaders or elders are mentioned." (France)

c. **Whatever you bind on earth will be bound in heaven**: If this process is done humbly and according to the Word, this is quite binding in the eyes of God, even if the unrepentant ones just go to another church.

i. "The binding and loosing generically = exercising judgment on conduct; here specifically = treating sin as pardonable or the reverse." (Bruce)

ii. "Each church has the keys of its own door. When those keys are rightly turned by the assembly below, the act is ratified above." (Spurgeon)

3. (19-20) The power and blessing in fellowship that is denied the unrepentant.

"Again I say to you that if two of you agree on earth concerning anything that they ask, it will be done for them by My Father in heaven. For where two or three are gathered together in My name, I am there in the midst of them."

a. **If two of you agree on earth**: There is real power in agreement in prayer and in the presence of Jesus. This is exactly what the unrepentant ones miss out on.

> i. In the ancient Greek, **agree** is literally "to symphonize." Jesus wants us to complement each other like a great orchestra. "It is a metaphor taken from a number of musical instruments set to the same *key*, and playing the same *tune*: here, it means a perfect agreement of the hearts, desires, wishes, and voices, of *two* or more persons praying to God." (Clarke)

b. **It will be done for them by My Father in heaven**: We must take advantage of the power of agreement, which works on the principle related in Leviticus 26:8, where five set a hundred enemies to flight but a hundred set *ten thousand* enemies to flight. That's difference between one defeating 20 and one defeating 100. There is real power, exponential power in the prayer of agreement.

> i. "Perhaps the exact petition which they offer may not apparently be answered. Remember that God often hears the prayer of our prayers, and answers *that* rather than our prayers themselves." (Spurgeon)

c. **Where two or three are gathered**: Jesus here indicated that meetings of His people – indeed, meetings full of power and authority connected to heaven – do not need to be large gatherings. They can be of **two or three** of His followers at a time.

> i. "Jesus is just as much present in the little congregation as in the great mass meeting…He is not the slave of numbers." (Barclay)

> ii. A meeting of two or three is easy to gather. Someone is always close at hand, and it isn't hard to find a place to meet.

> iii. "Two or three are mentioned, not to encourage absence, but to cheer the faithful few who do not forget the assembling of themselves together, as the manner of some is." (Spurgeon)

- This shows us that *large numbers are not essential*.
- This shows us that *the rank of the people is not essential*.
- This shows us that *the particular place is not essential*.
- This shows us that *the particular time is not essential*.

- This shows us that the *particular form the meeting should take is not essential.*

d. **Are gathered together in My name**: This shows us that *meeting in Jesus' name is most essential.*

- Gathering together in His name means that we are known by Him and by His name.

- Gathering together in His name means that He is our point of gathering; we gather around Jesus.

- Gathering together in His name means gathering according to the character and nature of Jesus.

- Gathering together in His name means gathering in a manner that Jesus would endorse.

e. **I am there in the midst of them**: This means that Jesus isn't up front, closer to the minister or the leaders. He is **in the midst**, there to be close to all. It means that he should be proclaimed and revealed to all. Some people leave a church saying, "They have taken away my Lord, and I don't know where they have laid Him."

i. "Our meeting is *in the name of Jesus*, and therefore there he is; near, not only to the leader, or to the minister, but *in the midst*, and therefore near to each worshipper." (Spurgeon)

ii. **I am there in the midst of them**: "None but God could say these words, to say them with truth, because God alone is *everywhere present*, and these words refer to his *omnipresence*...Let it be observed, that Jesus is not among them to spy out their sins; or to mark down the imperfections of their worship; but to enlighten, strengthen, comfort, and save them." (Clarke)

C. Forgiveness in the Kingdom Community: The Parable of the Unforgiving Servant

1. (21-22) Peter's question about forgiveness and Jesus' answer.

Then Peter came to Him and said, "Lord, how often shall my brother sin against me, and I forgive him? Up to seven times?" Jesus said to him, "I do not say to you, up to seven times, but up to seventy times seven."

a. **Up to seven times?** Peter, in light of what Jesus said about agreement and unity, hoped to sound extremely loving by suggesting forgiving a repentant brother up to *seven* times when *three* times was the accepted limit taught by many Jewish rabbis of that time.

i. "The Rabbis discussed this question, and recommended not more than three times…Peter's *seven times* is therefore generous, but Jesus' reply does away with all limits and calculations." (France)

b. **Up to seventy times seven**: Jesus answered unexpectedly, saying we are to forgive the repentant an unlimited number of times. *Unlimited* is surely the idea behind **up to seventy times seven**; it would be strange if Jesus expected us to count offenses against us up to 490, and at the 491st offense, to deny forgiveness.

i. "His allusion to Genesis 4:24 neatly contrasts Lamech's unlimited vindictiveness with the unlimited forgiveness of the disciple." (France)

2. (23-24) The debt of the first servant.

"Therefore the kingdom of heaven is like a certain king who wanted to settle accounts with his servants. And when he had begun to settle accounts, one was brought to him who owed him ten thousand talents."

a. **Who wanted to settle accounts with his servants**: The king in this parable expected his servants to be faithful and honorable in the way they conducted his business. Therefore, one day he examined their work and would **settle accounts** with them.

b. **Who owed him ten thousand talents**: Commentators list the modern value of 10,000 talents as anywhere between $12 million and $1 billion USD. The figure clearly represents an unpayable debt.

3. (25-27) The master forgives the debt.

"But as he was not able to pay, his master commanded that he be sold, with his wife and children and all that he had, and that payment be made. The servant therefore fell down before him, saying, 'Master, have patience with me, and I will pay you all.' Then the master of that servant was moved with compassion, released him, and forgave him the debt."

a. **His master commanded that he be sold**: Of course, the man **was not able to pay**. Therefore the master commanded to sell the debtor, his family, and all he had. This would not satisfy the debt; slaves at their top price were sold at a talent each (and usually sold for much less). Yet it would bring some measure of justice.

i. "Top price for a slave fetched about one talent, and one-tenth that amount or less was more common." (Carson)

b. **Master, have patience with me, and I will pay you all**: The promise of the servant made no sense. He spoke as if all he needed were **patience**; that if he were given enough time he could actually pay this massive debt. The disciples listening to Jesus would think this was humorous.

> i. "Many a poor sinner is very rich in resolutions. This servant-debtor thought he only needed *patience*; but indeed he needed forgiveness!" (Spurgeon)

c. **The master of that servant was moved with compassion, released him, and forgave him the debt**: The master showed mercy prompted by **compassion**, forgiving a debt that obviously could never be repaid – despite whatever promises the servant made.

4. (28-30) The forgiven servant refuses to forgive.

"But that servant went out and found one of his fellow servants who owed him a hundred denarii; and he laid hands on him and took *him* by the throat, saying, 'Pay me what you owe!' So his fellow servant fell down at his feet and begged him, saying, 'Have patience with me, and I will pay you all.' And he would not, but went and threw him into prison till he should pay the debt."

a. **One of his fellow servants who owed him a hundred denarii**: The servant who had just been forgiven an unpayable debt **went out and found** the one who owed him money. Upon meeting him, he immediately assaulted him (**took him by the throat**) and demanded payment.

> i. The debt was real. 100 denarii was roughly equal to 100 days' wages. This was not an insignificant amount, but it was almost nothing compared to the debt forgiven by his master. It was actually 1/600,000 of the debt owed to the **master** by the first servant.

> ii. **He took him by the throat**. "There is no word I am acquainted with, which so fully expresses the meaning of the original…as the *Anglo-Saxon* term *throttle*: it signified (like the Greek) to *half choke* a person, by *seizing his throat*." (Clarke)

> iii. "The debt was very, very small, but the claim was urged with intense ferocity. Our little claims against our fellow men are too apt to be pressed upon them with unsparing severity." (Spurgeon)

b. **Have patience with me, and I will pay you all**: The man who owed the smaller debt used the exact same plea and promise that brought mercy to the man who had the greater debt. But it gained nothing, and the forgiven servant put the man into a debtor's **prison**.

5. (31-34) The judgment of the unforgiving servant.

"So when his fellow servants saw what had been done, they were very grieved, and came and told their master all that had been done. Then

his master, after he had called him, said to him, 'You wicked servant! I forgave you all that debt because you begged me. Should you not also have had compassion on your fellow servant, just as I had pity on you?' And his master was angry, and delivered him to the torturers until he should pay all that was due to him."

a. **When his fellow servants saw what had been done**: There is no mention in the parable of the first servant's conscience bothering him about his conduct. It was **his fellow servants** that recognized the wrong that was done.

i. "Others could see the evil of his conduct if he could not." (Spurgeon) Sometimes we are painfully – and to our embarrassment – blind to our own sinful, fleshly conduct.

b. **You wicked servant... delivered him to the torturers until he should pay all that was due to him**: When the master heard of this, he was understandably angry. It was just wrong for a man who has been forgiven so much to then be so unforgiving. He then gave the first servant what he deserved - justice instead of mercy.

6. (35) Genuine forgiveness, from the heart, is required of all who have been forgiven.

"So My heavenly Father also will do to you if each of you, from his heart, does not forgive his brother his trespasses."

a. **So My heavenly Father also will do to you**: The principle is clear. God has forgiven such a great debt, that any debt owed to us is absolutely insignificant in comparison. No man can possibly offend me to the extent that my sins have offended God. This principle must be applied in the little things done to us, but also to the great things done unto us.

i. "We incur greater wrath by refusing to forgive than by all the rest of our indebtedness." (Spurgeon)

b. **If each of you, from his heart, does not forgive his brother his trespasses**: With this, Jesus taught an important and often neglected principle regarding forgiveness. There are many sincere Christians who withhold forgiveness from others for mistaken reasons – and they feel entirely justified in doing so.

i. Their reasoning works like this: We should not forgive another person who sins against us until they are properly repentant. This is because repentance is mentioned in the context of our commands to forgive (such as in Luke 17:4), and because our forgiveness to others is to be modeled after God's forgiveness of us. Since God does not forgive us apart from repentance, so we should not forgive others unless they properly repent to us. We even have the *duty* to withhold such forgiveness and to judge their repentance, because it is ultimately in their best interest to do so.

ii. This thinking – even if it means well – is incorrect and ultimately dangerous. This parable shows us why it is incorrect for us to think, "God doesn't forgive me without my repentance; therefore I must withhold forgiveness from others who sin against me until they properly repent." That thinking is wrong, *because I do not stand in the same place as God in the equation, and I never can.* God stands as *One who has never been forgiven and never needed forgiveness*; I stand as one who has been forgiven and needs continual forgiveness.

iii. Therefore – if it were possible – we should be *far quicker* to forgive than God is, without precondition of repentance, because we stand as forgiven sinners who must also forgive. We have *an even greater obligation to forgive than God does.*

iv. Since we have been forgiven so much, we have no right to withhold forgiveness from others. We are the debtor forgiven almost an infinite debt; will we hold on to the small debts others owe to us? If anyone had the right to withhold forgiveness it is God - and He forgives more freely and more completely than anyone we know. What possible right do we have to hold on to our unforgiveness?

v. It is also important to understand that a distinction can and should be made between *forgiveness* and *reconciliation*. True reconciliation of relationship can only happen when both parties are agreeable to it, and this may require repentance on one or both of the parties in the conflict. Yet forgiveness can be one-sided.

vi. Furthermore, forgiveness does not necessarily shield someone from the civil or practical consequences of their sin. For example, a homeowner may personally forgive the man who robbed his house, yet it is still appropriate for the robber to be arrested and put in jail. On a personal level, forgiveness is required. On a civil and societal level, the man should be punished by the magistrates (Romans 13).

vii. Nevertheless, the principle clearly stands. In context, this parable was given to make us *more forgiving*, not *less forgiving*. No one could reasonably read this parable and think that Jesus was trying to restrict the forgiveness of His disciples.

viii. People who read this, "Therefore be somewhat stingy with forgiveness as your Father in heaven is somewhat stingy with forgiveness" miss the whole point of the parable. Instead, *Therefore be merciful, just as your Father also is merciful* (Luke 6:36).

ix. **From his heart**: This makes the command all the stronger. "If we forgive in words only, but *not from our hearts*, we remain under the same condemnation." (Spurgeon)

c. **So My heavenly Father also will do to you**: It would be wrong to make this into the idea that unforgiveness itself is the unforgivable sin. It is better to say that forgiveness is evidence of truly being forgiven, and that habitual unforgiveness may show that a person's heart has never really been touched by the love of Jesus.

i. "Those who will not forgive cannot expect to be forgiven." (France) As James later wrote, *judgment is without mercy to the one who has shown no mercy.* (James 2:13)

ii. Additionally, we remember the punishment of the unforgiving man in the parable of Jesus: the master **delivered him to the torturers**. There are many poor souls who are *tortured* by their own unforgiveness toward others.

Matthew 19 - Jesus Teaches on Marriage, Divorce, Riches, and Discipleship

A. Jesus teaches on marriage, divorce, and celibacy.

1. (1-2) Jesus heads towards Judea and Jerusalem.

Now it came to pass, when Jesus had finished these sayings, *that* He departed from Galilee and came to the region of Judea beyond the Jordan. And great multitudes followed Him, and He healed them there.

a. **He departed from Galilee and came to the region of Judea**: The records of Matthew, Mark, and Luke focus on the Galilean ministry of Jesus, and only emphasize His presence in Jerusalem right before His crucifixion and resurrection. Yet it would be a mistake to believe that this trip from **Galilee** to the **region of Judea** was unusual for Jesus. The Gospel of John tells us of many previous visits He made to **Judea** and Jerusalem.

i. "To the Judean territory by way of Peraea, *i.e.*, along the eastern shore of Jordan." (Bruce) Mark 10:1 and Luke 9:51 indicate the same journey.

ii. "It seems, therefore, most probable, that the course of Christ's journey led him *by the side* of the river Jordan, not *beyond* it. That the Greek word peran, especially with a *genitive* case as here, has sometimes this signification, see on John 6:22." (Clarke)

b. **Great multitudes followed Him, and He healed them there**: Matthew points this out so his readers understand that the popularity and power of Jesus was not restricted to Galilee. It was also evident in Judea.

i. "*He healed them*, the text saith; but it saith not, they believed in him." (Poole)

ii. They **followed Him**; "Some to be *instructed*-some to be *healed*-some through *curiosity*-and some to *ensnare* him." (Clarke)

2. (3) The Pharisees attempt to trap Jesus.

The Pharisees also came to Him, testing Him, and saying to Him, "Is it lawful for a man to divorce his wife for *just* any reason?"

a. **The Pharisees also came to Him, testing Him**: This continues the theme of conflict and controversy with the religious leaders. Previously in Matthew, they had questioned Jesus as He did His work in Galilee. Now Jesus, in Judea is questioned by them – and their questions were not *honest*. They asked this, **testing Him**. They hoped to trap Jesus.

b. **Is it lawful for a man to divorce his wife**: Divorce was a controversial topic in Jesus' day, with two main schools of thought, centered around two of its most famous proponents. The first was the school of Rabbi Shammai (a more strict and unpopular view) and second was the school of Rabbi Hillel (a more lax and popular view).

   i. Among the Jews of that day, marriage was a sacred duty. If a man was unmarried after the age of 20 – except to concentrate on the study of the law – he was guilty of breaking God's command to "be fruitful and multiply." According to Barclay, they said that by not having children he killed his own descendants, and lessened the glory of God on earth.

   ii. In theory, the Jews of that day had a high ideal of marriage. Yet they had a low view of women. "The Jews had very low views of women…A wife was bought, regarded as property, used as a household drudge, and dismissed at pleasure." (Bruce) Today, men also have a low view of women; tragically, *women also have a low view of women*, and often reject the idea that women should be different than men in any way.

   iii. Their low view of women meant that their high ideal of marriage was constantly compromised, and those compromises were made into law, as with the thinking of Rabbi Hillel. Under the thinking of Hillel, "a man could divorce his wife if she spoiled his dinner, if she spun, or went with unbound hair, or spoke to men in the streets, if she spoke disrespectfully of his parents in his presence, or if she was a brawling woman whose voice could be heard in the next house. Rabbi Akiba even went the length of saying…that a man could divorce his wife if he found a woman whom he liked better and considered more beautiful." (Barclay)

   iv. "Perhaps, too, they hoped that Jesus would say something that would entangle him in the Herod-Herodias affair so that he might meet the Baptist's fate." (Carson)

c. **For just any reason**: These words were the center of the debate. Each school of thought understood that the Mosaic law gave permission for divorce in Deuteronomy 24:1: *When a man takes a wife and marries her, and it happens that she finds no favor in his eyes because he has found some <u>uncleanness</u> in her, and he writes her a certificate of divorce, puts it in her hand, and sends her out of his house.* Each side knew and believed Deuteronomy 24:1; the question was, "What constitutes *uncleanness*?"

i. The school of Rabbi Shammai understood that *uncleanness* meant sexual immorality, and said this was the only valid reason for divorce. The school of Rabbi Hillel understood *uncleanness* to mean *any* sort of indiscretion; even to the point where for some rabbis, burning a husband's breakfast was considered valid grounds for divorce.

ii. Barclay says that the Rabbis had many sayings about bad marriages and the bad wife. They said that the man with a bad wife would never face hell, because he has paid for his sins on earth. They said that the man who is ruled by his wife has a life that is not life. They said that a bad wife is like leprosy to her husband, and the only way he could be cured is by divorce. They even said, "If a man has a bad wife, it is a religious duty to divorce her."

d. **Testing Him**: So in their question, the Pharisees tried to get Jesus to side with one teaching or the other. If He agreed with the lax school of Rabbi Hillel, it was clear that Jesus did not take the Law of Moses seriously. If He agreed with the strict school of Rabbi Shammai, then Jesus might become unpopular with the multitude, who generally liked access to an easy divorce. The religious leaders had reason to believe they had caught Jesus on the horns of a dilemma.

3. (4-6) Jesus' first answer to the Pharisees: get back to marriage.

And He answered and said to them, "Have you not read that He who made *them* at the beginning 'made them male and female,' and said, 'For this reason a man shall leave his father and mother and be joined to his wife, and the two shall become one flesh'? So then, they are no longer two but one flesh. Therefore what God has joined together, let not man separate."

a. **Have you not read**: The Pharisees wanted to talk about divorce and rabbinical opinions, but Jesus wanted to go back to the Scriptures and talk about marriage. Jesus began with the first marriage, between Adam and Eve. This emphasis on the Scriptures and on marriage, rather than divorce, is a wise approach for anyone interested in keeping a marriage together.

i. "Our Lord honors Holy Scripture by drawing his argument therefrom. He chose specially to set his seal upon a part of the story of creation – that story which modern critics speak of as if it were fable or myth." (Spurgeon)

ii. "By answering the question, not from *Shammai* or *Hillel*, but from *Moses*, our blessed Lord defeated their malice, and confounded their devices." (Clarke)

iii. "In the case of Adam and Eve divorce was not only inadvisable; it was not only wrong; it was completely impossible, for the very simple reason that there was no one else whom either of them could possibly marry." (Barclay)

iv. Divorce cannot be seen as a ready option when things are difficult in married life. Marriage is like a mirror; it reflects what we put into it. If one or both partners has divorce readily in their mind as a convenient option, divorce will be much more likely.

v. "If marriage is grounded in *creation*, in the way God has made us, then it cannot be reduced to a merely covenantal relationship that breaks down when the covenantal promises are broken." (Carson)

b. **He who made them at the beginning "made them male and female"**: In quoting Genesis 1:27, Jesus indicated first that *God* made men and women different, and that *God* joins men and women together in marriage. In this, Jesus asserts God's authority over marriage; it is God's institution, not man's – so it is fair to say that His rules apply.

i. By bringing the issue back to the Scriptural foundation of marriage, Jesus makes it plain that couples must forsake their singleness (**a man shall leave his father and mother**), and come together in a **one-flesh** relationship that is both a fact (**they are...one flesh**) and a goal (**shall become one flesh**).

ii. "The law of God was not, that a man should forsake his wife whenever he had a mind to it, but that he should rather forsake his father and mother than his wife; that he should cleave unto his wife, living and dwelling with her." (Poole)

c. **Be joined to his wife, and the two shall become one flesh**: Back to creation and Adam's statement in Genesis 1:23, we see that men and women (as husband and wife) are different; yet they are joined together as one, completing one another as *one flesh*.

i. Adam said this at the creation of Eve. It was as if Adam said, "You are different than me; but you were made for me and from me. We are not the same, but we are one." In Genesis, Adam tells us that men and women are different from creation:

- Different sources of creation.
- Different methods of creation.

- Different times of creation.

- Different names at creation.

ii. Despite these fundamental, creation-rooted differences between the natures of men and women, God calls a husband and wife to come together as **one**, as **one flesh**. This process of things not alike coming together is part of God's great work in marriage; the work of sanctifying, and the work of providing a good parental team.

iii. The idea that they **shall become one flesh** includes the sexual union, but also goes far beyond it. "Marriage is given, not that two people should do one thing together, but that they should do all things together." (Barclay) "Be glued to her." (Trapp)

iv. "The reference is primarily to the physical fleshly unity. But flesh in Hebrew thought represents the entire man, and the ideal unity of marriage covers the whole nature. It is a unity of soul as well as of body: of sympathy, interest, purpose." (Bruce)

v. **The two shall become one flesh** also prohibits polygamy, and shows that this was God's intention *from the beginning*. Though polygamy was allowed under the Old Testament, it was never God's best – and men should have known so from looking at Genesis 2:24.

d. **What God has joined together**: Jesus also reminded the Pharisees that marriage is spiritually binding before God. Marriage is not merely a social contract; and as God has joined, He expects man to honor what He **has joined** and to keep the marriage together.

i. **Joined together**: "*Yoked together*, as *oxen in the plough*, where each must pull *equally*, in order to bring it on. Among the ancients, when persons were newly married, they put a *yoke* upon their necks, or *chains* upon their arms, to show that they were to be *one*, closely united, and pulling equally together in all the concerns of life." (Clarke)

ii. "*One flesh* vividly expresses a view of marriage as something much deeper than either human convenience or social convention…To see divorce as *man* undoing the word of *God* puts the whole issue in a radically new perspective." (France)

4. (7-9) The Mosaic controversy: Jesus' second answer.

They said to Him, "Why then did Moses command to give a certificate of divorce, and to put her away?" He said to them, "Moses, because of the hardness of your hearts, permitted you to divorce your wives, but from the beginning it was not so. And I say to you, whoever divorces his wife, except for sexual immorality, and marries another, commits adultery; and whoever marries her who is divorced commits adultery."

a. **Why then did Moses command to give a certificate of divorce, and to put her away**: The Pharisees wrongly thought that God *commanded* divorce where there was uncleanness. One rabbinic saying of that day went: "If a man has a bad wife, it is a religious duty to divorce her." But Jesus noted the difference between "**command**" and "**permitted.**" God never commands divorce, but He does permit it.

i. The Pharisees thought that Moses was *creating* or *promoting* divorce. In fact, he was *controlling* it.

b. **Because of the hardness of your hearts**: Divorce is never commanded, but **permitted** by God in certain circumstances, and God permits it **because of the hardness** of human hearts. It was as if Jesus said this: "Here is the ideal; and here is the allowance of God when human sinfulness and hardness of heart has made the ideal unobtainable."

i. **Hardness of your hearts**: "The thought is not so much of the cruelty of men to their wives, as of their unresponsiveness to the mind and will of God." (France)

ii. Sometimes the heart of the *offending party* is hard, and they will not do what must be done to reconcile the relationship. Sometimes the heart of the *offended party* is hard, and they refuse to reconcile and get past the offence even when there is contrition and repentance. Often the **hardness of** heart is on *both sides*.

iii. "Divorce is never to be thought of as a God-ordained, morally neutral option but as evidence of sin, of hardness of heart." (Carson)

c. **Except for sexual immorality**: Jesus interpreted the meaning of the word *uncleanness* in the Mosaic Law, showing that it refers to **sexual immorality**, not just anything that might displease the husband. Therefore, divorce – and the freedom to remarry without sin – is only permitted in the case of **sexual immorality**.

i. The ancient Greek word for **sexual immorality** is *porneia*. It is a broad word, covering a wide span of sexual impropriety. One may be guilty of *porneia* without actually having consummated an act of adultery. "It must be admitted that the word *porneia* itself is very broad…*Porneia* covers the entire range of such sins…and should not be restricted unless the context requires it." (Carson)

ii. To this permission for divorce, the Apostle Paul added the case of abandonment by an unbelieving spouse (1 Corinthians 7:15).

iii. We note that incompatibility, not loving each other anymore, brutality, and misery are not grounds for divorce, though they may be proper grounds for a separation and consequent "celibacy within marriage" as Paul indicates in 1 Corinthians 7:11. These words of Paul show us that a Christian couple may in fact split up for reasons that do not justify a Biblical divorce. It may be because of a misguided sense of spirituality; it may be because of general unhappiness, or conflict, or abuse, or misery, addiction, or poverty. Paul recognizes (without at all encouraging) that one might *depart* in such circumstance, but they cannot consider themselves divorced, with the right to remarry, because their marriage had not split up for reasons that justify a Biblical divorce.

iv. These problems that are serious yet fall short of the Biblical permission for divorce may justify a separation, but the partners are expected to honor their marriage vows even in their separation, because as far as God is concerned, they are still married – their marriage covenant has not been broken for what God considers to be Biblical reasons.

d. **And marries another, commits adultery**: The reason why a person who does not have a legitimate divorce **commits adultery** upon remarrying is because they *are not* divorced in the eyes of God. Since their old marriage was never dissolved on Biblical grounds, that marriage is still valid and they are actually guilty of bigamy and adultery.

i. "He agrees with neither Shammai nor Hillel; for even though the school of Shammai was stricter than Hillel, it permitted remarriage when the divorce was not in accordance with its own Halakah (rules of conduct)." (Carson)

ii. This teaching of Jesus shows us that marriage, as a promise made to God, to our spouse and to the world, is a *binding promise*, and cannot be broken at our own discretion. If God does not recognize the promise being broken, then it is not.

iii. One must admit that this is a *hard teaching* from Jesus. There are many reasons people give today to justify divorce that do not fulfill the two Biblical allowances for divorce.

iv. There are also many situations where a marriage is separated or divorced for reasons that do not fulfill the Biblical allowance for divorce, *but later* one or more of the spouses goes on to give Biblical allowance, often by marriage or sexual relations with another.

v. We also remember what the Apostle Paul wrote in 1 Corinthians 7:17: *As the Lord has called each one, so let him walk.* In the context, one of Paul's ideas with this statement was a warning about trying to undo the past in regard to relationships; God tells us to repent of whatever sin is there and then to move on. If you are married to your second wife after wrongfully divorcing your first wife, and become a Christian, don't think you must now leave your second wife and go back to your first wife, trying to undo the past. As the Lord has called you, walk in that place right now.

5. (10-12) The disciples ask about marriage and celibacy.

His disciples said to Him, "If such is the case of the man with *his* wife, it is better not to marry." But He said to them, "All cannot accept this saying, but only *those* to whom it has been given: "For there are eunuchs who were born thus from *their* mother's womb, and there are eunuchs who were made eunuchs by men, and there are eunuchs who have made themselves eunuchs for the kingdom of heaven's sake. He who is able to accept *it*, let him accept *it*."

a. **If such is the case...it is better not to marry**: The disciples understood Jesus' teaching on marriage and divorce clearly. They understood that it was not a commitment to be entered into quickly or lightly, and considered that since marriage is so binding before God, then maybe **it is better not to marry**.

i. "It is not evil to marry, but good to be wary; to look ere one leap." (Trapp)

b. **All cannot accept this saying, but only those to whom it has been given**: Jesus recognized that celibacy is good for some, for the one **who is able to accept it** (such as Jesus and the Apostle Paul, 1 Corinthians 7:7-9).

i. "If there be any who can receive this saying, who can without marriage bridle his list, and so live in a solute and single state as not to sin against God by any extravagancy of lusts, and impure desires and affections, and desire, and shall do so, that he may be more spiritual, and serve God with less distraction, and be a more fit instrument to promote the kingdom of God in the world, let him do it." (Poole)

ii. "But this is not every man's happiness; and where it is, the pride of virginity is no less foul a sin than impurity, saith Augustine." (Trapp)

c. **For there are eunuchs who were born thus**: The term *eunuch* was used figuratively for those who voluntarily abstain from marriage. Jesus here gave three kinds of **eunuchs**.

• Those who are **born** without the capacity for sex and marriage.

• Those who are **made** by others without the capacity for sex and marriage.

• Those who *choose* to live without sex and marriage **for the kingdom of heaven's sake**.

i. Paul said that the one who is unmarried because of calling should *be holy both in body and in spirit* (1 Corinthians 7:34). Therefore these **eunuchs for the kingdom of heaven's sake** should come to peace with their celibacy both physically and spiritually; it should not be a consistent torment to them in either aspect.

6. (13-15) Jesus blesses little children.

Then little children were brought to Him that He might put *His* hands on them and pray, but the disciples rebuked them. But Jesus said, "Let the little children come to Me, and do not forbid them; for of such is the kingdom of heaven." And He laid *His* hands on them and departed from there.

a. **Then little children were brought to Him**: It is marvelous that in the midst of Jesus' teaching on marriage, parents brought their children to be blessed. Today, parents should still bring their children to Jesus; He wants to bless them and welcome them into **the kingdom of heaven**.

i. "It was a Jewish custom to bring a child to the elders on the evening of the Day of Atonement 'to bless him and pray for him' (Mishnah *Sopherim* 18:5)." (France)

ii. "These are termed by Luke, Luke 18:15, ta brefh, *infants*, very young children." (Clarke)

b. **Let the little children come to Me**: This also shows us something remarkable able Jesus' character. He was the kind of man that children liked, and children are often astute judges of character.

c. **He laid His hands on them**: With this, Jesus blessed the children. The laying on of hands is used Biblically as a way to bestow blessing on another (Acts 6:6, Acts 8:17, Acts 9:17, 1 Timothy 5:22, 2 Timothy 1:6).

i. "He did not baptize them, but he did bless them." (Spurgeon)

B. Jesus teaches on riches and following Him.

1. (16-17) A man asks Jesus about gaining eternal life.

Now behold, one came and said to Him, "Good Teacher, what good thing shall I do that I may have eternal life?" So He said to him, "Why do you call Me good? No one *is* good but One, *that is,* God. But if you want to enter into life, keep the commandments."

a. **What good thing shall I do to inherit eternal life**: This question demonstrates that this man, like all people by nature, had an orientation towards earning eternal life. He wanted to know what good work or noble deed he could **do to inherit eternal life**.

i. All three gospels (Matthew, Mark, and Luke) tell us this man was rich. Matthew tells us he was young (Matthew 19:22), and Luke tells us he was a ruler.

b. **Why do you call Me good?** In this, Jesus did not deny His own goodness. Instead, He asked the man, "Do you understand what you are saying when **you call Me good?**"

i. It was as if Jesus said, "You come to Me asking about what good thing you can do to inherit eternal life. But what do you really know about goodness?"

c. **If you want to enter into life, keep the commandments**: Jesus' answer to the man's question was straightforward. If you want to gain eternal life by your doing, you must **keep the commandments** - all of them, and keep them in the fullest sense.

i. "He would needs be saved by doing, Christ sets him that to do which no man living can do, and so shows him his error." (Trapp)

2. (18-20) Jesus tests him by the aspects of the Mosaic Law that deal with man's relationship to men.

He said to Him, "Which ones?" Jesus said, "'You shall not murder,' 'You shall not commit adultery,' 'You shall not steal,' 'You shall not bear false witness,' 'Honor your father and *your* mother,' and, 'You shall love your neighbor as yourself.'" The young man said to Him, "All these things I have kept from my youth. What do I still lack?"

a. **You shall not murder**: Jesus asked the man about the commandments which primarily deal with a man's relation to man. In response, the young man claimed, "**All these things I have kept from my youth**," thus claiming to fulfill all God's commands regarding how we must treat other people.

i. Both tables of the law will test every person before God. It isn't enough to do good by our fellow man and be decent folk; we must do right by God, and give Him the glory and honor He deserves.

b. **All these things I have kept from my youth**: It is fair to ask if this man really had kept these commandments. It is likely that he actually did keep them in a way that made him righteous in the eyes of men, in the sense that Paul could say *concerning the righteousness which is in the law, blameless* in Philippians 3:6. But he certainly did not keep them in the full and perfect sense which Jesus spoke of in the Sermon on the Mount.

i. Mark 10:21 tells us that in response to the man's answer, *Jesus loved him*. Jesus had compassion on this man, who was so misguided as to think that he really could justify himself before God.

c. **What do I still lack?** This alone tells us that this man had not perfectly kept the law, because he still knew that there was something missing in his life, prompting the question, "**What do I still lack?**" There was still something lacking in his life, reflecting something missing in his relationship with God.

    i. "The exemplary life *plus* the dissatisfaction meant much…'I am on the right road, according to your teaching; why then do I not attain the rest of the true, godly life?'" (Bruce)

3. (21-22) Jesus tests him by the aspects of the Mosaic Law which deal with man's relationship to God.

Jesus said to him, "If you want to be perfect, go, sell what you have and give to the poor, and you will have treasure in heaven; and come, follow Me." But when the young man heard that saying, he went away sorrowful, for he had great possessions.

a. **Sell all you have and give to the poor, and you will have treasure in heaven; and come, follow Me**: The call to forsake everything and follow Jesus is a call to put God first in all things. It is full obedience to the first table of the law, which dealt with a man's relation to God.

    i. We may make two mistakes here. The one is to believe this applies to *everyone*, when Jesus never made this a general command to all who would follow Him, but especially to this one rich man whose riches were clearly an obstacle to his discipleship. Instead, many rich people can do *more good* in the world by continuing to make money and using those resources for the glory of God and the good of others. The second mistake is to believe this applies to *no one*, when there are clearly those today for whom the best thing they could do for themselves spiritually is to radically forsake the materialism that is ruining them.

    ii. Yet we notice that Jesus simply called this man to be His disciple, in saying, "**Follow Me.**" He used similar language in calling many of His disciples (Matthew 4:19; 8:22; 9:9; Mark 2:14). Jesus simply called this man to be His follower; but for this man it meant leaving behind the riches he had set his heart upon.

    iii. "Think not, therefore, as many do, that there is no other hell but poverty, no better heaven than abundance." (Trapp)

b. **He went away sorrowful, for he had great possessions**: In this, the wealthy questioner failed utterly. Money was his god; he was guilty of idolatry. This is why Jesus, knowing the man's heart, asked him to renounce his possessions.

i. "He would be saved by works; yet he would not carry out his works to the full of the law's demand. He failed to observe the spirit both of the second and the first table. He loved not his poor brother as himself; he loved not God in Christ Jesus with all his heart and soul." (Spurgeon)

ii. The principle remains: God may challenge and require an individual to give something up for the sake of His kingdom that He still allows to someone else. There are many who perish because they will not forsake what God tells them to.

iii. **Sorrowful, for he had great possessions**: "And what were these in comparison of peace of conscience, and mental rest? Besides, he had unequivocal proof that these contributed nothing to his comfort, for he is now miserable even *while* he possesses them!" (Clarke)

4. (23-26) Riches as an obstacle to the kingdom.

Then Jesus said to His disciples, "Assuredly, I say to you that it is hard for a rich man to enter the kingdom of heaven. And again I say to you, it is easier for a camel to go through the eye of a needle than for a rich man to enter the kingdom of God." When His disciples heard *it*, they were greatly astonished, saying, "Who then can be saved?" But Jesus looked at *them* and said to them, "With men this is impossible, but with God all things are possible."

a. **Assuredly, I say to you**: We should not diminish the strength of Jesus' words, nor fail to see their application in our own affluent society. Who among us would not be considered richer than this rich young ruler was?

b. **It is hard for a rich man to enter the kingdom of heaven**: Riches are a problem because they tend to make us satisfied with this life, instead of longing for the age to come. As well, sometimes riches are sought at the expense of seeking God.

i. The illustration that Jesus used – **it is easier for a camel to go through the eye of a needle** – was meant to be somewhat humorous. We immediately think of this as being impossible.

ii. "The *camel*, the largest common animal, trying to squeeze through the smallest imaginable hole." (France)

iii. One problem with riches is that they encourage a spirit of false independence, very much like the church of Laodicea: "*I am rich, have become wealthy, and have need of nothing*" (Revelation 3:17).

c. **They were exceedingly amazed**: The great amazement of the disciples was based on the assumption that riches were always a sign of God's blessing and favor.

i. They had probably hoped that their following of Jesus would make them rich and influential, and prominent leaders in His Messianic government. "In a culture where wealth was regarded as a sign of God's blessing and where a religious teacher was therefore expected to be at least moderately wealthy, the lifestyle of Jesus and his disciples was conspicuously different." (France)

d. **With God all things are possible**: It is **possible** for the rich man to be saved. God's grace is enough to save the rich man; we have the examples of people like Zaccheus, Joseph of Arimathea, and Barnabas. These all were rich men still able to put God first, not their riches.

i. "Jesus is not saying that all poor people and none of the wealthy enter the kingdom of heaven. That would exclude Abraham, Isaac, and Jacob, to say nothing of David, Solomon, and Joseph of Arimathea." (Carson)

5. (27-30) Peter's blunt question: What do *we* get for following You?

Then Peter answered and said to Him, "See, we have left all and followed You. Therefore what shall we have?" So Jesus said to them, "Assuredly I say to you, that in the regeneration, when the Son of Man sits on the throne of His glory, you who have followed Me will also sit on twelve thrones, judging the twelve tribes of Israel. And everyone who has left houses or brothers or sisters or father or mother or wife or children or lands, for My name's sake, shall receive a hundredfold, and inherit eternal life. But many *who are* first will be last, and the last first."

a. **Therefore what shall we have?** In contrast to the rich young ruler, the disciples did leave all to follow Jesus - so what would be their reward? Jesus tells of special honor for the disciples: **you who have followed Me will also sit on twelve thrones, judging the twelve tribes of Israel**. The disciples will have a special role in the future judgment, probably in the sense of administration in the millennial Kingdom.

i. As well, the apostles had the honor of helping to provide a singular foundation for the church (Ephesians 2:20), and have a special tribute in the New Jerusalem (Revelation 20:14).

ii. "What Peter said was true, but it was not wisely spoken. It has a selfish, grasping look...After all, what have any of us to lose for Jesus compared with what we gain by him?" (Spurgeon)

b. **Everyone who has left houses or brothers or sisters**: But there will be universal honor for all who sacrifice for Jesus' sake; whatever has been given up for Him will be returned to us a hundred times over - in addition to **everlasting life**.

i. **Hundredfold** is obviously not literal in a *material* sense; otherwise, Jesus promises a hundred mothers and a hundred wives. Jesus will do more than make up what we have given up for His sake, but the return may be spiritual instead of material. **Hundredfold** certainly *is* literally true in the spiritual sense.

ii. Matthew Poole described some of the ways we get our hundredfold:

- Joy in the Holy Ghost, peace of conscience, the sense of God's love.

- Contentment. They shall have a contented frame of mind.

- God will stir up the hearts of others to supply their wants, and that supply shall be sweeter to them than their abundance was.

- God sometimes repays them in this life, as He restored Job after his trial to greater riches.

iii. The principle stands: God will be a debtor to no man. It is impossible for us to give more to God than He gives back to us.

c. **But many who are first will be last, and the last first**: In the previous words, Jesus promised that those who sacrificed for His sake and the sake of His kingdom would be rewarded. Then He said that though they would be rewarded, it would be different than man usually expects; because we usually believe that the first will be first and the last will be last. The parable in the following chapter will illustrate this principle.

i. "Jesus lays it down that there will be surprises in the final assessment… it may be that those who were humble on earth will be great in heaven, and that those who were great in this world will be humbled in the world to come." (Barclay)

ii. "You remember the old Romish legend, which contains a great truth. There was a brother who preached very mightily, and who had won many souls to Christ, and it was revealed to him one night, in a dream, that in heaven he would have no reward for all that he had done. He asked to whom the reward would go; and an angel told him that it would go to an old man who used to sit on the pulpit stairs, and pray for him. Well, it may be so, though it is more likely that both would share their Master's praise. We shall not be rewarded, however, simply according to our apparent success." (Spurgeon)

Matthew 20 - Jesus Teaches of Grace, Greatness, and Service

A. The parable of the workers in the vineyard.

1. (1-2) A landowner's workers early in the morning.

"For the kingdom of heaven is like a landowner who went out early in the morning to hire laborers for his vineyard. Now when he had agreed with the laborers for a denarius a day, he sent them into his vineyard."

a. **For the kingdom of heaven is like a landowner**: Like many of Jesus' parables, this story is about an employer and those who work for him. Jesus will use this story to answer a question from Matthew 19:27: *See, we have left all and followed You. Therefore what shall we have?* His reply came in stages.

- First, a promise of reward (Matthew 19:28).

- Second, a warning that God's manner of distributing reward is not necessarily the manner of men (*many who are the first will be last, and the last first*, Matthew 19:30).

- Finally, this parable that illustrates the principle that God's manner of rewarding is not like man's practice of giving rewards.

b. **To hire laborers for his vineyard**: The landowner went to the marketplace, which was the gathering place for day laborers. A man who wanted to work came there first thing in the morning, carrying his tools, and waited until someone hired him.

c. **Early in the morning**: This is literally "at dawn," usually reckoned to be about 6:00 in the morning. These workers hired at the very beginning of the working day **agreed** to work **for a denarius a day**, the common daily wage for a workingman. This was an entirely normal arrangement.

2. (3-7) Through the day, the landowner continues to hire workers.

"And he went out about the third hour and saw others standing idle in the marketplace, and said to them, 'You also go into the vineyard, and whatever is right I will give you.' So they went. Again he went out about the sixth and the ninth hour, and did likewise. And about the eleventh hour he went out and found others standing idle, and said to them, 'Why have you been standing here idle all day?' They said to him, 'Because no one hired us.' He said to them, 'You also go into the vineyard, and whatever is right you will receive.'"

a. **And he went out about the third hour**: The **third hour** was about 9:00 a.m.; the **sixth hour** was about 12 noon; the **eleventh hour** was about 5:00 in the evening. Through the day, the landowner went to the place where the laborers gathered, found some **standing idle in the marketplace**, and hired them to do the work in his **vineyard**.

i. "If the harvest was not ingathered before the rains broke, then it was ruined; and so to get the harvest in was a frantic race against time. Any worker was welcome, even if he could give only an hour to the work." (Barclay)

ii. The picture is that the landowner had an inexhaustible supply of work for those who wanted to work. The impression is that the landowner was *surprised* to find people **idle**, because he had plenty of work to give them.

iii. Spurgeon applied this to us spiritually: "Why is any one of *us* remaining idle towards God? Has nothing yet had power to engage us to sacred service? Can we dare to say, *'No man hath hired us?'*"

b. **Whatever is right I will give you… whatever is right you will receive**: The landowner promised the earliest workers a day's wage (*a denarius a day*). The other workers hired through the day were not promised a *specific* wage, only **whatever is right**. He promised to pay all the later workers fairly.

3. (8-10) The landowner pays his workers.

So when evening had come, the owner of the vineyard said to his steward, 'Call the laborers and give them *their* wages, beginning with the last to the first.' And when those came who *were hired* about the eleventh hour, they each received a denarius. But when the first came, they supposed that they would receive more; and they likewise received each a denarius.

a. **Call the laborers and give them their wages, beginning with the last to the first**: These are day laborers, so they are paid at the end of each day. When it came time to pay the workers, the men hired last were paid first - and paid for a full day of work!

i. The men who were hired at the **eleventh hour** - who worked only about one hour - were obviously elated about being paid first, and being paid for a full day.

b. **They supposed that they would receive more**: The men who worked for the landowner all day saw the men who worked for only an hour come away from the pay table, and they **supposed**, "If the landowner is paying these guys a full day's pay for one hour's work, then we will get far more."

i. The *order* of payment was important. If the first workers had been paid first, they would not have had time to develop the expectation of more pay for themselves. "Possibly *the first* felt their vanity wounded by being paid after the others. They used their waiting time in considering their own superiority to the latecomers." (Spurgeon)

c. **They likewise received a denarius**: Yet the men hired first - early in the day, and who had worked all day - got paid exactly what the landowner had promised them (*a denarius a day*, Matthew 20:2). The landowner did exactly as promised, but their supposition of more pay than promised was disappointed.

4. (11-15) The complaint of the early workers.

"And when they had received *it*, they complained against the landowner, saying, 'These last *men* have worked *only* one hour, and you made them equal to us who have borne the burden and the heat of the day.' But he answered one of them and said, 'Friend, I am doing you no wrong. Did you not agree with me for a denarius? Take *what is* yours and go your way. I wish to give to this last man *the same* as to you. Is it not lawful for me to do what I wish with my own things? Or is your eye evil because I am good?'"

a. **They complained against the landowner**: After being paid, the men hired first took up their complaint with the landowner. They were offended that the landowner gave the men who worked less **equal to us who have borne the burden and the heat of the day**.

i. "The money was paid by the overseer, but he was standing by enjoying the scene." (Bruce)

ii. It is easy to sympathize with these who had worked all day. They worked while the others were idle. They worked in **the heat of the day** while others shaded themselves. Yet they were paid exactly the same.

b. **Friend, I am doing you no wrong. Did you not agree with me for a denarius?** The landowner reminded them that he had been completely fair to them. He did them **no wrong**, and had broken no promise.

c. **I wish to give to this last man the same as to you**: The landowner did nothing to *explain* why he did it, other than simply to say "**I wish**." The reasons for the landowner's generosity were completely in the landowner himself, and *not in the ones who received*.

d. **Is it not lawful for me to do what I wish with my own things? Or is your eye evil because I am good?** The landowner rebuked them for their jealousy and resentment of the landowner's generosity towards others. He also strongly claimed his right to do what he wanted with what was his.

> i. The "evil eye" was a jealous, envious eye. The landowner asked if they were jealous because the landowner was generous to other people. "The 'evil eye' was an idiom used to refer to jealousy (cf. Deuteronomy 15:9; 1 Samuel 18:9)." (Carson)

> ii. "An *evil eye* was a phrase in use, among the ancient Jews, to denote an *envious, covetous* man or disposition; a man who repined at his neighbour's prosperity, loved his own money, and would do nothing in the way of charity for God's sake." (Clarke)

5. (16) The parable applied: the principle of God's reward.

"So the last will be first, and the first last. For many are called, but few chosen."

a. **So the last will be first, and the first last**: Peter and the disciples knew they had given up a great deal to follow Jesus. Peter wanted to know what they would get in return. Through this parable Jesus assured Peter and the disciples that they will be rewarded - but the principle of *many who are first will be last and the last first* (Matthew 19:30) meant that God may not reward as man expects – even as the parable illustrated.

> i. Some think this parable speaks of the way that people come to God at different stages of their life. They may come at the beginning of their life, in their youth, in adulthood, in old age, or at the very end. Others think it refers to how the gospel first dawned with John the Baptist, then the preaching of Jesus, then the preaching at Pentecost, then to the Jews, and finally to the Gentiles. It is best understood as a parable about grace and reward.

> ii. The disciples should expect to be rewarded; but they should not be surprised if, when rewards are distributed, God will reward others in unexpected ways.

b. **Last will be first, and the first last**: This is the essence of God's *grace*, when He rewards and blesses man according to His will and pleasure, not necessarily according to what men deserve.

i. The system of law is easy to figure out: you get what you deserve. The system of grace is foreign to us: God deals with us according to who *He* is, not according to who *we* are.

ii. It is important to see that the landowner did not treat anyone *unfairly*, though he was more *generous* to some than to others. We can be assured that God will never, ever be unfair to us, though He may - for His own purpose and pleasure - bestow greater blessing on someone else who seems less deserving.

iii. The point isn't that all have the same reward – though all God's people do go to the same heaven (where they will have reward in different measure). The point is that God rewards on the principle of grace, and we should therefore expect surprises. He will never be *less* than fair, but reserves the right to be *more* than fair as pleases Him. God's grace always operates righteously.

iv. This parable is not a perfect illustration of God's grace, because the principle of working and deserving is involved. The grace of God does not give us *more* blessing than we deserve - it gives blessing to us completely apart from the principle of deserving.

v. Living under grace is sort of a two-edged sword. Under grace, we can't come to God complaining, "Don't I deserve better than this"; because God will reply, "Does this mean that you really want Me to give you what you deserve?"

vi. Grace should be especially manifested in our service; it is of grace, not works.

- All our service is already due to God; it belongs to Him.
- The ability to serve God is the gift of His grace.
- The call to serve God is the gift of His grace.
- Every opportunity to serve is a gift of His grace.
- Being in the right state of mind to do the Lord's work is a gift of grace.
- Successful service to God is the gift of His grace.

vii. "My last word to God's children is this: what does it matter, after all, whether we are first or whether we are last? Do not let us dwell too much upon it, for *we all share the honor given to each*. When we are converted, we become members of Christ's living body; and as we grow in grace, and get the true spirit that permeates that body, we shall say, when any member of it is honored, 'This is honor for us'…If any brother shall be greatly honored of God, I feel honored in his honor.

If God shall bless your brother, and make him ten times more useful than you are, then you see that he is blessing you — not only blessing him, but you. If my hand has something in it, my foot does not say, 'Oh, I have not got it!' No, for if my hand has it, my foot has it; it belongs to the whole of my body." (Spurgeon)

c. **For many are called, but few chosen**: This was said in the context of this illustration of grace. Jesus emphasized that both the calling and the choosing of God is based on His grace – *especially* His choosing.

B. Jesus teaches about status in the kingdom.

1. (17-19) Jesus again reveals the fate waiting for Him at Jerusalem.

Now Jesus, going up to Jerusalem, took the twelve disciples aside on the road and said to them, "Behold, we are going up to Jerusalem, and the Son of Man will be betrayed to the chief priests and to the scribes; and they will condemn Him to death, and deliver Him to the Gentiles to mock and to scourge and to crucify. And the third day He will rise again."

a. **Behold, we are going up to Jerusalem**: This was not a surprise to the disciples. Even if Jesus had not specifically told them, their movement south from Galilee at about the time of the Passover feast made it easy to figure out that Jesus and the disciples would be in **Jerusalem** for Passover.

b. **The Son of Man will be betrayed**: Jesus again told the disciples what awaited Him in Jerusalem, but no reaction from the disciples is noted. A reaction might especially be expected when Jesus said He would **be betrayed**.

i. "This he said in the hearing of the disciple who would act the traitor: did no compunction visit his base heart?" (Spurgeon)

ii. "And still is he *betrayed!* If the gospel dies in England, write on its tomb, 'Betrayed.' If our churches lose their holy influence among men, write on them, 'Betrayed.' What care we for infidels? What care we for those who curse and blaspheme? They cannot hurt the Christ. His wounds are those which he receives in the house of his friend." (Spurgeon)

iii. Seemingly, the disciples did not really listen when Jesus said these things. Their expectation was so focused on Jesus establishing an immediate political kingdom, and these words from Jesus were so contrary to that anticipation, these words just went over their heads.

iv. "But Luke saith, *they understood none of these things;* that is, surely they believed none of them, the *saying was hid from them.*" (Poole)

v. "When our Lord told the twelve that he would die, they imagined that it was a parable, concealing some deep mystery. They looked at one another, and they tried to fathom where there was no depth, but where the truth lay on the surface." (Spurgeon)

vi. It is often more agonizing to contemplate the painful future than it is to actually live it. Jesus openly acknowledged the suffering and agony that awaited Him. Jesus thought about how He would fulfill the will of His Father in the future. There was value for Him to look at His coming trial, and to think and say, "I will complete what My Father has given Me to do. I will obey to the end."

c. **Betrayed…they will condemn Him to death… deliver Him to the Gentiles to mock and to scourge and to crucify. And the third day He will rise again**: Jesus was remarkably specific in this announcement of His fate, and foretold many things over which He had no apparent control.

i. **Will be betrayed**: Conceivably, Jesus could have been delivered to the religious authorities without this. Certainly, He did not arrange His own betrayal. Yet He confidently said it would happen.

ii. **They will condemn Him to death**: Jesus confidently predicted that the religious leaders would do this; yet this was not something He could plan.

iii. **Deliver Him to the Gentiles**: Jesus knew that the religious leaders of the Jews did not have authority to carry out capital punishment themselves; yet sometimes they executed men despite this prohibition (Acts 7:54-60). Yet Jesus was confident that He would be delivered **to the Gentiles**.

iv. **To mock and to scourge**: Jesus predicted these specific aspects of His coming agony – which on a human level He could not arrange. "They plucked his hair, they smote his cheeks, they spat in his face. Mockery could go no farther. It was cruel, cutting, cursed scorn." (Spurgeon)

v. **And to crucify**: Crucifixion was not the only way criminals were executed under the Romans, yet Jesus knew that this was how He would be put to death. "Here is the first mention of the mode of Jesus' death and of the Gentiles' part in it (only the Romans could crucify people)." (Carson)

vi. Taken together, the entire picture is one of great suffering.

- Suffering from the disloyalty of friends.
- Suffering from injustice.

- Suffering from deliberate insult.

- Suffering from physical pain.

- Suffering from great humiliation and degradation.

vii. **And the third day He will rise again**: Most important, this was something that Jesus had *no apparent control over*. Yet He confidently announced to His disciples that this would happen.

2. (20-21) The mother of James and John asks for a place of special status for her sons.

Then the mother of Zebedee's sons came to Him with her sons, kneeling down and asking something from Him. And He said to her, "What do you wish?" She said to Him, "Grant that these two sons of mine may sit, one on Your right hand and the other on the left, in Your kingdom."

a. **The mother of Zebedee's sons came to Him**: This mother of James and John (Matthew 4:21) came with a request that would make a mother proud and the sons very happy.

i. She "was a regular member of the disciple group who accompanied Jesus (Matthew 27:56), so her involvement in her sons' ambitious ideas is hardly surprising." (France)

b. **Grant that these two sons of mine may sit**: Asking on behalf of her sons (note to whom Jesus replies in Matthew 20:22-23), she wanted prominent positions for them in the messianic administration of Jesus.

i. "The 'right hand' and 'left hand' suggest proximity to the King's person and so a share in his prestige and power." (Carson)

ii. "The promise of Matthew 19:28 forms the background to this request; the 'thrones' are already assured, leaving only the question of precedence." (France)

3. (22-23) Jesus answers James and John: when you ask for a place of special status, do you know what you ask for?

But Jesus answered and said, "You do not know what you ask. Are you able to drink the cup that I am about to drink, and be baptized with the baptism that I am baptized with?" They said to Him, "We are able." So He said to them, "You will indeed drink My cup, and be baptized with the baptism that I am baptized with; but to sit on My right hand and on My left is not Mine to give, but *it is for those* for whom it is prepared by My Father."

a. **Are you able to drink the cup that I am about to drink**: Their answer ("**We are able**") seems to come a little too quick. Jesus recognized that they didn't really understand, but they would.

i. "But these men slept in Gethsemane, forsook the Master when He was arrested, and one of them at least failed Him at the cross…we can only follow Christ in his cup and baptism, after we have been endued with the Spirit of Pentecost." (Meyer)

b. **You will indeed drink My cup, and be baptized with the baptism that I am baptized with**: Both James and John had to be **baptized** in suffering as Jesus was, but their "cups" and "baptisms" were different. James was the first martyr among the apostles, and John was the only apostle to *not* die through martyrdom - though not from a lack of trying.

i. James had to be ready to be the first to die among the disciples; John had to be ready to live the longest Christian life and testimony among them. "A Roman coin was once found with the picture of an ox on it; the ox was facing two things – an altar and a plough; and the inscription read: 'Ready for either.'" (Barclay)

ii. This is a good example of the word **baptism** having the sense of "immersion" or being "swallowed up in."

c. **But to sit on My right hand and on My left is not Mine to give**: Jesus here showed remarkable submission to His Father. He would not even claim the right to choose how His servants were rewarded, but yield that to His Father.

i. "He comes to do not his own will, but the will of him that sent him, and so he correctly says of rank in his kingdom, *It is not mine to give.* How thoroughly did our Lord take a lowly place for our sakes! In this laying aside of authority, he gives a silent rebuke to our self-seeking." (Spurgeon)

4. (24-28) The disciples' reaction; Jesus sets forth true greatness.

And when the ten heard *it*, they were greatly displeased with the two brothers. But Jesus called them to *Himself* and said, "You know that the rulers of the Gentiles lord it over them, and those who are great exercise authority over them. Yet it shall not be so among you; but whoever desires to become great among you, let him be your servant. And whoever desires to be first among you, let him be your slave; just as the Son of Man did not come to be served, but to serve, and to give His life a ransom for many."

a. **They were greatly displeased**: The other ten disciples mistakenly thought that a unique honor had just been bestowed on James and John. They did not know that Jesus could have made the same promise of suffering to come to any of them (if they really wanted it!).

> i. "The indignation of the ten doubtless sprang less from humility than jealousy plus fear that they might lose out." (Carson)

b. **Yet it shall not be so among you**: Their desire for position and status showed they did not yet know the nature of Jesus in respect to leadership and power. **The rulers of the Gentiles lord it over them**, but it should be different among the people of God.

> i. **Yet it shall not be so among you** is a stinging rebuke to the manner in which the modern church looks to the world for both its substance and style. Plainly, the church isn't to operate the way the world does.

c. **Whoever desires to become great among you, let him be your servant**: In the Kingdom community, status, money, popularity should never be the prerequisites for leadership. Humble service is the great prerequisite, as shown by Jesus' own ministry.

> i. "In the pagan world humility was regarded, not so much as a virtue, but as a vice. Imagine a slave being given leadership!" (Carson)

d. **Just as the Son of Man did not come to be served, but to serve**: Real ministry is done for the benefit of those ministered to, not for the benefit of the minister. Many people are in the ministry for what they can receive (either materially or emotionally) from their people instead of for what they can give.

> i. "He received nothing from others; his was a life of giving, and the giving of a life...No service is greater than to redeem sinners by his own death, no ministry is lowlier than to die in the stead of sinners." (Spurgeon)

> ii. "He does not come to be served, but to serve. Does not this suit you, poor sinner — you who never did serve him, you who could not, as you are, minister to him? Well, he did not come to get your service; he came to give you his services; not that you might first do him honor, but that he might show you mercy." (Spurgeon)

e. **And to give His life a ransom for many**: The death of Jesus – the giving of **His life** – purchased the freedom of His people. The idea is that His people were in bondage as slaves, and He paid their price.

> i. **Ransom** "was most commonly used as the purchase price for freeing slaves." (Carson) "*Lytron* ('ransom') and the preposition *anti* ('for', literally 'instead of') point clearly to the idea of his 'taking our place'." (France)

ii. These words of Jesus gave rise to an old and complicated theological question: *to whom did Jesus pay the* **ransom**? Origen said it was the devil; Gregory of Nyssa objected that this put the devil on the same level as God, and allowed the devil to dictate terms to God. Gregory the Great said that Jesus was like a baited hook meant to catch Satan, and Peter the Lombard said the cross was like a mousetrap to catch the devil, baited with the blood of Christ. All of this takes the simple picture Jesus gave too far. "A ransom is something paid or given to liberate a man from a situation from which it is impossible to free himself." (Barclay)

iii. "Had all the sinners that ever lived in the world been consigned to hell, they could not have discharged the claims of justice. They must still continue to endure the scourge of crime they could never expiate. But the Son of God, blending the infinite majesty of his Deity with the perfect capacity to suffer as a man, offered an atonement of such inestimable value that he has absolutely paid the entire debt for his people." (Spurgeon)

iv. "Most scholars have also recognized in 'the many' a clear reference to Isaiah." (Carson) *By His knowledge My righteous Servant shall justify many, for He shall bear their iniquities* (Isaiah 53:11) *He was numbered with the transgressors, and He bore the sin of many* (Isaiah 53:12)

C. Jesus heals two blind men.

1. (29-31) Two blind men gain the attention of Jesus.

Now as they went out of Jericho, a great multitude followed Him. And behold, two blind men sitting by the road, when they heard that Jesus was passing by, cried out, saying, "Have mercy on us, O Lord, Son of David!" Then the multitude warned them that they should be quiet; but they cried out all the more, saying, "Have mercy on us, O Lord, Son of David!"

a. **When they heard that Jesus was passing by**: They knew this might be their last time to meet Jesus. They had the desperation appropriate for those who know that *today* is the day of salvation.

i. "It is the end of the account of Jesus' itinerant ministry, and its setting *as they went out of Jericho* points forward to the next town on the road, Jerusalem." (France)

b. **Have mercy on us, O Lord, Son of David!** The earnestness of these men was marvelous; they were *desperate* to be healed, and ignored the crowd that tried to quiet them (**they cried out all the more**).

i. "When the world and the devil begin to rebuke, in this case, it is a proof that the salvation of God is *nigh*; therefore, let such *cry out a great deal the more*." (Clarke)

c. **Lord, Son of David**: However, in their desperation they glorified Jesus. They gave Him full honor with this title.

2. (32-34) Jesus heals the two blind men.

So Jesus stood still and called them, and said, "What do you want Me to do for you?" They said to Him, "Lord, that our eyes may be opened." So Jesus had compassion and touched their eyes. And immediately their eyes received sight, and they followed Him.

a. **Jesus stood still**: Nothing could stop Him on His journey to Jerusalem; yet He **stood still** to answer a persistent plea for mercy.

b. **What do you want Me to do for you?** This is a wonderful, simple question God has not stopped asking. Sometimes we go without when God would want to give us something simply because we will not answer this question, and we *do not have because we do not ask* (James 4:2).

i. Jesus asked this question with full knowledge that these men were blind. He knew what they needed and what they wanted, but God still wants us to tell Him our needs as a constant expression of our trust and reliance on Him.

c. **And they immediately followed Him**: This was a great result. Not only were they healed, but they also followed the One who did great things for them.

i. "Reader, whosoever thou art, act in behalf of thy soul as these blind men did in behalf of their sight, and thy salvation is sure. Apply to the Son of David; lose not a moment; he is *passing by*, and thou art *passing* into *eternity*, and probably wilt never have a more favourable opportunity than the present. The Lord increase thy earnestness and faith!" (Clarke)

Matthew 21 - The Beginning of Jesus' Last Week

A. The triumphal entry.

1. (1-6) Jesus instructs His disciples regarding preparation for His triumphal entry into Jerusalem.

Now when they drew near Jerusalem, and came to Bethphage, at the Mount of Olives, then Jesus sent two disciples, saying to them, "Go into the village opposite you, and immediately you will find a donkey tied, and a colt with her. Loose *them* and bring *them* to Me. And if anyone says anything to you, you shall say, 'The Lord has need of them,' and immediately he will send them." All this was done that it might be fulfilled which was spoken by the prophet, saying:

"Tell the daughter of Zion,
'Behold, your King is coming to you,
Lowly, and sitting on a donkey,
A colt, the foal of a donkey.'"

So the disciples went and did as Jesus commanded them.

> a. **When they drew near Jerusalem**: Jesus knew that the religious leaders were going to arrest Him and condemn Him and mock Him and scourge Him and deliver Him to the Romans for crucifixion (Matthew 20:19). Yet He had the courage to not only enter Jerusalem, but to enter in as public a way as possible. This contrasts to His previous pattern of suppressing publicity.

> > i. If Jesus had not deliberately suppressed the popular enthusiasm over Him and His credentials as Messiah – if Jesus had *wanted it*, this would have happened long ago and many times.

> > ii. "Jesus could not have chosen a more dramatic moment; it was into a city surging with people keyed up with religious expectations that he came." (Barclay)

iii. "The applause and the crowds were not manipulated; they would have occurred in any case. But the ride on a colt, because it was planned, could only be an acted parable, a deliberate act of self-disclosure... Secrecy was being lifted." (Carson)

b. **You will find a donkey tied, and a colt with her**: Jesus would ride upon the younger of these animals, the **colt**. He told the disciples how they would find these animals, and instructed them to bring both animals.

i. The Hebrew text of Zechariah 9 mentions *one* animal, not two. "If we assume that Matthew understood Hebrew, the full quotation affirms that Jesus rode on the 'colt,' not its mother. Mark and Luke say the animal was so young that it had never been ridden. In the midst, then, of this excited crowd, an unbroken animal remains calm under the hands of the Messiah who controls nature." (Carson)

ii. "Mark tells us that the colt had never before been ridden (Mark 11:2), so that it would be only prudent to bring its mother as well to reassure it among the noisy crowd." (France)

iii. "*Hath need of them*: not for any weariness: he who had travelled on foot from Galilee to Bethany, could have gone the other two miles; but that he might enter into Jerusalem as was prophesied of him, Zechariah 9:9." (Poole)

iv. "What a singular conjunction of words is here, 'the Lord' and 'hath need!' Jesus, without laying aside his sovereignty, had taken a nature full of needs; yet, being in need, he was still the Lord and could command his subjects and requisition their property." (Spurgeon)

c. **All this was done that it might be fulfilled which was spoken by the prophet**: Here, Jesus deliberately worked to fulfill prophecy, especially the prophecy of Daniel's Seventy Weeks, which many feel Jesus fulfilled to the exact day on His triumphal entry (Daniel 9:24-27).

i. "It is possible that Matthew presents these verses as having been spoken by Jesus." (Carson)

d. **Your King is coming to you, lowly, and sitting on a donkey**: Jesus came to Jerusalem in humility, yet with appropriate dignity. Instead of coming on a horse as a conquering general, He came on a **colt**, as was customary for royalty. He came to Jerusalem as the Prince of Peace.

i. "Asses were of old beasts that great persons used to ride on, Judges 10:4; 12:14. But after Solomon's time the Jews got a breed of horses; so as only poor people rode upon asses, mostly reserved for burdens." (Poole)

ii. "Therefore for those with eyes to see, Jesus was not only proclaiming his messiahship and his fulfillment of Scripture but showing the kind of peace-loving approach he was now making to the city." (Carson)

iii. "This entry into Jerusalem has been termed the *triumph* of Christ. It was indeed the triumph of *humility* over *pride* and worldly grandeur; of *poverty* over *affluence*; and of *meekness* and *gentleness* over *rage* and *malice*." (Clarke)

2. (7-11) Jesus receives and encourages adoration as the Messiah.

They brought the donkey and the colt, laid their clothes on them, and set *Him* on them. And a very great multitude spread their clothes on the road; others cut down branches from the trees and spread *them* on the road. Then the multitudes who went before and those who followed cried out, saying:

"Hosanna to the Son of David!
'Blessed *is* He who comes in the name of the LORD!'
Hosanna in the highest!"

And when He had come into Jerusalem, all the city was moved, saying, "Who is this?" So the multitudes said, "This is Jesus, the prophet from Nazareth of Galilee."

a. **Laid their clothes on them...spread their clothes on the road; others cut down branches from the trees and spread them on the road**: All this was done to honor Jesus as a great, triumphant person coming into Jerusalem in the season of Passover.

i. Wiseman says of the spreading out of garments for Jehu in 2 Kings 9:13: "The act of spreading out the garment was one of recognition, loyalty and promise of support." (Wiseman)

ii. "Carrying palm and other branches was emblematical of victory and success. See 1 Maccabees 13:51; 2 Maccabees 10:7; and Revelation 7:9." (Clarke) *On the twenty-third day of the second month, in the year one hundred and seventy-one, the Jews entered the citadel with shouts of jubilation, waving of palm branches, the music of harps and cymbals and lyres, and the singing of hymns and canticles, because a great enemy of Israel had been destroyed.* (1 Maccabees 13:51)

iii. In one way, this crowd was glorious. "It is a mark of Christ's presence when the church becomes enthusiastic. We sometimes hear complaints about revivals being too exciting. Perhaps the censure is deserved, but I would like to see a little of the fault. This age does not generally sin in the direction of being too excited concerning divine things. We have erred so long on the other side that, perhaps, a little excess in the direction of fervor might not be the worst of all calamities; at any rate, I would not fear to try it." (Spurgeon)

iv. In another way, this crowd was ridiculous – in worldly eyes. "Why, if Pilate himself had heard about it he would have said — 'Ah! There is nothing much to fear from that. There is no fear that that man will ever upset Caesar; there is no fear that he will ever overturn an army. Where are their swords? There is not a sword among them! They have no cries that sound like rebellion; their songs are only some religious verses taken out of the Psalms.' 'Oh!' says he, 'the whole thing is contemptible and ridiculous.'" (Spurgeon)

b. **Hosanna to the Son of David!** This was open Messianic adoration of Jesus. They look to Jesus for salvation (**Hosanna** means "save now!" and was addressed to kings, as in 2 Samuel 14:4 and 2 Kings 6:26). They openly give Jesus the titles appropriate for the Messiah (**Son of David…He who comes in the name of the LORD**).

i. Jesus received and indeed encouraged this worship. Again, this was because *this is the day that the LORD has made* (Psalm 118:24), the day when the Messiah came as Savior to Jerusalem in fulfillment of Daniel's prophecy.

ii. "'Hosanna' transliterates the Hebrew expression that originally was a cry for help: 'Save!'… In time it became an invocation of blessing and even an acclamation… The people praise God in the highest heavens for sending the Messiah and, if 'Hosanna' retains some of its original force, also cry to him for deliverance." (Carson)

iii. "Essentially it is a people's cry for deliverance and for help in the day of their trouble; it is an oppressed people's cry to their saviour and their king." (Barclay)

iv. "'*Vox populi, vox Dei*' they used to say; but the saying is false: the voice of the people may seem to be the voice of God when they shout 'Hosanna in the highest'; but whose voice is it when they yell out, 'Crucify him, crucify him'?" (Spurgeon)

c. **When He had come into Jerusalem, all the city was moved**: Jesus also showed that He wasn't afraid of chief priests and Pharisees. He knew they were plotting to kill Him, yet He came openly to the city as Messiah.

i. "When the Magi came looking for the King of Jews, 'all Jerusalem' was troubled (Matthew 2:3). Now when the king arrives *all the city is stirred*." (France)

ii. "How strange is it that these same people…should, about five days after, change their hosannas for, *Away with him! Crucify him! Crucify him!* How fickle is the multitude! Even when they get *right*, there is but little hope that they will continue so long." (Clarke)

iii. It was here, before He entered the city, that He looked over the city and wept, knowing the judgment that would come upon Jerusalem (Luke 19:41-44).

iv. "Our Lord loves his people to be glad. His tears he kept to himself, as he wept over Jerusalem; but the gladness he scattered all around, so that even the boys and girls in the streets of Jerusalem made the temple courts to ring with their merry feet and gladsome songs." (Spurgeon)

d. **This is Jesus, the prophet from Nazareth of Galilee**: This continues the earlier identification of Jesus with Nazareth (Matthew 2:23). It would sound strange to many – especially to the religious establishment – that a **prophet** would come from the obscure and unnoted city of **Nazareth**.

i. "When our Lord grants revivals to his church, the congregations and the multitude outside begin to ask, 'Wherefore this stir? What meaneth all this? Who is this Christ, and what is his salvation?' This spirit of inquiry is eminently desirable. It is just now a matter to be sought for by importunate prayer." (Spurgeon)

ii. "They had not profited so much, or made so far progress in the mystery of Christ, as to know him to have been born a Bethlehemite." (Trapp)

B. Jesus cleanses the temple.

1. (12-13) Jesus forcibly stops the commercial desecration of the temple.

Then Jesus went into the temple of God and drove out all those who bought and sold in the temple, and overturned the tables of the money changers and the seats of those who sold doves. And He said to them, "It is written, 'My house shall be called a house of prayer,' but you have made it a 'den of thieves.'"

a. **Drove out all those who bought and sold in the temple**: This seems distinct from the cleansing of the temple courts mentioned in John 2:13-22, which happened towards the beginning of Jesus' earthly ministry. Yet the purpose was the same; to drive out the merchants, who in cooperation with the priests cheated visitors to Jerusalem by forcing them to purchase approved sacrificial animals and currencies at high prices.

i. Barclay notes, "A pair of doves could cost as little as 4p outside the Temple and as much as 75p inside the Temple." This is almost *20 times* more expensive.

ii. Yet Jesus' anger was against **all those who bought** as well as those **who sold**. "Sellers and buyers viewed as one company – kindred in spirit, to be cleared out wholesale...The traffic was necessary, and might have been innocent; but the trading spirit soon develops abuses which were doubtless rampant at that period." (Bruce)

iii. What Jesus did was important more as an acted-out parable than for what it accomplished in itself. "There is no indication, nor is it likely, that any lasting reform was achieved; no doubt the tables were back for the rest of the week, and Jesus took no further action." (France)

iv. France says that there was a contemporary expectation that the Messiah would cleanse the temple, both approving it after the pagan conquerors (such as Antiochus Epiphanes and Pompey), but also from the false worship from God's own people.

v. "I do not believe we shall thoroughly purify any church by Acts of Parliament, nor by reformation associations, nor by agitation, nor by any merely human agency. No hand can grasp the scourge that can drive out the buyers and sellers, but that hand which once was fastened to the cross. Let the Lord do it and the work will be done, for it is not of man, nor shall man accomplish it." (Spurgeon)

b. **My house shall be called a house of prayer**: The merchants operated in the outer courts of the temple, the only area where Gentiles could come and pray. Therefore, this place of prayer was made into a marketplace, and a dishonest one (**a 'den of thieves'**).

i. Mark's record contains the more complete quotation of Jesus' reference to Isaiah 56:7: *Is it not written, "My house shall be called a house of prayer for all nations?"* (Mark 11:17). The point was that Isaiah prophesied, and Jesus demanded that the temple be a place for *all nations* to pray. The activity of **all those who bought and sold in the** outer courts made it impossible for any seeking Gentile to come and pray.

ii. "In that uproar of buying and selling and bargaining and auctioneering prayer was impossible. Those who sought God's presence were being debarred from it from the very people of God's House." (Barclay)

2. (14) Jesus carries on God's compassionate work in the temple courts.

Then *the* blind and *the* lame came to Him in the temple, and He healed them.

a. **The blind and the lame came to Him**: The bold action of Jesus when He drove out the merchants and money changers from the temple courts did not discourage the needy from coming to Him.

i. The **blind and the lame** were restricted to the court of the Gentiles; they could not go closer to the temple and could not go to the altar to sacrifice. After purging the court of the Gentiles of merchants and robbers, Jesus then ministered to the outcasts who congregated there.

b. **And He healed them**: After driving out the moneychangers and the merchants from the temple courts, Jesus didn't establish "The Society for the Cleansing of the Temple." He got back to doing the business of the Messiah, a significant part of which was showing the power of God in the context of compassion and mercy.

3. (15-17) The indignation of the Jewish leaders.

But when the chief priests and scribes saw the wonderful things that He did, and the children crying out in the temple and saying, "Hosanna to the Son of David!" they were indignant and said to Him, "Do You hear what these are saying?" And Jesus said to them, "Yes. Have you never read, 'Out of the mouth of babes and nursing infants You have perfected praise'?" Then He left them and went out of the city to Bethany, and He lodged there.

a. **They were indignant**: This was their response to **the wonderful things that He did**, and to the praise of **children** for Jesus in the temple courts. The hypocrisy of the religious leaders is evident. Greed and theft in the temple didn't bother them, but praise to Jesus did.

i. "It was a common thing among the Jews for the children to be employed in public acclamations; and thus they were accustomed to hail their celebrated rabbins. This shouting of the children was therefore no strange thing in the land: only they were exasperated, because a person was celebrated against whom they had a rooted hatred." (Clarke)

ii. This reminds us that **children** can have a real relationship with God and spiritual life, yet they will still be **children**. "For a boy to put on the air and manners of a man is not sanctification; that is to spoil him, not to sanctify him. And for a girl to be other than a girl, and to assume the air and tone of her careful mother, should be very mischievous. God does not sanctify children into men, but he sanctifies children in their own childlike way." (Spurgeon)

b. **Do You hear what these are saying?** Jesus answered this question from **the chief priests and scribes**. The answer was clear: *Yes*, He had heard **what these are saying** – and it was **perfected praise** in the ears of God.

i. "Luther was greatly encouraged when he found that the children met together for prayer. He said, 'God will hear *them*. The devil himself cannot defeat us now the children begin to pray.'" (Spurgeon)

c. **He left them and went out of the city to Bethany, and He lodged there**: At the time of Passover, thousands and thousands of pilgrims crowded into Jerusalem. It was common for some to stay in the surrounding villages, and **Bethany** was close by.

i. "At Passover time quarters could not easily be got in the city, but the house of Martha and Mary would be open to Jesus (*cf.* Luke 21:37)." (Bruce)

C. The lesson of the fig tree.

1. (18-19) Jesus rebukes a fig tree.

Now in the morning, as He returned to the city, He was hungry. And seeing a fig tree by the road, He came to it and found nothing on it but leaves, and said to it, "Let no fruit grow on you ever again." Immediately the fig tree withered away.

a. **He was hungry**: Some wonder why Jesus would be hungry in the morning leaving the home of Martha and Mary. Spurgeon speculated it was because He woke early to have time with His heavenly Father, and took no time to eat.

i. "He was perfectly human and therefore physically hungry, for hunger is a sign of health." (Morgan)

b. **Let no fruit grow on you ever again**: In a dramatic way, Jesus performed one of His few *destructive* miracles. His curse made the **fig tree** to wither away.

i. It is worth noting that the two destructive miracles of Jesus (this and the events that ended in the destruction of the herd of pigs, Matthew 8:30-32) were not directed towards people.

c. **Found nothing on it but leaves**: This explains why Jesus did this destructive miracle. Essentially, the tree was a picture of false advertising, having **leaves**, but no figs. This should not be the case with these particular fig trees, which customarily did not bear leaves apart from figs.

i. "The first Adam came to the fig tree for leaves, but the Second Adam looks for figs." (Spurgeon)

ii. In this acted-out-parable, Jesus warned of coming judgment upon an unfruitful Israel. It showed God's disapproval of people who are all leaves and no fruit. "The story is clear and simple, and its point obvious, that what counts is not promise but performance." (France)

2. (20-22) How did Jesus do this?

And when the disciples saw *it*, they marveled, saying, "How did the fig tree wither away so soon?" So Jesus answered and said to them, "Assuredly, I say to you, if you have faith and do not doubt, you will not only do what was done to the fig tree, but also if you say to this mountain, 'Be removed and be cast into the sea,' it will be done. And whatever things you ask in prayer, believing, you will receive."

a. **How did the fig tree wither away so soon?** Jesus explained that this miracle was really the result of a prayer made in faith (**if you have faith and do not doubt**). He then encouraged His marveling disciples to also have this kind of faith, trusting that God would hear them also.

b. **And whatever things you ask in prayer, believing, you will receive**: This promise of God's answer to the prayer of faith was made to disciples, not to the multitude. This is a promise to those who are following Jesus.

i. "Nothing is too big for true faith to obtain, but that faith must have a promise to lean upon." (Poole)

ii. "We can only believe for a thing when we are in such union with God that his thought and purpose can freely flow into us, suggesting what we should pray for, and leading us to that point in which there is a perfect sympathy and understanding between us and the divine mind. Faith is always the product of such a frame as this." (Meyer)

D. Jesus answers the Jewish leaders.

1. (23-27) Jesus is questioned by the religious leaders as He comes back into the temple.

Now when He came into the temple, the chief priests and the elders of the people confronted Him as He was teaching, and said, "By what authority are You doing these things? And who gave You this authority?" But Jesus answered and said to them, "I also will ask you one thing, which if you tell Me, I likewise will tell you by what authority I do these things: The baptism of John; where was it from? From heaven or from men?" And they reasoned among themselves, saying, "If we say, 'From heaven,' He will say to us, 'Why then did you not believe him?' But if we say, 'From men,' we fear the multitude, for all count John as a prophet." So they answered Jesus and said, "We do not know." And He said to them, "Neither will I tell you by what authority I do these things."

a. **The chief priests and the elders of the people confronted Him as He was teaching**: In His previous visit on the day before, Jesus drove out the moneychangers and merchants from the temple courts. Now He returned there to teach, unafraid of the religious leaders.

i. "When we think of the extraordinary things Jesus had been doing we cannot be surprised that the Jewish authorities asked him what right he had to do them." (Barclay)

b. **By what authority are You doing these things?** The religious leaders raised the question of Jesus' authority, and He answered by raising the question of their competence to judge such an issue. Their ability to judge John the Baptist and his ministry was a measure of their ability to judge Jesus as well (**The baptism of John: where was it from?**).

i. "His question is far more profound. If the religious authorities rightly answer it, they will already have the correct answer to their own question." (Carson)

ii. "Hence now-a-days those Popish questions to the professors of the truth: By what authority do you do these things? Where had you your calling, your ordination? Where was your religion before Luther? Whereunto it was well answered by one once, 'In the Bible, where yours never was.'" (Trapp)

c. **We do not know**: They answered only after carefully calculating the political consequences of either answer. They didn't seem interested in answering the question honestly, only cleverly. This showed they were more interested in the opinions of the multitude rather than the will of God, so Jesus didn't answer their question to Him.

i. "They could not say, 'Of men,' for they were cowards. They would not say, 'Of heaven,' for they were hypocrites." (Morgan)

ii. Jesus kindly and compassionately met the needs of the hurting multitude, as demonstrated in Matthew 21:14. But Jesus didn't show much patience with those who arrogantly questioned Him and hoped to trap Him in His own words. Jesus never fell into their trap.

2. (28-32) The parable of the two sons.

"But what do you think? A man had two sons, and he came to the first and said, 'Son, go, work today in my vineyard.' He answered and said, 'I will not,' but afterward he regretted it and went. Then he came to the second and said likewise. And he answered and said, 'I go, sir,' but he did not go. Which of the two did the will of *his* father?" They said to Him, "The first." Jesus said to them, "Assuredly, I say to you that tax collectors and harlots enter the kingdom of God before you. For John came to you in the way of righteousness, and you did not believe him; but tax collectors and harlots believed him; and when you saw *it*, you did not afterward relent and believe him."

a. **A man had two sons**: This parable shows us two different kinds of sons. They were in the same house, and we could say that the father had a right to the services of both his sons. Perhaps they wished that the father would just leave them alone, but he did not. It was good and right for the father to expect that the sons would work for him.

i. By general Biblical principle, we can say that it is not our duty to separate them except through exhortation and appeal to conscience. Their sure separation must await the end of the age; until then, the tares and the wheat grow together.

b. **Son, go work today in my vineyard**: There is much to see in these simple words of the father to the son.

- The father spoke to this son individually; he did not speak to the sons together. Though the same invitation was given to both sons (**he came to the second and said likewise**), it was an individual call to work.

- The father appealed to him first as a **son**. Knowing he was the son of his father should have made him willing to do his will.

- The father asked the son to **work**; to participate together in the family business. Yet it was **work** and not play.

- The father asked the son to work **today**, not in some distant time.

- The father asked the son to work in "**my vineyard**." It belonged to the father, so it should have mattered to the son.

c. **He answered and said, "I will not," but afterward he regretted it and went**: The first son refused to work for his father. He didn't want to bend to the father's will. Yet later **he regretted it and went**. He spoke wrong, but did right.

d. **He answered and said, "I go, sir," but he did not go**: The second son said the right thing and he said it with respect (**sir**), but he did not do what he said he would.

i. There are many churchgoers that imitate the second son.

- They admit that the Word of God is true.

- They intend to get serious about it someday.

- They talk about doing the Father's work.

- They keep up the external appearance of religion, but their heart is not right with God.

- They think that words and promises are enough.

ii. "The second son said, 'I go, sir,' but he went not; and these people do not go. They talk of repenting, but they do not repent. They speak of believing, but they never believe. They think of submitting to God, but they have not submitted themselves to him yet. They say it is time they broke up the fallow ground, and sought the Lord, but they do not seek him. It all ends in a mere promise." (Spurgeon)

iii. *They are sinning against the light, because they know better.* This is dangerous, because it is lying to the Holy Spirit; it is dangerous, because it hardens the conscience.

e. **Which of the two did the will of his father?** The point of this parable is clear. What matters is living for God, not saying the right words. The religious leaders were good at talking righteous talk, but their stubbornly unrepentant hearts showed that repentant sinners would **enter the kingdom before** them.

i. "The shock value of Jesus' statement can only be appreciated when the low esteem in which tax collectors were held, not to mention prostitutes, is taken into account." (Carson)

f. **When you saw it, you did not afterward relent and believe him**: These proud religionists should have repented all the more when they saw the notorious sinners repenting, but they did not.

3. (33-41) The parable of the wicked servants.

"Hear another parable: There was a certain landowner who planted a vineyard and set a hedge around it, dug a winepress in it and built a tower. And he leased it to vinedressers and went into a far country. Now when vintage-time drew near, he sent his servants to the vinedressers, that they might receive its fruit. And the vinedressers took his servants, beat one, killed one, and stoned another. Again he sent other servants, more than the first, and they did likewise to them. Then last of all he sent his son to them, saying, 'They will respect my son.' But when the vinedressers saw the son, they said among themselves, 'This is the heir. Come, let us kill him and seize his inheritance.' So they took him and cast *him* out of the vineyard and killed *him*. Therefore, when the owner of the vineyard comes, what will he do to those vinedressers?" They said to Him, "He will destroy those wicked men miserably, and lease *his* vineyard to other vinedressers who will render to him the fruits in their seasons."

a. **There was a certain landowner who planted a vineyard and set a hedge around it**: Jesus told of a **landowner** who prepared his vineyard carefully and hired men to manage it (**the vinedressers**). The men who were supposed to manage his vineyard mistreated and **killed** the messengers sent by the landowner. Finally he sent his son, and they killed him also – foolishly believing they would take control of the vineyard. Yet the response of the landowner was not to yield to the **vinedressers** but to judge and **destroy** them.

i. The Old Testament often used the picture of a vineyard to speak of Israel (Deuteronomy 32:32, Psalm 80:8, Jeremiah 2:21, and especially Isaiah 5:1-7).

b. **They will respect my son...This is the heir. Come, let us kill him and seize his inheritance**: Jesus portrayed the madness of the chief priests and elders who plotted to kill the Father's Son sent to the rebellious leaders of Israel.

i. "The husbandmen treat the messengers in the most barbarous and truculent manner: beating, killing, stoning to death; highly improbable in the natural sphere, but another instance in which parables have to violate the natural probability in order to describe truly men's conduct in the spiritual sphere." (Bruce)

ii. "By the *servants* here sent to the husbandmen are doubtless to be understood those extraordinary prophets." (Poole)

iii. "*They caught him* in the garden of Gethsemane; *they cast him out* in their Council in the hall of Caiaphas, and when he was led without the gate of Jerusalem; *they slew him* at Calvary." (Spurgeon)

c. **He will destroy those wicked men miserably**: The message of this parable is clear enough. With this answer, the chief priests and elders understood what the wicked servants deserved. Truly, those who rebel against their master this way deserve judgment.

i. They knew the **owner of the vineyard** had the right to expect **the fruits in their seasons**. In the same way, God looked for fruit from Israel's leadership, but found little (as shown in the fig tree incident).

ii. "Oh, that the Lord may raise up a race of men '*who shall render him the fruits in their seasons!*' The hallmark of a faithful minister is his giving to God all the glory of any work that he is enabled to do. That which does not magnify the Lord will not bless men." (Spurgeon)

d. **And lease his vineyard to other vinedressers who will render to him the fruits in their seasons**: The leaders of Israel were so corrupt that God was transferring leadership to others – specifically, to the apostles and then to the Jewish/Gentile church they would lead.

4. (42-46) Jesus warns the religious leaders of the result of their rejection.

Jesus said to them, "Have you never read in the Scriptures:

'The stone which the builders rejected
Has become the chief cornerstone.
This was the LORD's doing,
And it is marvelous in our eyes'?

Therefore I say to you, the kingdom of God will be taken from you and given to a nation bearing the fruits of it. And whoever falls on this stone will be broken; but on whomever it falls, it will grind him to powder." Now when the chief priests and Pharisees heard His parables, they perceived that He was speaking of them. But when they sought to lay hands on Him, they feared the multitudes, because they took Him for a prophet.

a. **Have you never read the Scriptures**: This manner of speaking to the chief priests and elders of Israel must have angered them. Jesus speaks to the leading theologians of Israel and asks them if they have ever read their **Scriptures**.

b. **The stone which the builders rejected has become the chief cornerstone**: Jesus quoted this from Psalm 118 to remind them that their rejection of Him said more about their guilt and coming judgment than it said about Jesus Himself. Though they reject Him, He is still **the chief cornerstone**, fulfilling the great Messianic Psalm 118.

i. Like a painting from a great master, Jesus is not on trial – those who look at Him are. These leaders who rejected Jesus had to hear the eventual consequences of their rejection.

ii. Clearly, Jesus claimed to be the rejected stone of Psalm 118:22-24 that God appointed to become the chief cornerstone. He is also the stone of Isaiah 8:13-15 that people stumble over, the foundation stone and precious cornerstone of Isaiah 28:16, and the stone of Daniel 2:34, 44-45 that destroys the world in rebellion to God.

c. **The kingdom of God will be taken from you and given to a nation bearing the fruits of it**: Jesus warned the religious leaders that if they continued their rejection of God and His Messiah, they could expect that God would pass the leadership of His work on earth to others.

i. "The doom is forfeiture of privilege, the kingdom is taken from them and given to others." (Bruce)

ii. "The sphere in which we must look for God at work in salvation is no longer the nation of Israel but another *nation*. This is not the Gentiles as such (that would require the plural *ethnesin*, not the singular *ethnei*), but a people of God derived from all nations, Jew and Gentile." (France)

iii. "What a warning is this to our own country! We, too, are seeing the sacrifice and deity of our Lord questioned, and his Sacred Word assailed by those who should have been its advocates. Unless there is speedy amendment, the Lord may take away the candlestick out of its place and find another race which will prove more faithful to him and his Gospel than our own has been." (Spurgeon)

d. **Whoever falls on this stone will be broken; but on whomever it falls, it will grind him to powder**: The choice before the religious leaders is the choice before every person. We can be **broken** in humble surrender before God or be completely broken in judgment.

e. **They sought to lay hands on Him**: Instead of repenting, the religious leaders responded with anger, continuing to increase the greatness of their sin of rejecting Jesus.

i. **They perceived that He was speaking of them**: "Who told them so, but their own guilty consciences?" (Trapp)

Matthew 22 - Jesus Answers and Asks Difficult Questions

A. The parable of the wedding feast.

1. (1-3) The first invitation is refused.

And Jesus answered and spoke to them again by parables and said: "The kingdom of heaven is like a certain king who arranged a marriage for his son, and sent out his servants to call those who were invited to the wedding; and they were not willing to come."

a. **Jesus answered and spoke to them again by parables**: Jesus continued to explain to the religious leaders and to the listening crowds the danger of rejecting Him.

b. **A certain king who arranged a marriage for his son**: A **wedding** is often the most significant social event of a one's life. The wedding of a prince would be a spectacular event, and an invitation would be prized.

i. This parable is similar in many ways to one found in Luke 14:15-24. Yet the differences between the two parables are even more evident. "Most preachers will use a good story more than once, and in different forms to suit different contexts, and there is no improbability in Jesus doing likewise." (France)

c. **They were not willing to come**: It seems strange that those invited refused an invitation to a royal wedding. This illustrates the principle that there is no *logical* reason God's good gifts are refused.

2. (4-7) The second invitation is refused and the king reacts.

"Again, he sent out other servants, saying, 'Tell those who are invited, "See, I have prepared my dinner; my oxen and fatted cattle *are* killed, and all things *are* ready. Come to the wedding."' But they made light of it and went their ways, one to his own farm, another to his business.

And the rest seized his servants, treated *them* spitefully, and killed *them*. But when the king heard *about it,* he was furious. And he sent out his armies, destroyed those murderers, and burned up their city."

a. **Tell those who are invited, "See, I have prepared"**: The king persisted in making the invitation as attractive as possible. He really *wanted* those invited to come.

> i. Barclay says that when a great social event happened in the Jewish culture of that day, people were invited but without a set time. On the appropriate day, when the host was ready to receive the guests, they sent out messengers to say that all things were ready and it was time to come to the feast.

> ii. "So, then, the king in this parable had long ago sent out his invitations; but it was not till everything was prepared that the final summons was issued – and insultingly refused." (Barclay)

> iii. **All things are ready** is the message of the gospel. You don't come to God's feast and prepare your own meal. He has made it **ready** for you; you come to receive.

b. **But they made light of it and went their ways**: The reaction of those invited made no sense, but it does give an accurate description of the reaction of many to the gospel. Many **made light of it**; others go back to their **business**.

> i. "The rebel seemed to say, 'Let the King do as he likes with *his* oxen and *his* fatlings; I am going to look after *my* farm, or attend to *my* merchandise." (Spurgeon)

c. **He was furious...and he sent out his armies, destroyed those murderers**: The king rightfully brought judgment upon the offenders. Not only did they reject his invitation, but they also murdered his messengers.

> i. This was a prophecy of what would happen to Jerusalem, the city whose religious leaders so strongly rejected Jesus and His gospel.

3. (8-10) The third invitation.

"Then he said to his servants, 'The wedding is ready, but those who were invited were not worthy. Therefore go into the highways, and as many as you find, invite to the wedding.' So those servants went out into the highways and gathered together all whom they found, both bad and good. And the wedding *hall* was filled with guests."

a. **As many as you find, invite to the wedding**: The king was determined that he would not have an empty banquet hall, so an invitation was given to all who would hear.

b. **Those servants went out into the highways and gathered together all whom they found, both good and bad**: When the first and second invitations were so dramatically rejected, the third invitation was made more broadly. All were invited, whether **good** or **bad**.

> i. In this sense, we can say this is a parable about grace. Those who were invited – and who came – were utterly undeserving of the invitation, much less the wedding feast itself.

4. (11-14) The man without a wedding garment.

"But when the king came in to see the guests, he saw a man there who did not have on a wedding garment. So he said to him, 'Friend, how did you come in here without a wedding garment?' And he was speechless. Then the king said to the servants, 'Bind him hand and foot, take him away, and cast *him* into outer darkness; there will be weeping and gnashing of teeth.' For many are called, but few *are* chosen."

a. **When the king came to see the guests**: The king carefully examined his guests to see if they all wore the garments that were customarily offered to those attending a wedding feast.

b. **A man there who did not have on a wedding garment**: The man without a robe was conspicuous by his difference. He came inappropriately dressed and the king noticed.

> i. There is debate among commentators as to if it was customary for a king or nobleman to offer his guests a garment to wear at such an occasion. There seems to have been some tradition of this among the Greeks, but no evidence of the practice in the days of Jesus.
>
> ii. Quite apart from who supplied the proper garments, the man clearly was out of place. "Is it fit to come to such a feast in thy worst? In the leathern coats, in the tattered rags and menstruous clouts of wretched old Adam?" (Trapp)
>
> iii. "He came because he was invited, but he came only in appearance. The banquet was intended to honor the King's Son, but this man meant nothing of the kind; he was willing to eat the good things set before him, but in his heart there was no love either for the King or his well-beloved Son." (Spurgeon)
>
> iv. **He was speechless**: "He was muzzled or haltered up, that is, he held his peace, as though he had had a bridle or a halter in his mouth. This is the import of the Greek word here used." (Trapp)

c. **Cast him into outer darkness**: The man who did as he pleased at the wedding feast, instead of honoring the king and conforming to his expectations, suffered a terrible fate.

i. "He had, by his action, if not in words, said, 'I am a free man, and will do as I like.' So *the king said to the servants, 'Bind him.'* Pinion him; let him never be free again. He had made too free with holy things; he had actively insulted the King." (Spurgeon)

ii. This parable demonstrates that those *indifferent* to the gospel, those *antagonistic* against the gospel, and those *unchanged* by the gospel share the same fate. None of them enjoyed the king's feast.

d. **For many are called, but few are chosen**: This statement of Jesus, in this context, touches on the great working together of the choices of man and the choosing of God. Why did they not come to the wedding party? *Because they refused the invitation.* Why did they not come to the wedding party? *Because they were called, but not chosen.*

B. Question from the Pharisees.

1. (15-17) After flattery, the Pharisees ask Jesus a problematic question.

Then the Pharisees went and plotted how they might entangle Him in *His* talk. And they sent to Him their disciples with the Herodians, saying, "Teacher, we know that You are true, and teach the way of God in truth; nor do You care about anyone, for You do not regard the person of men. Tell us, therefore, what do You think? Is it lawful to pay taxes to Caesar, or not?"

a. **Plotted how they might entangle Him in His talk**: Here the Pharisees and the Herodians worked together. This was evidence of their great hatred of Jesus, because they were willing to put aside their own differences for the sake of uniting against Jesus.

i. **The Herodians**: "The name of this party probably originated in a kind of hero-worship for Herod the Great." (Bruce)

ii. Jesus had been directly accusing and exposing the religious leaders; now they are fighting back. "Now we see the Jewish leaders launching their counterattack; and they do so by directing at Jesus carefully formulated questions." (Barclay)

b. **We know that You are true, and teach the way of God in truth; nor do you care about anyone, for You do not regard the person of men**: Their plotting led them to approach Jesus with flattery. They hoped He was insecure or foolish enough to be impressed by their hollow praise.

i. "Here is a fair glove, drawn upon a foul hand." (Trapp)

ii. "The compliment, besides being treacherous, was insulting, implying that Jesus was a reckless simpleton who would give Himself away, and a vain man who could be flattered." (Bruce)

c. **Is it lawful to pay taxes to Caesar, or not?** Jesus' dilemma with this question was simple. If He said that taxes *should* be paid, He could be accused of denying the sovereignty of God over Israel (making Himself unpopular with the Jewish people). If He said that taxes *should not* be paid, He made Himself an enemy of Rome.

i. "*Lawful* does not refer to Roman law (there was no question about that!), but to the law of God; is it permissible for the people of God to express allegiance to a pagan emperor?" (France)

ii. Barclay claims there were three regular taxes. There was the *ground tax*, which was a 10% tax on grain production and a 20% tax on oil and wine. There was the *income tax*, which was 1% of a man's income. And there was the *poll tax*, paid by every man from 14 to 65 years of age and every woman from 12 to 65 years of age; this tax was a denarius a year.

iii. This particular tax was the poll tax. "Paying the poll tax was the most obvious sign of submission to Rome...Zealots claimed the poll tax was a God-dishonoring badge of slavery to the pagans." (Carson)

2. (18-22) Jesus answers: give to Caesar what is his, but give to God what belongs to God.

But Jesus perceived their wickedness, and said, "Why do you test Me, *you* hypocrites? Show Me the tax money." So they brought Him a denarius. And He said to them, "Whose image and inscription *is* this?" They said to Him, "Caesar's." And He said to them, "Render therefore to Caesar the things that are Caesar's, and to God the things that are God's." When they had heard *these words*, they marveled, and left Him and went their way.

a. **Whose image and inscription is this**: Again, with His wise answer, Jesus showed that He was in complete control. He rebuked the wickedness and hypocrisy of the Pharisees and Herodians.

b. **Render therefore to Caesar the things that are Caesar's**: Jesus affirmed that the government makes legitimate requests of us. We are responsible to God in all things, but we must be obedient to government in matters civil and national.

i. Peter said it like this: *Fear God. Honor the king.* (1 Peter 2:17)

ii. "Every Christian has a double citizenship. He is a citizen of the country in which he happens to live. To it he owes many things. He owes the safety against lawless men which only a settled government can give; he owes all public services." (Barclay)

iii. "*Render* generally means 'give back' (whereas the verb they had used in verse 17 was simple 'give'). It is the verb for paying a bill or settling a debt; they owe it to him." (France)

c. **And to God the things that are God's**: Everyone has the image of God impressed upon them. This means that we belong to God, not to Caesar, or not even to ourselves.

i. "By treating them as distinct Jesus said in effect: The kingdom of God is not of this world, it is possible to be a true citizen of the kingdom and yet quietly submit to the civil rule of a foreign potentate." (Bruce)

ii. "It establishes the *limits*, regulates the *rights*, and distinguishes the *jurisdiction* of the two *empires* of *heaven* and *earth*. The *image* of *princes* stamped on their *coin* denotes that temporal things belong all to their government. The *image* of God stamped on the *soul* denotes that all its faculties and powers belong to the Most High, and should be employed in his service." (Clarke)

iii. Had the Jews rendered unto God His due, they would have never had to render *anything* to Caesar. In New Testament times, they would never have endured the occupying oppression of the Roman Empire if they had been obedient to their covenant with God.

C. Question from the Sadducees.

1. (23-28) The Sadducees attempt to ridicule the idea of the resurrection.

The same day the Sadducees, who say there is no resurrection, came to Him and asked Him, saying: "Teacher, Moses said that if a man dies, having no children, his brother shall marry his wife and raise up offspring for his brother. Now there were with us seven brothers. The first died after he had married, and having no offspring, left his wife to his brother. Likewise the second also, and the third, even to the seventh. Last of all the woman died also. Therefore, in the resurrection, whose wife of the seven will she be? For they all had her."

a. **The Sadducees, who say there is no resurrection**: The Sadducees were the ancient version of the modern liberal theologians. They were anti-supernaturalistic, only accepting the first five books of Moses as authentic - and disregarding what was written in those books when it pleased them to do so.

i. "The Sadducees were not many in number; but they were the wealthy, the aristocratic, and the governing class." (Barclay)

ii. "At Jesus' time Judaism as a whole held surprising diverse views of death and what lies beyond it." (Carson)

b. **Now there were with us seven brothers**: The Sadducees asked Jesus a hypothetical - and ridiculous - question, hoping to show that the idea of the resurrection is nonsense. Based on Deuteronomy 25:5-10, if a married man died childless, it was his brother's responsibility to impregnate his brother's widow and then count the child as the deceased husband's descendant. The Pharisees imagined elaborate circumstances along these lines and raised the question, "**Therefore, in the resurrection, whose wife of the seven will she be?**"

i. This practice of a brother-in-law marrying the widow of his brother is known as *levirate marriage*. The term comes from the Latin "lavir," meaning "brother-in-law." This is the specific idea in the question. "*Marry* is not the normal Greek word, but a technical term for the performance of the levirate duty." (France)

ii. "Probably, this was one of the stock stories they were in the habit of telling in order to cast ridicule upon the resurrection." (Spurgeon)

2. (29) Jesus' reply: you don't know the Scriptures, and you don't know the power of God.

Jesus answered and said to them, "You are mistaken, not knowing the Scriptures nor the power of God."

a. **You are mistaken**: The Sadducees connected their thoughts to a Biblical passage, but did not think through the passage correctly. These highly-trained men were **mistaken** in their basic understanding of Biblical truth.

b. **Not knowing the Scriptures nor the power of God**: Their mistake was rooted in two causes. First, they did not know **the Scriptures** (though they thought they did). Second, they did not know **the power of God**, being basically anti-supernaturalists. This was true of them, even though religion was their career and they were highly trained.

i. **Not knowing the Scriptures**: It is possible for a person to have much Bible knowledge, yet not fundamentally know the **Scriptures**. Paul later told Timothy to *hold fast the pattern of sound words which you have heard from me* (2 Timothy 1:13). This suggests that Biblical truth has a *pattern* to it, a pattern that can be detected by the discerning heart. It also suggests that one can lose this pattern (thus the command to *hold fast*). The Sadducees had Bible knowledge, but they did not *hold fast the pattern of sound words*; many today are like them in this respect.

ii. **Nor the power of God**: The Sadducees denied supernatural truths such as the existence of angelic beings and the bodily resurrection. They had a fundamental doubt of **the power of God** to do beyond what they could measure and understand in the material world; many today are like the Sadducees in this respect.

iii. "If you knew the power of God, you would know that God is able to raise the dead…If you knew the Scriptures, you would know that God will raise the dead." (Poole)

3. (30-33) Jesus answers: resurrection life is different.

"For in the resurrection they neither marry nor are given in marriage, but are like angels of God in heaven. But concerning the resurrection of the dead, have you not read what was spoken to you by God, saying, 'I am the God of Abraham, the God of Isaac, and the God of Jacob'? God is not the God of the dead, but of the living." And when the multitudes heard *this*, they were astonished at His teaching.

a. **In the resurrection they neither marry nor are given in marriage**: First, Jesus reminded them that life in the resurrection is quite different from this life. It does not merely continue this world and its arrangements, but it is life of a completely different order.

i. This passage has made many wonder if marriage relationships will exist in heaven, or if those who are husband and wife on earth will have no special relationship in heaven. We are not told enough about life in the world beyond to answer in great detail, but we can understand a few principles.

- Family relationships will still be known in life in the world beyond. The rich man Jesus described in the afterlife was aware of his family relationships (Luke 16:27-28).

- The glory of heaven will be a relationship and connection with God that surpasses anything else, including present family relationships (Revelation 21:22-23).

ii. If it seems that life **in the resurrection** that Jesus spoke of here does not include some of the pleasures of life we know on earth, it is only because the enjoyments and satisfactions of heaven far surpass what we know on earth. We can't be completely certain what life in glory beyond will be like, but we can know with certainty that no one will be disappointed with the arrangements (Revelation 22:1-5).

iii. This question is not merely theoretical. There will be many in heaven who have had more than one spouse, for any number of reasons. Jesus here told us that jealousy and exclusion will have no place in heaven.

iv. This Biblical understanding of heaven is dramatically different from the more sensual dreams of heaven, such as those found in Islamic and Mormon theology. "Mahomet, as he professed that himself had a special license given him by God to know what woman he would, and to put them away when he would; so he promised to all his votaries and adherents the like carnal pleasures at the resurrection." (Trapp)

b. **Are like the angels of God in heaven**: Jesus here said that **the angels of God in heaven** do not marry; we presume this includes that they do not have sexual relationships.

i. The most obvious point must not be neglected: Jesus told the Sadducees that angels were real. "In fact, Jesus' use of angels contains a double thrust since the Sadducees denied their existence." (Carson)

ii. Angels are always represented in the Bible as male figures, and never specifically as female figures (Genesis 18:2, 16; Genesis 19:1-11).

iii. This raises a question because of the probable connection of fallen angelic beings and human sexuality described in Genesis 6:1-8 and Jude 6-7. Yet the words of Jesus do not exclude such a connection.

- Jesus spoke of **the angels of God in heaven**, not the fallen angelic beings indicated in the Genesis and Jude passages.

- Jesus did not say that angelic beings were incapable of sexual expression, only that such relationships did not exist among the angels in heaven.

- We can't be certain of the type of sexual connection indicated in the Genesis and Jude passages. It is entirely possible that the connection was not between material appearances of these angelic beings and humans, but that the evil angelic beings expressed themselves through uniquely demon-possessed humans.

c. **But concerning the resurrection of the dead, have you not read what was spoken to you by God**: Jesus demonstrated the reality of the resurrection using only the Torah; the five books of Moses, which were the only books the Sadducees accepted as authoritative. If Abraham, Isaac and Jacob did not live on in resurrection, then God would say that *He was the God of Abraham*, instead of saying "*I am* **the God of Abraham**."

i. "The living God is the God of living men; and Abraham, Isaac, and Jacob are still alive and identified as the same persons who lived on earth." (Spurgeon)

ii. "As no man can be a father without children, nor a king without a people, so, strictly speaking, the Lord cannot be called the God of any but the living." (Calvin, cited in France)

D. Question from a Scribe.

1. (34-36) Question from a lawyer among the Pharisees: which is the greatest commandment?

But when the Pharisees heard that He had silenced the Sadducees, they gathered together. Then one of them, a lawyer, asked *Him a question*, testing Him, and saying, "Teacher, which *is* the great commandment in the law?"

    a. **When the Pharisees heard that He had silenced the Sadducees, they gathered**: Matthew gives us the fascinating scene of the opponents of Jesus working hard to embarrass Him – and working unsuccessfully.

        i. "*They came together* probably echoes deliberately the plotting of the heathen against God's anointed in Psalm 2:2." (France)

    b. **Asked Him a question, testing Him**: This question was also planned to trap Jesus. In asking Jesus to choose one **great commandment**, they hoped to make Jesus show neglect for another area of the law.

        i. "The Rabbins reckoned up 613 commandments of the law; and distinguished them into the greater and the lesser. These later they thought might be neglected or violated with little or no guilt." (Trapp)

2. (37-40) Jesus answers: Loving God and your neighbor.

Jesus said to him, "'You shall love the Lord your God with all your heart, with all your soul, and with all your mind.' This is *the* first and great commandment. And *the* second *is* like it: 'You shall love your neighbor as yourself.' On these two commandments hang all the Law and the Prophets."

    a. **Jesus said to him**: Perfectly understanding the essence of the law, Jesus had no difficulty answering. Instead of promoting one command over another, Jesus defined the law in its core principles: **love the Lord** with everything you have and **love your neighbor** as yourself.

        i. It is clear enough what it means to **love the Lord** with all we are, though it is impossible to do perfectly. But there has been much confusion about what it means to love **your neighbor as yourself**. This doesn't mean that we must love ourselves before we can love anyone else; it means that in the same way we take care of ourselves and are concerned about our own interests, we should take care and have concern for the interests of others.

        ii. **The first and great commandment**: "In respect of order, quantity, and dignity." (Trapp)

b. **On these two commandments hang all the Law and the Prophets**: God's moral expectation of man can be briefly and powerfully said in these two sentences. If the life of God is real in our life, it will show by the presence of this love for God and others.

i. "Moses summed up all in the ten commandments, to which, truly interpreted, all the precepts of Scripture are reducible. Christ here brings the ten to two." (Poole)

E. Jesus asks a question of His opponents.

1. (41-42a) Jesus asks about the lineage of the Messiah.

While the Pharisees were gathered together, Jesus asked them, saying, "What do you think about the Christ? Whose Son is He?"

a. **While the Pharisees were gathered together**: Before they could think of another question to test Him, Jesus asked them a question.

b. **What do you think about the Christ? Whose Son is He?** This was similar to the question Jesus asked of His disciples in Matthew 16:13-15 (*Who do you say that I am?*). Jesus confronted His opponents with the need to decide who He was, connecting Himself to the Old Testament understanding of the Messiah (**the Christ**).

2. (42b) The Pharisees identify the lineage of the Messiah.

They said to Him, *"The Son* of David."

a. **The Son of David**: This is one of the great Old Testament titles of the Messiah. Founded on the covenant God made with King David in 2 Samuel 7, it identifies the Christ as the chosen descendant of King David's royal line (see also Jeremiah 23:5-6, Isaiah 9:6-7, and Luke 1:31-33).

b. **The Son of David**: It is possible that the Pharisees did not know or had forgotten that Jesus was of the line of King David and was even born in Bethlehem, the city of David. When Jesus recently entered Jerusalem, it was noted that He was from Nazareth, and perhaps His connection to King David had been unknown or forgotten (Matthew 21:11).

3. (43-45) Jesus is not only David's Son; He is also David's Lord.

He said to them, "How then does David in the Spirit call Him 'Lord,' saying:

'The LORD said to my Lord,
"Sit at My right hand,
Till I make Your enemies Your footstool"'?

If David then calls Him 'Lord,' how is He his Son?"

a. **How then does David in the Spirit call Him "Lord"**: The Pharisees were partially right in saying that the Messiah is the Son of David. But they didn't have a complete understanding of who the Messiah is. He is not only David's Son (a reference to His humanity), but He is also David's **Lord** (a reference to the deity of Jesus, the Messiah).

i. "The force of Jesus' argument depends on his use of Psalm 110, the most frequently quoted OT chapter in the NT." (Carson)

ii. This is the idea communicated in Revelation 22:16: *I am the root and the offspring of David*, and Romans 1:4, which shows Jesus as both the *Son of David* and the *Son of God*. We must not neglect either facet of Jesus' person. He is truly man and truly God, and can only be our Savior if He is both.

b. **If David then calls Him "Lord," how is He his Son?** Jesus' brilliantly simple explanation of the Scriptures put the Pharisees on the defensive. They did not want to admit that the Messiah was also the LORD God, but Jesus showed this is true from the Scriptures.

i. "What did Jesus mean? He can have meant only one thing – that the true description of him is *Son of God*. *Son of David* is not an adequate title; only *Son of God* will do." (Barclay)

4. (46) Jesus' enemies in retreat.

And no one was able to answer Him a word, nor from that day on did anyone dare question Him anymore.

a. **No one was able to answer Him a word**: The religious leaders hoped to trap Jesus and embarrass Him in front of the Passover pilgrims that crowded Jerusalem and heard Him teach. Yet Jesus embarrassed them instead.

i. "Yet even their silence was a tribute. The teacher who never attended the right schools (John 7:15-18) confounds the greatest theologians in the land. And if his question (Matthew 22:45) was unanswerable at this time, a young Pharisee, who may have been in Jerusalem at the time, was to answer it in due course (Romans 1:1-4; 9:5)." (Carson)

b. **Nor from that day on did anyone dare question Him anymore**: Logic and rhetoric proved useless in attacking Jesus. Now His enemies would use treachery and violence instead.

i. Jesus was done debating with the religious leaders. "From now on he will not debate with the authorities, but will go over their heads to the crowd." (France)

Matthew 23 - Woes to the Scribes and the Pharisees

A. Jesus rebukes the scribes and the Pharisees.

1. (1-4) They lay oppressive burdens on others.

Then Jesus spoke to the multitudes and to His disciples, saying: "The scribes and the Pharisees sit in Moses' seat. Therefore whatever they tell you to observe, *that* **observe and do, but do not do according to their works; for they say, and do not do. For they bind heavy burdens, hard to bear, and lay** *them* **on men's shoulders; but they** *themselves* **will not move them with one of their fingers."**

a. **Then Jesus spoke to the multitudes and to His disciples**: Jesus spoke to these groups, but He spoke *about* the **scribes** and **Pharisees**. Of course, these hardened opponents of Jesus listened; but in a sense Jesus was finished speaking to them. Instead he intended to warn the people and His followers about them.

i. "The true target of the whole discourse is the crowds and disciples who need to break free from Pharisaic legalism." (France)

ii. "Perhaps a year earlier Jesus had begun to denounce the Pharisees (Matthew 15:7). Subsequently he warned his disciples of the teaching of the Pharisees and Sadducees (Matthew 16:5-12). Now his warning and denunciations are public." (Carson)

iii. According to William Barclay, the Talmud describes seven different types of Pharisees; six of the seven are bad.

- The *Shoulder Pharisee*, who wore all his good deeds and righteousness on his shoulder for everyone to see.
- The *Wait-a-Little Pharisee*, who always intended to do good deeds, but always found a reason for doing them later, not now.

- The *Bruised* or *Bleeding Pharisee*, who was so holy that he would turn his head away from any woman seen in public – and was therefore constantly bumping into things and tripping, thus injuring himself.

- The *Hump-Backed Pharisee*, who was so humble that he walked bent over and barely lifting his feet – so everyone could see just how humble he was.

- The *Always-Counting Pharisee*, who was always counting up his good deeds and believed that he put God in debt to him for all the good he had done.

- The *Fearful Pharisee*, who did good because he was terrified that God would strike him with judgment if he did not.

- The *God-Fearing Pharisee*, who really loved God and did good deeds to please the God he loved.

b. **Whatever they tell you to observe, that observe and do**: Jesus said that respect was due to the scribes and the Pharisees; not because of their conduct, but because they **sit in Moses' seat**. They should be respected because they hold an office of authority, ordained by God.

i. "Let not the law of God lose its authority with you because of these wicked men." (Poole)

ii. **Moses' seat**: "Synagogues had a stone seat at the front where the authoritative teacher [sat]." (Carson) "The Jews spoke of the teacher's seat as we speak of a professor's chair." (Bruce)

c. **They bind heavy burdens, hard to bear, and lay them on men's shoulders**: The scribes and Pharisees were bad examples because they expected more of others than they did of themselves. They set **heavy burdens** on others, yet **they themselves will not move them with one of their fingers**.

d. **Heavy burdens**: The burden of the religious leaders contrasts sharply to Jesus' burden. His burden is light, and His yoke is easy (Matthew 11:30). These religious leaders were burden bringers; Jesus was a burden taker.

i. The first accusation against these religious leaders could apply to many religious leaders today. Many teach as if the essence of Christianity were a set of burdensome rules to follow.

ii. The early church rejected this legalism when it insisted that obedience to the Mosaic Law is not a foundation for the Christian life. Peter told the legalists in Acts 15:10: *"Why do you test God by putting a yoke on the neck of the disciples which neither our fathers nor we were able to bear?*

2. (5-10) They do their works to be seen, and they live for the praise of men.

"But all their works they do to be seen by men. They make their phylacteries broad and enlarge the borders of their garments. They love the best places at feasts, the best seats in the synagogues, greetings in the marketplaces, and to be called by men, 'Rabbi, Rabbi.' But you, do not be called 'Rabbi'; for One is your Teacher, the Christ, and you are all brethren. Do not call anyone on earth your father; for One is your Father, He who is in heaven. And do not be called teachers; for One is your Teacher, the Christ."

a. **All their works they do to be seen by men**: The religious leaders were guilty of advertising their righteous deeds. They acted out the religious spirit Jesus spoke against in the Sermon on the Mount (Matthew 6:1-6).

b. **They make their phylacteries broad and enlarge the borders of their garments**: Both the **phylacteries** (small leather boxes with tiny scrolls with scriptures on them, tied to the arm and head with leather straps) and the **borders of their garments** were worn in the attempt to conform to the Mosaic Law (Deuteronomy 11:18, Numbers 15:38-40).

i. "These were called phylacteries, from [the ancient Greek word], to keep, things wherein the law was kept." (Poole)

ii. It was natural for these religious leaders to believe that *broader* phylacteries and *larger* borders on their garments showed them to be more spiritual. The idea of wearing the **phylacteries** and the special **borders of their garments** was obedience to what God commanded Israel under the covenant given at Mount Sinai. The use of those things to promote an image of super-spirituality was the fault of human sinfulness, not of the command itself.

c. **They love the best places...greetings in the marketplaces**: Not content to display their supposed spirituality, the religious leaders loved it when people *admired* their supposed spirituality. They coveted the seats of honor at banquets and at the synagogue, and they loved the honoring titles such as **Rabbi** and **father**.

i. "There is therefore an emphasis to be put upon the word *love*; they might take salutations, and the upper rooms, if offered them as their due, for keeping civil order, but not affect them." (Poole)

d. **But you, do not be called "Rabbi"; for One is your Teacher, the Christ, and you are all brethren**: Jesus warned the people that they should *not* imitate the scribes and the Pharisees at this point. His followers should always remember that "**you are all brethren**" and that one should not be exalted above others by titles that are either demanded or received.

i. "An exhortation which today's church could profitably take more seriously, not only in relation to formal ecclesiastical titles ('Most Reverend', 'my Lord Bishop', *etc.*), but more significantly in its excessive deference to academic qualifications or to authoritative status in the churches." (France)

e. **Do not be called "Rabbi"... Do not call anyone on earth your father... do not be called teachers**: Jesus warned His listeners and us against giving anyone inappropriate honor. One may have a **father** or **teachers** in a normal human sense, but should not regard them in a sense that gives them excessive spiritual honor or authority.

i. "In the Church of Christ, all titles and honors which exalt men and give occasion for pride are here forbidden." (Spurgeon)

ii. From the rest of Scripture, we can see that Jesus did not intend this as an absolute prohibition, rather as speaking to the heart that loves, collects, and cherishes such titles. We know this because, under inspiration of the Holy Spirit, godly men spoke of themselves with some of these titles.

- Jesus was called Rabbi: Matthew 26:25 and 26:49; John 1:38 and 3:26.

- Paul called himself a father: 1 Corinthians 4:15, Philippians 2:22.

- Paul called other Christians his children: Galatians 4:19.

- Paul called himself a teacher: 1 Timothy 2:7, 2 Timothy 1:11.

iii. "That which he forbids is, 1. An affectation of such titles, and hunting after them. 2. *Rom tituli*, the exercise of an absolute mastership, or a paternal, absolute power." (Poole)

iv. Nevertheless, this command is often ignored and violated today in the way people give and receive titles such as prophet, apostle, most reverend, and so on. It is also seen in the expected etiquette for closing a letter to the Pope: "Prostrate at the feet of Your Holiness and imploring the favor of its apostolic benediction, I have the honor to be, Very Holy Father, with the deepest veneration of Your Holiness, the most humble and obedient servant and son/daughter."

v. "We must say that the risen Christ is as displeased with those in his church who demand unquestioning submission to themselves and their opinions and confuse a reputation for showy piety with godly surrender to his teachings as he ever was with any Pharisee." (Carson)

3. (11-12) The way of Jesus: service and humility.

"But he who is greatest among you shall be your servant. And whoever exalts himself will be humbled, and he who humbles himself will be exalted."

a. **He who is greatest among you shall be your servant**: Normally, people estimate greatness by how many people serve and honor them. Jesus reminded His followers that in His kingdom it should be different, and that we should estimate greatness by how we serve and honor others.

i. "In a word, like all their successors in *spirit* to the present day, they were *severe to others*, but very *indulgent to themselves.*" (Clarke)

ii. Since Jesus truly was the **greatest among** them, He spoke of Himself as a **servant**. It is unfortunate that many of the followers of Jesus imitate the leadership philosophy and style of the scribes and Pharisees more than the style of Jesus.

b. **Whoever exalts himself will be humbled, and he who humbles himself will be exalted**: This promise is absolutely true, but sometimes is only known in the measure of eternity.

B. The eight woes to the religious leaders.

These woes stand in contrast to the eight beatitudes of Matthew 5:3-11. Jesus spoke harshly here, yet this was not the language of personal irritation but of divine warning and condemnation. "Such series of 'woes' are familiar from the Old Testament prophets (e.g. Isaiah 5:8-23; Habakkuk 2:6-19), where the tone is of condemnation, and that is the emphasis here too." (France)

1. (13) Woe to those who shut up the kingdom.

"But woe to you, scribes and Pharisees, hypocrites! For you shut up the kingdom of heaven against men; for you neither go in *yourselves*, nor do you allow those who are entering to go in."

a. **Woe to you, scribes and Pharisees, hypocrites!** Literally, the word "**hypocrites**" refers to an actor, someone playing a part. Jesus exposed the corruption covered by the spiritual image of the **scribes and Pharisees**.

b. **You shut up the kingdom of heaven against men**: The religious leaders kept people from the kingdom of heaven by making human traditions and human religious rules more important than God's Word. This was clearly seen in the way that they opposed and rejected Jesus; if they had *opened* the kingdom of heaven to men, they would have welcomed and received Jesus as the Messiah and Son of God.

i. "It was written of old, that *the priest's lips should preserve knowledge*: God that committed the key of knowledge to the ministers and guides of his church, not that they should take it away, but that the people might *seek the law of their mouths, because they are the messengers of the Lord of hosts*, Malachi 2:7." (Poole)

c. **You neither go in yourselves, nor do you allow those who are entering to go in**: It is bad for someone not to enter into heaven themselves, but it is far worse to prevent another person from entering in (Matthew 18:6).

    i. "In ancient times the rabbins carried a *key*, which was the symbol or emblem of knowledge." (Clarke)

2. (14) The religious leaders steal from the vulnerable.

Many Bible translations do not include this verse or place it in the margin. D.A. Carson writes: "Verse 14 must be taken as an interpolation...This is made clear, not only by its absence from the best and earliest Matthew MSS, but from the fact that the MSS that do include it divide on where to place it – before or after verse 13." Nevertheless, it is certainly present in the Mark 12 and Luke 20 passages.

"Woe to you, scribes and Pharisees, hypocrites! For you devour widows' houses, and for a pretense make long prayers. Therefore you will receive greater condemnation."

a. **You devour widows' houses**: Using clever and dishonest dealing, the scribes and Pharisees stole **widows' houses** – careful to cover it up in the name of good business or stewardship.

b. **For a pretense make long prayers**: Their **long**, falsely spiritual prayers were used to build a spiritual image, often for the sake of big donations.

    i. "He respecteth not the arithmetic of our prayers, how many they are; nor the rhetoric of our prayers, how eloquent they are; nor the music of our prayers, the sweetness of our voice, nor the logic of our prayers, or the method of them, but the divinity of our prayers is that which he so much esteemeth." (Trapp)

c. **Therefore you will receive greater condemnation**: The greatness of their sin demanded a **greater condemnation** than others will endure. Under this concept we can say that no one will have it good in Hell, but we can trust that some will have it worse than others will.

    i. "These words prove that there are degrees of punishment, as there are gradations in glory. All the ungodly will be judged and condemned by the Righteous Judge, but 'the greater condemnation' will be reserved for the hypocrites." (Spurgeon)

3. (15) The religious leaders led their converts on the wrong path.

"Woe to you, scribes and Pharisees, hypocrites! For you travel land and sea to win one proselyte, and when he is won, you make him twice as much a son of hell as yourselves."

a. **You travel land and sea to win one proselyte**: Their zeal in evangelism did not prove they were right with God. These religious leaders went to great lengths to **win** others, but they brought people to darkness, not light.

i. Paul had the same idea in Romans 10:2 where he observed that some of the Jewish people of his day had *a zeal for God, but not according to knowledge*.

ii. "The word *proselyte* is an English transliteration of a Greek word *proselutos*, which means *one who has approached* or *drawn near*. The *proselyte* was the full convert who had accepted the ceremonial law and circumcision and who had become in the fullest sense a Jew." (Barclay)

iii. "A sizable body of scholarship convincingly argues that the first century A.D. till the Fall of Jerusalem marks the most remarkable period of Jewish missionary zeal and corresponding success." (Carson)

b. **When he is won, you make him twice as much a son of hell as yourselves**: Through their great energy they could **win** some, but to no lasting good to those who were won.

i. "Their business was not to turn men from sin unto God, but merely to convert them to an opinion." (Poole)

ii. In this respect, the religious leaders were similar to Mormons and Jehovah's Witnesses today. They were courageous and energetic messengers, but with a false message.

iii. "Jesus did not criticize the *fact* of the Pharisees' extensive missionary effort but its *results*…they 'out-Phariseed' the Pharisees." (Carson)

4. (16-22) The religious leaders made false and deceptive oaths.

"Woe to you, blind guides, who say, 'Whoever swears by the temple, it is nothing; but whoever swears by the gold of the temple, he is obliged *to perform it*.' Fools and blind! For which is greater, the gold or the temple that sanctifies the gold? And, 'Whoever swears by the altar, it is nothing; but whoever swears by the gift that is on it, he is obliged *to perform it*.' Fools and blind! For which is greater, the gift or the altar that sanctifies the gift? Therefore he who swears by the altar, swears by it and by all things on it. He who swears by the temple, swears by it and by Him who dwells in it. And he who swears by heaven, swears by the throne of God and by Him who sits on it."

a. **Whoever swears by the temple, it is nothing**: Out of obedience to God's Word they refused to swear by the name of God (as commanded in Exodus 20:7). Yet they constructed an elaborate system of oaths, some of which were binding and some were not. It was a way of making a promise while keeping fingers crossed behind one's back.

i. "To the Jew an oath was absolutely binding, *so long as it was a binding oath.* Broadly speaking, a binding oath was an oath which definitely and without equivocation employed the name of God; such an oath must be kept, no matter what the cost. Any other oath might be legitimately broken." (Barclay)

b. **For which is greater, the gift or the altar that sanctifies the gift?** Here Jesus emphasized that the altar itself is greater than the sacrifice made upon it. The altar is the established meeting place between God and man, and our altar is Jesus Himself and His work on the cross.

i. Having never been separated from God the Father by sin, Jesus Himself needed no altar. He had a free and glorious relationship with His Father. It was the freedom of Adam before the fall – or even more so, because Jesus had a *history* of relationship with His Father that Adam did not know.

ii. It is worthy to think of the greatness of the Old Testament altar:

- The *purpose* of the altar is significant: it sanctified what was put upon it, and it sustained and bore up the sacrifice until it was consumed.

- The *location* of the altar is significant: it shows that we come to Jesus and His atoning work first.

- The *shape* of the altar is significant: it is square and perfectly proportioned, stable and unshakeable.

- The *horns* of the altar are significant: they show the power of God inherent in Jesus.

- The *position* of the altar is significant: it is not raised, but is low enough for all to approach; it has no steps that would reveal human flesh.

- The *appearance* of the altar is significant: it is smeared with the blood of sacrifice.

- The *material* of the altar is significant: it is brass, forged in the fire and able to endure the judgment of the flames.

c. **He who swears by the temple, swears by it and by Him who dwells in it**: Jesus reminded them that every oath is binding and God holds the oath-maker to account, even if they excuse themselves.

5. (23-24) They are obsessed with trivialities, and ignoring the weighty matters.

"Woe to you, scribes and Pharisees, hypocrites! For you pay tithe of mint and anise and cummin, and have neglected the weightier *matters*

of the law: justice and mercy and faith. These you ought to have done, without leaving the others undone. Blind guides, who strain out a gnat and swallow a camel!"

a. **You pay tithe of mint and anise and cummin**: Their tithing was meticulous and noteworthy; but hypocritical because it served to sooth the guilt of their neglect of the **weightier matters of the law**. It is both possible and common to be distracted with relatively trivial matters while a lost world perishes.

i. "The 'weightier' matters do not refer to the 'more difficult' or 'harder' but to the 'more central,' 'most decisive.'" (Carson)

ii. Jesus gave a cursory description of these **weightier matters of the law** with the words, **justice and mercy and faith**. "This phrase recalls the summary of true religion (in contrast to extravagant sacrifice) in Micah 6:8." (France)

b. **Blind guides, who strain out a gnat and swallow a camel**: Jesus illustrated their folly with a humorous picture of a man so committed to a kosher diet that he would not swallow a **gnat** because it was not bled properly in accord with kosher regulations. Yet the same man would swallow a whole **camel** instead.

i. "This is a humorous picture which must have raised a laugh, of a man carefully straining his wine through gauze to avoid swallowing a microscopic insect and yet cheerfully swallowing a camel. It is the picture of a man who has completely lost his sense of proportion." (Barclay)

6. (25-26) The religious leaders are impure both inside and out.

"Woe to you, scribes and Pharisees, hypocrites! For you cleanse the outside of the cup and dish, but inside they are full of extortion and self-indulgence. Blind Pharisee, first cleanse the inside of the cup and dish, that the outside of them may be clean also."

a. **You cleanse the outside of the cup**: The scribes and Pharisees were satisfied with a superficial cleansing and the *appearance* of righteousness.

b. **Inside they are full of extortion and self-indulgence**: While greatly concerned with their outward appearance of righteousness, they were unconcerned with an **inside** full of sin and corruption.

c. **First cleanse the inside of the cup and dish, that the outside of them may be clean also**: Jesus did not call them to choose between outer righteousness and inner righteousness. He called them to be concerned with both, but to **first** address the **inside**. True outward righteousness starts on the **inside**.

7. (27-28) The religious leaders have the appearance of good, but without spiritual life in the inner man.

"Woe to you, scribes and Pharisees, hypocrites! For you are like whitewashed tombs which indeed appear beautiful outwardly, but inside are full of dead *men's* bones and all uncleanness. Even so you also outwardly appear righteous to men, but inside you are full of hypocrisy and lawlessness."

> a. **You are like whitewashed tombs**: It was the custom of the Jews of that time to whitewash the tombs in the city of Jerusalem before Passover so that no one would touch one accidentally, thus making themselves ceremonially unclean. Jesus said these religious leaders were like these **whitewashed tombs** - pretty on the outside, but dead on the inside.

> > i. So Paul called the High Priest a *whitewashed wall* in Acts 23:3.

> b. **You also outwardly appear righteous to men**: Men might see them as **righteous**, but God did not. God is never fooled by what we show on the outside. He sees what we actually are, not what we appear to be to other men.

8. (29-36) The religious leaders honor dead prophets, but murder the living prophets.

"Woe to you, scribes and Pharisees, hypocrites! Because you build the tombs of the prophets and adorn the monuments of the righteous, and say, 'If we had lived in the days of our fathers, we would not have been partakers with them in the blood of the prophets.' Therefore you are witnesses against yourselves that you are sons of those who murdered the prophets. Fill up, then, the measure of your fathers' *guilt*. Serpents, brood of vipers! How can you escape the condemnation of hell? Therefore, indeed, I send you prophets, wise men, and scribes: *some* of them you will kill and crucify, and *some* of them you will scourge in your synagogues and persecute from city to city, that on you may come all the righteous blood shed on the earth, from the blood of righteous Abel to the blood of Zechariah, son of Berechiah, whom you murdered between the temple and the altar. Assuredly, I say to you, all these things will come upon this generation."

> a. **You build the tombs of the prophets and adorn the monuments of the righteous**: They professed to venerate dead prophets but they rejected living prophets. In doing so they showed that they really were the children of those who murdered the prophets in the days of old (**you are sons of those who murdered the prophets**).

i. We express the same thought when we think. "I wouldn't have denied Jesus like the other disciples did."

b. **Fill up, then, the measure of your fathers' guilt**: Jesus prophesied about how these leaders would complete the rejection of the prophets their fathers began by persecuting His disciples, whom He would send to them.

i. "No amount of argument can rob these words of their terrible import. They stand upon the page for evermore speaking to us of 'the wrath of the Lamb.'" (Morgan)

ii. "This is one of the most terrible sentences that ever fell from Christ's lips. It is like his message to Judas, 'That thou doest, do quickly'…This crowning sin would fill up the measure of their fathers' guilt and bring down upon them the righteous judgment of God." (Spurgeon)

c. **Serpents, brood of vipers**: This phrase has the idea of "family of the devil." These religious leaders took an unmerited pride in their heritage, thinking they were spiritual sons of Abraham. Instead, they were more like sons of the devil, not of Abraham.

i. Jesus spoke so strongly about these religious leaders for two reasons. First, He did not want others to be deceived by them. Second, He loved these men. These men were the farthest from God and they needed to be warned of coming judgment. What Jesus really wanted was their repentance, not their judgment.

d. **From the blood of righteous Abel to the blood of Zechariah, son of Berechiah**: Jesus here spoke of *all* the righteous martyrs of the Old Testament. **Abel** was clearly the first, and in the way that the Hebrew Bible was arranged, **Zechariah** was the last. 2 Chronicles is the last book of the Hebrew Bible, and Zechariah's story is found in 2 Chronicles 24.

i. Abel's blood cried out (Genesis 4:10), and Zechariah asked that his blood be remembered (2 Chronicles 24:22).

ii. There is a problem with the description of **Zechariah** as the son of Berechiah, because the 2 Chronicles text describes him as the son of Jehoiada (2 Chronicles 24:20). Clarke summarizes the best resolutions to this problem. First, that double names were frequent among the Jews (1 Samuel 9:1 and 1 Chronicles 8:33; Matthew 9:9 and Mark 2:14, and other examples as well). Second, that the names *Jehoiada* and *Berechiah* have much the same meaning: the *praise* or *blessing of Jehovah*.

iii. "One can almost feel the withering force of His strong and mighty indignation – indignation directed, not against the people, but against their false guides. And yet behind it all is His heart, and the 'woes' merge into a wail of agony, the cry of a mother over her lost child." (Morgan)

9. (37-39) Jesus laments for Jerusalem.

"O Jerusalem, Jerusalem, the one who kills the prophets and stones those who are sent to her! How often I wanted to gather your children together, as a hen gathers her chicks under *her* wings, but you were not willing! See! Your house is left to you desolate; for I say to you, you shall see Me no more till you say, 'Blessed *is* He who comes in the name of the LORD!'"

a. **O Jerusalem, Jerusalem**: Luke 19:41 tells us that Jesus wept as He looked over the city of Jerusalem, thought about its coming judgment, and said these words. Jesus wanted to protect them from the terrible judgment that would eventually follow their rejection of Him.

i. It is written that Jesus wept two times: here, at the pain of knowing what would befall those who reject Him; and also at the tomb of Lazurus, weeping at the power and pain of death.

ii. This heartfelt cry is another way to see that Jesus didn't hate these men He rebuked so strongly. His heart broke for them. When we sin, God does not hate us; He genuinely sorrows for us, knowing that in every way our sin and rebellion only destroys our life. We should hope to share God's sorrow for lost humanity.

b. **How often I wanted to gather your children together, as a hen gathers her chicks under her wings**: Jesus wanted to protect, nourish, and cherish His people the Jews, even as a mother bird protects the young chicks.

i. "The image of a *hen* (Greek is simply 'bird') protecting its young is used in the Old Testament for God's protection of his people (Psalm 17:8; 91:4; Isaiah 31:5; *etc.*)." (France)

ii. This picture of **a hen** and **her chicks** tells us something about what Jesus wanted to do for these who rejected Him.

- He wanted to make them safe.
- He wanted to make them happy.
- He wanted to make them part of a blessed community.
- He wanted to promote their growth.
- He wanted them to know His love.
- This could only happen if they came to Him when He called.

iii. "Jesus' longing can only belong to Israel's Savior, not to one of her prophets." (Carson)

iv. The words **how often I wanted** are a subtle indication that Matthew knew Jesus had visited Jerusalem many times before (as clearly recounted in the Gospel of John), even though he only mentions this last visit. "Jesus could not have said what he says here unless he had paid repeated visits to Jerusalem and issued to the people repeated appeals." (Barclay)

c. **But you were not willing!** The problem was not the willingness of Jesus to rescue and protect them; the problem was that they **were not willing**. Therefore the predicted destruction would come upon them.

i. "What a picture of pity and disappointed love the King's face must have presented when, with flowing tears, he uttered these words!" (Spurgeon)

ii. "We hold tenaciously that salvation is all of grace, but we also believe with equal firmness that the ruin of man is entirely the result of his own sin. It is the will of God that saves; it is the will of man that damns." (Spurgeon)

iii. In a wonderful sermon on this text (*I Would; But Ye Would Not*), Spurgeon described the kind of will that *does* come to Jesus.

- It is a *real* will.
- It is a *practical, doing* will.
- It is an *immediate* will.
- It is a *settled* will.

d. **You shall see Me no more till you say, "Blessed is He who comes in the name of the LORD!"** Jesus here revealed something of the conditions surrounding His Second Coming. When Jesus comes again, the Jewish people will welcome Him as the Messiah saying, "**Blessed is He who comes in the name of the LORD!**"

i. "Till after the fulness of the Gentiles is brought in, when the word of life shall again be sent unto you; then will ye rejoice, and bless, and *praise* him *that cometh in the name of the Lord*, with full and final salvation for the lost sheep of the house of Israel." (Clarke)

ii. It will take a great deal to bring Israel to that point, but God will do it. It is promised that Israel will welcome Jesus back, even as the Apostle Paul said in Romans 11:26: *And so all Israel will be saved*.

Matthew 24 - Jesus' Olivet Discourse

A. The destruction of the temple and its implications.

1. (1-2) Jesus predicts the destruction of the temple.

Then Jesus went out and departed from the temple, and His disciples came up to show Him the buildings of the temple. And Jesus said to them, "Do you not see all these things? Assuredly, I say to you, not *one* stone shall be left here upon another, that shall not be thrown down."

a. **Then Jesus went out and departed from the temple**: Jesus would contend no more with the religious leaders, and never again come to the temple in His earthly ministry. With emphasis, He **went out and departed**.

   i. **Went out and departed**: "There is an emphasis on the idea of the verb. He was going away, like one who did not mean to return." (Bruce)

   ii. "They came to their Master, going before in a deeply preoccupied mood, and tried to change the gloomy current of His thoughts by inviting Him to look back at the sacred structure." (Bruce)

b. **His disciples came up to show Him the buildings of the temple**: After the destruction of Solomon's temple, this temple was originally built by Zerubbabel and Ezra (Ezra 6:15). Herod the Great (who ruled when Jesus was born) greatly expanded and improved it. This temple was the center of Jewish life for almost a thousand years - so much so, that it was customary to swear by the temple (Matthew 23:16), and speaking against the temple could be considered blasphemy (Acts 6:13).

   i. "Josephus the Jew (Antiquities 15.14) tells us that for eight whole years together he kept 10,000 men a-work about it; and that for magnificence and stateliness, it exceeded Solomon's temple." (Trapp)

   ii. After Herod's work, the temple was huge: nearly 500 yards or meters long and 400 yards or meters wide. Herod's plan for rebuilding started in 19 B.C. and was only completed in A.D. 63, taking more than 80 years. The temple was finished only seven years before it was destroyed.

iii. But the Second Temple wasn't just big; it was also beautiful. The Jewish historian Josephus said that the temple was covered with gold plates, and when the sun shone on them it was blinding to look at. Where there was no gold, there were blocks of marble of such a pure white that from a distance strangers thought there was snow on the temple.

c. **Do you not see all these things?** The disciples wanted Jesus to look at the beautiful **buildings**; Jesus told them to turn around and take a good look at those **things**.

i. "These *things*, not building, implying indifference to the splendours admired by the disciples." (Bruce)

d. **Not one stone shall be left here upon another**: Some 40 years after Jesus said this, there was a widespread Jewish revolution against the Romans in Palestine, and they enjoyed many early successes. But ultimately Roman soldiers crushed the rebels. In A.D. 70 Jerusalem was leveled, including the temple - just as Jesus said would happen.

i. "Titus (it is said) would have preserved the temple, as one of the world's wonders, from being burnt, but could not; such was the fury of his soldiers, set a-work by God doubtless." (Trapp)

ii. It is said that at the fall of Jerusalem, the last surviving Jews of the city fled to the temple, because it was the strongest and most secure building in the city. Roman soldiers surrounded it, and one drunken soldier started a fire that soon engulfed the whole building. Ornate gold detail work in the roof melted down in the cracks between the stone walls of the temple, and to retrieve the gold, the Roman commander ordered that the temple be dismantled stone by stone. The destruction was so complete that today they have true difficulty learning exactly where the foundation of the temple was.

iii. "Josephus says the stones were white and strong; fifty feet long, twenty-four broad, and sixteen thick. Antiq. b. 15. c. xi." (Clarke)

e. **That shall not be thrown down**: This prophecy was fulfilled literally. There was a real temple, and it was really destroyed. The literal fulfillment of this prophecy establishes the tone for the rest of the prophecies in the chapter. We should expect a literal fulfillment for these as well.

i. "We may also observe how little God values splendid houses of prayer when they are made dens of thieves." (Poole)

2. (3) Jesus' prediction brings up two questions.

Now as He sat on the Mount of Olives, the disciples came to Him privately, saying, "Tell us, when will these things be? And what *will be* **the sign of Your coming, and of the end of the age?"**

a. **As He sat on the Mount of Olives**: Removed from the temple, yet overlooking it, the disciples asked Jesus questions about His bold prediction concerning the destruction of the temple.

> i. It was an appropriate time for such a discourse. The religious leaders rejected Jesus, and would soon deliver Him to the Romans for crucifixion. He knew the bitter fate awaiting Jerusalem, and He wanted to give hope and confidence to His disciples who would soon be greatly tested.

b. **When will these things be?** Jesus said the temple would be completely destroyed. It was logical that the disciples wanted to know when it would happen. Jesus will speak to this question, but only in the context of answering their next two questions.

c. **And what will be the sign of Your coming, and of the end of the age?** The disciples probably thought they asked only one question. In their minds, the destruction of the temple and the **end of the age** were probably connected. But really, they asked two questions (some say three), and this second question is answered in the remainder of the chapter.

> i. "The disciples did not so tabulate their questions. In all probability they presented them as one request, supposing that all these things would happen simultaneously. Jesus' answer was directed mainly to correct this misapprehension." (Morgan)

> ii. It may also be that this second question was asked as they remembered the events surrounding the first temple's destruction: Solomon's Temple was destroyed in the context of national judgment and exile.

d. **And what will be the sign of Your coming, and of the end of the age?** As Jesus answers this important second question, He will make many specific comments and predictions about the end times. These predictions have been the source of significant disagreement among Christians who have tried to understand them. Why didn't Jesus simply say it so clearly that there was no possibility anyone could misunderstand Him?

> i. One reason why prophecy may seem vague or imprecise is because God wants every age to have reasons to be ready for Jesus' return. We should not think of Jesus' return as an event far off on a time line,

but something we have been running parallel with since the day of Pentecost.

ii. Others suggest that God's intention was to keep the future somewhat vague and clouded to confound the Devil, even as the resurrection of the Messiah was vague in the Old Testament.

iii. Though some prophetic interpretations are different, we are sure of this: *He is coming again*, and we must be ready.

B. The flow of history until Jesus' return.

1. (4-8) Jesus describes general world conditions during the period between His Ascension and the time immediately preceding His second coming.

And Jesus answered and said to them: "Take heed that no one deceives you. For many will come in My name, saying, 'I am the Christ,' and will deceive many. And you will hear of wars and rumors of wars. See that you are not troubled; for all *these things* must come to pass, but the end is not yet. For nation will rise against nation, and kingdom against kingdom. And there will be famines, pestilences, and earthquakes in various places. All these *are* the beginning of sorrows."

a. **Take heed that no one deceives you**: From the outset, Jesus warned the disciples that many would be deceived as they anticipated His return. There have been times in the history of the church when rash predictions were made and then relied upon resulting in great disappointment, disillusionment, and falling way.

i. One notable example of this was the prophetic expectation in 1846 with William Miller in the United States. Because of his prophetic interpretations, calculations, and publications, there were hundreds of thousands in the United States who were convinced that Jesus would return in 1846. When He did not, there was great disappointment, with some falling away, and some cultic groups spawned from the prophetic fervor.

b. **See that you are not troubled; for all these things must come to pass, but the end is not yet**: The kind of things Jesus mentions in this section are *not* the things that mark specific signs of the end. Things like false messiahs, **wars**, **famines**, **pestilences**, **and earthquakes** have certainly marked man's history since the time of Jesus' Ascension - but were not specific signs of the end. In effect Jesus said, "Catastrophes will happen, but these will not signal the end."

i. In the midst of any great war or any great famine or any great earthquake, it is natural to believe that the world is coming to an end.

But Jesus said there is a far more specific sign that would indicate His return, and He describes this later.

ii. "One clear aim of this chapter is to prevent *premature excitement* about the parousia." (France)

c. **All these are the beginning of sorrows**: Though none of those events are the specific sign of the end, collectively they *are* a sign. When Jesus described these calamities as **the beginning of sorrows**, He literally called them *the beginning of labor pains*. Just as is true with labor pains, we should expect that the things mentioned - **wars**, **famines**, **earthquakes**, and so on - would become *more frequent* and *more intense* before the return of Jesus – without any one of them being the specific sign of the end.

i. "The *beginning*: such an accumulation of horrors might well appear to the inexperienced the end, hence the remark to prevent panic." (Bruce)

2. (9-14) Jesus describes what His disciples must expect during the time between His Ascension and Second Coming.

"Then they will deliver you up to tribulation and kill you, and you will be hated by all nations for My name's sake. And then many will be offended, will betray one another, and will hate one another. Then many false prophets will rise up and deceive many. And because lawlessness will abound, the love of many will grow cold. But he who endures to the end shall be saved. And this gospel of the kingdom will be preached in all the world as a witness to all the nations, and then the end will come."

a. **They will deliver you to tribulation and kill you**: In the period after Jesus ascends to heaven and before He comes again, His disciples should expect to be persecuted. This may make His followers believe the end is near, but this also is not the specific sign of His return.

i. "Rather, *Then they will deliver you up to affliction*…By a bold figure of speech, *affliction* is here *personified*. They are to be delivered into affliction's own hand, to be harassed by all the modes of inventive torture." (Clarke)

ii. **Will betray one another**: "Persecution would reveal the traitors within the Church as well as the enemies without." (Spurgeon)

b. **False prophets will arise and deceive many**: In the period after Jesus ascends to heaven and before He comes again, the disciples of Jesus will see many false prophets, and their success. But these also are not the specific signs of His return.

i. **Deceive many**: "Alas, that such teachers would have *any* disciples! It is doubly sad that they should be able to lead astray '*many.*' Yet, when it so happens, let us remember that the King said that it would be so." (Spurgeon)

c. **Lawlessness will abound, the love of many will grow cold**: In the period after Jesus ascends to heaven and before He comes again, His disciples should expect to see society become worse and worse. But this also is not the specific sign of His return.

i. "And lawlessness will lead to the cooling off of *love*, a connection to be noted. *Most men's love* is literally 'the love of the many.'" (France)

ii. "Here is something to tremble at: 'Because iniquity shall abound,' — that is worse than pestilence; 'the love of many shall wax cold,' — that is worse than persecution. As all the water outside a vessel can do it no hurt until it enters the vessel itself, so outward persecutions cannot really injure the Church of God, but when the mischief oozes into the Church, and the love of God's people waxes cold, — ah, then the barque is in sore distress." (Spurgeon)

iii. "If the heart grows cold, everything will be coldly done. When love declines, what cold preaching we have! All moonlight light without heat; polished like marble, and as chill. What cold singing we get, — pretty music, made by pipes and wind, but oh, how little soul-song! — how little singing in the Holy Ghost, making melody in the heart unto God ! And what poor praying! Do you call it praying? What little giving! When the heart is cold, the hands can find nothing in the purse; and Christ's Church, and Christ's poor, and the heathen may perish, for we must needs hoard up for ourselves, and live to grow rich. Is there anything that goes on as it ought to go when love waxes cold?" (Spurgeon)

d. **This gospel of the kingdom will be preached in all the world as a witness to all the nations, and then the end will come**: Jesus also promised that before the end, the gospel would go out to the whole world. The persecution, false prophets, and general downgrade of society would not prevent the spread of the gospel.

i. "Some claim this has already been done, and that therefore the end of the age is necessarily close at hand. This conclusion is open to grave doubt. Everything depends on the meaning of the words, 'for a testimony.'" (Morgan)

ii. The church is to take this seriously as their duty. However, God assured that it *will* happen: *I saw another angel flying in the midst of heaven, having the everlasting gospel to preach to those who dwell on the earth - to every nation, tribe, tongue and people - saying with a loud voice. "Fear God and give glory to Him, for the hour of His judgment has come."* (Revelation 14:6-7)

C. Jesus describes the sign of His coming and the end of the age.

1. (15) The sign: the abomination of desolation, spoken of by Daniel.

"Therefore when you see the 'abomination of desolation,' spoken of by Daniel the prophet, standing in the holy place" (whoever reads, let him understand),"

a. **When you see the "abomination of desolation"**: Essentially, the **abomination of desolation** speaks of the ultimate desecration of a Jewish temple, the establishment of an idolatrous image in the **holy place** itself, which will inevitably result in the judgment of God. It is the **abomination** that brings desolation.

i. In the vocabulary of Judaism of that time, an **abomination** was an especially offensive form of idolatry. Jesus described a gross form of idolatry, **standing in the holy place**, that brings with it great destruction (**desolation**).

ii. "*The desolating sacrilege* is a literal Greek rendering of the phrase... An 'abomination' in Old Testament idiom is an idolatrous affront to the true worship of God." (France)

b. **Standing in the holy place**: This means that the **abomination of desolation** takes place in the Jewish temple. This is the only plain meaning of the phrase **holy place**. Some believe it happened in a *prior* Jewish temple, before it was destroyed in A.D. 70. Others - more properly - believe it *will happen* in the **holy place** of a rebuilt temple.

i. For centuries, there was only a small Jewish presence in Judea and Jerusalem. Their presence in the region was definite, and continuous, but small. It was unthinkable that this weak Jewish presence could rebuild a temple. Therefore the fulfillment of this prophecy was highly unlikely until Israel was gathered again as a nation in 1948. The restoration of a nation that the world had not seen for some 2,000 years is a remarkable event in the fulfillment and future fulfillment of prophecy.

ii. Those who believe that the events of Matthew 24 were all or mostly all fulfilled in A.D. 70 have a difficulty here. There is no good evidence at all that what they believe was the abomination of desolation (the Roman armies or their ensigns) were ever set up as idolatrous images in the **holy place** of the temple. Instead, the temple was destroyed before the Romans entered.

iii. Therefore, those with this interpretive approach often re-define what the **holy place** is, as does Bruce: "One naturally thinks of the temple or the holy city and its environs, but a 'holy place' in the prophetic style might mean the holy *land*."

iv. "The normal meaning of *hagios topos* ('holy place') is the temple complex… But by the time the Romans had actually desecrated the temple in A.D. 70 it was too late for anyone in the city to flee." (Carson)

c. **As spoken of by Daniel the prophet**: The mention of the **abomination of desolation** is taken from the book of Daniel. *They shall defile the sanctuary fortress; then they shall take away the daily sacrifices, and place there the abomination of desolation* (Daniel 11:31). This describes a complete desecration of the temple, prefigured by Antiochus Epiphanies in the period between the Old Testament and the New Testament.

i. Paul elaborates on the future fulfillment of this in 2 Thessalonians 2:3-4: *That day will not come unless the falling away comes first, and the man of sin is revealed, the son of perdition, who opposes and exalts himself above all that is called God or that is worshipped, so that he sits as God in the temple of God, showing himself that he is God.*

ii. "The discourse itself is undoubtedly a source for the Thessalonian Epistles… we may say that Jesus himself sets the pattern for the church's eschatology." (Carson)

iii. Daniel 12:11 gives additional insight: *And from the time that the daily sacrifice is taken away, and the abomination of desolation is set up, there shall be 1,290 days* (until the end). When this sign is set up, the end may be determined - there will be almost three and one-half years to go until the consummation of all things.

iv. Through the centuries, the most common interpretive approach to the predictions Jesus made in this chapter is to see them all or mostly all fulfilled in the great destruction that came upon Jerusalem and Judea in A.D. 70. This approach is attractive in some ways, especially in that it makes the words of Jesus in Matthew 24:34 easy to understand. Yet the approach that sees this chapter as all or mostly all fulfilled in A.D. 70 is *completely inadequate in its supposed fulfillment of the abomination of desolation*. In this approach, the **abomination of desolation** is almost always understood to be the Roman armies or the ensigns they carried.

v. Yet when we understand the importance and what is said about this event – the abomination of desolation – we must give priority to this event, even more than the easiest interpretation of Matthew 24:34.

• It is the *critical sign* mentioned in Matthew 24.

- It is the *warning to flee* mentioned in Matthew 24.
- It is the *sign of the consummation of all things* in Daniel 9:27.
- It is the sign *foreshadowed by Antiochus Epiphanies* in Daniel 11:31.
- It is the precise marker of days to the end in Daniel 12:11.
- It is the *revelation of the man of sin* in 2 Thessalonians 2:3-4.
- It is the *image of the beast* in Revelation 13:14-15.

vi. Taking these passages in their most plain meaning, the **abomination of desolation** cannot be the Roman armies or the ensigns they marched under; it cannot be totalitarian governments or any other conjecture. The **abomination of desolation** must be some kind of image of the Antichrist set in an actual temple, and is the decisive sign for the end. This means that for the most part, Jesus' predictions in Matthew 24 have not been fulfilled; or at least that the destruction of Jerusalem in A.D. 70 was a foreshadowing fulfillment, even as the desecration of the temple under Antiochus Epiphanies was a foreshadowing of the ultimate **abomination of desolation**.

d. **Whoever reads, let him understand**: Here Jesus (assuming that He said these words, and that they were not added by Matthew) directed us again to the central place of understanding, the **abomination of desolation**. It was almost as if Jesus said, "Don't miss this. If you don't understand this, you won't understand many other things." And this is *exactly* the error of many who, with good intentions, misunderstand the plain meaning of the **abomination of desolation**. **Let him understand**!

2. (16-20) Jesus warns what should be done when the abomination of desolation appears: flee immediately.

"Then let those who are in Judea flee to the mountains. Let him who is on the housetop not go down to take anything out of his house. And let him who is in the field not go back to get his clothes. But woe to those who are pregnant and to those who are nursing babies in those days! And pray that your flight may not be in winter or on the Sabbath."

a. **Then let those who are in Judea flee**: These are warnings specifically addressed to Israelites. **Judea**, **housetops**, and **Sabbath** all speak to a Jewish environment.

i. "A refugee's lot is hard enough without extra impediments." (France)

ii. In light of the broader context in this chapter, these words of Jesus should be understood as having primary application to those who see the abomination of desolation in the very last days, during the great tribulation – events that are yet to occur.

iii. Yet there is no doubt that in some ways the catastrophe that came upon Judea and especially Jerusalem in A.D. 70 was a prefiguring of that future event; an imperfect foreshadow of the ultimate fulfillment. For this reason, virtually all the Christians fled Jerusalem and Judea in the years leading up to A.D. 70, when the Roman armies arrived in the area intent on putting down the Jewish rebellion in the Roman province of Palestine.

iv. "There is reasonably good tradition that Christians abandoned the city, perhaps in A.D. 68, about halfway through the siege." (Carson)

v. "*Eusebius* and *Epiphanius* say, that at this juncture, after *Cestius Gallus* had raised the siege, and Vespasian was approaching with his army, all who believed in Christ left Jerusalem and fled to Pella, and other places beyond the river Jordan; and so they all marvellously escaped the general shipwreck of their country: not one of them perished." (Clarke)

vi. Sadly, that was *not* what the Jewish people did. "Jesus' advice was that when that day came men ought to flee to the mountains. They did not; they crammed themselves into the city and into the walls of Jerusalem from all over the country, and that very folly multiplied the grim horror of the famine of the siege a hundredfold." (Barclay)

b. **Then let those who are in Judea flee**: This is because at the appearance of the abomination of desolation, the desolation will first be poured out at Judea, and because the church will not be a factor at this time, having already been caught up to meet Jesus in the air (1 Thessalonians 4:16-17).

i. Because Jesus told His disciples about the abomination of desolation (which is set up by the Antichrist in the middle of the Great Tribulation) and warned them of this coming destruction in the Great Tribulation, some Christians believe that all Christians *will go through* the Great Tribulation. To them, it seems evident. Why would Jesus say these things to His disciples if His disciples would not experience them?

ii. The answer is simple. We know from this passage and other passages that God will remove His church before the fury of the Great Tribulation, catching them away to meet Jesus in the air (1 Thessalonians 4:16-17). Yet this information is valuable for the followers of Jesus so they can understand His plan for the future. This information is especially valuable for those who *will become* His disciples in the Great Tribulation after the church is gone.

iii. We do well to remember that the disciples who heard Jesus say these words saw none of these things. Yet it was still good for them to hear it. Even if Christians will not go into the Great Tribulation, it is good for them - and those who will become Christians in the tribulation - to know what will happen during that time. Jesus spoke to all ages here.

3. (21-28) Coming after the abomination of desolation: **great tribulation**.

"For then there will be great tribulation, such as has not been since the beginning of the world until this time, no, nor ever shall be. And unless those days were shortened, no flesh would be saved; but for the elect's sake those days will be shortened. Then if anyone says to you, 'Look, here *is* the Christ!' or 'There!' do not believe *it*. For false christs and false prophets will rise and show great signs and wonders to deceive, if possible, even the elect. See, I have told you beforehand. Therefore if they say to you, 'Look, He is in the desert!' do not go out; *or* 'Look, *He is* in the inner rooms!' do not believe *it*. For as the lightning comes from the east and flashes to the west, so also will the coming of the Son of Man be. For wherever the carcass is, there the eagles will be gathered together."

a. **Great tribulation, such as has not been since the beginning of the world until this time**: Jesus said that this will be the most awful time in all history. When we think of the terrible wars, plagues, famines, and genocide history has seen, this is a sobering statement. When God pours out His wrath on a God rejecting world, it will be truly **great tribulation**.

i. Those who believe that the events of Matthew 24 were all or mostly all fulfilled in A.D. 70 are in the unenviable position of arguing that the calamity that befell Jerusalem at that time was the worst catastrophe of all history. This is not possible to adequately defend historically. As bad as the catastrophe of A.D. 70 was, there have been subsequent wars and calamities even worse. This reminds us that this **great tribulation** – this time of catastrophe **such as has not been since the beginning of the world until this time** – has not yet been fulfilled.

b. **Look, here is the Christ**: No one should be deceived about the nature of Jesus' coming. It will not be secret or private, but as plain as **lightning** that **flashes** across the sky. But in the midst of such tribulation, there will be a temptation to look for false messiahs (**false christs and false prophets will rise**).

i. **As the lightning comes from the east and flashes to the west, so also will be the coming of the Son of Man**: "Christ's coming will be sudden, startling, universally visible, and terrifying to the ungodly." (Spurgeon)

ii. **The coming of the Son of Man**: "*Parousia* ('coming') is used only in this chapter in the Gospels (vv. 3, 27, 37, 39), though in the Epistles it is used several times of Jesus' return in glory. Its literal meaning is 'presence' (as in 2 Corinthians 10:10), but it was used for official visits by high-ranking persons, state visits, and also for divine visitations, hence its technical use for Jesus' ultimate 'visitation'." (France)

c. **For wherever the carcass is, there the eagles will be gathered together**: This is a difficult statement. It was probably a figure of speech with the idea, "when judgment is ripe, it will surely come."

4. (29-31) Coming after the great tribulation: the return of Jesus Christ.

"Immediately after the tribulation of those days the sun will be darkened, and the moon will not give its light; the stars will fall from heaven, and the powers of the heavens will be shaken. Then the sign of the Son of Man will appear in heaven, and then all the tribes of the earth will mourn, and they will see the Son of Man coming on the clouds of heaven with power and great glory. And He will send His angels with a great sound of a trumpet, and they will gather together His elect from the four winds, from one end of heaven to the other."

a. **The sun will be darkened, the moon will not give its light**: Several prophetic passages describe the cosmic disturbances that will precede and surround the glorious return of Jesus (Joel 2:10, Revelation 6:12-14, Isaiah 34:4).

b. **The sign of the Son of Man will appear in heaven**: It is difficult to say exactly what this **sign** is. It seems to precede His return as described in Revelation 19:11. Perhaps this sign is somehow related to the incredible cosmic disturbances that will precede the great event.

i. Some, in light of the Roman Emperor Constantine's vision, thought the **sign of the Son of Man** would be a cross in the sky. More probably it is simply a way to describe the physical, visible return of Jesus to the earth from heaven.

ii. "Others point out that *semeion* is the LXX translation for the 'standard' or 'banner' referred to in the Old Testament as a signal for the gathering of God's people." (France)

iii. Barclay on *semeion*: "It is the regular word for the arrival of a governor into his province or for the coming of a king to his subjects. It regularly describes a coming in authority and in power."

c. **They will see the Son of Man coming on the clouds of heaven with power and great glory**: This is the fulfillment of the end, indicated by the sign of *the abomination of desolation*. Since this has not happened yet, neither has the abomination of desolation.

i. Again, those who claim that all or most of the events of Matthew 24 were fulfilled in the Roman conquest of Jerusalem and Judea in A.D. 70 are in an unenviable position. They often claim that Jesus fulfilled this **coming on the clouds of heaven** of **the Son of Man** with **power and great glory** by "coming" in judgment against the Jewish people in A.D. 70.

ii. Even some of those who believe that most the events of Matthew 24 were fulfilled in the fall of Jerusalem understand that this is a stretch too far. "From the foregoing exposition it appears that the coming of the Son of Man is not to be identified with the judgment of Jerusalem." (Bruce)

5. (32-35) Jesus speaks more regarding the timing of these events.

"Now learn this parable from the fig tree: When its branch has already become tender and puts forth leaves, you know that summer *is* near. So you also, when you see all these things, know that it is near; at the doors! Assuredly, I say to you, this generation will by no means pass away till all these things take place. Heaven and earth will pass away, but My words will by no means pass away."

a. **Learn this parable from the fig tree**: The **fig tree** has a regular pattern. The leaves appear, and then summer follows. When you see the leaves, you know summer is near.

i. The **fig tree** was a common fruit tree in Israel. It is mentioned many times in the Old Testament, especially as a description of the abundance of the land. Sometimes figs or fig trees are also used as symbols or pictures. In passages like Jeremiah 24:1-10 and Hosea 9:10, figs or fig trees are used as a representation of Israel.

ii. However, most Old Testament references to the **fig tree** use it as simply an example of agricultural blessing. It seems that Jesus' reference here is not so much on the "figness" of the fig tree, but on the way that the fig tree follows reliable growth cycles related to the seasons. This is especially evident when this passage is compared with Luke 21:29-31: *Look at the fig tree, and all the trees. When they are already budding, you see and know for yourselves that summer is now near. So you also, when you see these things happening, know that the kingdom of God is near.*

b. **So you also, when you see all these things, know that it is near; at the doors!** Jesus assured that when these signs appeared as He foretold (the abomination of desolation, followed by great tribulation, followed by signs in the heavens), His return to the earth *would* follow. When a fig tree buds, there is an inevitable result - summer is near and fruit is coming. In the same way, when these signs are seen, the coming of Jesus in glory with His church to this world will inevitably follow.

i. Really, it was just as Daniel prophesied in Daniel 12:11. The end *will come* 1,290 days after the abomination of desolation. Jesus assures that the agonies of the Great Tribulation will not continue indefinitely; they will have an end.

ii. Up to this point, Jesus has given an important outline for end-times events.

- There will arise catastrophes and persecutions, but those in themselves are not the sign of the end.

- There will arise a pivotal sign: the abomination of desolation.

- When the abomination of desolation appears, there are warnings to Israel to flee after the abomination.

- On the heels of the abomination of desolation comes great tribulation, and cosmic disturbances.

- In culmination, Jesus Christ will return in glory to the earth.

c. **Assuredly, I say to you, this generation will by no means pass away till all these things take place**: This statement of Jesus is one of the central reasons many have looked for all or most of the events of this chapter to be fulfilled in A.D. 70, approximately 40 years after Jesus spoke these words. Yet as previously argued, to assert this is to greatly stretch the most natural interpretation of the abomination of desolation, of the severity of the great tribulation, of the cosmic signs, and of the coming of the Son of Man. It is better to let those passages have their most natural meaning and to fit this promise into that framework.

i. The **generation** Jesus meant cannot be the generation of the disciples, because they never saw Jesus return in glory as described in Matthew 24:30. It is undoubtedly the generation that sees these signs. These events and Jesus' return won't be on some 1,000-year timetable, but will happen in succession.

ii. It has been suggested that the word **generation** could also be translated "race," and is a promise that the Jewish race would not be extinguished and would survive to the end. This would be a valuable promise, but some commentators (such as France) claim this is an embarrassingly wrong translation. Yet others – such as Adam Clarke, who strongly believed the events of this chapter were almost all fulfilled in A.D. 70 – writes, "*This race*; i.e. the Jews shall not cease from being a *distinct people*, till all the counsels of God relative to *them* and the *Gentiles* be fulfilled."

D. More on His coming, but from a different approach.

1. (36) Jesus says that the day and hour of His return is unknowable by men, and even unknowable by angels.

"But of that day and hour no one knows, not even the angels of heaven, but My Father only."

a. **Of that day and hour no one knows**: Here, Jesus refers back to the original question of Matthew 24:3 (*what will be the sign of Your coming?*). His answer is somewhat unexpected, saying **of that day and hour no one knows**.

i. To give this idea the strongest emphasis, Jesus claimed that this knowledge was reserved for His **Father only**. If Jesus Himself – at least during His earthly ministry – did not know this **day and hour**, it emphasizes the foolishness of any later person making certain predictions regarding the prophetic timetable.

b. **No one knows**: Based on what He had told us about the abomination of desolation, we might have expected that the exact day and hour *could* be known. After all, Daniel set the day of Jesus' return as being exactly 1,290 days after the abomination of desolation (Daniel 12:11).

i. In this, there is a dilemma. How can the day of Jesus' coming be both completely unknown, and at the same time be known to the day according to Daniel 12:11?

2. (37-39) Jesus says that His coming will be when the world is as it was in **the days of Noah**.

"But as the days of Noah *were*, so also will the coming of the Son of Man be. For as in the days before the flood, they were eating and drinking, marrying and giving in marriage, until the day that Noah entered the ark, and did not know until the flood came and took them all away, so also will the coming of the Son of Man be."

a. **As the days of Noah were**: Jesus explained what He meant by **the days of Noah**. It means life centered around the normal things: **eating and drinking, marrying and giving in marriage**. In other words, life will be business as usual; reprobate perhaps, but usual.

i. **Eating and drinking, marrying and giving in marriage**: Bruce notes that "Some charge these with sinister meaning: [**eating**], hinting at gluttony because often used of beasts, though also, in the sense of eating, of men…[**marrying and giving in marriage**], euphemistically pointing at sexual licences on both sides." Yet he comes to the conclusion, "The idea rather seems to be that all things went on as usual, as if nothing were going to happen."

ii. We should also remember that the days of Noah were also marked by violence and demonic oppression (Genesis 6:1-5).

b. **And did not know until the flood came and took them all away**: Those in the days of Noah were warned, and judgment eventually came. To those who had ignored the warnings, it came suddenly and unexpectedly.

i. "That the coming of the Son of Man takes place at an unknown time can only be true if in fact life seems to be going on pretty much as usual – just as in the days before the Flood." (Carson)

ii. In this, there is a dilemma. How can Jesus come to a "business-as-usual" world, and a world experiencing the worst calamities ever seen on earth?

3. (40-44) Jesus cautions His disciples to be ready for an unexpected coming.

"Then two *men* will be in the field: one will be taken and the other left. Two *women will be* grinding at the mill: one will be taken and the other left. Watch therefore, for you do not know what hour your Lord is coming. But know this, that if the master of the house had known what hour the thief would come, he would have watched and not allowed his house to be broken into. Therefore you also be ready, for the Son of Man is coming at an hour you do not expect."

a. **Then two men will be in the field: one will be taken and the other left**: Jesus here pointed to curious disappearances; to a catching away of some at the coming of the Son of Man (as also described in 1 Thessalonians 4:16-17).

i. "*Taken* is the same verb used, *e.g.*, in 1:20; 17:1; 18:16; 20:17; it implies to take someone to be with you, and therefore here points to the salvation rather than the destruction of the one 'taken'." (France)

b. **Watch therefore, for you do not know what hour your Lord is coming**: Since the day and hour of this coming are unknowable, Jesus' followers must be on constant guard for His coming.

i. Here again is the Second Coming dilemma.

- Is it at an unexpected hour or is it positively predicted?
- Is it business as usual or worldwide cataclysm?

- Is it meeting Him in the air (1 Thessalonians 4:16-17) or is He coming with the saints (Zechariah 14:5)?

ii. William Barclay describes one aspect of the difficulty here: "It is in two sections and they seem to contradict each other. The first (verses 32-35) seem to indicate that, as a man can tell by the signs of nature when summer is on the way, so he can tell by the signs of the world when the Second Coming is on the way... The second section (verses 36-41) says quite definitely that no one knows the time of the Second Coming, not the angels, not even Jesus himself, but only God; and that it will come upon men with the suddenness of a rainstorm out of a blue sky."

iii. The dilemma is resolved by seeing that there are actually *two* second comings. One is in the air, for the church - commonly known as the *rapture*. The other is to the world, coming with the church, commonly known as the Second Coming of Jesus. The "contradictions" in Matthew 24 (and much of the rest of prophecy) are often solved by seeing there are really references to "two" returns of Jesus.

c. **Therefore you also be ready, for the Son of Man is coming at an hour you do not expect**: We must not escape the emphasis. We must be ready, because His coming for us is without warning. Jesus follows with a few parables to drive home this point.

i. "Suetonius tells us that it was a piece of Julius Caesar's policy never to fore-acquaint his soldiers of any set time of removal or onset, that he might ever have them in readiness to draw forth whithersoever he would." (Trapp)

E. Parable of the two servants.

1. (45-47) The faithful servant.

"Who then is a faithful and wise servant, whom his master made ruler over his household, to give them food in due season? Blessed *is* that servant whom his master, when he comes, will find so doing. Assuredly, I say to you that he will make him ruler over all his goods."

a. **Blessed is that servant whom his master, when he comes, will find so doing**: Jesus told us that we must carry on with diligence while the Lord is gone. We must be that **faithful and wise servant** who takes care of his master's business while the master is away.

b. **Assuredly, I say to you that he will make him ruler over all his goods**: Jesus also promised that we will be rewarded for our diligence. The servants serve the master, but the master knows how to take care of and reward the servants.

2. (48-51) The evil servant.

"But if that evil servant says in his heart, 'My master is delaying his coming,' and begins to beat *his* fellow servants, and to eat and drink with the drunkards, the master of that servant will come on a day when he is not looking for *him* and at an hour that he is not aware of, and will cut him in two and appoint *him* his portion with the hypocrites. There shall be weeping and gnashing of teeth."

a. **If that evil servant says in his heart, "My master is delaying his coming"**: Jesus warns us of the attitude which says, "**my master is delaying his coming**." We must live in constant anticipation of Jesus' return, and that means being about our business for Him *now*.

i. The most dangerous lie is not "There is no God," not "there is no hell"; but the most dangerous lie of Satan is "there is no hurry." It is no small thing to say "Jesus is not coming today or for several years," because your system of prophecy demands it. We need to be ready for the *imminent return* of Jesus Christ.

b. **Begins to beat his fellow servants, and to eat and drink with the drunkards**: The evil servant, who was not ready for the master's return, sinned in at least three ways.

- He was not about the business that the master left for him.
- He fought with and mistreated **his fellow servants**.
- He gave himself to the pleasures of the world instead of serving his master.

i. This emphasis on constant readiness is a challenge for the Christian today. It can be said that many Christians are not ready in the same three ways. Each reader should be greatly impressed by the urgency of Jesus' appeal.

c. **Cut him in two and appoint him his portion with the hypocrites**: The faithful and wise servant was rewarded, but so was the evil servant. He was rewarded for His wickedness, and he would have the **portion with the hypocrites** he deserved.

i. **Cut him in two**: "The probable meaning is: will cut him in two (so to speak) with a *whip* = thrash him, the base slave, unmercifully. It is a strong word, selected to sympathy with the master's rage." (Bruce)

Matthew 25 - Jesus' Olivet Discourse (Part 2)

A. The parable of the ten virgins.

1. (1) Ten virgins go out to meet a bridegroom at a wedding.

"Then the kingdom of heaven shall be likened to ten virgins who took their lamps and went out to meet the bridegroom."

a. **Then the kingdom of heaven**: Matthew 24 ended with a parable meant to emphasize the idea of readiness for the coming of Jesus. Matthew 25 begins with another parable upon the same principle.

b. **To ten virgins who took their lamps and went out to meet the bridegroom**: There were three stages to a Jewish wedding in that day. The first was *engagement* - a formal agreement made by the fathers. The second was *betrothal* - the ceremony where mutual promises are made. The third was *marriage* - approximately one year later when the bridegroom came at an unexpected time for his bride.

i. "When the bridegroom came, the bride-maids, who were attending the bride, went forth to meet the bridegroom, with lamps lighted, to conduct him and his companions into the house, and to her who was to be the bride." (Poole)

ii. Some ask why Jesus described **ten virgins** and not another number. Reportedly, Talmudic authorities said there were usually **ten** lamps in a bridal procession. It was a common size of a wedding party.

iii. "The point is not these girls' virginity, which is assumed, but simply that they are ten (a favorite round number . . .) maidens invited to the wedding." (Carson)

c. **Went to meet the bridegroom**: In this parable, the first two stages have already taken place. Now the wedding party (**the ten virgins**) waits for the coming of the **bridegroom** for the bride.

i. "To see the bridegroom as Jesus himself seems warranted in light of Matthew 9:15. This would be a bold figure for Him to use, as the Old Testament frequently describes *God* (not the Messiah) as the bridegroom, and Israel as the bride (Isaiah 54:4-5; 62:5; Jeremiah 2:2; Hosea 1-3, *etc.*)." (France)

2. (2-13) The young women caught unprepared are denied entry.

"Now five of them were wise, and five *were* foolish. Those who *were* foolish took their lamps and took no oil with them, but the wise took oil in their vessels with their lamps. But while the bridegroom was delayed, they all slumbered and slept. And at midnight a cry was *heard:* 'Behold, the bridegroom is coming; go out to meet him!' Then all those virgins arose and trimmed their lamps. And the foolish said to the wise, 'Give us *some* of your oil, for our lamps are going out.' But the wise answered, saying, 'No, lest there should not be enough for us and you; but go rather to those who sell, and buy for yourselves.' And while they went to buy, the bridegroom came, and those who were ready went in with him to the wedding; and the door was shut. Afterward the other virgins came also, saying, 'Lord, Lord, open to us!' But he answered and said, 'Assuredly, I say to you, I do not know you.' Watch therefore, for you know neither the day nor the hour in which the Son of Man is coming."

a. **Now five of them were wise, and five were foolish**: Some in the wedding party were **wise** and prepared for the coming of the bridegroom. Some in the wedding party were **foolish** and unprepared.

i. "Foolish, wise, not bad and good, but prudent and imprudent, thoughtless and thoughtful." (Bruce)

b. **While the bridegroom was delayed, they all slumbered and slept**: All ten of the maidens slept, because the bridegroom was **delayed**. In this parable both the wise and foolish maidens slept, but the wise ones were prepared to act immediately when they were unexpectedly awakened. The foolish maidens were not prepared.

i. "They are waiting to escort the bridegroom in festal procession, probably in the last stage of the ceremonies as he brings his bride home for the wedding feast." (France)

ii. **Slumbered and slept**: "'Nodded off and were sound asleep' would get the sense of the Greek tenses." (France)

c. **Took their lamps and took no oil with them**: The five foolish virgins *appeared* to be ready for the bridegroom, because they had their lamps in hand. But they really were not ready, because they **took no oil with them**.

i. "It is apparently a torchlight procession, the *lamps* probably being 'torches' (of oil-soaked rags wrapped on a stick) rather than standing lamps, which are described by a different word in Matthew 5:15 and 6:22; the word used here regularly means 'torch'." (France)

ii. "Their *torches* consisting of a wooden staff held in the hand, with a dish at the top, in which was a piece of cloth or rope dipped in oil or pitch." (Bruce)

iii. **Oil in their vessels**: The wise maidens had an *extra supply* of oil.

d. **At midnight a cry was heard: "Behold, the bridegroom is coming"… all those virgins arose and trimmed their lamps**: At an unexpected hour the bridegroom came for the wedding. The wedding party (**all those virgins**) immediately began to prepare their lamps for lighting.

i. "*Trimmed their lamps* is literally 'put their torches in order'." (France)

ii. "It is a warning addressed specifically to those inside the professing church who are not to assume that their future is unconditionally assured; all ten are expecting to be at the feast, and until the moment comes there is no apparent difference between them – it is the crisis which will divide the ready from the unready." (France)

e. **Give us some of your oil, for our lamps are going out**: The **foolish** virgins were unprepared because they lacked oil for their lamps. In many Biblical passages **oil**, is an emblem of the Holy Spirit (such as Zechariah 4:1-7). Without **oil** the wedding party was not ready for the bridegroom. Without the Holy Spirit, no one is ready for the return of Jesus.

i. Olive oil is a good representation of the Holy Spirit for many reasons.

- Oil *lubricates* when used for that purpose - there is little friction and wear among those who are lubricated by the Spirit of God.

- Oil *heals* and was used as a medicinal treatment in Biblical times (Luke 10:34) - the Spirit of God brings healing and restoration.

- Oil *lights* when it is burned in a lamp - where the Spirit of God is, there is light.

- Oil *warms* when it is used as fuel for a flame - where the Spirit of God is, there is warmth and comfort.

- Oil *invigorates* when used to massage - the Holy Spirit invigorates us for His service.

- Oil *adorns* when applied as a perfume - the Holy Spirit adorns us and makes us more pleasant to be around.

- Oil *polishes* when used to shine metal - the Holy Spirit wipes away our grime and smooths out our rough edges.

ii. No one can be a true Christian without the indwelling Holy Spirit, as it says in Romans 8:9: *Now if anyone does not have the Spirit of Christ, he is not His.* In this parable Jesus probably did not intend a separation between "Spirit-filled" and "Non-Spirit-filled" Christians; the distinction is likely between true Christians and false believers.

iii. Nevertheless, a key to Christian readiness is to be constantly being filled with the Holy Spirit (Ephesians 5:18). Much of the weakness, defeat and lethargy in our spiritual lives can be explained if we are not constantly being filled with the Holy Spirit.

f. **The door was shut... "Assuredly, I say to you, I do not know you"**: The penalty was severe for the foolish maidens. They were not allowed to come to the wedding, and the **door was shut** against them in the strongest terms.

i. "The girls' appeal and the bridegroom's response recall the chilling words of Matthew 7:22-23; here, as there, *I do not know you* is a decisive formula of rejection, rather than a mere statement of fact." (France)

ii. "When that door is once shut, it will never be opened. There are some who dote and dream about an opening of that door, after death, for those who have died impenitent; but there is nothing in the Scriptures to warrant such an expectation. Any 'larger hope' than that revealed in the Word of God is a delusion and a snare." (Spurgeon)

g. **Watch therefore, for you know neither the day nor the hour in which the Son of Man is coming**: The point of this parable is simple - *be ready*. The price for failing to be ready is too high.

B. The parable of the talents.

1. (14-15) Jesus describes a master who gives instructions to his servants before departing on a long journey.

"For *the kingdom of heaven is* like a man traveling to a far country, *who* called his own servants and delivered his goods to them. And to one he gave five talents, to another two, and to another one, to each according to his own ability; and immediately he went on a journey."

a. **A man traveling to a far country, who called his servants and delivered his goods to them**: This was not a strange idea in the ancient world, where **servants** (slaves) were often given great responsibility. This was often the safest and smartest thing a man could do with his money.

i. "The best thing he could do with his money in his absence, dividing it among carefully selected slaves, and leaving them to do their best with it." (Bruce)

ii. "This parable takes up the question which that of the bridesmaids left unanswered: what *is* 'readiness'?" (France)

b. **To one he gave five talents, to another two, and to another one**: A **talent** was not an *ability* (though this parable has application to our abilities), but a unit of *money* worth at least $1,200 in modern terms, and likely much more.

i. "The *talent* was not a *coin*, it was a *weight*; and therefore its value obviously depended on whether the coinage involved was copper, gold, or silver." (Barclay)

ii. "The English use of 'talent' for a natural (or supernatural) aptitude derives from this parable...But of course the Greek *talanton* is simply a sum of money...it was generally regarded as equal to 6,000 denarii." (France) "If a talent were worth six thousand denarii, then it would take a day laborer twenty years to earn so much." (Carson)

iii. In the application of this parable it is appropriate to see these **talents** as life resources - such as time, money, abilities, and authority.

c. **To each according to his own ability**: The servants were given different amounts of money according to their **ability**. One servant only received one talent, yet we should see that this was not an insignificant amount. Some received more; but everyone received something and everyone received *a large amount*.

i. "The talent which each man has suits his *own* state best; and it is only *pride* and *insanity* which lead him to *desire* and *envy* the graces and talents of another. *Five* talents would be *too much* for some men: *one* talent would be *too little*." (Clarke)

2. (16-18) The servants manage the master's money.

"Then he who had received the five talents went and traded with them, and made another five talents. And likewise he who *had received* two gained two more also. But he who had received one went and dug in the ground, and hid his lord's money."

a. **He who had received the five talents went and traded with them**: Each of those who had received **talents** from their master did with them as they saw fit. Two of them **traded with** their talents and earned more talents (**made another five talents...gained two more also**).

i. **Went and traded** implies direct action. "The point is that the good servants felt the responsibility of their assignment and went to work without delay." (Carson)

ii. We aren't told how they **traded with** their talents. Perhaps they loaned the money at interest, perhaps they used the money and bought things and sold them for more money. The point is that they used what they had and gained more by using.

iii. We can say many good things about the work of the first two servants:

- They did their work *promptly*.
- They did their work with *perseverance*.
- They did their work with *success*.
- They were *ready* to give an account to their master.

b. **He who had received one went and dug in the ground, and hid his lord's money**: The third servant did almost *nothing* with his master's money. He took some care that it would not be lost (by hiding it), but he did nothing *positive* with his master's money, in contrast to the first two servants.

3. (19-23) The first two servants are judged.

"After a long time the lord of those servants came and settled accounts with them. So he who had received five talents came and brought five other talents, saying, 'Lord, you delivered to me five talents; look, I have gained five more talents besides them.' His lord said to him, 'Well *done*, good and faithful servant; you were faithful over a few things, I will make you ruler over many things. Enter into the joy of your lord.' He also who had received two talents came and said, 'Lord, you delivered to me two talents; look, I have gained two more talents besides them.' His lord said to him, 'Well *done*, good and faithful servant; you have been faithful over a few things, I will make you ruler over many things. Enter into the joy of your lord.'"

a. **After a long time the lord of those servants came**: The long delay would tempt the servants to think that they would *never* give an account for their management, yet they most certainly would.

b. **You have been faithful over a few things, I will make you ruler over many things**: The reward was the same for both servants, even though one was given **five talents** and the other was given **two talents**. Each performed the same according to the resources they had received.

c. **Well done, good and faithful servant**: This shows that the master looked for goodness and faithfulness in His servants. Whatever financial success these servants enjoyed came because they were **good and faithful**. The master looked first for these character qualities, not for a specific amount of money.

i. "It is not 'Well done, thou good and brilliant servant;' for perhaps the man never shone at all in the eyes of those who appreciate glare and glitter. It is not, 'Well done, thou great and distinguished servant;' for it is possible that he was never known beyond his native village." (Spurgeon)

ii. "It is better to be faithful in the infant-school than to be unfaithful in a noble class of young men. Better to be faithful in a hamlet over two or three score of people, than to be unfaithful in a great-city parish, with thousands perishing in consequence. Better to be faithful in a cottage meeting, speaking of Christ crucified to half-a hundred villagers, than to be unfaithful in a great building where thousands congregate." (Spurgeon)

d. **Enter into the joy of your lord**: This has the echo of heaven in it. The idea is that there is a place of **joy** belonging to the master of these servants, and they are invited to join the master in that place. There is a sense of heaven about this destiny for the two faithful servants.

i. "This is not the servant's portion, but the Master's portion shared with his faithful servants…not so much that we shall have a joy of our own as that we shall enter into the joy of our Lord." (Spurgeon)

ii. We can say of the reward for the first two servants:

- They received praise from their master.
- They received a promise of future blessing.
- They received glory, "**the joy of your lord**."

4. (24-30) The third servant gives account.

"Then he who had received the one talent came and said, 'Lord, I knew you to be a hard man, reaping where you have not sown, and gathering where you have not scattered seed. And I was afraid, and went and hid your talent in the ground. Look, *there* you have *what is* yours.'"

a. **Then he who had received the one talent came**: The master judged each of the servants *individually*. If they were taken as a group, they did very well: 8 talents given and 15 talents returned. Yet each one was judged on their individual faithfulness and effort.

i. "Remember, my hearer, that in the day of judgment thy account must be personal; God will not ask you what your church did – he will ask you what you did yourself." (Spurgeon)

b. **I knew you to be a hard man, reaping where you have not sown**: The servant who merely buried his talent tried to excuse himself because of his master's great power. In fact, he believed his master to be in some sense omnipotent: **reaping where you have not sown, and gathering where you have not scattered seed**.

i. **A hard man**: "Grasping, ungenerous, taking all to himself, offering no inducements to his servants." (Bruce)

ii. F.B. Meyer expressed the thinking of this servant: "I can do very little; it will not make much difference if I do nothing: I shall not be missed; my tiny push is not needed to turn the scale."

iii. "It is the genius of wicked men to lay the blame of their miscarriages upon others, oftentimes upon God himself." (Poole)

c. **Look, there you have what is yours**: The third servant seemed proud of himself. Because the master was so powerful and (in the mind of the servant) didn't need his help, the third servant thought that the master would be *pleased* that he did nothing and could say, "**Look, there you have what is yours**." He seemed to have no idea how much he had displeased his master.

i. We can say in the third servant's favor that at least he still understood that what he had been given belonged to his master. He said, "**you have what is yours**." Many modern servants of God think that when God gives them something, it no longer belongs to God; it belongs to *them* and they can do with it as they please.

ii. Yet "albeit this man was doing nothing for his master, he did not think himself an unprofitable servant. He exhibited no self-depreciation, no humbling, no contrition. He was as bold as brass, and said unblushingly, 'Lo, there thou hast that is thine.'" (Spurgeon)

iii. We can say of the work of the third servant:

- He didn't *think*.
- He didn't *work*.
- He didn't even *try*.
- He made *excuses*.

5. (26-30) The third servant is judged.

"But his lord answered and said to him, 'You wicked and lazy servant, you knew that I reap where I have not sown, and gather where I have not scattered seed. So you ought to have deposited my money with the bankers, and at my coming I would have received back my own with

interest. Therefore take the talent from him, and give *it* to him who has ten talents. For to everyone who has, more will be given, and he will have abundance; but from him who does not have, even what he has will be taken away. And cast the unprofitable servant into the outer darkness. There will be weeping and gnashing of teeth.'"

a. **You wicked and lazy servant, you knew that I reap where I have not sown**: The condemnation of this third servant – here called a **wicked and lazy servant** – was strong. The sovereignty of the master never excused the laziness of the servant. It condemned that laziness all the more.

> i. Those who don't work for the Lord, or pray, or don't evangelize because God is sovereign condemn themselves by their laziness. By their actions (or lack of action) they show that they are like the wicked servant in the parable. They do not know their Master's heart at all. "The lord of the unprofitable servant tells him, that the fault lay in his own sloth and wickedness, and his dread of his lord's security was but a mere frivolous pretence and unreasonable excuse." (Poole)

> ii. The charge against this servant who merely buried his talent was that he was **wicked and lazy**. We rarely see laziness as a real sin, something that must be repented of before the Lord. If laziness were a calling or a spiritual gift, this man would have been excellent.

> iii. "Not dishonest – the master had not misjudged as to that – but indolent, unenterprising, timid…Slothful, a poor creature altogether: suspicious, timid, heartless, spiritless, idle." (Bruce)

> iv. We might say that this servant did not have a proper fear of his master, but an unfitting fear of risk and failure.

b. **So you ought to have deposited my money with the bankers, and at my coming I would have received back my own with interest**: This man could have done *something* with what he had. Even if it had not doubled, it would have gained some **interest** for the master's money.

> i. "If we cannot trade directly and personally on our Lord's account, if we have not the skill nor the tact to manage a society or an enterprise for him, we may at least contribute to what others are doing, and join our capital to theirs, so that, by some means, our Master may have the interest to which he is entitled." (Spurgeon)

> ii. "The Old Testament forbade Israelites from charging interest against one another (Exodus 22:25; Leviticus 25:35-37; Deuteronomy 23:19; cf. Psalm 15:5…); but interest on money loaned to Gentiles was permitted (Deuteronomy 23:20)…By New Testament times Jewish

scholars had already distinguished between 'lending at interest' and 'usury' (in the modern sense)." (Carson)

c. **For to everyone who has, more will be given... but from him who does not have, even what he has will be taken away**: There are those who have things (like the servant with one talent), but hold them in such a way that it is as if they have nothing. These ones will find what they had **taken away**. Those who hold what they have received as faithful men and women, to them **more will be given**.

> i. "See that ye receive not any grace of God in vain; neither envy those that have much; a proportion is expected." (Trapp)

> ii. "We need not wait for the great future, to obtain this multiplication or withdrawal of our talents. They are already waxing or waning in our hands." (Meyer)

d. **Cast the unprofitable servant into the outer darkness**: Because he was **wicked and lazy**, the third servant demonstrated that he was not a true servant of his master at all. It is fitting that he (and those who show the same heart) was cast forever out of the master's presence.

> i. Just as there was a sense of heaven in the destiny for the two faithful servants, there is a strong sense of *hell* in the destiny for the **wicked and lazy servant**.

> ii. In the larger context of Matthew 25, the main point of this parable is clear: our readiness for Jesus' return is determined by our stewardship of the resources that He has given us.

> iii. Some think that readiness for Jesus' return is a very spiritual and abstract thing. It really isn't - it is a matter of being about our business for the Lord. In light of this parable, we must ask ourselves: What have we done with our knowledge? Our time? Our money? Our abilities? The sins of *omission* [what we don't do] may ultimately be more dangerous than the sins of *commission* [what we do].

C. The judgment of the nations.

1. (31-33) The nations are gathered before God's throne and separated.

"When the Son of Man comes in His glory, and all the holy angels with Him, then He will sit on the throne of His glory. All the nations will be gathered before Him, and He will separate them one from another, as a shepherd divides *his* sheep from the goats. And He will set the sheep on His right hand, but the goats on the left.

a. **When the Son of Man comes in His glory**: This is not really a parable; it is a description of a future scene of judgment after the glorious second coming of Jesus (described in Matthew 24:30).

b. **He will sit on the throne of His glory**: Jesus here was either guilty of megalomania (delusion about one's own power or importance) or He is indeed the Lord of **glory**, who will judge the nations from His **throne**. Seemingly this throne is present on earth, because it happens when **the Son of Man comes in His glory**.

> In three days He would be crucified; yet He spoke of "**When the Son of Man comes in His glory**."

> He had around Him a handful of disciples – one would betray Him, one deny Him, and the others forsake Him; yet He spoke of "**all the holy angels with Him**."

> He lived in utter simplicity, almost poverty – and was rejected by almost all the great and mighty men of the world; yet He said He would "**sit on the throne of His glory**."

c. **All the nations will be gathered before Him, and He will separate them one from another**: This particular judgment seems distinct from the *great white throne judgment* described in Revelation 20:11-15. This judgment of the nations is distinct from the final judgment for several reasons.

- It happens at a different *time*. The Great White Throne judgment of Revelation 20:11-15 clearly happens *after* the 1,000-year reign of Jesus Christ and His saints. The Judgment of the Nations of Matthew 25 happens immediately after the glorious return of Jesus (Matthew 25:31-32).

- It happens at a different *place*. The Great White Throne judgment of Revelation 20 happens in heaven; the Judgment of the Nations of Matthew 25 happens on earth.

- It happens unto different *subjects*. The Great White Throne judgment of Revelation 20 emphatically includes all unredeemed men and women. The Judgment of the Nations of Matthew 25 seems only to include the *nations* – that is Gentiles who are judged in large measure on their kindness and care towards [in part] the Jewish people (*My brethren*). It may be that Jewish people who survive the Great Tribulation will not be in this Judgment of the Nations.

- It happens on a different *basis*. This is described in the following section.

d. **He will set the sheep on His right hand, but the goats on the left**: The Son of Man – Jesus Himself – has the authority to divide humanity in this judgment. There are not *three* categories, but only two: **sheep** and **goats**, **right** and **left**.

i. "In the countryside sheep and goats mingled during the day. At night they were often separated: sheep tolerate the cool air, but goats have to be herded together for warmth." (Carson)

ii. This is true of the final judgment, when humanity will be divided into two groups and only two. Yet in the opinion of this commentator (definitely a minority opinion), Jesus spoke here not of the final judgment, but of the separation that will happen after the glorious return but before the final judgment to deal with those who have survived the Great Tribulation.

iii. By the end of the Great Tribulation (mentioned in Matthew 24:21 and other passages), the population of the earth will be greatly reduced by several factors:

- The rapture of the church (described in 1 Thessalonians 4:16-17) will take many millions of believers from the earth.

- The persecution and martyrdom of many of those who believe on Jesus after the rapture and during the Great Tribulation will take many from the earth.

- The terrible death and destruction of the Great Tribulation will take many from the earth.

- The catastrophe of the Battle of Armageddon and Jesus' glorious return to the earth will take many from the earth.

iv. Nevertheless, one can assume that even with the greatness of all these, that there will be many people – perhaps 3 billion or more – still remaining on the earth after Jesus returns in power and glory at the end of the last seven-year period. Among these will be the 144,000 who were specially sealed and preserved through the Great Tribulation and who stand with the Lamb of God on Mount Zion at His glorious return (Revelation 14:1-5). It is fair to ask, "What happens with all these people – perhaps 3 billion or more – who survive the Great Tribulation and Armageddon?" This judgment of the nations answers that question.

2. (34-40) The judgment and reward of those on the right hand.

Then the King will say to those on His right hand, 'Come, you blessed of My Father, inherit the kingdom prepared for you from the foundation

of the world: for I was hungry and you gave Me food; I was thirsty and you gave Me drink; I was a stranger and you took Me in; I *was* naked and you clothed Me; I was sick and you visited Me; I was in prison and you came to Me.' Then the righteous will answer Him, saying, 'Lord, when did we see You hungry and feed *You,* or thirsty and give *You* drink? When did we see You a stranger and take *You* in, or naked and clothe *You*? Or when did we see You sick, or in prison, and come to You?' And the King will answer and say to them, 'Assuredly, I say to you, inasmuch as you did *it* to one of the least of these My brethren, you did *it* to Me.'

a. **Come, you blessed of My Father, inherit the kingdom prepared for you**: The reward for **those on His right hand** (the sheep) is that they enter into the Father's kingdom.

b. **For I was hungry and you gave Me food; I was thirsty and you gave Me drink**: They were approved on the basis of their works. There is no mention of faith or even forgiveness here. This judgment was based purely on their moral kindness.

c. **Inasmuch as you did it to one of the least of these my brethren, you did it to Me**: This is another clear distinction between this judgment of the nations and the final judgment. The Great White Throne judgment of Revelation 20 is based on what is written in the Book of Life; the Judgment of the Nations in Matthew 25 is based on the humane treatment of others, especially Christians and the Jewish people (who will be particularly hated and persecuted the last half of the Great Tribulation).

i. Though the Christian and Jewish **brethren** of Jesus may be first in mind, knowing the nature of Jesus, we can say that it does not exclude others. "The brethren are the Christian poor and needy and suffering, in the first place, but ultimately and inferentially any suffering people anywhere." (Bruce)

3. (41-46) The judgment and condemnation of those on the left hand.

Then He will also say to those on the left hand, 'Depart from Me, you cursed, into the everlasting fire prepared for the devil and his angels: for I was hungry and you gave Me no food; I was thirsty and you gave Me no drink; I was a stranger and you did not take Me in, naked and you did not clothe Me, sick and in prison and you did not visit Me.' Then they also will answer Him, saying, 'Lord, when did we see You hungry or thirsty or a stranger or naked or sick or in prison, and did not minister to You?' Then He will answer them, saying, 'Assuredly, I say to you, inasmuch as you did not do *it* to one of the least of these, you

did not do *it* to Me.' And these will go away into everlasting punishment, but the righteous into eternal life."

a. **Inasmuch as you did not do it to one of the least of these, you did not do it to Me**: The charge against the lost ones did not concern any obvious moral violation, but their indifferent attitude toward Jesus (and His people). Their indifference sealed their doom. Throughout this chapter, the point has been emphasized: the price of indifference is too high to pay.

- We cannot afford to be indifferent towards Jesus and His return.
- We can't afford to be indifferent towards the Holy Spirit who makes us ready for the return of Jesus.
- We can't afford to be indifferent towards the resources that God gives us.
- We can't afford to be indifferent towards the needy people all around us.
- We can't afford to be indifferent towards lost humanity that will stand in judgment.

  i. "The 'guilt' of the cursed arises not so much from doing wrong things as from failure to do right…to do nothing is seen as the road to condemnation." (France)

b. **Depart from Me, you cursed, into the everlasting fire prepared for the devil and his angels**: Jesus clearly points out that hell was **prepared for the devil and his angels**. Men only go there because they have willingly cast their lot with the devil and his angels.

  i. "They had joined the devil in refusing allegiance to the Lord; so it was but right that, imitating his rebellion, they should share his punishment." (Spurgeon)

  ii. **Everlasting fire…everlasting punishment**: The literal meaning of this ancient Greek word is "age-long." As Bruce says, "The strict meaning of [everlasting]: agelong, not everlasting." Because of this, some have thought that the suffering of the **cursed** is not eternal. Some suggest that the **cursed** are eventually rehabilitated and brought to heaven (the *larger hope* idea); others believe they will eventually cease to exist (the *annihilation* idea).

  iii. Yet there are good reasons for believing that the sense of *aionion* in this passage is indeed **eternal**. "*Aionion* can refer to life or punishment in the age to come, or it can be limited to the duration of the thing to which it refers (as in Matthew 21:19). But in apocalyptic and eschatological contexts, the word not only connotes 'pertaining to the [messianic] age' but, because that age is always lived in God's presence, also 'everlasting'." (Carson)

iv. In addition, in Matthew 25:46 **everlasting** and **eternal** both translate the exact same ancient Greek word. If the righteous experience **life** forever, then we must say that the guilty experience **punishment** forever. "But some are of opinion that this punishment shall have *an end*: this is as likely as that the glory of the righteous shall have *an end*: for the same word is used to express the *duration* of the punishment, as is used to express the duration of the state of glory." (Clarke)

v. "They shall go into *everlasting punishment*, not a punishment for a time, as Origen thought." (Poole)

vi. "But they have a will to sin ever; and being worthless they cannot satisfy God's justice in any time; therefore is their fire everlasting." (Trapp)

c. **Everlasting punishment...eternal life**: This mention of **eternal life** makes most believe that Jesus spoke about the final judgment. But for those who survive the Great Tribulation, certainly entrance into the millennial kingdom *is the gateway* to eternal life. Those who do not enter the millennial kingdom will also certainly have **everlasting punishment**.

i. The purpose of this Judgment of the Nations is to separate peoples before the beginning of Jesus' millennial kingdom. The wicked and cruel will not enter; the moral and good will enter.

Matthew 26 - Jesus' Betrayal and Arrest

A. The stage is set for the arrest and crucifixion of Jesus.

1. (1-2) Jesus reminds His disciples of His coming suffering and crucifixion.

Now it came to pass, when Jesus had finished all these sayings, *that* **He said to His disciples, "You know that after two days is the Passover, and the Son of Man will be delivered up to be crucified."**

a. **When Jesus had finished all these sayings**: In Matthew's Gospel, the teaching of Jesus is finished here. In these last days leading up to His betrayal and crucifixion, He warned the multitudes about the corrupt religious leadership and He spoke to His disciples about things to come. Now, it was time for Jesus to fulfill His work on the cross.

i. "Having *instructed* his disciples and the Jews by his *discourses, edified* them by his *example, convinced* them by his *miracles*, he now prepares to *redeem* them by his *blood*!" (Clarke)

b. **You know that after two days...the Son of Man will be delivered up to be crucified**: Perhaps after the triumphal descriptions of the coming kingdom, the disciples were strengthened in their idea that it was impossible that the Messiah should suffer. Jesus reminded them that this was not the case.

2. (3-5) The plot against Jesus.

Then the chief priests, the scribes, and the elders of the people assembled at the palace of the high priest, who was called Caiaphas, and plotted to take Jesus by trickery and kill *Him*. But they said, "Not during the feast, lest there be an uproar among the people."

a. **Then the chief priests, the scribes, and the elders... plotted to take Jesus by trickery and kill Him**: The long controversy between Jesus and the religious leaders had finally come to this.

i. According to Carson, the use of both **assembled** and **plotted** is deliberately suggestive of Psalm 31:13: *For I am the slander of many; fear is on every side; while they take counsel together against me, they scheme to take away my life.*

ii. **The high priest, who was called Caiaphas**: "Annas was deposed by the secular authorities in A.D. 15 and replaced by Caiaphas, who lived and ruled till his death in A.D. 36. But since according to the Old Testament the high priest was not to be replaced till after his death, the transfer of power was illegal. Doubtless some continued to call either man 'high priest.'" (Carson)

iii. "Between 37 B.C. and A.D. 67…there were no fewer than twenty-eight High Priests. The suggestive thing is that Caiaphas was High Priest from A.D. 18 to A.D. 36. This was an extraordinarily long time for a High Priest to last, and Caiaphas must have brought the technique of co-operating with the Romans to a fine art." (Barclay)

iv. "About *two* years after our Lord's crucifixion, Caiaphas and Pilate were both deposed by Vitellius, then governor of Syria, and afterwards emperor. Caiaphas, unable to bear this disgrace, and the stings of his conscience for the murder of Christ, killed himself about A.D. 35. See Joseph. Antiquities b. xviii. c. 2-4." (Clarke)

b. **Not during the feast, lest there be an uproar**: They didn't want to put Jesus to death during Passover, but that is exactly how it happened. This is another subtle indication that Jesus was in control of events, as they in fact killed Him on the very day that they didn't want to.

i. "The leaders were right in fearing the people. Jerusalem's population swelled perhaps fivefold during the feast; and with religious fervor and national messianism at a high pitch, a spark might set off an explosion." (Carson)

3. (6-13) A woman anoints Jesus before His death.

And when Jesus was in Bethany at the house of Simon the leper, a woman came to Him having an alabaster flask of very costly fragrant oil, and she poured *it* on His head as He sat *at the table*. But when His disciples saw *it*, they were indignant, saying, "Why this waste? For this fragrant oil might have been sold for much and given to *the* poor." But when Jesus was aware of *it*, He said to them, "Why do you trouble the woman? For she has done a good work for Me. For you have the poor with you always, but Me you do not have always. For in pouring this fragrant oil on My body, she did *it* for My burial. Assuredly, I say to you, wherever this gospel is preached in the whole world, what this woman has done will also be told as a memorial to her."

a. **A woman came to Him having an alabaster flask of very costly fragrant oil**: We know from John 12 that this **woman** was Mary, the sister of Lazarus and Martha. Mary, who sat at the feet of Jesus (Luke 10:39), made this extravagant display of love and devotion to Jesus.

> i. There is some measure of debate, and sometimes confusion, about this anointing of Jesus and those mentioned in Mark, Luke, and John. The best solution seems to be that Matthew, Mark, and John record one occasion of anointing in Bethany and Luke records a separate event in Galilee.

> ii. "*Simon the leper* is otherwise unknown to us. He was presumably a well-known local figure, perhaps one whom Jesus had cured (as one who was still a *leper* could not entertain guests to dinner) but whose nickname remained as a reminder of his former disease." (France)

> iii. Morris on the **alabaster flask**: "It had no handles and was furnished with a long neck which was broken off when the contents were needed...We may fairly deduce that this perfume was costly. Jewish ladies commonly wore a perfume flask suspended from a cord round the neck, and it was so much a part of them that they were allowed to wear it on the sabbath." (Commentary on Luke)

b. **Why this waste?** The disciples criticized this display of love and honor for Jesus. Specifically, the critic was Judas (John 12:4-6). But Jesus defended Mary as an example of someone who simply did **a good work** for Him. Her extravagant - reckless really - giving for Jesus would be remembered as long as the gospel was preached (**as a memorial to her**).

> i. "What they call waste, Jesus calls 'a beautiful thing.'" (Carson)

> ii. "Is anything wasted which is all for Jesus? It might rather seem as if all would be wasted which was not given to him." (Spurgeon)

> iii. "Judas could not breathe freely amid the odours of the ointment and all it emblemed." (Bruce)

c. **You have the poor with you always, but Me you do not have always**: Jesus did not say this to discourage generosity and kind treatment of the poor. In fact, His recent words about the judgment of the nations had just radically *encouraged* kindness to those in need (Matthew 25:31-46). Jesus pointed to the appropriate nature of *that moment* to honor Him in an extravagant way.

> i. "The beauty of this woman's act consisted in this, that it was all for Christ. All who were in the house could perceive and enjoy the perfume of the precious ointment; but the anointing was for Jesus only." (Spurgeon)

d. **She did it for My burial**: Even if she did not understand the full significance of what she did, Mary's act said something that the disciples didn't say or do. She gave Jesus the love and attention He deserved before His great suffering. She understood more because she was in the place of greatest understanding – being at the feet of Jesus.

> i. Kings were anointed. Priests were anointed. Each of these would have been true in the case of Jesus, yet He claimed that she anointed Him for His *burial*.

> ii. "She probably did not know all that her action meant when she anointed her Lord for his burial. The consequences of the simplest action done for Christ may be much greater than we think…She thus showed that there was, at least, one heart in the world that thought nothing was too good for her Lord, and that the best of the very best ought to be given to him." (Spurgeon)

> iii. "Mary's name now smells as sweet in all God's house as ever her ointment did; when Judas' name rots, and shall do to all posterity." (Trapp)

e. **What this woman has done will also be told as a memorial to her**: What Mary did was remarkable for its *motive* – a pure, loving heart. It was remarkable in that it was done *for Jesus alone*. And it was remarkable in that it was *unusual* and *extraordinary*.

> i. "All those who have done wonders for Christ have always been called eccentric and fanatical. Why, when Whitfield first went on Bennington Common to preach, because he could not find a building large enough, it was quite an unheard of thing, to preach in the open air. How could you expect God to hear prayer, if there was not a roof over the top of the people's heads? How could souls be blessed, if the people had not seats, and regular high-backed pews to sit in! Whitfield was thought to be doing something outrageous, but he went and did it; he went and broke the alabaster box on the head of his Master, and in the midst of scoffs and jeers, he preached in the open air. And what came of it? A revival of godliness, and a mighty spread of religion. I wish we were all of us ready to do some extraordinary thing for Christ – willing to be laughed at, to be called fanatics, to be hooted and scandallized because we went out of the common way, and were not content with doing what everybody else could do or approve to be done." (Spurgeon)

4. (14-16) Judas makes a sinister agreement with the religious leaders.

Then one of the twelve, called Judas Iscariot, went to the chief priests and said, "What are you willing to give me if I deliver Him to you?"

And they counted out to him thirty pieces of silver. So from that time he sought opportunity to betray Him.

a. **Then one of the twelve**: The sense from Matthew is that the matter with Mary was the final insult to Judas, even though it may have happened some days before. After that, he was determined to **betray** Jesus to the religious leaders who wanted to kill Him.

b. **What are you willing to give me if I deliver Him to you?** Through the centuries, many suggestions have been offered regarding the *motive* of Judas in betraying Jesus.

  i. Matthew 10:4 calls him *Judas Iscariot*; it may be that he was from Kerioth, a city in southern Judea. This would make Judas the only Judean among the other disciples, who were all Galileans. Some wonder if Judas resented the leadership of the Galilean fishermen among the disciples, and finally had enough of it.

  ii. Perhaps Judas was disillusioned with the type of Messiah Jesus revealed Himself to be; wanting a more political, conquering Messiah.

  iii. Perhaps Judas watched the ongoing conflict between Jesus and the religious leaders and concluded that they were winning and Jesus was losing; therefore, he decided to cut his losses and join the winning side.

  iv. Perhaps he came to the conclusion that Jesus simply was not the Messiah or a true Prophet, even as Saul of Tarsus had believed.

  v. Some even suggest that Judas did this from a noble motive; that he was impatient for Jesus to reveal Himself as a powerful Messiah, and he thought that this would force Him to do this.

  vi. Whatever the specific reason, the Scriptures present no sense of *reluctance* in Judas, and only one motivation: *greed*. The words stand: **"What are you willing to give me if I deliver Him to you?"**

c. **And they counted out to him thirty pieces of silver**: According to the Bible, there was no noble intention in Judas' heart. His motive was simply money, and his price wasn't too high: **thirty pieces of silver** was worth perhaps $25.

  i. The exact value of **thirty pieces of silver** is somewhat difficult to determine, but it was undeniably a *small* amount, not a great amount. "It was a known set price for the basest slave, Exodus 21:31; Joel 3:3, 6. For so small a sum sold this traitor so sweet a Master." (Trapp)

  ii. "Though therefore Judas was covetous enough to have asked more, and it is like the malice of these councilors would have edged them to have given more, yet it was thus ordered by the Divine council. Christ must be sold cheap, that he might be the more dear to the souls of the redeemed ones." (Poole)

iii. "Yet many have sold Jesus for a less price than Judas received; a smile or a sneer has been sufficient to induce them to betray their Lord." (Spurgeon)

B. A Last Supper with the disciples.

1. (17-20) Preparations for the Passover: remembering redemption.

Now on the first *day* of the *Feast of* the Unleavened Bread the disciples came to Jesus, saying to Him, "Where do You want us to prepare for You to eat the Passover?" And He said, "Go into the city to a certain man, and say to him, 'The Teacher says, "My time is at hand; I will keep the Passover at your house with My disciples."'" So the disciples did as Jesus had directed them; and they prepared the Passover. When evening had come, He sat down with the twelve.

a. **Now on the first day of the Feast of the Unleavened Bread**: This must have been a very moving commemoration for Jesus. Passover remembers the deliverance of Israel from Egypt, which was the central act of redemption in the Old Testament. Jesus now provided a new center of redemption to be remembered by a new ceremonial meal.

i. This mention of **the first day of the Feast of the Unleavened Bread** brings up complicated issues of the precise calendar chronology of these events. The main complicating issue is that Matthew, Mark, and Luke present this meal Jesus will have with His disciples as the Passover meal – normally eaten with lamb which was sacrificed on the day of Passover with a great ceremony at the temple. Yet John seems to indicate that the meal took place before the Passover (John 13:1), and that Jesus was actually crucified on the Passover (John 18:28).

ii. Another solution is suggested by Adam Clarke: "It is a common opinion that our Lord ate the Passover some hours before the Jews ate it; for the Jews, according to custom, ate theirs at the *end* of the *fourteenth* day, but Christ ate his the preceding even, which was the beginning of the same sixth day, or Friday; the Jews begin their day at *sunsetting*, we at midnight. Thus Christ ate the Passover on the *same day* with the Jews, but not on the *same hour*."

iii. "The simplest solution…is that Jesus, knowing that he would be dead before the regular time for the meal, deliberately held it in secret one day early. Luke 22:15-16 indicates Jesus' strong desire for such a meal with his disciples before his death, and his awareness that the time was short." (France)

iv. One is inclined to agree with Bruce regarding precise chronological analysis: "The discussions are irksome, and their results uncertain; and they are apt to take the attention off far more important matters."

b. **When evening had come, He sat down with the twelve**: Since the Jewish day began at sundown, Jesus ate the Passover and was killed on the same day according to the Jewish calendar.

i. If it is true that Jesus ate this at the beginning of the Jewish day (evening), when most Jews would normally eat the Passover at the end of the day (following the night and the morning), it explains why there is no mention of Jesus eating lamb with His disciples at this meal. They ate it before the Passover lambs were sacrificed at the temple. This would correspond with John's chronology that indicates Jesus was crucified at the same approximate time the Passover lambs were being sacrificed.

ii. However, it would be wrong to say that there was no Passover lamb at this last supper Jesus had with His disciples; *He* was the Passover lamb. Paul would later refer to *Christ, our Passover, was sacrificed for us* (1 Corinthians 5:7).

iii. **He sat down with the twelve**: "With Judas among the rest; though Hilary hold otherwise, for what reason I know not." (Trapp)

2. (21-25) Jesus gives Judas a last opportunity to repent.

Now as they were eating, He said, "Assuredly, I say to you, one of you will betray Me." And they were exceedingly sorrowful, and each of them began to say to Him, "Lord, is it I?" He answered and said, "He who dipped *his* hand with Me in the dish will betray Me. The Son of Man indeed goes just as it is written of Him, but woe to that man by whom the Son of Man is betrayed! It would have been good for that man if he had not been born." Then Judas, who was betraying Him, answered and said, "Rabbi, is it I?" He said to him, "You have said it."

a. **Assuredly, I say to you, one of you will betray Me**: In the midst of their Passover meal, Jesus made a startling announcement. He told His disciples that one of their own – these twelve who had lived and heard and learned from Jesus for three years – would **betray** Him.

i. If we are familiar with this story it is easy not to appreciate its impact. It's easy to lose appreciation for how terrible it was for one of Jesus' own to **betray** Him. For good reason Dante's great poem about heaven and hell places Judas in the lowest place of hell.

ii. "This was a most unpleasant thought to bring to a feast, yet it was most appropriate to the Passover, for God's commandment to Moses concerning the first paschal lamb was, 'With bitter herbs they shall eat it.'" (Spurgeon)

b. **He who dipped his hand with Me in the dish will betray Me**: Jesus said this not to point out a specific disciple, because they *all* **dipped** with Him. Instead, Jesus identified the betrayer as a *friend*, someone who ate at the same table with Him.

i. This idea is drawn from Psalm 41:9: *Even my own familiar friend in whom I trusted, who ate my bread, has lifted up his heel against me.* "My fellow-commoner, my familiar friend, Psalm 41:9. This greatly aggravateth the indignity of the matter." (Trapp)

c. **Rabbi, is it I?** It was noble for the 11 other disciples to ask this question (**Lord, is it I?**); it was terrible hypocrisy for Judas to ask it. For Judas to ask, "**Rabbi, is it I?**" while knowing he had already arranged the arrest of Jesus was the height of treachery.

i. "It is a beautiful trait in the character of the disciples that they did not suspect one another, but *every one of them* inquired, almost incredulously, as the form of the question implies, '*Lord, is it I?*' No one said, 'Lord is it Judas?'" (Spurgeon)

d. **You have said it**: Jesus did not say this to condemn Judas, but to call him to repentance. It is fair to assume that He said it with love in His eyes, and Jesus showed Judas that He loved him, even knowing his treachery.

3. (26-29) Jesus institutes the Lord's Supper.

And as they were eating, Jesus took bread, blessed and broke *it*, and gave *it* to the disciples and said, "Take, eat; this is My body." Then He took the cup, and gave thanks, and gave *it* to them, saying, "Drink from it, all of you. For this is My blood of the new covenant, which is shed for many for the remission of sins. But I say to you, I will not drink of this fruit of the vine from now on until that day when I drink it new with you in My Father's kingdom."

a. **As they were eating**: Sometime during or after this dinner, Jesus washed the disciples' feet (John 13:1-11). Following this, Judas left (John 13:30). Then Jesus gave the extended discourse with His disciples and prayer to God the Father described in John 13:31-17:26.

i. Was Judas present for the first celebration of the Lord's Supper? The debate centers on the manuscript of John 13:2. Some textual traditions say, *And supper being ended*, which would imply that Jesus washed their feet and that Judas left *after* the institution of the Lord's Supper. Other textual traditions read, *And during supper* at John 13:2. This would indicate that Jesus washed feet and Judas left sometime during the meal, and therefore may have left before the institution of the Lord's Supper.

ii. Since John did not describe the institution of the Lord's Supper in his gospel account, there is debate as to if Judas was present when the Lord's Supper was first given, as described in the following passage. Most confidently believe Judas was not part of this part of the Lord's Supper (such as Morgan: "Before the new feast was instituted, Judas had gone out (John 13:30)."). The issue is very difficult to determine with certainty.

b. **Jesus took bread, blessed and broke it**: When the bread was lifted up at Passover, the head of the meal said: "This is the bread of affliction which our fathers ate in the land of Egypt. Let everyone who hungers come and eat; let everyone who is needy come and eat the Passover meal." Everything eaten at the Passover meal had symbolic meaning. The bitter herbs recalled the bitterness of slavery; the salt water remembered the tears shed under Egypt's oppression. The main course of the meal - a lamb freshly sacrificed for that particular household - did not symbolize anything connected to the agonies of Egypt. It was the sin-bearing sacrifice that allowed the judgment of God to pass over the household that believed.

i. The Passover created a nation; a mob of slaves were freed from Egypt and became a nation. This new Passover also creates a people; those united in Jesus Christ, remembering and trusting His sacrifice.

c. **Take, eat; this is My body... This is My blood of the new covenant**: Jesus didn't give the normal explanation of the meaning of the foods. He reinterpreted them in Himself, and the focus was no longer on the suffering of Israel in Egypt, but on the sin-bearing suffering of Jesus on their behalf.

i. "The words 'this is my body' had no place in the Passover ritual; and as an innovation, they must have had a stunning effect, an effect that would grow with the increased understanding gained after Easter." (Carson)

ii. This is how we *remember* what Jesus did for us. As we eat the **bread**, we should remember how Jesus was broken, pierced, and beaten with stripes for our redemption. As we drink the **cup**, we should remember that His blood, His life was poured out on Calvary for us.

iii. This is how we *fellowship* with Jesus. Because His redemption has reconciled us to God, we can now sit down to a meal with Jesus, and enjoy each other's company.

d. **This is My blood of the new covenant**: Remarkably, Jesus announced the institution of a **new covenant**. No mere man could ever institute a **new**

covenant between God and man, but Jesus is the God-man. He has the authority to establish a **new covenant**, sealed with blood, even as the old covenant was sealed with blood (Exodus 24:8).

i. The **new covenant** concerns a transformation that cleanses from all sin: *For I will forgive their iniquity, and their sin I will remember no more* (Jeremiah 31:34). This transformation puts God's Word and will in us: *I will put My law in their minds, and write it on their hearts* (Jeremiah 31:33). This covenant is all about a new, close relationship with God: *I will be their God, and they shall be My people* (Jeremiah 31:33).

ii. We can say that the **blood** of Jesus made the **new covenant** possible, and it also made it sure and reliable. It is confirmed with the life of God Himself.

iii. Because of what Jesus did on the cross, we have can have a **new covenant** relationship with God. Sadly, many followers of Jesus live as if it never happened.

- As if there is no inner transformation
- As if there is no true cleansing from sin.
- As if there is no Word and will of God in our hearts.
- As if there is no new and close relationship with God.

iv. **Which is shed for many**: "In that large word 'many' let us exceedingly rejoice. Christ's blood was not shed for the handful of apostles alone. There were but eleven of them who really partook of the blood symbolized by the cup. The Savior does not say, 'This is my blood which is shed for you, the favored eleven;' but 'shed for many.'" (Spurgeon)

e. **This is My body… this is My blood**: The precise understanding of these words from Jesus have been the source of great theological controversy among Christians.

i. The Roman Catholic Church holds the idea of *transubstantiation*, which teaches that the bread and the wine *actually* become the body and blood of Jesus.

ii. Martin Luther held the idea of *consubstantiation*, which teaches the bread remains bread and the wine remains wine, but by faith they are the same as Jesus' actual body. Luther did not believe in the Roman Catholic doctrine of transubstantiation, but he did not go far from it.

iii. John Calvin taught that Jesus' presence in the bread and wine is real, but only spiritual, not physical. Zwingli taught that the bread and wine are significant symbols that represent the body and blood of Jesus. When the Swiss Reformers debated the issue with Martin Luther at Marburg, there was a huge contention. Luther insisted on some kind of physical presence because Jesus said, "**this is My body**." He insisted over and over again, writing it on the velvet of the table, *Hoc est corpus meum* – "**this is My body**" in Latin. Zwingli replied, "Jesus also said I am the vine," and "I am the door," but we understand what He was saying. Luther replied, "I don't know, but if Christ told me to eat dung I would do it knowing that it was good for me." Luther was so strong on this because he saw it as an issue of believing Christ's words; and because he thought Zwingli was compromising, he said he was of *another spirit* (*andere geist*). Ironically, Luther later read Calvin's writings on the Lord's Supper (which were essentially the same as Zwingli's) and seemed to agree with, or at least accept Calvin's views.

iv. Scripturally, we can understand that the **bread** and the **cup** are not *mere* symbols, but they are powerful pictures to partake of, to enter into, as we see the Lord's Table as the new Passover.

v. "Let the papists and Lutherans say what they can, here must be two figures acknowledged in these words. The *cup* here is put for the wine in the cup; and the meaning of these words, *this is my blood of the new testament*, must be, this wine is the sign of the new covenant. Why they should not as readily acknowledge a figure in these words, *This is my body*, I cannot understand." (Poole)

vi. "What is certain is that Jesus bids us commemorate, not his birth, nor his life, nor his miracles, but his death." (Carson)

f. **Take, eat**: Beyond the debate over what the **bread** and the **cup** mean, we must remember what Jesus said to *do with them*. We must **take** and **eat**.

i. **Take** means that it won't be *forced* upon anyone. One must actually receive it. "I anticipate that someone will say, 'Am I then to have Jesus Christ by only taking him?' Just so. Dost thou need a Savior? There he is; take him…Take him in; take him in; that is all that thou hast to do." (Spurgeon)

ii. **Eat** means that this is absolutely vital for everyone. Without food and drink, no one can live. Without Jesus, we perish. It also means that we must take Jesus into our innermost being. Everyone must also **eat** for themselves; no one else can do it for them.

iii. "If you have any question as to whether you have drunk, I will tell you how to solve it — *drink again!* If you have been eating, and you have really forgotten whether you have eaten or not — such things do occur to busy men, who eat but little; if, I say, you would be sure that you have eaten, *eat again!* If thou wilt be assured that thou hast believed in Jesus, believe again!" (Spurgeon)

g. **He gave thanks**: In the ancient Greek language, **thanks** is the word *eucharist*. This is why the commemoration of the Lord's Table is sometimes called the *Eucharist*.

> i. This tells us something of Jesus' own attitude and heart at this moment: "Observe, Jesus was in the mood, and able, at that hour, to thank and praise, confident that good would come out of evil. In Gethsemane He was able only to *submit*." (Bruce)

> ii. This tells us something of our own receiving of the Lord's Supper: "What, then, do we mean when at the Supper we lift that sacred cup to our lips? Are we not saying by that significant act, Remember thy covenant? Are we not reminding Jesus that we are relying upon Him to do His part? Are we not pledging ourselves to Him as his own, bound to Him by indissoluble ties, and satisfied with his most blessed service?" (Meyer)

> iii. This tells us something of the sometimes declined condition of the people of God and their leaders: "Once there were wooden cups, golden priests; now there are golden cups, but wooden priests." (Trapp)

h. **Until that day when I drink it new with you in My Father's kingdom**: Jesus looked forward to a future celebration of the Passover in heaven, one that He has not yet celebrated with His people. He is waiting for all His people to be gathered to Him, and then there will be a great supper - *the marriage supper of the Lamb* (Revelation 19:9). This is the fulfillment **in My Father's kingdom** that Jesus longed for.

4. (30) Jesus sings with His disciples and goes out to the Mount of Olives.

And when they had sung a hymn, they went out to the Mount of Olives.

a. **When they had sung a hymn**: We don't often think of Jesus singing, but He did. He lifted His voice in adoration and worship to God the Father. We can endlessly wonder what His voice sounded like, but we know for certain that He sang with more than His voice, and He lifted His whole heart up in praise. This reminds us that God *wants* to be praised with singing.

> i. "These words, interpreted by a reverent imagination, present one of the most wonderful pictures... They sing, and it is impossible to doubt that He led the singing." (Morgan)

> ii. It is remarkable that Jesus could sing on this night before His crucifixion. Could we sing in such circumstances? Jesus can truly be our worship leader. We should sing to God our Father - *just as Jesus*

did - because this is something that pleases Him; and when we love someone, we want to do the things that please *them*. It really doesn't matter if it does or doesn't please *us*.

iii. "No sweeter singing, no mightier music ever sounded amid the darkness of the sad world's night than the singing of Jesus and His first disciples, as they moved out to the Cross of His Passion, and their redemption." (Morgan)

b. **Sung a hymn**: It is wonderful that Jesus sang, but *what* did He sing? A Passover meal always ended with singing three Psalms known as the *Hallel*, Psalms 116-118. Think of how the words of these Psalms would have ministered to Jesus as He sang them on the night before His crucifixion:

- *The pains of death surrounded me, and the pangs of Sheol laid hold of me; I found trouble and sorrow. Then I called upon the name of the LORD: "O LORD, I implore You, deliver my soul!"* (Psalm 116:3-4)

- *For You have delivered my soul from death, My eyes from tears, and my feet from falling. I will walk before the LORD in the land of the living.* (Psalm 116:8-9)

- *I will take up the cup of salvation, and call upon the name of the LORD. I will pay my vows to the LORD now in the presence of all His people. Precious in the sight of the LORD is the death of His saints.* (Psalm 116:13-15)

- *Praise the LORD, all you Gentiles! Laud Him, all you peoples!* (Psalm 117:1)

- *You pushed me violently, that I might fall, but the LORD helped me. The LORD is my strength and song, and He has become my salvation.* (Psalm 118:13-14)

- *I shall not die, but live, and declare the works of the LORD. The LORD has chastened me severely, but He has not given me over to death. Open to me the gates of righteousness; I will go through them, and I will praise the LORD.* (Psalm 118:17-19)

- *The stone which the builders rejected Has become the chief cornerstone. This was the Lord's doing; It is marvelous in our eyes.* (Psalm 118:22-23)

- *God is the LORD, and He has given us light; bind the sacrifice with cords to the horns of the altar. You are my God, and I will praise You; You are my God, I will exalt You.* (Psalm 118:27-28)

i. "When Jesus arose to go to Gethsemane, Psalm 118 was upon his lips. It provided an appropriate description of how God would guide his Messiah through distress and suffering to glory." (Lane)

ii. "If, beloved, you knew that at--say, ten o'clock tonight, you would be led away to be mocked, and despised, and scourged, and that tomorrow's sun would see you falsely accused, hanging, a convicted criminal, to die upon a cross, do you think that you could sing tonight, after your last meal?" (Spurgeon)

5. (31-35) Jesus predicts the desertion of the disciples.

Then Jesus said to them, "All of you will be made to stumble because of Me this night, for it is written:

'I will strike the Shepherd,
And the sheep of the flock will be scattered.'

But after I have been raised, I will go before you to Galilee." Peter answered and said to Him, "Even if all are made to stumble because of You, I will never be made to stumble." Jesus said to him, "Assuredly, I say to you that this night, before the rooster crows, you will deny Me three times." Peter said to Him, "Even if I have to die with You, I will not deny You!" And so said all the disciples.

a. **All of you will be made to stumble because of Me this night**: Jesus said this not to condemn His disciples, but to show them that He really was in command of the situation, and to demonstrate that the Scriptures regarding the suffering of the Messiah *must* be fulfilled.

b. **After I have been raised**: Jesus already was looking beyond the cross. His eyes were set on *the joy set before Him* (Hebrews 12:2).

c. **Even if I have to die with You, I will not deny You!** Peter was tragically unaware of both the spiritual *reality* and the spiritual *battle* that Jesus clearly saw. Peter felt brave at the moment and had no perception beyond the moment. Soon, Peter would be intimidated before a humble servant girl, and before her Peter would deny that he even knew Jesus.

d. **Assuredly, I say to you that this night, before the rooster crows, you will deny Me three times**: Jesus knew that Peter would fail in what he thought was his strong area - courage and boldness. Through this solemn warning Jesus gave Peter an opportunity to take heed and consider his own weakness.

i. Jesus said it so clearly to Peter. "Peter, you will be made to stumble. You will forsake Me, your Master. You will do it this very night – before the rooster crows. You will deny that you have any association with Me, or even know Me. And you won't only do it once; you will do it *three times.*" "Was not this warning enough to him not to trust in his own strength, but to depend on God?" (Clarke)

ii. It was an opportunity that Peter did not use. Instead he said, **"If I have to die with You, I will not deny You!"** Jesus knew Peter far better than Peter did, and in over-estimating himself, Peter was ready for a fall.

iii. The rest of the disciples also overestimated their strength and did not rely on the Lord in the critical hour: **And so said all the disciples**.

iv. "Apparently it was usual for roosters in Palestine to crow about 12:30, 1:30, and 2:30 A.M.; so the Romans gave the term 'cock-crow' to the watch from 12:00 to 3:00 A.M." (Carson)

C. Jesus prays and is arrested in the Garden of Gethsemane.

1. (36-39) Jesus' prayer in deep distress.

Then Jesus came with them to a place called Gethsemane, and said to the disciples, "Sit here while I go and pray over there." And He took with Him Peter and the two sons of Zebedee, and He began to be sorrowful and deeply distressed. Then He said to them, "My soul is exceedingly sorrowful, even to death. Stay here and watch with Me." He went a little farther and fell on His face, and prayed, saying, "O My Father, if it is possible, let this cup pass from Me; nevertheless, not as I will, but as You *will*."

a. **Then Jesus came with them to a place called Gethsemane**: This is just east of the temple mount area in Jerusalem, across the ravine of the Brook Kidron, and on the lower slopes of the Mount of Olives. Surrounded by ancient olive trees, **Gethsemane** means "olive press." There, olives from the neighborhood were crushed for their oil. So too, the Son of God would be crushed here.

i. "And again, he chose that garden, amongst others contiguous to Jerusalem, because Judas knew the place. He wanted retirement, but he did not want a place where he could skulk and hide himself. It was not for Christ to give himself up-that were like suicide; but it was not for him to withdraw and secrete himself-that were like cowardice." (Spurgeon)

b. **He began to be sorrowful and deeply distressed**: Jesus was disturbed; in part from knowing the physical horror waiting for Him at the cross. As He came to Gethsemane from central Jerusalem, He crossed the Brook Kidron, and saw in the full moon of Passover the stream flowing red with sacrificial blood from the temple.

i. "The words in the Greek are expressive of the greatest sorrow imaginable." (Poole)

c. **My soul is exceedingly sorrowful, even to death**: But more so, Jesus was distressed at the spiritual horror waiting for Him on the cross. Jesus would stand in the place of guilty sinners and receive all the spiritual punishment sinners deserve; He *who knew no sin* would *be sin for us* (2 Corinthians 5:21).

i. **Exceedingly sorrowful** "is a rather weak translation for a phrase which contains Matthew's favourite word for violent emotion, even shock (used in 17:6, 23; 18:31; 19:25; 27:54)." (France)

ii. Jesus did not die as a martyr. "Jesus went to his death knowing that it was his Father's will that he face death completely alone (Matthew 27:46) as the sacrificial, wrath-averting Passover Lamb. As his death was unique, so also his anguish; and our best response to it is hushed worship." (Carson)

iii. "Hence the Greek Litany, 'By thine unknown sufferings, good Lord, deliver us." (Trapp)

iv. Yet in this hour of special agony, God the Father sent special help to His Son. Luke 22:43 says that angels came and ministered to Jesus in the garden.

d. **If it is possible**: Of course, there is a sense in which all things are possible with God (Matthew 19:26). Yet this is true only in a sense, because there are things that are *morally* impossible for God. It is impossible for God to lie (Hebrews 6:18) and impossible to please Him without faith (Hebrews 11:6). It was not *morally possible* for God to atone for sin and redeem lost humanity apart from the perfect, wrath-satisfying sacrifice that Jesus prepared Himself for in Gethsemane.

e. **If it is possible, let this cup pass from Me**: God the Father would never deny the Son any request, because Jesus prayed according to the heart and will of the Father. Since Jesus drank the **cup** of judgment at the cross, we know that it is not **possible** for salvation to come any other way. Salvation by the work of Jesus at the cross is the only **possible** way; if there is any other way to be made right before God, then Jesus died an unnecessary death.

i. Repeatedly in the Old Testament, the **cup** is a powerful picture of the wrath and judgment of God.

• *For in the hand of the LORD there is a cup, and the wine is red; it is fully mixed, and He pours it out; surely its dregs shall all the wicked of the earth drain and drink down.* (Psalm 75:8)

- *Awake, awake! Stand up, O Jerusalem, you who have drunk at the hand of the LORD the cup of His fury; you have drunk the dregs of the cup of trembling, and drained it out.* (Isaiah 51:17)

- *For thus says the LORD God of Israel to me: "Take this wine cup of fury from My hand, and cause all the nations, to whom I send you, to drink it."* (Jeremiah 25:15)

ii. Jesus became, as it were, an enemy of God, who was judged and forced to drink the **cup** of the Father's fury, so we would not have to drink from that cup - *this* was the source of Jesus' agony.

iii. The **cup** didn't represent death, but judgment. Jesus was unafraid of death, and when He had finished His work on the cross – the work of receiving and bearing and satisfying the righteous judgment of God the Father upon our sin – when He finished that work, He simply yielded Himself to death as His choice.

f. **Nevertheless, not as I will, but as You will**: Jesus came to a point of decision in Gethsemane. It wasn't that He had not decided before nor had consented before, but now He had come upon a unique point of decision. He drank the cup at Calvary, but He *decided* once for all to drink it at Gethsemane.

i. "'Not your will but mine' changed Paradise to desert and brought man from Eden to Gethsemane. Now 'Not my will but yours' brings anguish to the man who prays it but transforms the desert into the kingdom and brings man from Gethsemane to the gates of glory." (Carson)

ii. This struggle at Gethsemane - the place of crushing - has an important place in fulfilling God's plan of redemption. If Jesus failed here, He would have failed at the cross. His success here made the victory at the cross possible.

iii. The struggle at the cross was first won in *prayer* in Gethsemane. Jesus **fell on His face, and prayed**.

2. (40-46) Jesus wins the battle of prayer.

Then He came to the disciples and found them asleep, and said to Peter, "What? Could you not watch with Me one hour? Watch and pray, lest you enter into temptation. The spirit indeed *is* willing, but the flesh *is* weak." Again, a second time, He went away and prayed, saying, "O My Father, if this cup cannot pass away from Me unless I drink it, Your will be done." And He came and found them asleep again, for their eyes were heavy. So He left them, went away again, and prayed the third time, saying the same words. Then He came to His disciples and said to

them, "Are *you* still sleeping and resting? Behold, the hour is at hand, and the Son of Man is being betrayed into the hands of sinners. "Rise, let us be going. See, My betrayer is at hand."

a. **Could you not watch with Me one hour?** Jesus valued and desired the help of His friends in this battle of prayer and decision. But even without their help, He endured in prayer until the battle was won.

i. "But they not only not help him, but wound him by their dullness unto duty, and instead of wiping off his bloody sweat, they draw more out of him." (Trapp)

b. **Watch and pray, lest you enter into temptation**: Jesus knew Peter would fail; yet He encouraged him to victory, knowing that the resources were found in *watching* and *praying*. If Peter woke up (both physically and spiritually), and drew close in dependence on God, he could have kept from denying Jesus at the critical hour.

i. "By watching, he directeth them to the use of such means as were within their power to use; by adding *pray*, he lets them know, that it was not in their power to stand without God's help and assistance, which must be obtained by prayer." (Poole)

ii. Jesus found victory at the cross by succeeding in the struggle in Gethsemane. Peter - just like us - failed in later **temptation** because he failed to **watch and pray**. The spiritual battle is often *won* or *lost* before the crisis comes.

iii. Speaking kindly about the disciples Jesus said, "**The spirit indeed is willing, but the flesh is weak**." "Their Master might find an excuse for their neglect; but oh! How they would blame themselves afterwards for missing that last opportunity of watching with their wrestling Lord!" (Spurgeon)

iv. **He went away and prayed**: "Fervent prayer loves privacy, and Christ by this teaches us that secret prayer is our duty." (Poole)

v. **He came and found them asleep again, for their eyes were heavy**: "That is, they could not keep them open. Was there nothing *preternatural* in this? Was there no influence here from the powers of darkness?" (Clarke)

c. **Prayed the third time, saying the same words**: This shows us that it is not unspiritual to make the same request to God several times. Some hyper-spiritual people believe that if we ask for something more than once, it proves that we don't have faith. That may be true for some in some situations, but Jesus shows us that repeated prayer can be completely consistent with steadfast faith.

d. **Rise, let us be going. See, My betrayer is at hand**: Jesus knew Judas and those who would arrest Him were on the way. He could have run and escaped the agony waiting for Him at the cross, but Jesus rose to meet Judas. He was in complete control of all events.

i. "*Let us be going* could suggest a desire to escape, but the verb implies rather going into action, advance rather than retreat." (France)

3. (47-50) Judas betrays Jesus in the Garden of Gethsemane.

And while He was still speaking, behold, Judas, one of the twelve, with a great multitude with swords and clubs, came from the chief priests and elders of the people. Now His betrayer had given them a sign, saying, "Whomever I kiss, He is the One; seize Him." Immediately he went up to Jesus and said, "Greetings, Rabbi!" and kissed Him. But Jesus said to him, "Friend, why have you come?" Then they came and laid hands on Jesus and took Him.

a. **With a great multitude with swords and clubs**: They clearly regarded Jesus as a dangerous man and came to take Him with great force.

i. **Behold, Judas**: "What he received payment for was probably information as to where Jesus could be arrested in a quiet setting with little danger of mob violence." (Carson) Perhaps he led the soldiers first to the upper room; when he found that Jesus and the disciples were not there, he could guess where they would be.

ii. "Judas knew where to find them. Jesus could easily have foiled his plan by choosing a different place for this night, but…this was not his intention." (France)

iii. "Those skilled in the Jewish learning tell us, that the ordinary guard of the temple belonged to the priests, and such officers as their employed; but upon their great festivals, the Roman governors added a band of soliders, who yet were under the command of the priests." (Poole)

b. **Greetings, Rabbi!** Judas warmly greeted Jesus, even giving Him the customary **kiss**. But the **kiss** only precisely identified Jesus to the authorities who came to arrest Jesus. There are no more hollow, hypocritical words in the Bible than "**Greetings, Rabbi!**" in the mouth of Judas. The loving, heartfelt words of Jesus - calling Judas "**Friend**" - stand in sharp contrast.

i. **And kissed Him**: "Kissed Him heartily…What a tremendous contrast between the woman in Simon's house (Luke 8) and Judas! Both kissed Jesus fervently: with strong emotion; yet the one could have died for Him, the other betrays Him to death." (Bruce)

ii. "This *sign* of Judas was typical of the way in which Jesus is generally *betrayed*. When men intend to undermine the inspiration of the Scriptures, how do they begin their books? Why, always with a declaration that they wish to promote the truth of Christ! Christ's name is often slandered by those who make a loud profession of attachment to him, and then sin foully as the chief of transgressors." (Spurgeon)

c. **Then they came and laid hands on Jesus and took Him**: This happened only *after* they had all fallen to the ground when Jesus announced Himself as the "*I am*" (John 18:6).

i. "It is strange that, after this, they should dare to approach him; but the Scriptures must be fulfilled." (Clarke)

4. (51-56) The arrest of Jesus in Gethsemane.

And suddenly, one of those *who were* with Jesus stretched out *his* hand and drew his sword, struck the servant of the high priest, and cut off his ear. But Jesus said to him, "Put your sword in its place, for all who take the sword will perish by the sword. Or do you think that I cannot now pray to My Father, and He will provide Me with more than twelve legions of angels? How then could the Scriptures be fulfilled, that it must happen thus?" In that hour Jesus said to the multitudes, "Have you come out, as against a robber, with swords and clubs to take Me? I sat daily with you, teaching in the temple, and you did not seize Me. But all this was done that the Scriptures of the prophets might be fulfilled." Then all the disciples forsook Him and fled.

a. **One of those who were with Jesus stretched out his hand and drew his sword, struck the servant of the high priest, and cut off his ear**: Matthew doesn't tell us, but we know from John 18:10 that this unnamed swordsman was Peter.

i. "A wonderful work of God it was surely, that hereupon he was not hewn in an hundred pieces by the barbarous soldiers." (Trapp)

ii. "It would have been far better if Peter's hands had been clasped in prayer." (Spurgeon)

iii. "But how came Peter to have a sword? Judea was at this time so infested with robbers and cut-throats that it was not deemed safe for any person to go unarmed. He probably carried one for his mere personal safety." (Clarke)

b. **He will provide Me with more than twelve legions of angels**: Had Jesus wanted Divine help at this moment, He could have had it. There were **more than twelve legions of angels** ready to come to His aid.

i. "A legion is judged to be six thousand foot and seven hundred horse. And this great army of angels is by prayer despatched from heaven in an instant." (Trapp) The number is impressive, especially considering that one angel killed up to 185,000 soldiers in one night (2 Kings 19:35).

ii. With one sword, Peter was willing to take on a small army of men, yet he couldn't pray with Jesus for one hour. Prayer is the best work we can do, and often the most difficult.

iii. With his sword, Peter accomplished very little. He only cut off one ear, and really just made a mess that Jesus had to clean up by healing the severed ear (Luke 22:51). When Peter moved in the power of the world, he only cut off ears. But when he was filled with the Spirit, using the Word of God, Peter pierced hearts for God's glory (Acts 2:37).

iv. "Our Lord had thus the means of self-defense; something far more powerful than a sword hung at his girdle; but he refused to employ the power within his reach. His servants could not bear this test; they had no self-restraint, the hand of Peter is on his sword at once. The failure of the Servants in this matter seems to me to illustrate the grand self-possession of their Master." (Spurgeon)

v. At the moment when it seemed that Jesus had nothing and no advantage, He knew that He still had a Father in heaven, and access to His Father and all His resources through prayer.

c. **All this was done that the Scriptures of the prophets might be fulfilled**: With all power at His disposal, Jesus was in total command. He was not the victim of circumstance, but He managed circumstances for the fulfillment of prophecy.

d. **Then all the disciples forsook Him and fled**: At this point, all the disciples scattered, running for their own safety. A few (Peter and John, at least) followed back to see what would happen at a distance. None of them stood beside Jesus and said, "I have given my life to this Man. What you accuse Him of, you may accuse me of also." Instead, it was fulfilled what Jesus said: *All of you will be made to stumble because of Me* (Matthew 26:31).

i. "We never know our hears upon the prospect of great trials, until we come to grapple with them, and to be engaged in them. These disciples had all said they would not forsake him; when it comes to the push, not one of them stands by him." (Poole)

D. The trial before the Sanhedrin.

1. (57-61) Jesus is taken to the home of Caiaphas.

And those who had laid hold of Jesus led *Him* away to Caiaphas the high priest, where the scribes and the elders were assembled. But Peter followed Him at a distance to the high priest's courtyard. And he went in and sat with the servants to see the end.

a. **And those who had laid hold of Jesus led Him away to Caiaphas the high priest**: This was not the first appearance of Jesus before a judge or official on the night of His betrayal. On that night and the day of His crucifixion, Jesus actually stood in trial several times before different judges.

i. Before Jesus came to the home of **Caiaphas** (the official high priest), He was led to the home of Annas, who was the ex-high priest and the "power behind the throne" of the high priest (according to John 18:12-14 and John 18:19-23).

b. **Where the scribes and the elders were assembled**: Caiaphas had gathered a group of the Sanhedrin to pass judgment on Jesus.

i. After the break of dawn, the Sanhedrin gathered again, this time in official session, and they conducted the trial described in Luke 22:66-71.

c. **Peter followed Him at a distance...to see the end**: Peter was determined to prove wrong Jesus' prediction that He would deny and forsake Him at His death.

2. (59-61) The first trial before the Sanhedrin.

Now the chief priests, the elders, and all the council sought false testimony against Jesus to put Him to death, but found none. Even though many false witnesses came forward, they found none. But at last two false witnesses came forward and said, "This *fellow* said, 'I am able to destroy the temple of God and to build it in three days.'"

a. **Now the chief priests, the elders, and all the council**: This nighttime trial was illegal according to the Sanhedrin's own laws and regulations. According to Jewish law, all criminal trials must begin and end in the daylight. Therefore, though the decision to condemn Jesus was already made, they conducted a second trial in daylight (Luke 22:66-71), because they knew the first one - the *real* trial - had no legal standing.

i. This was only one of many illegalities made in the trial of Jesus. According to Jewish law, only decisions made in the official meeting place were valid. The first trial was held at the home of Caiaphas, the high priest.

• According to Jewish law, criminal cases could not be tried during the Passover season.

- According to Jewish law, only an acquittal could be issued on the day of the trial. Guilty verdicts had to wait one night to allow for feelings of mercy to rise.

- According to Jewish law, all evidence had to be guaranteed by two witnesses, who were separately examined and could not have contact with each other.

- According to Jewish law, false witness was punishable by death. Nothing was done to the **many false witnesses** in Jesus' trial.

- According to Jewish law, a trial always began by bringing forth evidence for the innocence of the accused, before the evidence of guilt was offered. This was not the practice here.

ii. "These were the Sanhedrin's own rules, and it is abundantly clear that, in their eagerness to get rid of Jesus, they broke their own rules." (Barclay)

iii. "Neither in the annals of the historian nor in the realm of fiction is there anything that can equal the degradation of the unholy trial, the base devices to find a charge to prefer against the Prisoner, the illegal tricks to secure a verdict of guilty which would ensure a death penalty." (Morgan)

b. **The council sought false testimony against Jesus to put Him to death, but found none**: This is a remarkable testimony to the life and integrity of Jesus. For having lived such a public life and performed such a public ministry, it was difficult to find even **false testimony** against Him.

c. **This fellow said, "I am able to destroy the temple of God and to build it in three days"**: After all the false witnesses had their say, Jesus was finally charged with threatening to destroy the temple (as in a modern-day bomb threat). Clearly, Jesus said "*Destroy this temple, and in three days I will raise it up*" (John 2:19). But this glorious prophecy of His resurrection was twisted into a terrorist threat. John 2:21 makes it clear that *He was speaking of the temple of His body*.

3. (62-64) Jesus testifies at His trial.

And the high priest arose and said to Him, "Do You answer nothing? What *is it* these men testify against You?" But Jesus kept silent. And the high priest answered and said to Him, "I put You under oath by the living God: Tell us if You are the Christ, the Son of God!" Jesus said to him, "*It is as* you said. Nevertheless, I say to you, hereafter you will see the Son of Man sitting at the right hand of the Power, and coming on the clouds of heaven."

a. **Do You answer nothing?** Jesus sat silently until He was commanded by the office of the high priest to answer the accusations against Him.

i. "The high priest expected a long defence, and so to have had matter of accusation against him out of his own mouth." (Poole)

ii. Remarkably, Jesus **kept silent and answered nothing** until it was absolutely necessary in obedience for Him to speak. Jesus *could* have mounted a magnificent defense here, calling forth all the various witnesses to His deity, power and character. The people He taught, the people He healed, the dead risen, the blind who see, even the demons themselves testified to His deity. But Jesus *opened not His mouth; He was led as a lamb to the slaughter, and as a sheep before its shearers is silent, so He opened not His mouth* (Isaiah 53:7).

iii. "His was the silence of patience, not of indifference; of courage, not of cowardice." (Spurgeon)

b. **And the high priest answered and said to Him, "I put You under oath by the living God: Tell us if You are the Christ, the Son of God!"** Seeing the trial going badly, Caiaphas confronted Jesus, acting more as an accuser than an impartial judge.

i. "*I adjure you* is a rare and formal expression (*cf.* 1 Kings 22:16 for a similar Old Testament formula), invoking the name of God in order to compel a true answer. This is therefore the climax of the hearing." (France)

ii. "The high priest, frustrated by Jesus' silence, tried a bold stroke that cut to the central issue: Was Jesus the Messiah or was he not?" (Carson)

iii. "It was a tacit confession that Christ had been proved innocent up till then. The high priest would not have needed to draw something out of the accused one if there had been sufficient material against him elsewhere. The trial had been a dead failure up to that point, and he knew it, and was red with rage. Now he attempts to bully the prisoner that he may extract some declaration from him which may save all further trouble of witnesses, and end the matter." (Spurgeon)

c. **It is as you said**: Instead of defending Himself, Jesus simply testified to the truth. He was indeed **the Christ, the Son of God**. He answered as briefly and directly as possible.

i. The high priest probably asked the question with sarcasm or irony. "The wording of Caiaphas' question (especially in Mark) probably suggests that it did not even sound like a dispassionate enquiry: 'Are *you* the Messiah?' (you, the abandoned, helpless, prisoner!)." (France)

d. **You will see the Son of Man sitting at the right hand of the Power**: Jesus added this one word of warning. He warned them that though they sat in judgment of Him now, He would one day sit in judgment of them - and with a far more binding judgment.

> i. **Hereafter**: "'Hereafter!' 'Hereafter!' Oh, when that hereafter comes, how overwhelming it will be to Jesus' foes! Now where is Caiaphas? Will he now adjure the Lord to speak? Now, ye priests, lift up your haughty heads! Utter a sentence against him now! There sits, your victim upon the clouds of heaven. Say now that he blasphemes, and hold up your rent rags, and condemn him again. But where is Caiaphas? He hides his guilty head he is utterly confounded, and begs the mountains to fall upon him." (Spurgeon)

> ii. **Of the Power**: "*Power* is a typically Jewish reverential expression to avoid pronouncing the sacred name of God (which might have laid Jesus open to the charge of blasphemy, though ironically it was precisely that charge on which he was condemned, Matthew 26:65!)." (France)

4. (65-68) The Sanhedrin react with horror and brutality.

Then the high priest tore his clothes, saying, "He has spoken blasphemy! What further need do we have of witnesses? Look, now you have heard His blasphemy! What do you think?" They answered and said, "He is deserving of death." Then they spat in His face and beat Him; and others struck *Him* with the palms of their hands, saying, "Prophesy to us, Christ! Who is the one who struck You?"

a. **He has spoken blasphemy!** The accusation of **blasphemy** would have been correct, except that Jesus *was* whom He said He was. It is no crime for the Christ, the Son of God, to declare who He really is.

b. **He is deserving of death**: Their verdict reveals the depths of man's depravity. God, in total perfection, came to earth, lived among men, and this was man's reply to God.

c. **They spat in His face and beat Him**: They spit on Him; they hit Him with their fists; they slapped Him with their open hands. It is easy to think that they did this because they didn't know who He was. That is true in one sense, because they would not admit to themselves that He was indeed the Messiah and the Son of God. Yet in another sense it is not true at all, because by nature man is an enemy of God (Romans 5:10, Colossians 1:21). For a long time man waited to *literally* hit, slap, and spit in God's face.

i. "Be astonished, O heavens, and be horribly afraid. His face is the light of the universe, his person is the glory of heaven, and they 'began to spit on him.' Alas, my God, that man should be so base!" (Spurgeon)

ii. Spurgeon suggested some ways that men still spit in the face of Jesus.

- Men spit in His face by denying His deity.
- Men spit in His face by rejecting His gospel.
- Men spit in His face by preferring their own righteousness.
- Men spit in His face by turning away from Jesus.

iii. As these religious leaders vented their hatred, fear, and anger upon Jesus, spitting in His face and beating Him, it was remarkable that the immediate judgment of God did not rain down from heaven. It was remarkable that a legion of angels did not spring to the defense of Jesus. This shows the amazing forbearance towards sin that God has, and the staggering riches of His mercy.

iv. "As one reads this story one wonders more and more at the greatest miracle of all, the patient suffering of the spotless One." (Morgan)

5. (69-75) Fearing association with Jesus, Peter denies his relationship with Jesus three times.

Now Peter sat outside in the courtyard. And a servant girl came to him, saying, "You also were with Jesus of Galilee." But he denied it before *them* all, saying, "I do not know what you are saying." And when he had gone out to the gateway, another *girl* saw him and said to those *who were* there, "This *fellow* also was with Jesus of Nazareth." But again he denied with an oath, "I do not know the Man!" And a little later those who stood by came up and said to Peter, "Surely you also are *one* of them, for your speech betrays you." Then he began to curse and swear, *saying,* "I do not know the Man!" Immediately a rooster crowed. And Peter remembered the word of Jesus who had said to him, "Before the rooster crows, you will deny Me three times." So he went out and wept bitterly.

a. **A servant girl came to him**: Peter was not questioned before a hostile court or even an angry mob. Peter's own fear made **a servant girl** and **another girl** hostile monsters in his eyes, and he bowed in fear before them.

b. **I do not know the Man!** Peter's sin of denying his association with Jesus grew worse with each denial. First, he merely lied; then he took an **oath** to the lie; then **he began to curse and swear**.

i. **Those who stood by**: "Loungers; seeing Peter's confusion, and amusing themselves by tormenting him." (Bruce)

ii. "The Galileans spoke with a burr; so ugly was their accent that no Galilean was allowed to pronounce the benediction at a synagogue service." (Barclay)

iii. And, as if it would help distance himself from association with Jesus, Peter **began to curse and swear**. "To call down curses on himself, sign of irritation and desperation; has lost self-control completely." (Bruce) When we hear that kind of language, we normally assume the person is not a follower of Jesus.

c. **Peter remembered the word of Jesus…so he went out and wept bitterly**: Peter finally remembered and took to heart what Jesus said, but in this case he did so too late. For now, all he could do was to weep **bitterly**. Yet Peter would be restored, showing a significant contrast between Judas (showing *apostasy*) and Peter (showing *backsliding*).

i. Apostasy is giving up the truth, as Judas did. Judas was sorry about his sin, but it was not a sorrow leading to repentance.

ii. Backsliding is a decline from a spiritual experience once enjoyed. Peter slipped, but he will not fall; his bitter weeping will lead to repentance and restoration.

d. **And wept bitterly**: This was the beginning of Peter's repentance. Several things brought him to this place.

i. The loving look of Jesus brought Peter to repentance. Luke tells us that just after the rooster crowed, *the Lord turned and looked at Peter* (Luke 22:61).

ii. The gift of remembering brought Peter to repentance; **Peter remembered the words of Jesus**. "Our memories serve us much in the business of repentance." (Poole)

Matthew 27 - Jesus' Trial, Death, and Burial

A. The death of Judas.

1. (1-2) Jesus is handed over to Pilate.

When morning came, all the chief priests and elders of the people plotted against Jesus to put Him to death. And when they had bound Him, they led Him away and delivered Him to Pontius Pilate the governor.

a. **All the chief priests and elders of the people plotted against Jesus to put Him to death**: This was the official gathering of the Sanhedrin following the informal (and illegal) night session, also described in Luke 22:66-71. As Luke shows, this **morning** trial was essentially the same as the previous, informal examination.

i. "But as it was contrary to all forms of law to proceed against a person's life by *night*, they seem to have separated for a few hours, and then, at the break of day, came together again, pretending to conduct the business according to the forms of law." (Clarke)

b. **They led Him away and delivered Him to Pontius Pilate**: The Sanhedrin gave Jesus over to **Pontius Pilate**, the Roman appointed governor over Judea, because they did not have the authority to put Him to death.

i. "Pilate was in fact appointed prefect or procurator by Tiberius Caesar in A.D. 26. Prefects governed small, troubled areas; and in judicial matters they possessed powers like those of the far more powerful proconsuls and imperial legates; in short, they held the power of life and death." (Carson)

ii. "The ordinary residence of procurators was Caesarea, on the sea coast, but it was their custom to be in Jerusalem at Passover time, with a detachment of soldiers, to watch over the public peace." (Bruce)

iii. Philo, the ancient Jewish scholar from Alexandria, described Pilate: "His corruption, his acts of insolence, his rapine, his habit of insulting people, his cruelty, his continual murders of people untried and uncondemned, and his never-ending gratuitous and most grievous inhumanity." (Barclay)

iv. The Jewish leaders had reason to expect a favorable result when they went to Pilate. Secular history shows us that he was a cruel, ruthless man, almost completely insensitive to the moral feelings of others. Surely, they thought, **Pilate** will put this Jesus to death.

v. Pilate would not be interested in the charge of blasphemy against Jesus, regarding that as a religious matter of no concern to Rome. So **all the chief priests and elders** essentially brought Jesus to Pilate with three false accusations: that Jesus was a revolutionary; that He incited the people to not pay their taxes; and that He claimed to be a king in opposition to Caesar (Luke 23:2).

2. (3-10) Judas' miserable end.

Then Judas, His betrayer, seeing that He had been condemned, was remorseful and brought back the thirty pieces of silver to the chief priests and elders, saying, "I have sinned by betraying innocent blood." And they said, "What *is that* to us? You see *to it!*" Then he threw down the pieces of silver in the temple and departed, and went and hanged himself. But the chief priests took the silver pieces and said, "It is not lawful to put them into the treasury, because they are the price of blood." And they consulted together and bought with them the potter's field, to bury strangers in. Therefore that field has been called the Field of Blood to this day. Then was fulfilled what was spoken by Jeremiah the prophet, saying, "And they took the thirty pieces of silver, the value of Him who was priced, whom they of the children of Israel priced, and gave them for the potter's field, as the LORD directed me."

a. **Was remorseful and brought back the thirty pieces of silver**: Judas was filled with *remorse*, not repentance. Even though he knew exactly what he did (**I have sinned by betraying innocent blood**), Judas was more sorry for the result of his sin than for the sin itself. There is a huge difference in being sorry *about* sin, and being sorry *for* sin.

i. By throwing the money into the **temple** (the "*naos*, properly the inner sanctuary, where only the priests were allowed to go" according to France), Judas wanted to implicate the priests in his crime. It was his way of saying, "You also are guilty of this."

ii. "The act of a desperate man, determined that they should get the money, and perhaps hoping it might be a kind of atonement for his sin." (Bruce)

iii. All this happened **seeing that He had been condemned**. "Perhaps *Judas* expected that Jesus would miraculously deliver himself from his captors; and *when he saw that he was condemned*, remorse seized him, and he carried back to his fellow criminals the reward of his infamy." (Spurgeon)

iv. **Innocent blood**: "Judas had been with our Lord in public and in private; and if he could have found a flaw in Christ's character, this would have been the time to mention it; but even the traitor, in his dying speech, declared that Jesus was 'innocent.'" (Spurgeon)

b. **It is not lawful to put them into the treasury, because they are the price of blood**: The hypocrisy of the chief priests was transparent. They didn't want to defile themselves with **the price of blood**, even though it was a price that they themselves paid.

i. The religious leaders treated their servant Judas badly. "Tempters never make good comforters. Those who are the devil's instruments, to command, entice, or allure men to sin, will afford them no relief when they have come to be troubled for what they have done." (Poole)

ii. "God, Deuteronomy 23:18, had forbidden to bring the price of a whore, or a dog, into the temple; this they had interpreted of all filthy gain." (Poole)

iii. "The *treasury*, perhaps the source from which the money had been paid to Judas, would be the natural place to deposit money left in the temple, but its use as *blood money* made it unclean. A burial ground (itself an unclean place) would be a suitable use for it." (France)

c. **Went and hanged himself**: In his unrepentant remorse and despair, Judas committed suicide. Being *the son of perdition* (John 17:12), we are assured he went to eternal punishment.

i. Some hold that Matthew's account of Judas' death is at variance with Acts 1:18-19, which says that Judas fell headlong into a field, burst open in the middle, and all his entrails gushed out. Most reconcile this by suggesting that Judas hanged himself, and then his body was cast down on the ground, bursting open.

ii. "If Judas hanged himself, no Jew would want to defile himself during the Feast of Unleavened Bread by burying the corpse; and a hot sun might have brought on rapid decomposition till the body fell to the ground and burst open." (Carson)

d. Then was fulfilled what was spoken by Jeremiah the prophet: There has been much question about the quotation attributed to **Jeremiah**, because it is found in Zechariah 11:12-13. Matthew says the word **was spoken by Jeremiah the prophet**, though we find it recorded in Zechariah.

i. Some think it could be a copyist error. Perhaps Matthew wrote *Zechariah*, but an early copyist mistakenly put **Jeremiah** instead, and this rare mistake was repeated in subsequent copies.

ii. Some think that **Jeremiah** spoke this prophecy and Zechariah recorded it - the word **spoken by Jeremiah**, but *recorded* by Zechariah.

iii. Some think that Matthew refers to *scroll* of **Jeremiah**, which included the book of Zechariah.

B. Jesus before Pilate.

1. (11-14) Jesus greatly impresses Pilate.

Now Jesus stood before the governor. And the governor asked Him, saying, "Are You the King of the Jews?" So Jesus said to him, *"It is as* you say." And while He was being accused by the chief priests and elders, He answered nothing. Then Pilate said to Him, "Do You not hear how many things they testify against You?" But He answered him not one word, so that the governor marveled greatly.

a. **Now Jesus stood before the governor**: History shows us Pontius Pilate was a cruel and ruthless man, unkind to the Jews and contemptuous of almost everything but raw power. Here, he seems out of character in the way he treated Jesus. Jesus seems to have profoundly affected him.

i. Matthew condenses the full account, telling us only of the *second* appearance of Jesus before Pilate. The first appearance before Pilate is described in Luke 23:1-6. Hoping to avoid making a judgment about Jesus, Pilate sent Him to Herod, the sub-ruler of Galilee (Luke 23:6-12). Jesus refused to say *anything* to Herod, so He returned to Pilate as here described in Matthew.

b. **Are You the King of the Jews?** When they brought Him to Pilate, the Jewish leaders accused Jesus of promoting Himself as a king in defiance of Caesar (Luke 23:2). They wanted to make Jesus seem like a dangerous revolutionary against the Roman Empire. Therefore, Pilate asked Jesus this simple question.

i. "The question reveals the form in which the Sanhedrists presented their accusation." (Bruce)

ii. Of course, we can only wonder what Pilate thought when he first set eyes on Jesus, when he saw this beaten and bloodied Man before him. Jesus didn't look especially regal or majestic as He stood before Pilate, so the Roman **governor** was probably sarcastic or ironic when he asked, **"Are You the King of the Jews?"**

iii. "Pilate was evidently not alarmed by the charge brought against Jesus. Why? Apparently at first glance he saw that the man before him was not likely to be a pretender to royalty in any sense that he need trouble himself about…The [you] in an emphatic position in verse 11 suggests this = *You* the King of the Jews!" (Bruce)

c. **It is as you say**: No majestic defense, no instant miracle to save His own life. Instead, Jesus gave Pilate the same simple reply He gave to the high priest (Matthew 26:64). This amazed Pilate; he asked, **"Do You not hear how many things they testify against You?"** Pilate couldn't believe that such a strong, dignified man - as beaten and bloody as He was - would stand silent at these accusations. **The governor marveled greatly**.

i. There is a time to defend one's cause or one's self, but those times are rare. When we rise to our own defense, we would usually be better off to keep silent and to trust God to defend us.

ii. Spurgeon explained why Pilate **marveled greatly**: "He had seen in captured Jews the fierce courage of fanaticism; but there was no fanaticism in Christ. He had also seen in many prisoners the meanness which will do or say anything to escape from death; but he saw nothing of that about our Lord. He saw in him unusual gentleness and humility combined with majestic dignity. He beheld submission blended with innocence." (Spurgeon)

2. (15-18) Pilate hopes to release Jesus.

Now at the feast the governor was accustomed to releasing to the multitude one prisoner whom they wished. And at that time they had a notorious prisoner called Barabbas. Therefore, when they had gathered together, Pilate said to them, "Whom do you want me to release to you? Barabbas, or Jesus who is called Christ?" For he knew that they had handed Him over because of envy.

a. **At the feast the governor was accustomed to releasing to the multitude one prisoner whom they wished**: Judging there was something different – and innocent – about Jesus, Pilate hoped this custom of **releasing** a prisoner might help solve the problem.

b. **A notorious prisoner called Barabbas**: Mark 15:7 tells us what made Barabbas **notorious**. He was one of several *insurrectionists*, who had *committed murder in the insurrection*. We would today regard a man like Barabbas as something like a revolutionary terrorist.

c. **For he knew that they had handed Him over because of envy**: Pilate saw through the manipulative words of the religious leaders. He knew their motive was **envy**, not any other concern.

i. **Because of envy**: "Let it be remembered that *malice* as often originates from *envy* as it does from *anger*." (Clarke)

3. (19-20) Pilate influenced by both his wife and the religious leaders.

While he was sitting on the judgment seat, his wife sent to him, saying, "Have nothing to do with that just Man, for I have suffered many things today in a dream because of Him." But the chief priests and elders persuaded the multitudes that they should ask for Barabbas and destroy Jesus.

a. **While he was sitting on the judgment seat**: As Pilate sat in judgment of Jesus, he failed to give the accused justice. Pilate had all the evidence he needed to do the right thing – to release Jesus.

- He saw the strength and dignity of Jesus, and he knew this was no criminal or revolutionary.

- He knew that it was no just charge that brought Jesus before his judgment seat - it was only the **envy** of the religious leaders.

- He saw that Jesus was a man so at peace with His God that He didn't need to answer a single accusation.

- He already declared Jesus an innocent man (*I find no fault in this Man*, Luke 23:4).

b. **His wife sent to him, saying**: In addition to all of these, Pilate also had a unique and remarkable messenger – his wife's dream. We can only conjecture what she saw in this **dream**. Perhaps she saw Jesus, an innocent man, crowned with thorns and crucified. Maybe she saw Him coming in glory with the clouds of heaven. Maybe she saw Him at the Great White Throne of judgment, and she and her husband facing Jesus.

i. We know that the vision of Jesus in her dream made her *suffer* (**I have suffered many things today in a dream because of Him**). "Whatever it was, she had suffered repeated painful emotions in the dream, and she awoke startled and amazed." (Spurgeon)

ii. It was a remarkable occurrence. She awoke late in the morning, disturbed by the dream. She asked where her husband was, and her attendants told her that he was called away early to his business as a governor – the religious leaders of Jerusalem sent over a prisoner for judgment. Immediately, she asked a messenger to go to her husband with news of her dream.

iii. "Most dreams we quite forget; a few we mention as remarkable, and only now and then one is impressed upon us so that we remember it for years. Scarcely have any of you had a dream which made you send a message to a magistrate upon the bench." (Spurgeon)

iv. Because of all this, there was a great urgency about her message to Pilate. She was bold to send it, and she implored him to simply having nothing to do with this man Jesus. "Let Him go. Send Him away. Don't punish Him even a little." It was an influence, a warning that he tragically ignored. All of this was God's merciful message to Pilate; a merciful message that he rejected.

c. **But the chief priests and elders persuaded the multitudes that they should ask for Barabbas and destroy Jesus**: The religious leaders knew the best way to influence Pilate. Not through his own judgment of Jesus, not through his wife, and not through the religious leaders themselves directly. The best way to push Pilate in a certain direction was by the voice of the **multitudes**.

i. Here is a man who knows the right thing to do – and knows it by many convincing ways. Yet he will do the *wrong* thing, a *terrible* thing, in obedience to the **multitudes**.

ii. "But this it appears they did at the instigation of the chief priests. We see here how dangerous wicked priests are in the Church of Christ; when pastors are corrupt, they are capable of inducing their flock to prefer *Barabbas* to *Jesus*, the *world* to *God*, and the *pleasures of sense* to the *salvation of their souls*." (Clarke)

4. (21-23) The crowd demands release for Barabbas and crucifixion for Jesus.

The governor answered and said to them, "Which of the two do you want me to release to you?" They said, "Barabbas!" Pilate said to them, "What then shall I do with Jesus who is called Christ?" *They* all said to him, "Let Him be crucified!" Then the governor said, "Why, what evil has He done?" But they cried out all the more, saying, "Let Him be crucified!"

a. **"Which of the two do you want me to release to you?" They said, "Barabbas!"** The voice of the crowd is not *always* the voice of God. The mob did not answer Pilate's request for evidence or proof when he asked, **"What evil has He done?"** They only continued to shout for Jesus' death. They called for more than His death - they called for Him to be executed by torture through crucifixion (**"Let Him be crucified!"**).

i. "The call *Let him be crucified* is remarkable on the lips of a Jewish crowd, for crucifixion was a Roman punishment, abhorrent to most Jews." (France)

ii. **They all said to him**: "There were none in the crowd silently sympathizing with the Saviour; they *all* said, 'Let him be crucified.'" (Spurgeon)

iii. When the crowd chose Barabbas instead of Jesus, it reflected the fallen nature of all humanity. The name "Barabbas" sounds very much like *son of the father*. They chose a false, violent *son of the father* instead of the true Son of the Father. This prefigures the future embrace of the ultimate Barabbas - the one popularly called the Antichrist.

iv. "I impeach humanity again of the utmost possible folly; because, in crucifying Christ, it crucified its best friend. Jesus Christ was not only the friend of man, so as to take human nature upon himself, but he was the friend of sinners, so that he came into the world to seek and to save that which was lost." (Spurgeon)

v. People today still reject Jesus and choose another. Their Barabbas might be lust, it might be intoxication, it might be self and the comforts of life. "This mad choice is every day made, while men prefer the lusts of their flesh before the lives of their souls." (Trapp)

b. **They said, "Barabbas!"** If anyone knew what it meant that Jesus died in his place, it was **Barabbas**. He was a terrorist and a murderer, yet he was set free while Jesus was crucified. The cross Jesus hung on was probably originally intended for Barabbas.

i. We can imagine Barabbas, in a dark prison cell with a small window, waiting to be crucified. Through the window he could hear the crowd gathered before Pilate, not far away from the Fortress Antonia where he was imprisoned. Perhaps he could not hear Pilate ask, "**Which of the two do you want me to release to you?**" But surely he heard the crowd shout back, "**Barabbas.**" He probably could not hear Pilate's one voice ask, "**What then shall I do with Jesus who is called Christ?**" But he certainly heard the crowd roar in response, "**Let Him be crucified.**" If all Barabbas heard from his cell was his name shouted by the mob, then the "**Let Him be crucified**," when the soldiers came to his cell, he surely thought it was time for him to die a tortured death. But when the soldiers said, "Barabbas, you are a guilty man - but you will be released because Jesus will die in your place," Barabbas knew the meaning of the cross better than most. We wonder if he ever took it to heart.

5. (24-25) Pilate tries to avoid responsibility for Jesus' fate.

When Pilate saw that he could not prevail at all, but rather *that* a tumult was rising, he took water and washed *his* hands before the multitude,

saying, **"I am innocent of the blood of this just Person. You see *to it*."** **And all the people answered and said, "His blood *be* on us and on our children."**

a. **When Pilate saw that he could not prevail at all**: It was out of character for Pilate to bend this way to the religious leaders and the crowd. He *could have* chosen differently.

b. **He took water and washed his hands before the multitude**: Pilate washed his hands saying, "It's out of my control. Personally I wish this Jesus no harm, but these things happen." Yet *the power and responsibility of what to do with Jesus rested with him*. Saying "I find no fault in Him" was not enough. Looking for a clever solution in releasing a prisoner at Passover was no solution. Washing his hands was meaningless. Therefore he could not escape responsibility, and is forever associated with the crime of sending Jesus to the cross, echoed through history in the creeds (*crucified under Pontius Pilate*).

i. "Oh, the daring of Pilate thus in the sight of God to commit murder and disclaim it. There is a strange mingling of cowardliness and courage about many men; they are afraid of a man, but not afraid of the eternal God who can destroy both body and soul in hell." (Spurgeon)

c. **I am innocent of the blood of this just Person**: Hidden in Pilate's attempt at self-justification is a declaration of Jesus' innocence. When he called Jesus "**this just Person**," he admitted that Jesus was the innocent man - not Pilate. Just because Pilate *said* "**I am innocent**" doesn't mean that he was **innocent**.

i. Strangely, in later periods of Christian anti-Semitism, some Christians tried to rehabilitate Pilate, wanting to put all the blame on the Jews. Some even said that Pilate and his wife became Christians, and "to this day the Coptic Church ranks both Pilate and his wife as saints." (Barclay)

d. **His blood be on us and on our children**: They really had no understanding of what they asked for. They didn't understand the glory of Jesus' cleansing blood, and how wonderful it would be to have **His blood...on us and on our children**. They also didn't understand the enormity of the crime of calling for the execution of the sinless Son of God, and the judgment that would be visited on their children some forty years later in the destruction of Jerusalem.

i. This is one of the passages wrongly used as a justification by wicked and misguided Christians who persecuted or allowed persecution of the Jews. They did not understand that even if this *did* put these people and their descendants under a curse, it was *never* the duty of the church to bring this curse to bear upon the Jews. Indeed, as God promised Abraham, *I will bless those who bless you, and I will curse him who curses you* (Genesis 12:3). Those Christians wicked and foolish enough to curse the Jews have indeed been cursed by God in one way or another.

C. The suffering of Jesus Christ.

1. (26) Scourging: a customary prelude to crucifixion.

Then he released Barabbas to them; and when he had scourged Jesus, he delivered *Him* to be crucified.

a. **When he had scourged Jesus**: The blows came from a whip with many leather strands, each having sharp pieces of bone or metal at the ends. It reduced the back to raw flesh, and it was not unusual for a criminal to die from a scourging, even before crucifixion.

i. "Scourging was a legal preliminary to every Roman execution, and only women and Roman senators or soldiers (except in cases of desertion) were exempt." (Dr. William Edwards in the article "On the Physical Death of Jesus Christ" from the *Journal of the American Medical Association*, 3/21/86)

ii. The goal of the scourging was to weaken the victim to a state just short of collapse and death. "As the Roman soldiers repeatedly struck the victim's back with full force, the iron balls would cause deep contusions, and the leather thongs and sheep bones would cut into the skin and subcutaneous tissues. Then, as the flogging continued, the lacerations would tear into the underlying skeletal muscles and produce quivering ribbons of bleeding flesh. Pain and blood loss generally set the stage for circulatory shock. The extent of blood loss may well have determined how long the victim would survive the cross." (Edwards)

iii. "The severe scourging, with its intense pain and appreciable blood loss, most probably left Jesus in a pre-shock state. Moreover, hematidrosis had rendered his skin particularly tender. The physical and mental abuse meted out by the Jews and the Romans, as well as the lack of food, water, and sleep, also contributed to his generally weakened state. Therefore, even before the actual crucifixion, Jesus' physical condition was at least serious and possibly critical." (Edwards)

b. **When he had scourged Jesus**: Commonly the blows of scourging would lessen as the criminal confessed to his crimes. Jesus remained silent, having no crimes to confess, so the blows continued with full strength.

2. (27-31) Jesus is beaten and mocked.

Then the soldiers of the governor took Jesus into the Praetorium and gathered the whole garrison around Him. And they stripped Him and put a scarlet robe on Him. When they had twisted a crown of thorns, they put *it* on His head, and a reed in His right hand. And they bowed the knee before Him and mocked Him, saying, "Hail, King of the Jews!" Then they spat on Him, and took the reed and struck Him on the head. And when they had mocked Him, they took the robe off Him, put His *own* clothes on Him, and led Him away to be crucified.

a. **Gathered the whole garrison around Him**: They only needed a regular group of four soldiers – called a *quaternion* – to carry out the execution. Yet they **gathered the whole garrison around Him**. It wasn't to prevent His escape. It wasn't to prevent a hostile crowd from rescuing Him. It wasn't to keep the disciples away.

  i. "Take heed of sinning in a crowd. Young man, abandon the idea that you may sin in a crowd. Beware of the notion that, because many do it, it is less a guilt to any one of them." (Spurgeon)

  ii. "*The soldiers of the governor* were auxiliaries, not Roman legionaries, and would be recruited from non-Jewish inhabitants of the surrounding areas (*e.g.* Phoenicians, Syrians, perhaps Samaritans)." (France)

  iii. **Garrison**: "The detachment is called a *speira*; in a full *speira* there were six hundred men. It is not likely that there were as many as that in Jerusalem. These soldiers were Pilate's bodyguard who accompanied him from Caesarea, where his permanent headquarters were." (Barclay)

  iv. **Praetorium**: "Called so from the *praetor*, a principal magistrate among the Romans, whose business it was to administer justice in the absence of the *consul*. This place might be termed in English the *court house*, or *common hall*." (Clarke)

b. **Mocked Him, saying, "Hail, King of the Jews!"** Everything about this was intended to humiliate Jesus. The Jewish rulers had already mocked Jesus as the Messiah (Matthew 26:67-68). Now the Roman powers mocked him as king.

- **They stripped Him**: When a prisoner was crucified, they were often nailed to the cross naked, simply to increase their humiliation. Jesus hasn't been crucified yet, but His humiliation had begun, and He was publicly **stripped**.

- **Put a scarlet robe on Him**: Kings and rulers often wore **scarlet**, because the dyes to make fabrics that color were expensive. The **scarlet robe** was intended as cruel irony.

- **They had twisted a crown of thorns**: Kings wear crowns, but not crowns of torture. The specific thorn-bushes of this region have long, hard, sharp thorns. This was a crown that cut, pierced, and bloodied the head of the King who wore it.

- **A reed in His right hand**: Kings hold scepters, but glorious, ornate scepters that symbolize their power. In their mockery of Jesus, they gave Him a **scepter** - but a thin, weak **reed**.

- **They bowed the knee before Him**: Kings are honored, so they offered mocking worship to this King.

- **"Hail, King of the Jews!"** Kings are greeted with royal titles, so in their spite they mocked Jesus with this title. It was meant to humiliate Jesus, but also the **Jews** - saying, "This is the best King they can bring forth."

  i. We might say that in contrast, Jesus says to the kings and rulers of this age that their crowns are false and their scepters are reeds.

  ii. We can also decide to do the opposite of what these did to Jesus. "Oh, that we were half as inventive in devising honor for our King as these soldiers were in planning his dishonor! Let us offer to Christ the real homage that these men pretended to offer him." (Spurgeon)

c. **Then they spat on Him, and took the reed and struck Him on the head**: They now shifted from mockery to cruelty. They seized the ironic scepter, took off the mock-royal robe, and began to hurl their spit and their fists at the head of Jesus.

  i. "They spat on him and used the staff, the symbol of his kingly authority, to hit him on the head 'again and again' (cf. the imperfect tense of the verb)." (Carson)

  ii. Even the hands that drove the nails into His hands unto the cross did only what they were commanded to do. Yet they spat in His face just for the pleasure of doing it. "But, my brethren bad as man is, methinks he never was so bad — or rather, his badness never came out to the full so much — as when gathering all his spite, his pride, his lust his desperate defiance, his abominable wickedness into one mouthful he spat into the face of the Son of God himself." (Spurgeon)

  iii. Even in this, Jesus stood in the place of sinners. Rebellious man wants to be a king, yet he is a sorry kind of king. Even so, Jesus endured the mocking kind of royalty that man, left to himself, is capable of.

  iv. It is possible for us to mock Jesus today by the way we live. "You have mocked him by a feigned worship, and thus you have put the purple robe upon him. For that purple robe meant that they made him a nominal king, a king who was not in truth a king, but a mere show. Your Sunday religion, which has been forgotten in the week, has been a scepter of reed, a powerless ensign, a mere sham. You have mocked and insulted him even in your hymns and prayers, for your religion is a pretense, with no heart in it; you brought him an adoration that was no adoration, a confession that was no confession, and a prayer that was no prayer. Is it not so?" (Spurgeon)

v. Spurgeon wondered how Matthew heard of this crown of thorns and the mocking that went along with it. He wonders if it was not one of the soldiers that was later converted and came to faith in Jesus. "Our Lord's marred but patient visage preached such a sermon that one at least who gazed upon it felt its mysterious power, felt that such patience was more than human, and accepted the thorn-crowned Savior as henceforth his Lord and his King."

d. **And led Him away to be crucified**: The march to the place of crucifixion was useful advertising for Rome. It warned potential troublemakers that this was their fate should they challenge Rome. Normally a centurion on horseback led the procession, and a herald shouted the crime of the condemned.

i. "The criminal was led to the scene of crucifixion by as long a route as possible, so that as many as possible might see him and take warning from the grim sight." (Barclay)

ii. As Jesus was led away to be crucified, He was - like most victims of crucifixion - forced to carry the wood He would hang upon. The weight of the entire cross was typically 300 pounds. The victim only carried the crossbar, which weighed anywhere from 75 to 125 pounds. When the victim carried the crossbar, he was usually stripped naked, and his hands were often tied to the wood.

iii. The upright beams of a cross were usually permanently fixed in a visible place outside of the city walls, beside a major road. It is likely that on many occasions, Jesus passed by the very upright He would hang upon.

iv. When Jesus said, *If anyone desires to come after Me, let him deny himself, and take up his cross, and follow Me* (Matthew 16:24), this is exactly the scene He had in mind. Everyone knew what the cross was - an unrelenting instrument of death and only death. The cross wasn't about religious ceremonies; it wasn't about traditions and spiritual feelings. The cross was a way to execute people. But in these twenty centuries after the death of Jesus, we have sanitized and ritualized the cross. How would we receive it if Jesus said, "Walk down death row daily and follow Me"? Taking up your cross wasn't a journey; it was a one-way trip. There was no return ticketing; it was never a round trip.

3. (32-34) On the way to **Golgotha** (in Latin, *Calvary*).

Now as they came out, they found a man of Cyrene, Simon by name. Him they compelled to bear His cross. And when they had come to a place called Golgotha, that is to say, Place of a Skull, they gave Him sour wine mingled with gall to drink. But when He had tasted *it*, He would not drink.

a. **A man of Cyrene, Simon by name**: This man was probably a visitor to Jerusalem, there as a faithful Jew to celebrate the Passover. Visiting Jerusalem, he was far from **Cyrene** in North Africa (some 800 miles/1300 kilometers away).

b. **Him they compelled to bear His cross**: Simon knew little if anything about this Jesus, and had no desire to be associated with this Man who was condemned to die as a criminal. Yet the Romans ruled, and Simon was not given a choice. **Him they compelled to bear His cross**. Perhaps he was chosen because he was an obvious foreigner and more conspicuous in the crowd.

　i. Wonderfully, we have reason to believe that Simon came to know what it *really meant* to take up one's cross and follow Jesus. There is some evidence to suggest that his sons became leaders among the early Christians (Mark 15:21 and Romans 16:13).

　ii. "How easy it would have been to carry the cross had he known Jesus as he came to know Him afterwards!" (Meyer)

c. **A place called Golgotha, that is to say, Place of a Skull**: There was a specific place outside the city walls of Jerusalem, yet still very close, where people were crucified. At this **Place of a Skull** Jesus died for our sins, and our salvation was accomplished.

　i. **Golgotha** - in Latin, "Calvary" (Luke 23:33) means "**Place of a Skull**." It was called that because it was the established place where criminals were crucified. As a place of cruel, humiliating death it was outside the city walls, yet likely on a well-established road. It may also be that the hill itself had a skull-like appearance, as is the case with the site in Jerusalem known as Gordon's Calvary.

d. **They gave Him sour wine mingled with gall to drink. But when He had tasted it, He would not drink**: It was customary to give those about to be crucified a pain-numbing and mind-numbing drink, to lessen their awareness of the agony awaiting them. But Jesus refused any numbing drug. He chose to face the spiritual and physical terror with His senses awake.

i. "The wine would be the sour wine or *posca* used by Roman soldiers. In Mark Jesus declines the drink, apparently without tasting, desiring to suffer with a clear mind." (Bruce)

4. (35a) Jesus is crucified.

Then they crucified Him,

a. **They crucified**: We have yet to see an accurate, full depiction of crucifixion in modern media. If it were ever made, it would be limited to adult audiences, because of its intense horror and brutality.

i. The Bible spares us the gory descriptions of Jesus' physical agony, simply stating "**then they crucified Him**." This is because everyone in Matthew's day was well acquainted with the terror of crucifixion, but especially because the greater aspect of Jesus' suffering was spiritual, not physical

ii. "It originated in Persia; and its origin came from the fact that the earth was considered to be sacred to Ormuzd the god, and the criminal was lifted up from it that he might not defile the earth, which was the god's property." (Barclay)

iii. In 1986, Dr. William Edwards wrote a remarkable article in the prestigious *Journal of the American Medical Association* titled "On the Physical Death of Jesus Christ." Following are some of the observations of Dr. Edwards and his associates. The quotations belong to the article, and much of the other text is paraphrased from the article.

iv. "Although the Romans did not invent crucifixion, they perfected it as a form of torture and capital punishment that was designed to produce a slow death with maximum pain and suffering."

v. The victim's back was first torn open by the scourging, then opened again as the congealing, clotting blood came off with the clothing that was removed at the place of crucifixion. When thrown on the ground to nail the hands to the crossbeam, the wounds were again opened, deepened, and contaminated with dirt. With each breath attached to the upright cross, the painful wounds on the back scraped against the rough wood of the upright beam and were further aggravated

vi. Driving the nail through the wrist severed the large median nerve. This stimulated nerve caused bolts of fiery pain in both arms, and often resulted in a claw-like grip in the victim's hands.

vii. Beyond the severe pain, the major effect of crucifixion inhibited normal breathing. The weight of the body, pulling down on the arms and shoulders, tended to lock the respiratory muscles in an inhalation state, thus hindering exhalation. The lack of adequate respiration resulted in severe muscle cramps, which hindered breathing even further. To get a good breath, one had to push against the feet and flex the elbows, pulling from the shoulders. Putting the weight of the body on the feet produced more pain, and flexing the elbows twisted the hands hanging on the nails. Lifting the body for a breath also painfully scraped the back against the rough wooden post. Each effort to get a proper breath was agonizing, exhausting, and led to a sooner death.

viii. "Not uncommonly, insects would light upon or burrow into the open wounds or the eyes, ears, and nose of the dying and helpless victim, and birds of prey would tear at these sites. Moreover, it was customary to leave the corpse on the cross to be devoured by predatory animals."

ix. Death from crucifixion could come from many sources: acute shock from blood loss; being too exhausted to breathe any longer; dehydration; stress-induced heart attack; or congestive heart failure leading to a cardiac rupture. If the victim did not die quickly enough, the legs were broken, and the victim was soon unable to breathe.

x. A Roman citizen could not be crucified except by direct order of Caesar; it was reserved for the worst criminals and lowest classes. No wonder that the Roman statesman Cicero said of crucifixion: "It is a crime to bind a Roman citizen; to scourge him is an act of wickedness; to execute him is almost murder: What shall I say of crucifying him? An act so abominable it is impossible to find any word adequately to express." The Roman historian Tacitus called crucifixion "A torture fit only for slaves" – fit only for them because they were seen as sub-human.

xi. How bad was crucifixion? We get our English word *excruciating* from the Roman word "out of the cross." "Consider how heinous sin must be in the sight of God, when it requires such a sacrifice!" (Commentator Adam Clarke)

b. **Then they crucified Him**: It is significant to remember that Jesus did not suffer as the victim of circumstances. He was in control. Jesus said of His life in John 10:18, *no one takes it from Me, but I lay it down of Myself.* It is terrible to be forced to endure such torture, but to freely choose it out of love is remarkable. Can we ever rightly doubt God's love for us again? Has He not gone to the most extreme length to demonstrate that love?

5. (35b-37) The Roman soldiers at the crucifixion of Jesus.

And divided His garments, casting lots, that it might be fulfilled which was spoken by the prophet:

"They divided My garments among them,
And for My clothing they cast lots."

Sitting down, they kept watch over Him there. And they put up over His head the accusation written against Him: THIS IS JESUS THE KING OF THE JEWS.

    a. **Divided His garments, casting lots**: Jesus lost even His clothing at the cross. He was nailed to the cross as a naked, humiliated man.

        i. Jesus came all the way down the ladder to accomplish our salvation. He let go of absolutely everything - even His clothes - becoming completely poor for us, so we could become completely rich in Him.

    b. **That it might be fulfilled**: Yet even in all this sin, pain, agony, and injustice God guided all things to His desired fulfillment. It may seem that Jesus has *no control* over these events. Yet the invisible hand of God guided all things, so that specific prophecies were specifically fulfilled.

    c. **Sitting down, they kept watch over Him**: This was to prevent someone from rescuing Jesus from the cross. "Men were known to have lived after being taken down from a cross." (Carson)

    d. THIS IS JESUS THE KING OF THE JEWS: In John 19:21 we read that the religious leaders among the Jews objected to this title. They felt it was *false*, because they did not believe that Jesus was **the King of the Jews**. They also believed it was *demeaning*, because it showed Rome's power to humiliate and torture even the "**King of the Jews**." Yet Pilate would not alter this, and when asked to take down the inscription he answered, *What I have written, I have written* (John 19:22).

        i. "The written *charge* (or *titulus*) was normally carried before a criminal on the way to execution, or hung around his neck, and would then be fixed to the cross, thus reinforcing the deterrent effect of the punishment." (France)

        ii. "*Over his head* perhaps indicates that Jesus' cross was of the traditional t-shape, rather than the T-shape frequently used." (France)

6. (38-44) Jesus is mocked on the cross.

Then two robbers were crucified with Him, one on the right and another on the left. And those who passed by blasphemed Him, wagging their heads and saying, "You who destroy the temple and build *it* in three days, save Yourself! If You are the Son of God, come down from the

cross." Likewise the chief priests also, mocking with the scribes and elders, said, "He saved others; Himself He cannot save. If He is the King of Israel, let Him now come down from the cross, and we will believe Him. He trusted in God; let Him deliver Him now if He will have Him; for He said, 'I am the Son of God.'" Even the robbers who were crucified with Him reviled Him with the same thing.

a. **Then two robbers were crucified with Him, one on the right and another on the left**: In His crucifixion, Jesus stood right in the center of sinful humanity. With the mockery of the criminals, the rejection of Jesus by His people is complete. Even criminals rejected Him.

i. "The Jews placed him between these two, perhaps to intimate that he was the *worst* felon of the *three*." (Clarke)

ii. One of these **robbers** repented and trusted in Jesus, and one did not (Luke 23:39-43).

b. **And those who passed by blasphemed Him, wagging their heads**: In the midst of His staggering display of love, Jesus was not honored. Instead, He was **blasphemed** and His enemies sneered, saying, **"Save Yourself. If You are the Son of God, come down from the cross."**

i. "Nothing torments a man when in pain more than mockery. When Jesus Christ most wanted words of pity and looks of kindness, *they that passed by reviled him, wagging their heads.*" (Spurgeon)

ii. Significantly, they mocked Jesus for who He really was and is.

- They mocked Him as a Savior.
- They mocked Him as a King.
- They mocked Him as a believer who trusted in God.
- They mocked Him as the Son of God.

iii. They acted as if Jesus did what they said, they would **believe Him**. Yet it is precisely because He did *not* save Himself that He can save others. Love kept Jesus on the cross, not nails! Jesus did greater than come down from the cross; He rose from the dead, yet they did not believe even then.

iv. Jesus also showed us how we should regard the scorn and mocking of this world – that is, to not regard it at all. "Scorn! Let us scorn scorn. Does the world laugh at us? Let us laugh at the world's laughter, and say to it, 'Dost thou despise us? It is not one half as much as we despise thee. Our fathers despised thy sword, O world, thy dungeons, thy racks, thy gibbets, thy stakes, and dost thou think that we shall tremble at thy scoffs, and jeers?'" (Spurgeon)

c. **Even the robbers who were crucified with Him reviled Him with the same thing**: There were many low points to Jesus' ordeal on the cross, but this is surely one of the lowest. Even among the three crucified men, Jesus was put in the "lowest" position.

i. This was the peak of God's love for man: to endure this for our salvation. But it was also the summit of man's hatred for God; God came to earth, and this is what man did to Him.

ii. Jesus had to suffer this alone, outside the gate. He was cut off from the community; both so we could be joined to His community, and also so that our experiences of isolation can be redeemed and made into opportunities of fellowship with Him.

D. The death of Jesus.

1. (45) An unusual darkness on the land.

Now from the sixth hour until the ninth hour there was darkness over all the land.

a. **Now from the sixth hour until the ninth hour**: From the Roman reckoning of time, this was approximately from 12:00 noon until 3:00 in the afternoon. This unusual darkness lasted for some three hours, much longer than any natural eclipse.

i. This was not the entire time Jesus was on the cross, but the later part of that time. According to Mark 15:25 and 15:34, we can surmise that Jesus hung on the cross for about 6 hours (approximately between 9:00 in the morning and 3:00 in the afternoon).

ii. The first three hours of Jesus' ordeal on the cross were in normal daylight, so that all could see that it was in fact Jesus on the cross, and not a replacement or an impostor.

iii. This darkness was especially remarkable because it happened during a full moon – during which time Passover was always held – and during a full moon it is impossible that there be a *natural* eclipse of the sun.

b. **There was darkness over all the land**: The remarkable **darkness** all over the earth showed the agony of creation itself in the Creator's suffering.

i. "The darkness is the symbol of the wrath of God which fell on those who slew his only begotten Son. God was angry, and his frown removed the light of day...The symbol also tells us what our Lord Jesus Christ endured. The darkness outside of him was the figure of the darkness that was within him. In Gethsemane a thick darkness fell upon our Lord's spirit." (Spurgeon)

ii. There was contemporary evidence for this unusual darkness. "Origen (*Contra Celsus*, ii,33) and Eusebius (*Chron.*) quoted words from Phlegon (a Roman historian) in which he made mention of an extraordinary solar eclipse as well as of an earthquake about the time of the crucifixion." (Geldenhuys in his commentary on Luke)

iii. Phlegon, Roman historian wrote: "In the fourth year of the 202nd Olympiad, there was an extraordinary eclipse of the sun: at the sixth hour, the day turned into dark night, so that the stars in heaven were seen; and there was an earthquake." (Cited in Clarke)

2. (46-49) Jesus cries out to the Father in agony.

And about the ninth hour Jesus cried out with a loud voice, saying, "Eli, Eli, lama sabachthani?" that is, "My God, My God, why have You forsaken Me?" Some of those who stood there, when they heard *that*, said, "This Man is calling for Elijah!" Immediately one of them ran and took a sponge, filled *it* with sour wine and put *it* on a reed, and offered it to Him to drink. The rest said, "Let Him alone; let us see if Elijah will come to save Him."

a. **My God, My God**: In quoting Psalm 22, Jesus declared His fulfillment of that prophecy, in both its agony and in its exultation. The Psalm continues to say, *You have answered Me. I will declare Your name to My brethren; in the midst of the congregation I will praise You* (Psalm 22:21b-22).

i. "The probability is that Jesus spoke in Hebrew. It is no argument against this that the spectators might not understand what He said, for the utterance was not meant for the ears of men." (Bruce)

ii. "*Cried* (*anaboao*, used only here in the New Testament) is a strong verb indicating powerful emotion or appeal to God." (France)

iii. "This is, remarkably, the only time in the Synoptic Gospels where Jesus addressed God without calling him 'Father'." (France)

b. **Why have You forsaken Me?** Jesus had known great pain and suffering (both physical and emotional) during His life. Yet He had never known separation from His Father. At this moment, He experienced what He had not yet ever experienced. There was a significant sense in which Jesus rightly felt **forsaken** by the Father at this moment.

i. "His one moan is concerning his God. It is not, 'Why has Peter forsaken me? Why has Judas betrayed me?' These were sharp griefs, but this is the sharpest. This stroke has cut him to the quick." (Spurgeon)

ii. At this moment, a holy transaction took place. God the Father regarded God the Son as if He were a sinner. As the Apostle Paul would later write, *God made Him who knew no sin to be sin for us, that we might become the righteousness of God in Him.* (2 Corinthians 5:21)

iii. Yet Jesus not only endured the *withdrawal* of the Father's fellowship, but also the actual outpouring of the Father's *wrath* upon Him as a substitute for sinful humanity.

iv. Horrible as this was, it fulfilled God's good and loving plan of redemption. Therefore Isaiah could say, *Yet it pleased the Lord to bruise Him* (Isaiah 53:10).

v. At the same time, we cannot say that the separation between the Father and the Son at the cross was complete. Paul made this clear in 2 Corinthians 5:19: *God was in Christ reconciling the world to Himself* at the cross.

vi. "I even venture to say that, if it had been possible for God's love towards his Son to be increased, he would have delighted in him more when he was standing as the suffering Representative of his chosen people than ever he had delighted in him before." (Spurgeon)

c. **Why have You forsaken Me?** The *agony* of this cry is significant. It rarely grieves man to be separated from God or to consider that he is a *worthy* object of God's wrath, yet this was the true agony of Jesus on the cross. At some point before He died, before the veil was torn in two, before He cried out *it is finished*, an awesome spiritual transaction took place. God the Father laid upon God the Son all the guilt and wrath our sin deserved, and He bore it in Himself perfectly, totally satisfying the wrath of God for us.

i. As horrible as the physical suffering of Jesus was, this spiritual suffering - the act of being judged for sin in our place - was what Jesus really dreaded about the cross. This was the *cup* - the cup of God's righteous wrath - that He trembled at drinking (Luke 22:39-46, Psalm 75:8, Isaiah 51:17, Jeremiah 25:15). On the cross, Jesus became, as it were, an enemy of God who was judged and forced to drink the cup of the Father's fury. He did it so we would not have to drink that cup.

ii. Isaiah 53:3-5 puts it powerfully: *He is despised and rejected by men, a Man of sorrows and acquainted with grief. And we hid, as it were, our faces from Him; He was despised, and we did not esteem Him. Surely He has borne our griefs and carried our sorrows; yet we esteemed Him stricken, smitten by God, and afflicted. But He was wounded for our transgressions, He was bruised for our iniquities; the chastisement for our peace was upon Him, and by His stripes we are healed.*

iii. "His Father now dried up that sacred stream of peaceful communion and loving fellowship which had flowed hitherto throughout his whole earthly life…We lose but drops when we lose our joyful experience of heavenly fellowship; and yet the loss is killing: but to our Lord Jesus Christ the sea was dried up — I mean his sea of fellowship with the infinite God." (Spurgeon)

iv. We can imagine the answer to Jesus' question: Why? "Because My Son, You have chosen to stand in the place of guilty sinners. You, who have never known sin, have made the infinite sacrifice to become sin and receive My just wrath upon sin and sinners. You do this because of Your great love, and because of My great love." Then the Father might give the Son a glimpse of His reward – the righteously-robed multitude of His people on heaven's golden streets, "all of them singing their redeemer's praise, all of them chanting the name of Jehovah and the Lamb; and this was a part of the answer to his question." (Spurgeon)

v. Knowing this agony of the Son of God on the cross should affect how we see sin: "O sirs, if I had a dear brother who had been murdered, what would you think of me if I valued the knife which had been crimsoned with his blood? – If I made a friend of the murderer, and daily consorted with the assassin, who drove the dagger into my brother's heart? Surely I, too, must be an accomplice in the crime! Sin murdered Christ; will you be a friend to it? Sin pierced the heart of the Incarnate God; can you love it?" (Spurgeon)

d. **This man is calling for Elijah**: Sadly, Jesus was misunderstood and mocked until the bitter end. These observers thought it was all an interesting test case to see if **Elijah** would actually come.

i. As Jesus hung on the cross, His listeners misunderstood Him by taking the part for the whole. He said, "**Eli, Eli, lama sabachthani?**" Not only did they get wrong what they heard (Jesus said, "**Eloi**" not "**Elijah**"), but they also only heard *one word* of what He said. This will not do for the true follower of Jesus; we hear not only *one word* from Jesus, but every word that proceeds from the mouth of God.

ii. One of the first things we know about Jesus was that He was misunderstood. When Joseph and Mary left Him behind at Jerusalem, they didn't understand that He had to be about His Father's business. Now at the end of His earthly ministry, He is also misunderstood on the cross.

iii. Jesus knew what it was to have His *motives* misunderstood. He healed people, and others said He did it by the devil. He reached out to sinners, and people called Him a drunken pig. The followers of Jesus also sometimes have their *motives* misunderstood.

iv. Jesus knew what it was to have His *words* misunderstood. He said, "Destroy this temple and in three days I will raise it up again," no doubt motioning towards His own body as He said it. Still, people insisted that He spoke of the literal temple in Jerusalem. Another time He knew Lazarus was dead, and He told others that Lazarus was sleeping. They misunderstood Jesus and thought He meant Lazarus was getting much-needed rest. The followers of Jesus sometimes have their *words* misunderstood.

v. Jesus knew what it was to have His *silence* misunderstood. When He first appeared before Pilate, Pilate sent Him off to Herod. When Herod questioned Jesus, He didn't say a word. Herod misunderstood the silence of Jesus and saw it as weakness and powerlessness. Herod was blind to the power and dignity in the silence of Jesus. The followers of Jesus also sometimes have their *silence* misunderstood.

3. (50) The death of Jesus.

And Jesus cried out again with a loud voice, and yielded up His spirit.

a. **Jesus cried out again with a loud voice**: Most victims of crucifixion spent their last hours in complete exhaustion or unconsciousness before death. Jesus was not like this; though tremendously tortured and weakened, He was conscious and able to speak right up to the moment of His death.

i. "The Fathers found in the loud cry a proof that Jesus died voluntarily, not from physical exhaustion. Some modern commentators, on the contrary, regard the cry as the utterance as one dying of a ruptured heart." (Bruce)

ii. John 19:30 tells us that Jesus said, "*It is finished,*" which is one word in the ancient Greek - *tetelestai*, which means, "paid in full." This was the cry of a winner, because Jesus fully paid the debt of sin we owed, and finished the eternal purpose of the cross.

b. **And yielded up His spirit**: No one took Jesus' life from Him. Jesus, in a manner unlike any other man, **yielded up His spirit**. Death had no righteous hold over the sinless Son of God. He stood *in the place* of sinners, but never was or became a sinner Himself. Therefore He could not die unless He **yielded up His spirit**.

i. As Jesus said, *I lay down My life that I may take it again. No one takes it from Me, but I lay it down of Myself. I have power to lay it down, and I have power to take it again.* (John 10:17-18)

ii. "Every man, since the fall, has not only been *liable* to death, but has *deserved* it; as all have forfeited their lives because of sin. Jesus Christ, was born immaculate, and having never sinned, had not *forfeited* his life, and therefore may be considered as naturally and properly immortal." (Clarke)

iii. "He gave up his life because He willed it, when He willed it, and as He willed it." (Augustine)

4. (51-56) The immediate results of Jesus' death.

Then, behold, the veil of the temple was torn in two from top to bottom; and the earth quaked, and the rocks were split, and the graves were opened; and many bodies of the saints who had fallen asleep were raised; and coming out of the graves after His resurrection, they went into the holy city and appeared to many. So when the centurion and those with him, who were guarding Jesus, saw the earthquake and the things that had happened, they feared greatly, saying, "Truly this was the Son of God!" And many women who followed Jesus from Galilee, ministering to Him, were there looking on from afar, among whom were Mary Magdalene, Mary the mother of James and Joses, and the mother of Zebedee's sons.

a. **The veil of the temple was torn in two**: The **veil** was what separated the holy place from the most holy place in the temple. It was a vivid demonstration of the separation between God and man. Notably, the veil was torn from **top to bottom**, and it was God who did the tearing.

i. "As if shocked at the sacrilegious murder of her Lord, the temple rent her garments, like one stricken with horror at some stupendous crime." (Spurgeon)

ii. Acts 6:7 says that in the days of the early church, *a great many of the priests were obedient to the faith*. Perhaps this torn veil demonstrated to them the greatness of the work of Jesus. It is also probably *how* the torn veil became common knowledge.

iii. "It is not a slight rent through which we may see a little; but it is rent from the top to the bottom. There is an entrance made for the greatest sinners. If there had only been a small hole cut through it, the lesser offenders might have crept through; but what an act of abounding mercy is this, that the veil is rent in the midst, and rent from top to bottom, so that the chief of sinners may find ample passage!" (Spurgeon)

b. **The earth quaked, and the rocks were split**: Nature itself was shaken by the death of the Son of God.

i. "Men's hearts did not respond to the agonizing cries of the dying Redeemer, but the rocks responded: the rocks were rent. He did not die for rocks; yet rocks were more tender than the hearts of men, for whom he shed his blood." (Spurgeon)

ii. There should probably be a break between the end of Matthew 27:51 and the start of Matthew 27:52. We aren't to suppose that the earthquake that happened and split rocks during the crucifixion also opened graves of some of the righteous dead; who waited in those open graves for three days until **coming out of the graves after His resurrection**. It is better to understand that Matthew intended us to see that the earthquake happened on the day Jesus was crucified. Then, on the day He was revealed as resurrected, the radiating power of new life was so great that it resuscitated some of the righteous dead.

c. **Coming out of the graves after His resurrection**: This is one of the strangest passages in the Gospel of Matthew. We don't know about this event from any other source, and Matthew doesn't tell us very much. So we really don't know what this was all about, but apparently these resuscitated saints died once again, because they were raised from the dead in the sense that Lazarus was – not to resurrection life, but to die again.

i. They were raised, "Not to converse again, as heretofore, with men, but to accompany Christ, that raised them, into heaven; and to be as so many ocular demonstrations of Christ's quickening power." (Trapp)

ii. "These first miracles wrought in connection with the death of Christ were typical of spiritual wonders that will be continued till he comes again – rocky hearts are rent, graves of sin are opened, those who have been dead in trespasses and sins, and buried in sepulchers of lust and evil, are quickened, and come out from among the dead, and go unto *the holy city*, the New Jerusalem." (Spurgeon)

d. **Truly this was the Son of God!** The scene at the crucifixion of Jesus was so striking that even a hardened Roman centurion confessed that **this was the Son of God**. This man had supervised the death of perhaps hundreds of other men by crucifixion, but he knew there was something absolutely unique about Jesus.

i. **This was the Son of God**: The only thing wrong is his verb tense; Jesus *is* **the Son of God**. The Roman centurion seemed to assume that He was *no longer* the Son of God.

ii. "There are those that think that these soldiers, our Saviour's executioners, were truly converted by the miracles they had seen, according to what Christ had prayed for them, Luke 23:34." (Trapp)

e. **And many women who followed Jesus from Galilee, ministering to Him, were there looking on from afar**: Jesus not only made an impact upon rough and hardened men like the Roman centurion, but He also made an impact on women, even women like **Mary Magdalene** (the formerly demon-possessed woman who followed Jesus from Galilee, according to Luke 8:2).

> i. **Many women**: "To their everlasting honour, these women evidenced more *courage*, and *affectionate attachment* to their Lord and Master, than the disciples did, who had promised to *die* with him rather than forsake him." (Clarke)

> ii. Think of who was there at the cross.

> - Men and women.
> - Jews and Gentiles.
> - Rich and poor.
> - High class and no class.
> - Religious and irreligious.
> - Guilty and innocent.
> - Haters of Jesus and lovers of Jesus.
> - Oppressors and the oppressed.
> - Weepers and mockers.
> - Educated and uneducated.
> - The deeply moved and the indifferent.
> - Different races, different nationalities, different languages, different classes.

> iii. "That mixed crowd was surely a prophecy. All sorts and conditions of men have been attracted by that Cross." (Morgan)

E. The burial of Jesus.

1. (57-61) Joseph of Armithea sets Jesus in his own tomb.

Now when evening had come, there came a rich man from Arimathea, named Joseph, who himself had also become a disciple of Jesus. This man went to Pilate and asked for the body of Jesus. Then Pilate commanded the body to be given to him. When Joseph had taken the body, he wrapped it in a clean linen cloth, and laid it in his new tomb which he had hewn out of the rock; and he rolled a large stone against the door of the tomb, and departed. And Mary Magdalene was there, and the other Mary, sitting opposite the tomb.

> a. **This man went to Pilate and asked for the body of Jesus**: Customarily, the bodies of crucified criminals were left on their crosses to rot or to be

eaten by wild animals. But the Jews wanted no such horror displayed during the Passover season, and Romans were known to grant the corpses of executed men to friends or relatives for proper burial.

b. **He wrapped it in a clean linen cloth**: Joseph followed the burial customs of that day - the best he could, considering that they had very little time because *the Sabbath drew near* (Luke 23:54).

c. **Laid it in his new tomb**: He came into the world from a virgin's womb; He came forth again from a virgin tomb. No body had ever been set in that tomb, so that when a body came forth and the tomb was empty, there was no possible confusion as to which body came forth.

> i. "It was a new tomb, wherein no remains had been previously laid, and thus if he came forth from it there would be no suspicion that another had arisen, nor could it be imagined that he rose through touching some old prophet's bones, as he did who was laid in Elisha's grave." (Spurgeon)

d. **He rolled a large stone against the door of the tomb**: This was the customary way to seal an expensive tomb. A rich man like Joseph of Arimethea probably had a tomb carved into solid rock; this tomb was in a garden near the place of crucifixion (John 19:41). The tomb would commonly have a small entrance and perhaps one or more compartments where bodies were laid out after being somewhat mummified with spices, ointments, and linen strips. Customarily, the Jews left these bodies alone for a few years until they decayed down to the bones, then the bones were placed in a small stone box known as an ossuary. The ossuary remained in the tomb with the remains of other family members.

> i. The door to the tomb was typically made of a heavy, circular shaped stone, running in a groove and settled down into a channel, so it could not be moved except by several strong men. This was done to ensure that no one would disturb the remains.

> ii. **He rolled a large stone**: "The usual mode of shutting the door of the tomb; the Jews called the stone *golal*, the roller." (Bruce)

> iii. John 19:42 specifically tells us that the tomb of Joseph of Arimethea that Jesus was laid in was close to the place of Jesus' crucifixion (and each of the two suggested places for Jesus' death and resurrection bear this out). Joseph probably didn't like it that the value of his family tomb decreased because the Romans decided to crucify people nearby - yet it reminds us that the in God's plan, the cross and the power of the resurrection are always permanently and closely connected.

iv. Tombs like this were very expensive. It was quite a sacrifice for Joseph of Arimathea to give his up - but Jesus would only use it for a few days!

2. (62-66) The tomb is sealed and guarded.

On the next day, which followed the Day of Preparation, the chief priests and Pharisees gathered together to Pilate, saying, "Sir, we remember, while He was still alive, how that deceiver said, 'After three days I will rise.' Therefore command that the tomb be made secure until the third day, lest His disciples come by night and steal Him *away*, and say to the people, 'He has risen from the dead.' So the last deception will be worse than the first." Pilate said to them, "You have a guard; go your way, make *it* as secure as you know how." So they went and made the tomb secure, sealing the stone and setting the guard.

a. **Sir**: They gave Pilate a title of honor and respect. But the day before these same religious leaders rejected the King of Kings. They mocked and despised Him, putting Jesus to open shame, but they honored Pilate.

i. **On the next day**: "It must mean that the chief priests and Pharisees actually approached Pilate *on the Sabbath* with their request. If they did that, it is clear to see how radically they broke the Sabbath Law." (Barclay)

b. **We remember...how that deceiver said, "After three days I will rise"**: Ironically, the enemies of Jesus remembered His promise of resurrection better than His own disciples remembered.

c. **While He was still alive**: In this, the enemies of Jesus admit that Jesus is dead. They did not believe the "Swoon Theory," a conjecture that denies the resurrection, saying that Jesus never really died, but just "swooned" on the cross, and then somehow wonderfully revived in the tomb.

i. A humorous letter to the editor to a Christian magazine accurately evaluated the "Swoon Theory":

Dear Eutychus: Our preacher said, on Easter, that Jesus just swooned on the cross and that the disciples nursed Him back to health. What do you think? Sincerely, Bewildered

Dear Bewildered: Beat your preacher with a cat-of-nine-tails with 39 heavy strokes, nail him to a cross; hang him in the sun for 6 hours; run a spear through his heart; embalm him; put him in an airless tomb for 36 hours and see what happens. Sincerely, Eutychus

d. **Lest His disciples come by night and steal Him away**: They couldn't have been afraid of the **disciples**. They knew they were terrified and in hiding. They knew they were gone from the crucifixion scene. Their intelligence sources and informants let them know the disciples were terrified. Instead, they were afraid of the power of Jesus.

i. After all, look at their words: **And say to the people, "He has risen from the dead."** If that were to happen, why not just say to the disciples, "So where is Jesus? Produce the supposedly living body of your risen Lord!" They knew that it would do nothing for the disciples to steal the body of Jesus, because they could not present a dead body and pretend it was alive. That would prove nothing. *What they were really afraid of was the resurrection power of Jesus.*

ii. It is sad that the religious leaders were afraid of the resurrection power of Jesus, but at least they believed it was true. On Saturday morning, the chief priests and the Pharisees preached a better resurrection sermon than the disciples did.

iii. "Justin says that such stories were still being actively disseminated in the middle of the second century (*Dialogues* 108). The fact of such propaganda in itself indicates that it could not be denied that the tomb was empty; what was questioned was how it came to be empty." (France)

e. **Command that the tomb be made secure...you have a guard...make it as secure as you know how**: This shows that both the Jewish leaders and the Romans were well aware of the need to guard the tomb, and that they took all necessary measures to secure it. These security measures simply gave greater testimony to the miracle of the resurrection. If Jesus' tomb was unguarded, one might suggest that an unknown person or persons stole the body, and it would be difficult to refute. Yet because the tomb was so well guarded, we can be *certain* that His body wasn't stolen.

i. **You have a guard** was Pilate's promise to supply a Roman guard. "It is unlikely that the Jews would have needed Pilate's permission at all to deploy their own police; moreover the word for *guard* is (uniquely in the New Testament) a transliteration of the Latin word *custodia*. It is therefore more likely that it was Pilate's troops who were used; the Jewish leaders are going for maximum security." (France)

ii. "Vain men! As if the same power that was necessary to raise and quicken the dead could not also remove the stone, and break through the watch they had set. But by their excessive care and diligence, instead of preventing Christ's resurrection, as they intended, they have confirmed the truth and belief of it to all the world." (Poole)

f. **Sealing the stone and setting the guard**: This describes the measures taken to secure the tomb of Jesus.

i. The tomb was secured by a **stone**, which was a *material obstacle*. These stones were large, and set in an inclined channel. This was a real obstacle. For sure, the stone could not be rolled away from the inside. The disciples, if you had enough of them, could roll away the stone – but not quietly. Besides, they would have to work *together* to roll it away, and that didn't seem likely.

ii. The tomb was secured by a *seal*, which was an obstacle of *human authority*. The seal was a rope, overlapping the width of the stone covering the entrance to the tomb. On either side of the doorway, there was a glob of wax securing the rope over the stone. You could not move the rock without breaking the seal. It was important that the guards witness the sealing, because they were responsible for whatever was being sealed. These Roman guards would watch carefully as the stone was sealed, because they knew their careers, and perhaps their lives, were on the line. The Roman seal carried legal authority. It was more than yellow tape barricading a modern crime scene; to break a Roman seal was to defy Roman authority. That stone was secured by the authority of the Roman Empire.

iii. The tomb was secured by a **guard**, which was an obstacle of *human strength*. A typical Roman guard had four soldiers. Two watched while the others rested. This guard may have had more. The soldiers would be fully equipped – sword, shield, spear, dagger, armor. We should also remember that these were *Roman* soldiers. They didn't care about Jesus or Jewish laws or rituals. They were called to secure the tomb of a criminal. To them the only sacred thing at this tomb was the Roman seal, because if that were broken, their careers were ruined and they might be executed themselves. Soldiers cold-blooded enough to gamble over a dying man's clothes were not the kind of men to be tricked by trembling disciples, or would not jeopardize their necks by sleeping at their post.

iv. *None* of these obstacles mattered. They all fall away before Him!

- Material obstacles don't stand before the resurrected Jesus.
- Human authority doesn't stand before the resurrected Jesus.
- Human strength doesn't stand before the resurrected Jesus.

Matthew 28 - A Risen Lord Jesus and His Commission

A. The risen Jesus.

1. (1-3) Mary Magdalene and Mary of Bethany find an angel at the tomb.

Now after the Sabbath, as the first *day* of the week began to dawn, Mary Magdalene and the other Mary came to see the tomb. And behold, there was a great earthquake; for an angel of the Lord descended from heaven, and came and rolled back the stone from the door, and sat on it. His countenance was like lightning, and his clothing as white as snow.

a. **Mary Magdalene and the other Mary came to see the tomb**: They came to finish the preparation of Jesus' body, which was cut short by the Sabbath (Luke 24:1-3). So **after the Sabbath** on Sunday (**the first day of the week**), they came to the tomb – fully expecting to find the dead body of Jesus.

b. **There was a great earthquake**: Matthew alone notes this earthquake. The earthquake did not cause the stone to be rolled away; if anything, the angelic rolling of the stone prompted the earthquake.

i. "The earth shook both at Christ's passion and at his resurrection; then, to show that it could not bear his suffering; now, to show that it could not hinder his rising." (Trapp)

ii. Some think this was not a normal earthquake, but refers to the disturbance of the guards at the tomb (Matthew 28:4). "Seismov, a *shaking* or *commotion* of any kind: probably the word means no more than the *confusion* caused among the guards by the angel's appearance. All this had taken place before the women reached the sepulcher." (Clarke)

c. **An angel of the Lord descended from heaven, and came and rolled back the stone from the door, and sat on it**: When the women came to

435

the tomb, they saw the stone rolled away and an angel sitting on the stone. The door to the tomb was wide open.

> i. "Indeed there needed not any angel at all to remove the stone, if this had been all he had come down for; He that was quickened by the Spirit, could by the same power have rolled away the stone; but as it was fit that the angels, who had been witnesses of his passion, should also be witnesses of his resurrection." (Poole)

> ii. The stone that enclosed the body of Jesus in the tomb had been like the gate of a prison cell, trapping the body of Jesus in the grave. Now it became a place of rest, as the angel **sat on it**.

2. (4-6) The angel's message.

And the guards shook for fear of him, and became like dead *men*. But the angel answered and said to the women, "Do not be afraid, for I know that you seek Jesus who was crucified. He is not here; for He is risen, as He said. Come, see the place where the Lord lay."

a. **And the guards shook for fear of him, and became like dead men**: The Roman soldiers responsible for guarding the tomb were terrified. The angelic presence made these professional soldiers tremble and faint.

> i. "He does not appear to have drawn a flaming sword, nor even to have spoken to *the keepers*; but the presence of perfect purity overawed these rough legionaries." (Spurgeon)

> ii. "The resurrection of Christ is a subject of *terror* to the servants of sin, and a subject of consolation to the sons of God; because it is a proof of the resurrection of both, the one to shame and everlasting contempt-the other to eternal glory and joy." (Clarke)

b. **He is not here, for He is risen**: For the first time, the followers of Jesus – these faithful women – heard what they did not expect to hear. They heard that Jesus was not in the tomb, but **risen** to resurrection life.

> i. There are several examples in the Bible of people being *resuscitated* before this, such as the widow's son in the days of Elijah (1 Kings 17:17-24) and Lazarus (John 11:38-44). Each of these was resuscitated from death, but none of them were *resurrected*. Each of them was raised in the same body they died in, and raised from the dead to eventually die again. Resurrection isn't just living again; it is living again in a new body, based on our old body, perfectly suited for life in eternity. Jesus was not the first one brought back from the dead, but He was the first one *resurrected*.

ii. We should also say that Jesus *still* **is risen**. He ascended into heaven and continues to reign as resurrected man, still fully man and fully God.

iii. In Israel, one may see many graves and tombs - there is an ocean of tombs on the Mount of Olives, and vast sea of graves outside the eastern wall of the temple mount. You can see the tomb of Rebekka, the tomb of David, the tomb of Absalom - but you won't find the tomb of Jesus anywhere. **He is not here**.

iv. **As He said** reminded these women – and all the disciples – that they *should have* expected this. It was just what He promised.

c. **Come, see the place where the Lord lay**: The stone was not rolled away to let Jesus out. John 20:19 tells us that Jesus, in His resurrection body, could pass through material barriers. It was rolled away so that others could see in and be persuaded that Jesus Christ was raised from the dead.

i. "The invitation to *see the place where he lay* is appropriately addressed to the same people who had watched the body being deposited – so there is no possibility of a mistake." (France)

ii. "Come and see the niche in which he was laid-it is now empty; nor was there any other body in the place, for the tomb was a *new* one, in which no man had ever been laid, John 19:41; so there could be no deception in the case." (Clarke)

iii. The *fact* of the resurrection is clear enough. We must also grapple with the *meaning* of the resurrection. Simply, Jesus' resurrection proved that His death was an actual propitiation for sin and that the Father had accepted it as such. The cross was the payment, the resurrection the receipt, proving that the payment was fully accepted.

iv. Those women were later grateful that the angel told them to **see the place where they laid Him**. It would have - it should have - been enough to merely hear the testimony of the angel. Nevertheless, when they *saw* it, it gave them ground to stand on even more solid than the testimony of an angel. "One eye-witness is better than twenty ear-witnesses; men will believe what you have seen if they do not believe what you have heard." (Spurgeon)

- When we **see the place where they laid Him**, we see that the Father did not forsake Jesus.

- When we **see the place where they laid Him**, we see that death is conquered.

- When we **see the place where they laid Him**, we see that we have a living friend in Jesus.

3. (7-8) The angel's instructions to Mary Magdalene and Mary of Bethany.

"And go quickly and tell His disciples that He is risen from the dead, and indeed He is going before you into Galilee; there you will see Him. Behold, I have told you." So they went out quickly from the tomb with fear and great joy, and ran to bring His disciples word.

a. **Go quickly and tell His disciples that He is risen from the dead**: The angel commanded them to be the first messengers of the good news of Jesus' resurrection. Since these women were some of the few people courageous enough to publicly identify themselves with Jesus, it was an appropriate honor.

i. "Not first to them who were the heads of the Church, as it were, but first of all to lowly women, did the Lord appear; and the apostles themselves had to go to school to Mary Magdalene and the other Mary to learn that great truth, 'The Lord is risen indeed.'" (Spurgeon)

b. **He is going before you into Galilee; there you will see Him**: This assured the women *they would see the resurrected Jesus*. He wasn't simply raised from the dead; He was raised to continue His relationship with them.

i. Conceivably, the angel might have said: "He is risen, and has ascended to heaven!" That would have been better than knowing He was dead; but the truth was far better. He was risen, and risen to have and continue a real relationship with His disciples.

c. **Ran to bring His disciples word**: The women – filled with **fear and great joy** – did exactly what the angel told them to do. He told them to **go quickly** and they did.

i. "Saints running in the way of obedience are likely to be *met by Jesus*. Some Christians travel to heaven so slowly that they are overtaken by follies or by faults, by slumber or by Satan; but he who is Christ's running footman shall meet his Master while he is speeding on his way." (Spurgeon)

4. (9-10) Mary Magdalene and Mary of Bethany meet a risen Jesus.

And as they went to tell His disciples, behold, Jesus met them, saying, "Rejoice!" So they came and held Him by the feet and worshiped Him. Then Jesus said to them, "Do not be afraid. Go *and* tell My brethren to go to Galilee, and there they will see Me."

a. **As they went to tell His disciples**: The women met Jesus as they obeyed the command to tell the news of the resurrection.

b. **Jesus met them, saying "Rejoice!"** What else could Jesus say to these women? What else could they do other than **rejoice**?

i. The old King James Version translates **"Rejoice!"** with *All hail!* France observes, "'*Hail!*' represents the normal Greek greeting, an almost homely 'Hello!' in contrast with the fearsome appearance of the angel."

c. **So they came and held Him by the feet and worshiped Him**: When the women met Jesus, they felt compelled to worship Him. An hour before, they thought everything was lost because they thought Jesus was dead. Now they knew everything was gained because Jesus was alive.

i. Notably, Jesus *received the worship* of these ladies. If Jesus were not God, it would have been terribly sinful for Him to receive this worship. But being God, it was good and appropriate for Him to receive it.

d. **Do not be afraid. Go and tell My brethren to go to Galilee, and there they will see Me**: Jesus told the women to do the same thing that the angel told them to do.

i. **My brethren**: "This is the *first* time our Lord called his disciples by this endearing name: they no doubt thought that their Lord would reproach them with their past cowardice and infidelity; but, in speaking thus, he gives them a full assurance, in the most tender terms, that all that was passed was buried for ever." (Clarke)

5. (11-15) The cover-up of the resurrection begins with the bribery of the guards.

Now while they were going, behold, some of the guard came into the city and reported to the chief priests all the things that had happened. When they had assembled with the elders and consulted together, they gave a large sum of money to the soldiers, saying, "Tell them, 'His disciples came at night and stole Him *away* while we slept.' And if this comes to the governor's ears, we will appease him and make you secure." So they took the money and did as they were instructed; and this saying is commonly reported among the Jews until this day.

a. **Tell them, "His disciples came at night and stole Him away while we slept"**: This cover-up attempt shows the darkness of these priests. They knew the truth of the resurrection, yet they rejected that truth.

i. **A large sum of money**: "The Greek is literally 'sufficient money' – it would need to be large!" (France)

b. **While we slept**: The cover-up also shows their foolishness. If it was true that the guards were asleep, they could not know that it was **His disciples** that stole the body of Jesus.

> i. To believe this, we have to believe:
>
> - *All* the soldiers were asleep – all of them!
> - *All* the soldiers violated the strict law of the Roman military against sleeping on watch, punishable by death.
> - *All* the soldiers slept so deeply that none of them were awakened by the work and exertion and noise necessary to roll away the stone and carry out the body.
> - *All* the soldiers were so soundly asleep – yet they knew who it was who did this.
>
> ii. Clarke rightly comments, "Here is a whole heap of absurdities."

c. **This saying is commonly reported among the Jews until this day**: Through the years, there have been many objections suggested to the resurrection of Jesus. Some say He didn't die at all, but just swooned or fainted on the cross and spontaneously revived in the tomb. Others say He really died, but His body was stolen. Still others suggest He really died, but His desperate followers hallucinated His resurrection. A plain, simple understanding of these evidences of the resurrection of Jesus answers all of these theories, and shows they take far more faith to believe than the Biblical account does.

> i. "I suppose, brethren, that we may have persons arise, who will doubt whether there was ever such a man as Julius Caesar, or Napoleon Bonaparte; and when they do, - when all reliable history is flung to the winds, - then, but not till then, may they begin to question whether Jesus Christ rose from the dead, for this historical fact is attested by more witnesses than almost any other fact that stands on record in history, whether sacred or profane." (Spurgeon)
>
> ii. We sometimes sing: "You ask me how I know He lives; He lives, He lives inside my heart." But that is not the best way to prove Jesus lives. He lives because the historical evidence *demands* we believe in the resurrection of Jesus. If we can believe *anything* in history, we can believe the reliable, confirmed testimony of these eyewitnesses. Jesus rose from the dead.

B. The great commission.

1. (16-17) The disciples meet Jesus at Galilee.

Then the eleven disciples went away into Galilee, to the mountain which Jesus had appointed for them. When they saw Him, they worshiped Him; but some doubted.

a. **The eleven disciples went away into Galilee**: Matthew doesn't tell us about the Jerusalem appearances of Jesus to His disciples, as John does. Matthew was more interested in showing that the promise of Jesus in Matthew 26:32 was fulfilled.

i. **To the mountain which Jesus had appointed for them**: "The meeting place would be some familiar haunt...only imperfectly recorded in the Gospels." (Bruce)

b. **When they saw Him, they worshiped Him**: This was not their first meeting with the risen Jesus; but it was an important one. At this meeting, they received their apostolic commission.

c. **They worshiped Him; but some doubted**: The natural reaction to encountering the risen Jesus is worship, even if some had to overcome uncertainty and hesitation – probably from feeling it was too good to be true, and lingering shame from having forsaken Jesus during His suffering.

i. "When they recognized him, it was natural that *they worshipped him*, but the whole experience was so mysterious and overwhelming that *some doubted*...The verb *distazo* does not denote a settled unbelief, but a state of uncertainty and hesitation." (France)

ii. "Dunn sees Matthew's mention of this doubt as 'a genuine historical echo' – those who were there would never have forgotten the conflicting emotions and beliefs in that unique experience." (France)

iii. The fact that some of the disciples doubted argues against the theory that their seeing Jesus was simply a hallucination born of a desperate desire to see Him.

2. (18-20) Jesus instructs His disciples regarding their duty after His departure.

And Jesus came and spoke to them, saying, "All authority has been given to Me in heaven and on earth. Go therefore and make disciples of all the nations, baptizing them in the name of the Father and of the Son and of the Holy Spirit, teaching them to observe all things that I have commanded you; and lo, I am with you always, *even* to the end of the age." Amen.

a. **All authority has been given to Me in heaven and on earth**: This commission that follows is given in light of the authority of Jesus. This indicates that this is an authoritative command, not a suggestion. It is the same idea as if an officer reminded a private of his rank before he gave the order. Because He has this **authority**, He can send whomever He wills to do whatever He pleases.

   i. "'All' dominates Matthew 28:18-20 and ties these verses together: *all* authority, *all* nations, *all* things, *all* the days." (Carson)

   ii. "Power in the hands of some people is dangerous, but power in the hands of Christ is blessed. Oh, let him have all power! Let him do what he will with it, for he cannot will anything but that which is right, and just, and true, and good." (Spurgeon)

   iii. "We believe in this power, and we rest in it." (Spurgeon)

   • *We do not seek any other power.*

   • *We defy every other power.*

   • *We know our powerlessness will not hinder the progress of His kingdom.*

   • *We give all our power unto Him.*

   iv. "If Jesus Christ were not equal with the Father, could he have claimed this equality of power, without being guilty of impiety and blasphemy? Surely not; and does he not, in the fullest manner, assert his Godhead, and his equality with the Father, by claiming and possessing all the authority in heaven and earth?" (Clarke)

b. **Go therefore**: Because Jesus has this authority, we are **therefore** commanded to **go**. It is His authority that sends us, His authority that guides us, and His authority that empowers us. His work and message would continue to the world through His disciples.

   i. "These verses thus magnificently conclude the final section…but they also bring the whole Gospel to a dynamic conclusion, which is in fact more a beginning than an end." (France)

   ii. Jesus said, "**Go**" to some very imperfect disciples. "Who is to go out of that first band of disciples? It is Peter, the rash and the headstrong. It is John, who sometimes wishes to call fire from heaven to destroy men. It is Philip, with whom the Savior has been so long, and yet he has not known him. It is Thomas, who must put his finger into the print of the nails, or he will not believe him. Yet the Master says to them, 'Go ye; all power is given unto me, therefore go ye. You are as good for my purpose as anybody else would be. There is no power in you, I know, but then all power is in me, therefore go ye.'" (Spurgeon)

c. **Make disciples of all the nations**: The command is to **make disciples**, not merely converts or supporters of a cause. The idea behind the word **disciples** is of scholars, learners, or students.

i. **Make disciples** reminds us that disciples are *made*. **Disciples** are not spontaneously created at conversion; they are the product of a process involving other believers. This making of **disciples** is the power of spreading Christianity.

d. **Of all the nations**: In His previous ministry, Jesus deliberately restricted His work to the Jewish people (Matthew 15:24) and previously sent His disciples with the same restriction (Matthew 10:6). Only in rare exceptions did Jesus minister among the Gentiles (Matthew 15:21-28). Now all of that is in the past, and the disciples are commissioned to take the gospel to **all the nations**. There is no place on earth where the gospel of Jesus should not be preached and where disciples should not be made.

i. "The aim of Jesus' disciples, therefore, is to make disciples of all men everywhere, without distinction." (Carson)

ii. "*Christ* commands them to go and baptize the nations: but how much time was past before such a journey was taken! And when the time was now come that this work should be begun, *Peter* doth not enter upon it without a previous admonition given him from heaven." (Lightfoot, cited in Clarke)

e. **Baptizing them in the name of the Father and of the Son and of the Holy Spirit**: Significantly, when Jesus told them to go to **all the nations**, He did not tell them to *circumcise* those who became disciples. Instead, they were to baptize them, suggesting the break with traditional Judaism.

i. "*In the name* is literally '*into* the name', implying entrance into an allegiance." (France)

ii. The words and context certainly indicate that it is **disciples** who are baptized, those of age who can be taught and who can observe the things Jesus commanded.

iii. Those who favor infant baptism answer, albeit unconvincingly: "But it doth not therefore follow, that children of such professors are not to be baptized, for the apostles were commanded to baptize *all nations*; children are a great part of any nation." (Poole)

iv. **In the name of the Father and of the Son and of the Holy Spirit**: "The experience of God in these three Persons is the essential basis of discipleship. At the same time the singular noun *name* (not 'names') underlines the unity of the three Persons." (France)

f. **Teaching them to observe all things that I have commanded you**: Disciples are made through **teaching**. This **teaching** is not with words only, but with the power of the always-present Jesus. He will be present with His people until the job of making disciples is done - until the **end of the age**.

i. "Hitherto Jesus alone has been the teacher, and the verb has not been used by Matthew of his disciples' ministry. Now they take over his role of *teaching*." (France)

ii. The content of the teaching must be **all things that I have commanded you**. The followers of Jesus are responsible to present the whole counsel of God to those who are made disciples.

g. **Lo, I am with you always, even to the end of the age**: Jesus sent His disciples with a mission to fulfill, but He did not send them alone. The promise of His constant presence was more than enough to strengthen and guide the disciples as they obeyed Jesus in making **disciples of all the nations**.

i. The promise of His presence is complete. "The English adverb 'always' renders an expression found in the New Testament only here – strictly, 'the whole of every day'. Not just the horizon is in view, but each day as we live it." (Carson)

ii. His presence means *privilege*, because we work with a Great King. Paul understood this principle well in 1 Corinthians 3:9, where he wrote: *For we are God's fellow workers*. Since Jesus promised, "**I am with you always**," then we work together with Him in all our service. We certainly work *for* Jesus, but more than that, we work *with* Jesus.

iii. His presence means *protection*, because we are never out of His sight or supervision.

iv. His presence means *power*, because as we fulfill this great command, we work in His name.

v. His presence means *peace*, because it always reminds us that the church belongs to Jesus. It is His church, and His work. How, then, can we worry?

vi. "When Christ saith, 'I will be with you,' you may add what you will; to protect you, to direct you, to comfort you, to carry on the work of grace in you, and in the end to crown you with immortality and glory. All this and more is included in this precious promise." (Trapp)

Bibliography - The Gospel of Matthew

Barclay, William *The Gospel of Matthew, Volume 1* and *Volume 2* (Philadelphia: The Westminster Press, 1975)

Bruce. A.B. "The Synoptic Gospels" *The Expositor's Greek Testament, Volume 1* (London: Hodder and Stoughton, ?)

Calvin, John *A Harmony of the Gospels: Matthew, Mark, and Luke Volumes 1, 2, and 3* Translator: A.W. Morrison (Grand Rapids, Michigan: Eerdmans Publishing, 1972)

Carson, D.A. "Matthew" *The Expositor's Bible Commentary, Volume 8* (Grand Rapids. Michigan: Zondervan, 1984)

Clarke, Adam *The New Testament of Our Lord and Saviour Jesus Christ, Volume II* (New York: Eaton & Mains, 1832)

France, R.T. *The Gospel According to Matthew* (Leicester, England: Inter-Varsity Press, 1985)

Geldenhuys, Norval *Commentary on the Gospel of Luke* (Eerdmans Publishing, 1988)

Hill, David *The Gospel of Matthew* (Grand Rapids, Michigan: Eerdmans Publishing, 1981)

Lane, William L. *The Gospel of Mark* (Grand Rapids, Michigan: Eerdmans, 1974)

Maclaren, Alexander *Expositions of Holy Scripture, Volume 6* and *Volume 7* (Grand Rapids, Michigan: Baker Book House, 1984)

Meyer, F.B. *Our Daily Homily* (Westwood, New Jersey: Revell, 1966)

Morgan, G. Campbell *An Exposition of the Whole Bible* (Old Tappan, New Jersey: Revell, 1959)

Morgan, G. Campbell *Searchlights from the Word* (New York: Revell, 1926)

Morgan, G. Campbell *Commentary on the Gospel of Matthew* (Old Tappan, New Jersey: Revell, 1979)

Morris, Luke *Luke, an Introduction and Commentary* (Inter-Varsity Press, Leicester, England, 1988)

Poole, Matthew *A Commentary on the Holy Bible, Volume III: Matthew-Revelation* (London: Banner of Truth Trust, 1969, first published in 1685)

Robertson, A.T. *Word Pictures in the New Testament, Volume 1* (Nashville, Tennessee: Broadman Press, 1930)

Spurgeon, Charles Haddon *The Gospel of Matthew* (Old Tappan, New Jersey: Revell, 1987)

Spurgeon, Charles Haddon *The New Park Street Pulpit, Volumes 1-6* and *The Metropolitan Tabernacle Pulpit, Volumes 7-63* (Pasadena, Texas: Pilgrim Publications, 1990)

Stott, John *Christian Counter-Culture: The Message of the Sermon on the Mount* (Downers Grove, Illinois: Inter-Varsity Press, 1978)

Trapp, John *A Commentary on the Old and New Testaments, Volume Five* (Eureka, California: Tanski Publications, 1997)

Wessel, Walter W. "Mark" *The Expositor's Bible Commentary, Volume 8* (Grand Rapids, Michigan: Zondervan, 1984)

Wiersbe, Warren W. *The Bible Exposition Commentary, Volume 1*, Mark (Wheaton, Illinois: Victor Books, 1989)

As the years pass I love the work of studying, learning, and teaching the Bible more than ever. I'm so grateful that God is faithful to meet me in His Word. This commentary on the Gospel of Matthew is dedicated to our granddaughter Sirena in the year of her birth.

Thanks once again to Debbie Pollacia for her proofreading help. She's remarkably patient with my work, even when I make the same mistakes through a manuscript. Even more, I thank Debbie for her prayer support through the years.

We use the same cover format and artwork for this commentary series, so continued thanks to Craig Brewer who created the cover and helped with the layout. Kara Valeri helped with graphic design. Gayle Erwin provided both inspiration and practical guidance. I am often amazed at the remarkable kindness of others, and thanks to all who give the gift of encouragement. With each year that passes, faithful friends and supporters become all the more precious. Through you all, God has been better to me than I have ever deserved.

After more than 20 years of pastoral ministry in California and 7 years of work with Calvary Chapel Bible College Germany, David Guzik accepted the call to serve the congregation of Calvary Chapel Santa Barbara in July 2010. David and Inga-Lill live in Santa Barbara.

You can e-mail David at
ewm@enduringword.com

For more resources by David Guzik, go to
www.enduringword.com

CPSIA information can be obtained
at www.ICGtesting.com
Printed in the USA
BVHW092202170322
631650BV00001B/54

9 781565 990272